Report from the Synod

JOHN PAUL II
AND THE
BATTLE FOR VATICAN II

Richard Cowden-Guido

T0204452

TRINITY COMMUNICATIONS
MANASSAS, VIRGINIA

ISBN 0-937495-00-X

DEDICATION

This book is dedicated to John Cardinal Wright, from whom I received my first Holy Communion at the tomb of St. Peter on 14 April 1973.

And to Seattle Auxilliary Bishop Donald Wuerl, from whom I received instruction for my reception into the Church, as well as the copy of the documents of Vatican II that were used during the composition of this work.

ACKNOWLEDGMENTS

With apologies to those who have helped me in so many ways through the years, allow me to keep this brief by thanking only those who assisted me most directly during the Synod and in the composition of this book. These are: Patricia Stookley Clarke and Yasmine Renton who provided me with good conversation, good wine, and other Roman amenities while the Synod took place; Farley Clinton, who, as ever, provided me with many insights; Jeff Mirus, my publisher and editor, who demonstrated remarkable support and patience before various setbacks, and the evolution of the book into something beyond our original intentions; and, not least, the Italian beauty who not only condescended to marry me, but who reviewed every page of the manuscript, kept me going with—excepting her mother's—the very finest pasta sauce in the Western hemisphere, and who daily reminds me what a glorious thing it is to be alive.

Table of Contents

Publisher's Foreword

In the Fall of 1985, Trinity Communications commissioned Richard Cowden-Guido to write a report on the 1985 Extraordinary Synod of Bishops which Pope· John Paul II had called to ·evaluate the impact of the Second Vatican Council. At the time of the commission, people on all sides of the many issues dividing the Church were speculating wildly about what the Synod was likely to do. We determined to have our own man there to find out.

Over the past generation, nearly all the books which have covered major ecclesiastical events in this country have come from Modernist authors. These authors have literally made history by purveying a false image of the Church, and especially a false image of the Second Vatican Council. This book sets the record straight.

As his trip to Rome drew near, Mr. Cowden-Guido realized that under our present Pope the real story of the Synod was likely to be nothing less than the real story of Vatican II. It would be the story of a Council gone astray, of Bishops who had allowed that to happen, and of a Pope and a Cardinal who were determined that, in our lifetimes, Vatican II would be implemented after all.

As events proved, it was impossible to write *that* story without writing at the same time a major book, and so the project grew.

Those who desire a comprehensive and detailed account of what was actually said and done at the Synod will find it here, as originally planned, in Part V. But they will also find a complete analysis of the situation which made the Synod necessary, and of the events and strategies leading up to it. They will find a sad reminder of the difficulties of past years and a clear record of present triumphs. The author reveals what it means to take the Council seriously, and shows how determined John Paul II is to see this done.

In so doing, Mr. Cowden-Guido has written a book which will stand for years as a vital contribution to the Catholic historical record and to the life of the Church in the Western world. He has written our story and the story of our Church—and he has written well.

Jeffrey A. Mirus
April 16, 1986

The Proper Context:
An Introduction by the Author

"This Council was the 21st Ecumenical Council. It can only be understood in the continuity of which it is a part, in the contexts of the 20 councils that preceded it, and our entire Church tradition."
Jean-Marie Cardinal Lustiger, Archbishop of Paris

"There has seldom been a Council without great confusion after it."
John Henry Cardinal Newman

The first great Ecumenical Council of the Roman Catholic Church was held at Nicea in A.D. 325. It was called to confront the challenge of Arianism, a heresy not unlike that attacking the Church today, for at its heart was the denial of Christ's Divinity. The Council met the challenge head on, and formally declared that Christ shared the same Divine nature as His Father, a declaration which Catholics to this day affirm at each Sunday Mass in the Nicene Creed.

By 345, however—twenty years later—Arianism had swept through much of the Roman Empire, winning the support of vast numbers of bishops and, after the death of Constantine in 337, virtually the entire Roman political apparatus. With the exception of the great St. Athanasius, and a few others, even those bishops who remained Catholic were timid about proclaiming the faith; and even some of the Popes were weak about combatting its enemies. Matters, in fact, became so grim between 340 and 370 that St. Jerome felt compelled to make his famous observation that "the whole world awoke, and groaned in astonishment to find itself Arian."

St. Jerome's observation was not strictly accurate, though, for despite the mass defection of the clergy and the politicians, and mass conversions to Arianism from paganism on the part of Germanic barbarian tribes, most of the laity throughout the Empire remained strongly Catholic—in faith, if not always in morals—and eventually their resistance to Arian clericalism began to triumph. By 380 the Catholic Restoration was so powerful that it was embraced by the Emperor Theodosius. Then, in 381, the Council of Constantinople was called, which of course reaffirmed the mystery of Christ's Divinity, as well as that of the Holy Spirit, against the new heresy of Macedonius that had sprung up: and it was from this Council that the affirmations about the Holy Spirit—"with the Father and the Son He is worshipped and glorified"—were added to the Creed.

But Arianism did not quite die, and new heresies—Donatism, Manicheeism, Pelagianism, Nestorianism and a host of others—were convulsing the Empire. The Third Ecumenical Council of Ephesus, presided over by St. Cyril of Alexandria representing Pope Celestine I, was held in 431; it defined the true personal unity of Christ, declared Mary the Mother of God against Nestorius, and condemned the Pelagian idea that a man may achieve salvation by his own fine efforts, without the grace of God. But neither heresy died out right away, and in fact, there are pockets of Nestorianism in the Middle East and Monophysitism in North Africa that have a constant tradition from this period, though serious efforts at reunion have been made since the Second Vatican Council. Pelagianism, meanwhile, has come and gone throughout the course of history, and today flickers at the edges of more virulent attacks on the Mystery of the Incarnation, and Its implications.

The tumults continued. The Fourth Ecumenical Council of Chalcedon in 451 is considered among the most important in Catholic history, not least in these days, where it is under persistent attack from such media personalities as Hans Kueng and Edward Schillebeeckx. It defined the two natures, Divine and human, in the One Divine Person of Christ. So successful was it from a practical standpoint, that another Council—the Fifth, also at Constantinople—had to be called more than 100 years later in 553 in order to reaffirm Chalcedon against the clamor that had not died out against it. Whereupon the heresy took different forms, which the Sixth Council, again at Constantinople, condemned in 681 by defining the two wills of Christ, the Divine and the human, as two distinct entities. By the Seventh Council, held in Nicea in 787, Chalcedon had triumphed, and the Church now confronted the phenomenon of iconoclasm, or the smashing of statues and pictures. To be sure, the Church condemned this, but it went on for awhile anyway; though, like the challenge to the Divinity of Christ, the phenomenon of iconoclasm did not resurface within the Church until after the last Council, despite Vatican II's specific assertion that "the practice of placing sacred images in churches so that they may be venerated by the faithful is to be maintained," in section 125 of the Sacred Constitution on the Liturgy, *Sacrosanctum concilium.*

Then things really got bad. The Eighth Ecumenical Council in 869 was the last to be held in Constantinople—or in the East. It condemned a false council that had sought not only to oust Ignatius, the legitimate Patriarch of Constantinople, but to condemn the Roman Pontiff in the bargain. Eventually the fruits of this conflict led to the Eastern Schism, though not formally for another 185 years, and arguably to the Byzantine Empire's eventual fall to that most formidable heresy of all, Mohammedanism. Still, there were two more Councils, the Fourteenth, held in Lyons in 1274, and the Seventeenth, which closed in Florence in 1439, both of which formally ended the schism. The first of these was attended by Pope Gregory X, the Emperor Michael VIII, several prominent Orthodox prelates, including the Patriarch of Constantinople and also of Antioch, and the Archbishop of Nicea, who had with them letters of procuration from 50 metropolitans and another 500 Eastern Orthodox bishops. Along with the Pope, the Catholics provided 500 bishops of their own, among them 15 cardinals. The Emperor agreed to add the word *filioque* to the symbol of Constantinople, ending the chief theological dispute between Rome and the East. But the antagonisms between East and West had by then become too political, and Lyons was repudiated by Michael's successor. Indeed, the great Emperor was denied a Christian burial by an angry Orthodox clergy, supported by the populace. The Florence Council, a tumultuous affair only in part Ecumenical due to Pope Eugenius IV's refusal to recognize some of its decrees, nonetheless again achieved formal reunion with the East, and was approved and attended by the Byzantine Emperor John VIII and numerous Orthodox bishops, and was this time supported by John's successor, Constantine XI.

But again, it did not take with the Orthodox clergy or population, and the Grand Duke Lucas Notarus captured the general feeling when he said, "I would rather see the Moslem turban in the midst of the city than the Latin Mitre." A few years later, his wish was granted.

Every Council from the Ninth to the Eighteenth dealt with the Moslem occupation of Palestine. The Eleventh, held at the Lateran in 1179, issued numerous decrees for the reformation of morals, particularly among the clergy, though it took the arrival of Sts. Clare, Dominic and Francis to accomplish, for a time, any serious progress in that arena. The Fifteenth through the Eighteenth Ecumenical Councils were held respectively in 1311-1313, 1414-1418, 1431-1439, and 1512-1517—two centuries, in short, of severe decline for the Church and thus for Europe, during which time the Papacy was subjected first to the Avignon Captivity, then to the Great Schism which recognized two Popes, and finally to the scandal of a decadent clergy that occasionally reached to the seat of Peter itself. And yet, each of these Councils sought to correct the abuses and scandals, culminating in the reforms issued after the five year Council at the Lateran, that ended in 1517. Seven months after that, an Augustinian monk named Luther nonetheless launched a rebellion that eventually gave way to secularism, historicism, and evangelicalism, which, though checked by the Nineteenth Council of Trent, was not ended by it. Meanwhile, during the course of that Council, Catholicism was restored in England under Mary Tudor; upon the Council's conclusion, however, Queen Mary died, whereupon the Faith was subjected to furious persecution in that country, from which it has yet to recover.

Vatican I ended—not formally, and not by choice—with the occupation of Rome and the conquest of the papal states by Garibaldi and his troops.

Then came Vatican II.

THE COUNCIL

I. Who's Afraid of Vatican II?

1. Why Vatican II?

> *"Vatican II is upheld by the same authority as Vatican I and the Council of Trent ... whoever denies Vatican II denies the authority that upholds the other two councils ... whoever accepts Vatican II, as it has clearly expressed and understood itself, at the same time accepts the whole binding tradition of the Catholic Church, particularly also the two previous councils."*
>
> Joseph Cardinal Ratzinger

> *"Without the Council, would it have been possible to avoid the bursting of the dam?"*
>
> Godfried Cardinal Danneels

One quite uncharacteristic aspect of the Roman Catholic Church in the 20th century, at least on the surface and until the Second Vatican Council, was the degree of public unity that prevailed within her own bureaucratic and clerical organization for some three generations. Doubtless Providence had much to do with this, but, given the extreme political and even mental instability of the European powers in this era, it was a Providence that made much practical sense.

Those powers, let us recall, decided in this century to abandon the pursuit of a Christian civilization in favor of such curious alternatives as Communism, Nazism and Consumerism. When not busily massacring millions of their own civilian populations, they fought two of the most destructive and immorally conducted wars in history. And a consequence of this, as Pope Paul VI

14

seemed to grasp, was that Western Europe has rapidly receded into little more than an appendage of history, after having dominated it for almost a millenium.

Science, meanwhile, having successfully convinced the world that the battle between Galileo and the Church had been over the correctness of his calculations, as opposed to the considerable dangers of unrestrained scientific pride—proceeded unrestrained. As a result it produced many marvels and relieved much suffering, although not without exacting something of a stiff price. The strength of the totalitarian ethic, for example, could simply not exist without the power of scientific manipulation to back it up. The poisoning of the atmosphere, one suspects, is doubtless more serious than anyone is yet willing to admit. And, lest we forget, there is the Bomb.

One thing about the Bomb, however, is that it did reintroduce a certain edgy stability to international political life. But, not surprisingly, as people got accustomed to that stability, a long delayed agitation against the unity of the Church began to quiver again. While Europe had been tearing itself apart, and the new superpowers seemed inclined for a time to complete that process throughout the entire world, neither the Roman Curia nor the Catholic faithful were much interested in hearing attacks against the Divinity of Christ or the efficacy of the sacraments, and particularly not from priests or theologians hoping to represent such views as somehow Catholic. Accordingly, those who held them and yet refused formally to apostatize were as careful about what they said in public, as they were determined to organize allies in private.

This caution had another rationale besides the public rejection that would invariably have greeted any open promotion of such perspectives: it was the experience of the clerics who had last sought to do something of the kind. Centered around the English Jesuit George Tyrrell and the French Abbe Alfred Loisy in the late 19th and early part of this century, they advanced a heresy condemned under the name of Modernism by Pope St. Pius X; and which held as a primary thesis that the four gospels were historically false, in effect fantasies. That, however, was merely the methodology for obtaining the chief goal, which was little more than a new hybrid of Arianism; the denial—once again—of the central Christian claim that God had deigned to become man, and walk among us.

"The main facts about the Modernist conspiracy are well known," wrote an Anglican partisan of it, the Rev. W. R. Inge.[1] "The group of men whom Pope Pius X called Modernists are, or were, some of them philosophers, and some New Testament critics. In the latter capacity they tend to accept the extreme destructive position, holding with Loisy that the historical Jesus was merely an enthusiastic prophet," that "all the supernatural elements in the Gospel narrative are either openly rejected or tacitly set aside," that "the historical Jesus, according to these critics, founded no Church and instituted no sacraments," that "the real founder of Catholicism was St. Paul, who inaugurated the cult of the Lord Christ," that "the 'historical' articles in the Creed are, for the Modernists, myth, not fact," and that "the fatal error of Catholic theology has been the attempt to find a rationalistic foundation for faith."

"The Vatican made no terms with [such propositions]," the Rev. Inge continued. "Modernism was pronounced to be 'a compendium of all the heresies,' and its theses were anathematized in detail. A very searching anti-Modernist oath was exacted," which made it "impossible for any Modernist to hold office in the Catholic Church except by deliberate perjury."

The principal vehicle by which the Modernist heresy was condemned was the saint's rather stirring encyclical of 1907, *Pascendi dominici gregis* (in English, On the Doctrine of the Modernists). It was promulgated on July 3, along with the document *Lamentabili sane*,[2] which exposed 65 specific propositions, such as for example no. 24: "The exegete who constructs premises from which it follows that dogmas are historically false or doubtful is not to be reproved as long as he does not directly deny the dogmas themselves." All 65 were condemned as inimical to the Catholic Faith. When Tyrrell and Loisy publicly refused to accept this, they were formally excommunicated, and died unrepentant.

St. Pius' forceful measures proved strikingly, and, considering the history of heresies, uncharacteristically successful. "The vigorous action of the Pope," notes historian Philip Hughes,[3]

---

[1] In the July *Quarterly Review*. The article was titled *The Crisis of Roman Catholicism.*

[2] The complete text of *Lamentabili sane* is published in the Appendix.

[3] In *A Popular History of the Catholic Church*, Macmillan Press, 1947; from which I have drawn all of the Monsignor's quotes that appear in this book.

"forced the concealed Modernists out into the open and within a very short time the Church was rid of them." As late as 1957 a German Jesuit remarked that "hardly ever before in the history of the Church was a heresy overcome so rapidly and so completely."[4] But these analyses proved premature.

Without realizing it, Hughes also points to the reason why, for he discusses the early Modernist strategy of occupying "important posts in various seminaries and universities," and the "danger anticipated" that from this vantage point they "would gradually corrupt the faith of the clergy and the educated laity, perverting theology and philosophy and the whole theory of the spiritual life." Despite *Pascendi* and *Lamentabili*, and the Rev. Inge's observation that it was "impossible for any Modernist to hold office in the Catholic Church except by deliberate perjury," this strategy was not abandoned, though it was practiced by more subtle means than those employed by Messers. Loisy and Tyrrell.

One paradox of the success of *Pascendi* and *Lamentabili*, however, was that when Modernism broke into the open again after the Second Vatican Council, nobody recognized it for what it was. "The Modernists were never, indeed, very numerous," as Hughes observed, "and Pius X's acts against them . . . were to most Catholics the first news of their existence." When Pope John XXIII surprised the world—if perhaps not the Holy Spirit—by calling in 1959 for yet a new Ecumenical Council, everyone had long since forgotten the Modernist heresy—everyone, that is, except the Modernists themselves. And indeed, it is likely that many of its new partisans were simply naive, or had been unwittingly corrupted, to borrow the expression of Philip Hughes.

In addition, let us again recall the extraordinary degree of unity that had characterized Catholic purpose regarding faith, morals, doctrine and devotion, without serious rupture, for more than half a century. In 1962, vigilance hardly seemed the order of the day. Not only had nearly three generations grown used to what everyone admitted was a firm and apparently unassailable Catholic presence throughout the world—even where persecuted openly by Communists—but Catholic conversions, vocations, schools, missions, hospitals, orphanages, and the list goes on, were at an all-time high. When Pope John issued *Humanae salutis* on the Christmas before the Council was formally convened, he openly

---

[4]As noted by *National Catholic Register* columnist Paul Hallett in his introduction to *Partisans of Error*, by Michael Davies, Neumann Press, 1983.

exulted in how the Church had "opposed decisively the materialist ideologies which deny faith," how She had "witnessed the rise
and growth of the immense energies of the apostolate of prayer,
of action in all fields," had seen "the emergence of a clergy constantly better equipped in learning and virtue for its mission" as
well as "a laity which has become ever more conscious of its responsibilities within the bosom of the Church and, in a special
way, of its duty to collaborate with the Church hierarchy."

Still, there was a fundamental point Catholics seemed to
have forgotten. It was that this fifty year period of relative internal peace and unity was an unusual dispensation, not at all the
norm. Indeed, as the post-Council era has so painfully revealed,
there was in too many quarters during the immediate pre-
Council era something very much akin to the sin of complacency,
and its collapse, in a sense, would vindicate a central Catholic
doctrine: for Catholicism teaches, *contra* the fundamentalist
Evangelicals, that it is a grave error, indeed the sin of pride, to
ever assume that any present possession of God's favor means you
may relax in the presumption it must necessarily continue.

For the Catholic Church, it did not. To be sure, there are
any number of impressive passages in the documents of Vatican
II—though not all, as Pope John Paul II diplomatically acknowledged on 6 October 1985. And yet, when you consider how poised
the Modernist party was in 1962 to manipulate the Council for its
own purposes, and even more how unprepared so many bishops
were to counter or even understand the nature of this manipulation, perhaps the most impressive thing about Vatican II is how
utterly the Modernists failed to introduce any heretical propositions into the Council documents themselves. Without complacency—to be sure—it is yet cause for Catholics to feel some satisfaction about the claims of their Faith, when they ponder how
skillfully the Modernists managed everything else, but were unable to manage that. For, of course, it is a dogma of Catholicism
that, just as He protects a Pope who speaks *ex cathedra* on matters
of faith and morals, so will the Holy Spirit protect an Ecumenical
Council from promulgating formal error. Despite certain inevitable criticisms of confusion and ambiguity in some of the
Council documents, however, no one has ever been able to cite
any such error; for there are none to cite.

Indeed, when one considers the vast corruption both in the
Catholic priesthood and the religious orders that the Council revealed, and the relative ease by which these clerics ignored and in

fact repudiated its documents in the name of its "spirit"—or "anti-spirit" as this process has now been recognized and named—then it is fair to wonder just how much worse the situation of the Church might be today had the Council not been held: had Catholicism in short continued on longer with naive optimism about unity, while Modernism continued its conquest of the Western Catholic clergy. Consider, for example, that one of the striking differences between the festive years of Vatican II and the Extraordinary Synod was in the nature of the Vatican's relations with the press. During the Council, an eyewitness informs me, if *New York Times* religion editor Ed Fiske was late for a press conference, the bishops would not begin it until he arrived. The impression too often conveyed was of a synod of reporters, with bishops acting as a species of copy boy. This time, it was not only a synod of bishops, but—much to its dismay—the international media quickly became aware of the fact.

When one further considers how vague Pope John seemed to be about why he was calling a Council, how opposed the Curia was to the idea, and how it completely surprised everyone, then the argument that it was divinely inspired increases in stature in light of recent history. Leave aside that the Council had an immediate benefit in Africa, where seminaries are overflowing and the Catholic population has gone from 29 to 66 million since 1965, and conversions still continue at the rate of two million annually (as opposed to the United States where there were just over 91,000 conversions in 1984); or in South Korea, where a similar phenomenon takes place on a smaller scale; or in Poland; or in Central and South America, where vocations, and particularly native vocations, have never in history been higher, and the Catholic population in both areas is nearly twice what it was twenty years ago. Remember instead that in 1962 the Western world was preparing for a furious burst of nihilism—disguised at first, of course, as idealism—and that because of the complacency and ongoing corruption of its priesthood, the Catholic Church was in no position to oppose this destructive wave.

Yes, consider that in 1962 television was a relatively new wonder, and people did not realize (though the Catholic convert Marshall McLuhan did) what a hypnotic and potent force it was about to become. Or that the international media itself had only just begun to grasp the power and extent of its own peculiar influence, not to say of its ability to shape events by the disingenuous method of direct participation in them, while affecting to be mere detached observers. And then reflect on what might have happened had Pope John played the role of interim Pope that was expected of him, and left it to Paul VI to convene a Council, say, in 1972. By then the Arianism assaulting the Church and the nihilism assaulting the West might well have made such a measure seem imperative. But of course also by then the bishops would have had no more experience in how to deal with a hostile media, whereas the media—and the Modernists—would have exhibited far more sophistication than even the high level they displayed during the real Vatican II. It seems of no small import that, despite certain naive strains in the document itself, the very first Decree issued by the Second Vatican Council—on 4 December 1963, the same day the Constitution on the Sacred Liturgy was released—was *Inter mirifica*: On the Means of Social Communication.

Would it, indeed, have been impossible to avoid the bursting of the dam without Vatican II? And held precisely when it was? The fact is that throughout history virtually all the Ecumenical Councils have been called in order to clarify Church teaching, by purifying it of a false teaching that had grown popular among clerical heretics and their followers. With few exceptions, the heresies spread even more rapidly following the Councils, only to die down, and often enough to die out, with the passing decades and sometimes centuries. That, clearly, was also the purpose of Vatican II—not the only one, but the most fundamental—despite that nobody, no human agent, understood this at the time. Though the Church did not seem embattled in 1962, She was in fact naive and enfeebled; and though, as ever, the Council did not immediately alter that, it did very definitely lance the boil. With a huge resurgence of Arianism about to conquer the Western clergy (to the extent it had not already done so *in pectore*), Vatican II reaffirmed the importance of the laity; broke a false dependence on the clergy; broke Church dependence on the declining West (recall there were *no* third world cardinals when John became Pope); forcefully asserted all the ancient truths of the Faith, not least the primacy of the Papacy and the doctrine of infallibility; focused on the importance of the liturgy as well as on the Eastern Catholic churches and their rites; finished what had been the original intentions of Vatican I in defining the role of bishops; proclaimed the veracity of Scripture and its organic relation to Sacred Tradition; alerted Catholics to the importance and the growing power of the media; established firm principles for the renewal of religious life and missionary work and the training of priests; condemned anti-semitism and other forms of racism; condemned abortion and euthanasia and infanticide; called for serious efforts of ecumenism toward what history would soon reveal to be (except for fundamentalism) a dying Protestantism and resurgent Mohammedanism; reaffirmed the importance of chastity, the value of the contemplative life, the reality of purgatory, miracles, angels, guardian angels and the supernatural reality that permeates the temporal and brief life of man; and, not least, asserted the dignity of man in the face of a growing bureaucratic totalitarianism of which Modernism is but another gray example, and which indeed reflects, even as it feeds, that grim despair at the heart of the modern age.

2. What Happened to the West? Modernism and the Worship of History

> *"We are too charitable if we presume the atheist is always acting in good faith when he rejects faith."*
>
> Joseph Sobran

> *"The crisis in the Church today is before all else a crisis of priests and religious orders."*
>
> Joseph Cardinal Ratzinger

It is, as St. Paul reminds us, a fearful thing to fall into the hands of the living God. As the bloodshed in this century has so ruthlessly demonstrated, however, falling out of His hands is more fearsome still: for it means falling into the hands of men. "To the archetype of the new class," observes former *New Statesman* editor Paul Johnson in his remarkable history of the 20th century *Modern Times,*[5] "such as Lenin, Hitler, and Mao Tse-Tung, politics was the one legitimate form of moral activity. . . . This view, which would have struck an earlier age as fantastic, became to some extent the orthodoxy everywhere . . . it had also proved itself the great killer of all time. By the 1980's, state action had been responsible for the violent or unnatural deaths of over

---

[5]Harper & Row, 1983.

100 million people, more perhaps than it had hitherto succeeded in destroying during the whole of human history up to 1900."

Why, one wonders? What is it about our age that produced not only the virtually unprecedented phenomenon of the political zealot, but thousands, nay millions, who were willing to pay tribute to the "moral activity" of such men, and the rigid political states they created? What possessed the fathers of our century, the Lenins and the Hitlers and the Maos, and all their less formidable imitators, to devote their every waking hour, every sinew of their energy, to serving the Moloch of politics, or of history, as they liked to consider it? And why hasn't the empirical evidence inspired all the Leninettes, as it were, to re-examine the premises that have produced these horrors?

To the Christian, the answers to these questions, for all their complexity, have also about them a certain simplicity, as Alexander Solzhenitsyn observed during his speech at Buckingham Palace when he received the Templeton Prize in 1983. "If I were called upon to identify briefly the principal trait of the entire 20th century," he said, "I would be unable to find anything more precise and pithy than to repeat once again: men have forgotten God."

Indeed, one did not need to be Christian to recognize this. Friedrich Nietzsche struck an international chord more than a century before Solzhenitsyn when his fictional character announced the death of God, and went on to scream at the intellectual elite of his time, "and *you* have killed Him." In fact, that 19th century intellectual elite had concluded that the glories of Christendom were not the result of struggles to love Christ and discern His Will, and thus serve truth by organizing society in pursuit of these goals; but were rather something like the natural condition of men.

World War I was a setback to this view, but by 1918 the great heresy of history worship—against which the Marian apparitions the previous year in Portugal had warned—was firmly entrenched. The hubris of the 19th century, particularly with its great scientific advances, had proved too exhilarating for the new ruling classes to abandon; and so, despite the Great War, they did not turn to God. At the same time they remained uneasy, for there were certain ancient questions that the major Hegelian and history-worshipping offshoots like Marxism and Nazism, and as time went on Liberalism as well, were unable to answer—questions such as those posed by the present Roman

Pontiff during a general audience on 9 January 1985: "Where does man come from?" he asked. "Why does he exist? What are his relationships with God and the invisible world? How must he behave in order to achieve his life's goal? Why is he subject to suffering and death, and what is his hope?"

The chimera of "progress" that had entranced so many in the 19th century, was no longer tenable with Europe lying in rubble and consumed by a hunger for vengeance in 1918. And yet, the elite were still reluctant to pose the above queries with any seriousness, thereby creating a vacuum; and into the vacuum, with ferocious determination, marched the professional politician, the single-minded fanatic, the men who would soon be regarded as kings and lords and even demigods, because they spared the unbelieving intellectuals from having to confront either God or despair. They did this by the simple device of advocating *activity*, politics, a ceaseless devotion to the worship and formation and organization of the new god history, and by organizing it in a manner that would not leave time for threatening questions from the successor to St. Peter. Indeed, those with the temerity to inquire, say, about the fact that one day history would itself be as dead and silent as Mr. Lenin's formerly fevered brain, were at first never answered, but merely dismissed as outside the great flowing course of history for even asking the question; eventually they were shot; or else their societies were protected from them with such distractions as pornography, cocaine, and the carefully controlled concerns of the seven o'clock news. Meanwhile, the elite began devoting themselves to the one thing they think can create history: which is to say power.

"Never before," Solzhenitsyn also observed when he received the Templeton Prize, had the world "known a godlessness as organized, militarized, and tenaciously malevolent as that preached by Marxism. Within the philosophical system of Karl Marx and Nikolai Lenin and at the heart of their psychology," he continued, "hatred of God is the principal driving force, more fundamental than all their political and economic pretensions. Militant atheism is not merely incidental or marginal to communist policy: it is not a side effect, but the central pivot."

Essayist Joseph Sobran, who as a combination of Edmund Burke and Hilaire Belloc may be the finest writer in America today, is only slightly kinder to Liberalism than is Solzhenitsyn to Leninism. " 'The poor' are to liberalism roughly what 'the proletariat' is to Communism," he asserts. "A formalistic device for the assumption of power." As such, "if the American Left doesn't contemplate persecution of Christians, it has found its own alternative: seduction of the clergy. Why make martyrs of people who can be enlisted as allies? And the strange fact is that many of the clergy have accepted this role."[6]

For all its individual failures and sinners, the Church, the *teaching* Church, has always stood firmly in the path of mere power worship, by its simple and constant assertion that man does not exist for the state, nor for labor, not even for the Sabbath, and certainly not for history: but that all these things, that every created thing, exists for man. Indeed, this is so true, according to Catholicism, that even God Almighty did not disdain to humble Himself and become a man, simply (among other things) to drive that point home.

One can thus see that the worship of power, of history, of any idol at all, the promulgation of any heresy, can never wholly succeed until it first destroys or buries this idea: and it cannot do that without first destroying the religious and philosophical system that is Roman Catholicism. At the same time, those fascinated by power could not help but gaze longingly at the organization of the Catholic Church; and perhaps dream of the impact they might have on history should they succeed in garnering its services. Indeed, the historian Paul Johnson informs us how inviting a temptation this might be, upon noting that "The Roman Catholic Church is an enormous organization[7] ... a powerful educational and cultural force, since it ran 79,207 primary and over 28,000 secondary schools and provided nearly a million university places"[8] when Cardinal Karol Wojtyla became Pope John Paul II. It also had at that time, more than 400,000 priests, some 4500 deacons, nearly 70,000 lay religious and nearly a million nuns and lay-Sisters, and more than 125,000 catechists in the missions, as well as "331,960 parishes, composing some 2372 ecclesiastical territories; 1640 dioceses, 402 metropolitan sees, 54 archbishoprics, and 12 patriarchal sees. The Church," says Johnson, "runs an astonishing variety of different institutions, ranging from newspapers and

---

[6]From "Pensees: Notes For the Reactionary of Tomorrow," in the 31 December *National Review*.
     [7]In *Pope John Paul II and the Catholic Restoration*, Servant Books, 1981.
     8*Modern Times.*

radio stations to hospitals; but above all it is a major educational force in the world."[9]

Yes. Enemies of Catholicism, therefore, were, and are, faced with the dilemma of trying to crush Catholic influence either by direct force, as Queen Elizabeth I largely accomplished in England, but not in Ireland; or by the seduction of the clergy that Sobran addresses, which of late has proved immensely successful in the United States. Meanwhile, a violent or head-on confrontation with the Church might also seem less desirable to the historicist for the simple reason that the Church might win such a confrontation, even if She were to be temporarily conquered. Worshippers of history, in fact, might be particularly nervous on that point.

Accordingly, after the initial defeat of the Modernists by St. Pius X, their survivors began to adopt precisely the kind of frenetic intensity and determination that the professional politicians had used to win the power of the state, while excluding the inapplicable methods of direct violence, of course—although even for the state politicians, violence was but the handmaid of propaganda, at least until they had actually won power.

And it made sense. "The heresy that goes by the name of Modernism," according to Hughes, "was an attempt to make Catholicism palatable to the thought of the day, by repudiating its objective supernatural character." Having envied and adopted the philosophical systems of the historicists, but having failed to convince the Church She should follow suit—indeed, having won Her censure for trying—the Modernists had but two choices: formally to apostatize, or to employ from within the Church the organizational methods of their historicist mentors. What this meant in practical terms was the quiet insinuation, through deliberate perjury, of philosophical and then theological principles of the kind condemned by *Pascendi* and *Lamentabili*, but done in

---

[9]See footnote 7.

such a way as not to attract the attention of Rome.[10] With a specific agenda in mind, it became but a matter of eventually learning how to manipulate the bureaucratic organization of the Church, win a few converts among the hierarchy and heads of religious orders, and then, among other things, slowly establish political and administrative control of the seminaries, the universities, the catechetical establishments, the religious orders, and—*voila.*

Indeed, particularly in dioceses where the bishops were either part of the process, or timid, or simply not very astute, once a determined group wins positions wherein they can decide what questions are allowed to be asked, what categories of thought priests may be allowed to pursue (and of course, which to be dismissed or ignored), and not least who is to be promoted and who discharged from the administrative life of the diocese or seminary or university—then the power of those with a specific agenda in mind can only grow, unless detected and checked by a superior force. By way of analogy to the civil order in the United States, consider that there was no mass movement, merely a small group of determined activists, who wanted to legalize abortion, or insist that every neighborhood in the country was Constitutionally obliged to provide the most degrading pornography at the local drug store; yet by learning how to manipulate the levers of power and language of the fashionable elite, they

---

[10]Given the great intellectual and speculative tradition of the Church—She had, of course, founded the university system throughout Europe in the Middle Ages—this deception was not so difficult as it might seem, despite the very careful anti-Modernist oath the Rev. Inge has mentioned, which, with only specified exceptions, was required of all priests and bishops until Pope Paul VI, perhaps somewhat precipitately, decided in 1965 that it should be believed only as a matter of good will rather than formal oath.

In addition, though it is not the purpose of this book to investigate all the controversies and figures involved, I should note that part of the problem stems from the fact that deep but solid orthodox thinking can skirt close to Modernist thought in some instances; that speculative but genuinely Catholic thinkers can make mistakes; and that one of the mistakes these latter might be inclined to make, is to trust the intellectual honesty of those whose agenda was somewhat different than mere speculative theology subject to the approval of the Church. Add to that Aristotle's astute observation that "the least initial deviation from truth is later multiplied a thousand times," and one can perhaps see how much room the Modernists had in which to operate, despite the problems posed by St. Pius X's oath.

imposed both. And were followed in turn by the profiteers, who knew how to manipulate the weakness of men.

Within the Church, the luminous intelligence of *Pascendi* and the administrative measures that attended it provided that superior force which checked the Modernists for a season; for St. Pius had recognized that seduction of the clergy was the chief Modernist goal. Indeed, in warning of this, he charged in as early as the second paragraph of *Pascendi* "that the partisans of error are to be sought not only among the Church's open enemies; but, what is to be most dreaded and deplored, in her very bosom, and are the more mischievous the less they keep in the open." Among these, he noted in the following sentence, are those in "the ranks of the priesthood itself, who ... thoroughly imbibed with the poisonous doctrine taught by the enemies of the Church, and lost to all sense of modesty, put themselves forward as reformers of the Church, and, forming more boldly into lines of attack, assail all that is most sacred in the work of Christ, not sparing even the Divine Redeemer."

"Although they express their astonishment that we should number them amongst the enemies of the Church," paragraph 3 begins, "no one will be reasonably surprised that we should do so, if, leaving out of account the internal disposition of the soul, of which God alone is the Judge, he considers their tenets, their manner of speech, and their action. Nor indeed would he be wrong in regarding them as the most pernicious of all adversaries of the Church. For they put into operation their designs for Her undoing, not from without but from within. Hence, the danger is present almost in the very veins and heart of the Church, whose injury is the more certain from the very fact that their knowledge of her is more intimate. Moreover, they lay the ax not to the branches and shoots, but to the very root, that is, to the faith and its deepest fibers, [from where] they proceed to diffuse poison throughout the whole tree, so that there is no part of Catholic truth which they leave untouched, none that they do not strive to corrupt."

"Further," *Pascendi* continues, "none is more skillful, none more astute than they, in the employment of a thousand noxious devices: for they play the double part of rationalist and Catholic, and this so craftily that they easily lead the unwary into error; and as audacity is their chief characteristic, there is no conclusion of any kind from which they shrink or which they do not thrust forward with pertinacity and assurance."

This last sentence was to prove an eerily prophetic look at the role the Modernists would play during the Second Vatican Council and the years that have followed.

3. A Look at the Documents

> *"The greatest concern of the Ecumenical Council is this: that the Sacred Deposit of Christian Doctrine should be guarded and taught more efficaciously . . . to transmit that doctrine pure and integral without any attenuation or distortion which throughout twenty centuries, notwithstanding difficulties and contrasts, has become the common patrimony of men."*
>
> Pope John XXIII

> *"Return to the authentic texts of the original Vatican II . . . to defend true tradition means to defend the Council. Though it is also our fault if we have provided a pretext—to the 'right' and the 'left' alike—to view Vatican II as a 'break' and an abandonment of the tradition. There is, instead, a continuity. . . ."*
>
> Joseph Cardinal Ratzinger

Unlike the Council of Chalcedon, there were no bishops (as far as I know) who engaged in open fisticuffs during the course of Vatican II. To be sure, there was some baseness; but this was due, no doubt, as the Curial Clergy Prefect Silvio Cardinal Oddi remarked to me during an interview he granted in 1983, that "bishops are sons of Adam, are they not?" Indeed, given how often their actions have reminded us of this, both during and since the Council, one is again struck by the depth and orthodoxy of the actual documents Vatican II produced. Well, orthodoxy anyhow; and if some of what was produced contained a hint of naivete—certain wide-eyed passages of enthusiasm in *Gaudium et Spes* come to mind—this was more than counterbalanced by the profound insights of *Lumen Gentium*.[11] At the same time it could be observed, and indeed was, by Pope John Paul II in speaking of the Council on 6 October, that its "expression, in so far as it is human, can be imperfect, and remains open to ever more precise formulation." To address these imperfections was presumably one of the reasons he convened the Extraordinary Synod.

---

[11]Particularly in light of *Nota Praevia* Pope Paul VI collegially added to its beginning, in order to give it proper context.

In any event, on 25 January 1959, Pope John XXIII announced he would convene a Council in the course of his Pontificate; on June 5 the following year he established Preparatory Commissions and Secretariats to develop its schemas; then he released the Apostolic Constitution *Humanae salutis* on Christmas of 1961 formally convening the Council for the following year. On 20 July 1962 he invited non-Catholic denominations to send observers, which they agreed to do. Vatican II was formally opened on 11 October.

During the First Session, the Council Fathers voted by some sixty per cent against the first four schemas presented by the Preparatory Commission, in favor of addressing themselves first to the matter of the liturgy. Though the rules governing the Council had stated such a rejection needed a two-thirds vote of the Fathers, Pope John decided it better to go along with the majority feeling on the matter, and so work on *Sacrosanctum concilium* (*SC*) began. On 7 December, as the First Session came to a close, the Fathers voted 1922 to 11 in favor of the first chapter of that Constitution. The following day, on the Feast of the Immaculate Conception, the Session formally closed. On that same day, by the will of the Pope, the name of St. Joseph was placed into the Canon of the Mass.

Pope John died on June 3, 1963. Eighteen days later Giovanni Cardinal Montini, the Archbishop of Milan, became the successor to St. Peter and took the name of Paul VI. At that time, he had the authority to announce the end of the Council, but of course he did not, and its Second Session was convened on September 29. It closed on 4 December with the formal promulgation of *Sacrosanctum concilium* and *Inter mirifica*, the Decree on Social Communications.

There are 12,179[12] lines of text in the documents of Vatican II, so one can only give a flavor of them, and it is not quite possi-

---

[12]In regard to which (since His Holiness has explicitly bound no Catholic to consider the expression of Catholicism within the Council's documents as necessarily the best possible), it could perhaps be said that the least happy aspect of Vatican II is its length: the 12,179 lines are nearly half as many as the 25,548 lines that comprise the texts of all 20 previous Councils combined. Thus, in comparison to the average Council, (of 1277 lines) the last Council Fathers felt nearly 10 words were necessary for every one their more economic predecessors produced. Accordingly, Catholics who are hesitant to read all 12,179 lines, may prefer to rely in a general way on the *Final Report* of the Extraordinary Synod—to be found in the Appendix—which is a more pointed 700 to 800 lines.

ble here to refute the charges of ambiguity from various quarters that are leveled against them. I have read them twice, however, carefully, and do not think they contain any serious ambiguity; indeed, upon seeing (as we shall) how the Pope's and Cardinal Ratzinger's words and intentions have in the course of this year been distorted, I think it fair to suggest again that the Modernist onslaught would have happened regardless of what the documents said. At the same time, Cardinal Ratzinger's admission that the bishops themselves deserve censure for allowing deliberate distortions to take hold is well taken; but that is because the bishops did not defend Vatican II, and not because of the content of the documents themselves.

Allow a review of that content.

"The Church," *SC* asserts, "is . . . so constituted that in Her the human is directed toward and subordinated to the divine, the visible to the invisible, action to contemplation, and this present world to that city yet to come, the object of our quest" (Section 2). "Christ . . . achieved His task principally by the paschal mystery of His blessed passion, resurrection from the dead, and glorious ascension, whereby 'dying He destroyed our death, rising He restored our life' " (Sec. 5). "Popular devotions of the Christian people, provided they conform to the laws and norms of the Church, are to be highly recommended" (Sec. 13).

Section 22 states that the "Regulation of the sacred liturgy depends solely on the authority of the Church, that is, on the Apostolic See, and, as laws may determine, on the bishops. . . . Therefore no other person, not even a priest, may add, remove, or change anything in the liturgy on his own authority . . . ;" moreover (Sec. 30), "at the proper time a reverent silence should be observed," and (Sec. 54) "care must be taken to ensure that the faithful may also be able to say or sing together in Latin those parts of the Ordinary of the Mass which pertain to them."

Nonetheless, a survey of 19,000 U.S. parishes was published in the 13 October 1985 *National Catholic Register*, and revealed that only 100 of them abide by Conciliar Teaching on the Liturgy. The rest, by celebrating Mass exclusively in the vernacular, are still resisting Vatican II; though there is resistance in other areas as well.

Sec. 109 of *SC*, for example, also notes that catechesis, while pointing out the social consequences of sin, "must impress upon the minds of the faithful the distinctive character of penance as a detestation of sin because it is an offense against God." Sec. 124

exhorts bishops to "be careful to ensure that works of art which are repugnant to faith, morals, and Christian piety, and which offend true religious sense either by depraved forms or through lack of artistic merit or because of mediocrity or pretense, be removed from the houses of God and from other sacred places," and the next paragraph notes that "the practice of placing sacred images in churches so that they may be venerated by the faithful is to be maintained."

Among other things, *Inter mirifica* insists in Section 17 that in regard to "Catholic newspapers, periodicals, film-projects, radio and television stations and programs ... the main aim of all these is to propagate and defend the truth and to secure the permeation of society by Christian values."

The Third Session opened on 14 September 1964 and closed on 21 November. It was a stormy one, at the end of which the Decrees *Unitatis redintegratio* (on Ecumenism), *Orientalium ecclesiarum* (on Eastern Catholic Churches) and the Dogmatic Constitution on the Church *Lumen gentium* were promulgated. And on that same final day, to the fury of the Modernists, Pope Paul proclaimed the Blessed Virgin Mary to be the Mother of the Church.

Orientalium ecclesiarum insisted not only upon the equality of the Eastern Churches with the Latin, but also (Sec. 4) that provision must be made to protect and advance "these individual churches," and in section five noted "the great debt owed to the Eastern Churches by the Church Universal." It was also in this Decree, in Sec. 26, that Vatican II condemned "a mutual sharing in sacred things *communicatio in sacris*, which runs counter to the unity of the Church, or which involves formal adhesion to error or the danger of aberration in the faith, of scandal and of indifferentism."

This principle was applied to ecumenical discussion in Sec. 24 of the Ecumenism Decree, when the council Fathers insisted that "ecumenical activity cannot be other than fully and sincerely Catholic, that is, loyal to the truth we have received from the Apostles and the Fathers, and in harmony with the faith which the Catholic Church has always professed." At the same time Sec. 3 struck a reasonable and charitable chord, when it said that Catholics "cannot charge with the sin of separation those who at present are born into [Protestant or schismatic] communities and in them are brought up in the faith of Christ, and the Catholic Church accepts them with respect and affection as brothers. For men who believe in Christ and have been properly baptized are put in some, though imperfect, communion with the Catholic Church."

That same paragraph also asserts that "it is through Christ's Catholic Church alone, which is the universal help toward salvation, that the fullness of the means of salvation can be obtained. It was to the apostolic college alone, of which Peter is the head, that Our Lord entrusted all the blessings of the New Covenant, in order to establish on earth the one Body of Christ into which all those should be fully incorporated who belong in any way to the people of God."

Lumen gentium, which shall be considered in more detail later because of the controversies surrounding it, and because it is in one sense very much the heart of Vatican II, was composed, in addition to Pope Paul's *Nota praevia*, of eight chapters. These were: The Mystery of the Church; The People of God; The Hierarchy; The Laity; The Universal Call to Holiness; Religious; The Pilgrim Church which "will receive its perfection only in the glory of heaven" (this chapter in Sec. 50 thus exhorts the faithful to pray for the souls in purgatory); and the Conclusion—a song of praise to Mary, the Mother of God, Mediatrix of all graces, and Mother of the Church.

Lumen gentium also discusses the importance of union and collegiality, which—since some serious attention was finally given to these concepts during the Extraordinary Synod—one can hope will in the future be used to strengthen the Catholicity of the bishops rather than fragment it. Its *Nota praevia* point out that "there is no such thing as a college without its head," and that the distinction between the college and its head, the Vicar of Christ, "is not a distinction between the Roman Pontiff and the bishops taken together but between the Roman Pontiff by himself and the Roman Pontiff along with the bishops. The Pope alone, in fact, being the head of the college, is qualified to perform certain actions in which bishops have no competence whatsoever ... the Pope, as supreme pastor of the Church, may exercise his power at any time, as he sees fit, by reason of the demands of his office.... Clearly it is the connection of the bishops with their head that is in question throughout [*Lumen gentium*] and not the activity of the bishops independently of the Pope. In a case like that, in default of the Pope's action, the bishops cannot act as a college, for this is obvious from the idea of college itself."

Meanwhile, *Lumen gentium* begins with the ringing affirmation that "Christ is the light of humanity," a theme much developed in the encyclicals and discourses of John Paul II, particularly in his first encyclical *Redemptor hominis*; and should the reader wish to grasp the real spirit of Vatican II—without having to read all 12,179 lines—a perusal of this Constitution is doubtless the best approach.

For the moment, however, let us consider its observations in light of the Modernist revival that followed the Council, for "very often," as Sec. 16 notes, "deceived by the Evil One, men have become vain in their reasonings, have exchanged truth for a lie and served the world rather than the Creator."

Sec. 18: "Jesus Christ, the eternal pastor, set up the Holy Church by entrusting the apostles with their mission as He Himself had been sent by the Father," and "in order that the episcopate . . . might be one and undivided he put Peter at the head of the other apostles and in him set up a lasting and visible source and foundation of the unity of both faith and communion. This teaching concerning the institution, the permanence, the nature and import of the sacred primacy of the Roman Pontiff and his infallible teaching office, the sacred synod proposes anew to be firmly believed by all the faithful."

After discussing the collegial character of the bishopric—"in communion with one another and the Roman Pontiff in a bond of unity, charity and peace"—Sec. 22 also notes, however, that "the college or body of bishops has for all that no authority unless united with the Roman Pontiff, Peter's successor, as its head, whose primatial authority, let it be added, over all, whether pastors or faithful, remains in its integrity. For the Roman Pontiff, by reason of his office as Vicar of Christ, namely, and as pastor of the entire Church, has full supreme and universal power over the whole Church, a power which he can always exercise unhindered."

"The individual bishops," meanwhile, "are the visible source and foundation of unity in their own particular Churches, which are constituted after the model of the universal Church," and they "have the obligation of fostering and safeguarding the unity of the faith and upholding the discipline which is common to the whole Church" (Sec. 23). It is perhaps by considering this passage that a Catholic can determine whether a bishop is in reality a member of the college in union with the Pope, despite his juridical status.

The question of the teaching authority of episcopal conferences is also firmly dismissed in *Lumen gentium*, when it notes that "individual bishops, in so far as they are set over particular Churches, exercise their pastoral office over the portion of the People of God assigned to them, not over other Churches, nor the Church universal," and though every bishop is required to "have care and solicitude for the whole Church," this is "not exercised by any act of jurisdiction."

The chapter on the laity has many astute observations as well, but in light of recent controversies between the American Catholic faithful and their bishops, Sec. 37 seems particularly relevant: to the pastors, of whom *Lumen gentium* says Peter is such for the entire Church, "the laity should disclose their needs and desires with that liberty and confidence which befits children of God and brothers in Christ," as well as "manifest their opinion on those things which pertain to the good of the Church."

Interestingly, on the feast of St. Pius X, just eleven days before the final session of the Council opened, and a month before his trip to speak before the United Nations, Pope Paul VI issued the encyclical *Mysterium Fidei*, which condemned liturgical abuses already gaining ground throughout the West; and which drew the parallels between the teaching on the liturgy in *Sacrasanctum concilium* and the Councils of Trent and Vatican I.

The last session's formal opening was on 14 September 1965 (St. Pius's feast day has since been changed to 21 August). On 28 October three more Decrees were issued: *Christus Dominus (CD)*, On the Pastoral Office of Bishops; *Perfectae caritatis (PF)*, On Religious Life; and *Optatem totius (OT)*, On the training of priests; and two declarations: *Gravissimum educationis (GE)*, On Christian Education; and *Nostra aetate (NA)*, On the Relation of the Church to Non-Christian Religions.

Christus Dominus encouraged the formation of Bishops' Conferences. It did more than that, of course, although much of the Decree was but a repeat of things that had already been said in *Lumen gentium*. One of the ugliest things about the event of the Council, however, had been the relentless and not infrequently vicious attacks on members of the Roman Curia from the media, often in collusion with bishops who shared their perspectives. Against all that, however, *CD* asserted that "in exercising his supreme, full, and immediate authority over the universal Church, the Roman Pontiff employs the various departments of the Roman Curia, which act in his name and by his authority for the good of the churches and in the service of the sacred pastors" (Sec. 9). The Pope would draw attention to this teaching when he addressed the College of Cardinals three days before the opening of the Extraordinary Synod. *CD* also encouraged bishops to proclaim "how highly we should value the family, its unity and stability, the procreation and education of children" (Sec. 12); noted how "bishops should be especially concerned about catechetical instruction . . . to develop in men a living, explicit and active faith, enlightened by doctrine" (Sec. 14); and advised that "in forming a judg ment as to the suitability of a priest for governing a parish, the bishop should take into consideration not only his learning but also his piety" (Sec. 31).

Perfectae caritatis said that religious "should practice mortification and custody of the senses . . . and, by a kind of spiritual instinct, they should reject whatever endangers chastity" (Sec. 12). The next paragraph notes that "with regard to religious poverty it is by no means enough to be subject to superiors in the use of property. Religious should be poor in fact and in spirit, having their treasures in heaven." And Sec. 17: "The religious habit, as a symbol of consecration, must be simple and modest, at once poor and becoming."

The Modernists of course, hated and in practice attacked the teaching of *Optatam totius* as much as they did—well, all the rest of the documents. "Seminary superiors and professors," Sec. 5 insisted, "should receive a careful preparation in sound doctrine." Sec. 8 noted that "spiritual formation should be closely associated with doctrinal and pastoral formation," and Sec. 9 that "students should be thoroughly penetrated with the Mystery of the Church, which this Council has set particularly in relief." That same paragraph quotes St. Augustine: "A man possesses the Holy Spirit in the measure in which he loves the Church." Seminarians are warned in Sec. 10 to "be put on their guard against the dangers that threaten their chastity, especially in present-day society." And not least, Sec. 16 notes that "theological subjects should be taught in the light of faith, under the guidance of the magisterium of the Church."

Gravissimum educationis in section 3 insists upon the primacy of parents in the education of their children, and section 8 requires teachers to "work in close cooperation with the parents."

In *Nostra aetate*, the Church acknowledged that She "rejected nothing of what is true and holy in [non-Christian] religions," but that despite this, She "proclaims and is in duty bound to proclaim without fail, Christ, who is the way, the truth and the life" (Sec. 2). *NA* also sought to bury the hatchet of past disputes and blood-shed with the Moslems, and in condemning "every form of perse-cution against whomsoever it may be directed," it particularly deplored "all hatreds, persecutions, displays of anti-semitism lev-eled at any time or from any source against the Jews," in Sec. 4. It did not, of course, insist that enemies of Christianity were the sole possessors of the right to define anti-semitism.

On November 18, the Council promulgated the Dogmatic Constitution on Divine Revelation, *Dei Verbum*. It dogmatically asserted what all Catholics know, what *Pascendi* and *Lamentabili* defended, and what the Modernists had been denying from the beginning, albeit with particular ferocity within seminaries and universities since the Council: "God graciously arranged that the things he had once revealed for the salvation of peoples should remain in their entirety, throughout the ages, and be transmitted to all generations. Therefore, Christ the Lord, in whom the entire Revelation of the most high God is summed up, commanded the apostles to preach the Gospel, which had been promised before-hand by the prophets, and which He fulfilled in His own Person and promulgated with His own lips. . . . This Gospel was to be the source of all saving truth and moral discipline. This was faith-fully done: it was done by the apostles who handed on, by the spoken word of their preaching, by the example they gave, by the institutions they established, what they themselves had re-ceived—whether from the lips of Christ, from His way of life and His works, or whether they had learned it at the prompting of the Holy Spirit: it was done by those apostles and other men asso-ciated with the apostles who, under the inspiration of the same Holy Spirit, committed the message of salvation to writing." (Sec. 7)

Section 10 notes that "Sacred tradition and sacred Scripture make up a single sacred deposit of the Word of God, which is en-trusted to the Church." In a specific defense of *Pascendi* and *Dei Verbum* sec. 12 says "all that has been said about the matter of in-terpreting Scripture is ultimately subject to the judgment of the Church which exercises the divinely conferred commission and ministry of watching over and interpreting the Word of God." It is even more specific in affirming St. Pius' understanding, assert-ing in section 19 "that the four Gospels . . . whose historicity [the Church] unhesitatingly affirms, faithfully hand on what Jesus, the Son of God, while he lived among men, really did and taught for their eternal salvation, until the day He was taken up." That same section goes on to say that "the sacred authors, in writing the four Gospels, selected certain of the many elements which had been handed on, either orally or already in written form, others they synthesized or explained with an eye to the situation of the churches, the while sustaining the form of preaching, but always in such a way as they have told the honest truth about Jesus." This passage should be kept particularly in mind in light of subsequent, post-Conciliar developments, to be examined more thoroughly in a later chapter.

The Decree on the Apostolate of the Laity, *Apostolicam actuositatem*, was also issued on that day. And, with perhaps a growing understanding of the increasing strength of Modernism within the priesthood and even among their brother bishops—the Council was now four years old—the Council Fathers exhorted the laity by noting in sec. 6 that "at a time when ... grave errors aiming at undermining religion, the moral order and human society itself are rampant, the Council earnestly exhorts the laity to take a more active part ... in fidelity to the mind of the Church, in the explanation and defense of Christian principles and in the correct application of them to the problems of our times." Section 7 charged that "in our own days not a few, putting an immoderate trust in the conquests of science and technology, turn off into a kind of idolatry of the temporal; they become slaves of it rather than the masters." Section 11 exhorted the faithful "to assert with vigor the right and duty of parent and guardians to give their children a Christian upbringing," and "to defend the dignity and legitimate autonomy of the family: this has always been the duty of married persons; today, however, it has become the most important aspect of their apostolate." Alas, after Vatican II, it would become incumbent on the laity to exercise this charge particularly against bishops and the often shrill assaults of Church bureaucrats, clerics, and nuns, including one especially infamous document on sex education from the United State Catholic Conference which Father William Smith (whom John Cardinal O'Connor has called one of the top moral theologians in the country) denounced as a "dangerous perversion of true Christian education," which could "accomplish no more than instill a Planned Parenthood mentality in children at an age earlier than Planned Parenthood now succeeds in doing. If you held your breath between mentions of virtue in these guidelines," the priest added, "you'd die."[13]

The Laity Decree concludes with a prescient and "an earnest appeal" to all the laity to respond more forcefully "to the voice of Christ, who at this hour is summoning them more pressingly." And as we shall see in a later chapter, great numbers of Catholic lay men and women have taken this exhortation to heart, though they have in consequence been often viciously attacked by clerical opponents of Vatican II.

On 7 December, the final documents of Vatican II were promulgated. These included the Pastoral Constitution on the Church in the Modern World, *Gaudium et spes*, two Decrees, *Ad Gentes Divinitus* (On Missionary Activity) and *Presbyterorum ordinis* (On the Ministry and Life of Priests); and the Declaration *Dignitatis humanae* (On the Dignity of the Human Race or, more often, On Religious Liberty).

Ad Gentes Divinitus pointed out that "disciples of Christ . . . are not working for the merely material progress or prosperity of men; but in teaching the religious and moral truths, which Christ illumined with His light, they seek to enhance the dignity of men" (Sec. 12), and again urged the importance of "closely combining spiritual, doctrinal and pastoral formation" (Sec. 16).

"Priests," *Presbyterorum ordinis* admonishes in section 9, "are to be . . . the unwavering champions of truth, lest the faithful be carried about with every wind of doctrine." In section 14, priests are reminded that "faithfulness to Christ cannot be separated from faithfulness to His Church."

There has been much controversy about the fallible dictums in the Decree On the Dignity of the Human Person, which was composed, it is said, very much from an Americanist perspective by the Jesuit John Courtenay Murray. On the other hand, Bishop Karol Wojtyla is reported to have been very enthusiastic about this Decree; and, along with his Primate Stefan Cardinal Wyszinski, has since used it to good effect in Poland. Doubtless these two shrewd prelates would have survived even without the Decree, but they could not have been unhappy with *Dignitatus humanae's* insistence that "freedom of the Church is the fundamental principle governing relations between the Church and public authorities and the whole civil order" (Sec. 13), nor its condemnation of "forms of government under which, despite constitutional recognition of the freedom of religious worship, the public au-

---

[13]in the 11 April 1982 *National Catholic Register*.

thorities themselves strive to deter the citizens from professing their religion and make life particularly difficult and dangerous for religious bodies" (Sec. 15). Nor could any Catholic be unhappy with section 14's reminder that "the Catholic Church is by the will of Christ the teacher of truth," and that it is thus "Her duty to proclaim and teach with authority the truth which is Christ and, at the same time, to declare and confirm by Her authority the principles of the moral order which spring from human nature itself." The first section also points out that "while religious freedom which men demand in fulfilling their obligations to worship God has to do with freedom from coercion in civil society, it leaves intact the traditional Catholic teaching on the moral duty of individuals and societies towards the true religion and the one Church of Christ."

Its major point was that "in religious matters every form of coercion by men should be excluded," although "civil society has the right to protect itself against possible abuses committed in the name of religious freedom" (Sec. 7). It is, of course, the ancient teaching of the Church that the response of faith must be free.

At the same time, the Decree did include certain of the more gullible enthusiasms to which I've referred, such as its opening line that "contemporary man is becoming increasingly conscious of the dignity of the human person," when history indicates the opposite. *Gaudium et spes (GS)*, the Pastoral Constitution on the Modern World, suffers from this problem as well. The Anglican observer John Moorman in his book *Vatican Observed* rather captured the essence of the thing when he noted that too much of *GS* is simply "a bit pedestrian and banal. . . . The whole of the first part, which attempts to describe the conditions in which modern man lives, inevitably falls a bit flat. It has all been said so many times before."

And said better too. Still, there is much good in the document. Divorce is condemned as a "plague," abortion, infanticide, and euthanasia as "abominable crimes," and Catholics are reminded that the role of "conscience ought to be conformed to the law of the Church, which is the authentic interpreter of the divine law" (Sec. 50). It even condemned artificial birth control in section 51, noting that Catholics "are forbidden to use methods disapproved of by the Church in its interpretation of the divine law." Modernists were quick to say later that this did not of course mean the abortifacient pill, thus ignoring the specific footnote in *GS* added to that sentence, which by citing Pope Pius XI's observations on the matter in his encyclical *Casti connubii*, and Pius XII's in his Allocution to the Congress of Italian Midwives, made it quite clear that the pill and all other artificial means of birth control are precisely what Vatican II condemned.

The most relevant passage in *Gaudium et spes*, however—and arguably in any of the documents—to what was happening to the Church during the years when the bishops had been spending so much time away from their dioceses was to be found in section 43. It said, "by the power of the Holy Spirit the Church is the faithful spouse of the Lord and will never fail to be a sign of salvation in the world; but it is by no means unaware that down through the centuries there have been among its members, both clerical and lay, some who were disloyal to the Spirit of God. Today as well, the Church is not blind to the discrepancy between the message it proclaims and the human weakness of those to whom the Gospel has been entrusted. Whatever is history's judgment on these shortcomings, we cannot ignore them and must combat them earnestly, lest they hinder the spread of the Gospel."

By 8 December 1965, the newest name for hindering the spread of that Gospel was "The Spirit of Vatican II." And it was riding high.

II. The Anti-Spirit of Vatican II

1. Fertile Ground, and the Seed Among Rocks

"Obscured by ideologies and a thirst after sensation, the Council's spiritual nature never got through to Christians at the time. Strictly speaking, we had ears, but could not hear."
Jean-Marie Cardinal Lustiger, Archbishop of Paris

"If present trends continue, say some observers, the historic flow of missionaries from the West to the Third World could be reversed."
Religious News Service.

So what happened? Well, as previously mentioned, the reality of Vatican II has produced a great flowering of the Faith in what is known as the Third World, particularly, though not exclusively, in Africa. Indeed, there is no question that one of the chief accomplishments of the Council was to loosen the Church's historical dependence on Europe, and, one might say, in the nick of time.

Apart from the enormous number of conversions in Africa, which are running equal to Islamic conversions and are estimated at about two million annually, the African clergy and laity enthusiastically embrace the Council's teaching on abortion and contraception, not infrequently despite hostility from the State—and so are having children. Neither is the African hierarchy shy about defending Council teaching as elaborated by Pope Paul VI's encyclical *Humanae vitae.* One of the many examples of this—in contrast to the timidity of the U.S. hierarchy—was the immediate removal of Mill Hill missionary Father Hans Lofstra by the Kenyan Episcopal Conference when that priest publicly justified contraception.

In fact, the open battle between the Kenyan hierarchy and the State—as well as the largely U.S.-financed Multinational Population Control apparatus—became something of a major story in 1985, due to attention brought by the U.N. Conference on Women held in Nairobi in July, followed by the International Eucharistic Congress, which was attended by Pope John Paul II. Despite that attention, however, the battle between the faithful with their bishops against the Popcon establishment goes back at least to 1961, when the first Planned Parenthood affiliate was officially opened in Kenya. Today, the African headquarters of the International Planned Parenthood Federation (IPPF) is located in Nairobi, assisted by, among others, the Kenyan government, the (again largely U.S.-funded) United Nations Fund for Population Activities (UNFPA) and until recently by the U.S. Aid for International Development (USAID), which also has its own separate program of contraception advocacy. Though Kenya is an immense country of 245,000 square miles and only about 20 million people, its high birth rate is the key drawing card for Planned Parenthood and friends, whose influence has been further undermined by an extensive program of natural family planning (NFP) initiated by the bishops. NFP, of course, is as effective in postponing pregnancy as any artificial method—though it demands periodic abstinence and an understanding of the female cycle—with the exception of tubal sterilization.

As a consequence, according to Benedictine Father Paul Marx who runs Human Life International, many Kenyan women are "sterilized after childbirth, without knowledge or consent." Consequently, in 1984 the sixteen Kenyan bishops publicly denounced the government for allowing this, on the grounds that "such a mutilation of the reproductive organs for the direct purpose of preventing conception is against natural law. Aside from the religious and moral objections to such fertility destruction, the whole promotional approach of the camps [where the sterilizations took place] is an insult to the women and men of Kenya and a violation of human dignity." Then in late 1985, after the government allowed the IPPF to begin distributing contraceptives to children without parental knowledge, the Episcopal Conference took out advertisements in several Kenyan dailies denouncing contraception as a "violation of the clear law of God and of our true African traditions, and an affront to our youth and the respect that is due to them."

Shortly thereafter, Okiki Amayo, national chairman of Kenya's sole legal political party, the Kenya African National Union, publicly blasted and implicitly threatened the bishops for "challenging, undermining and subverting government efforts" to promote contraception.

Such forthright defense of the Council in Kenya and throughout Africa no doubt significantly contributes to what the German *Christliche Weltenzyklopedia* notes is, by a combination of births and conversion, an increase of 16,400 Christians a day on that continent, or roughly six million a year: to be compared with the daily decrease, according to the same source, of 7,200 Christians in Europe and North America.

There is further evidence of the impact Vatican II has had on the Third World. "One thing is certain," the 13 May 1985 edition of *L'Osservatore Romano* asserted (while the Pope was in Holland). "During these last twenty years the geography of vocations has been overturned. The more or less latent crisis denounced by the West regarding the blossoming of new vocations is contrasted by the ever more marked increase recorded in countries such as Africa, South America and, recently, Asia . . . the [African] Continent has not even felt slightly the crisis in the West," and as such, "we continue to receive requests for help for the erection of new seminaries."

That is putting it modestly. According to a *Religious News Service* report published in the 25 July 1985 issue of *The Wanderer,* the number of seminarians worldwide dropped 25% between 1967 and 1984—and by more than 50% in the United States, which was not the worst example in the West. France lost two-thirds of its seminarians in this period, Holland nearly that many, Spain more than half, Italy nearly half, and Australia, if she may be considered part of the West, lost an even greater percentage than France. There was not one Western country that did not suffer serious declines, including Ireland.

Whereas, this article continued, "a vastly different picture emerges in the Third World. The number of seminarians almost doubled between 1967 and 1984 in Asia, more than doubled in South America." The increase in Asia occurred primarily in the Philippines (though not exclusively, for between 1983 and 1984 the single largest increase was in South Korea) where the number of seminarians tripled during the 1967-1984 period. They also tripled in Argentina, nearly did so in Brazil, and *quintupled* in Chile. "Substantial increases," the article adds, "were also recorded in every other South American nation, as well as in the nations of Central America."

"Even sharper increases occurred in Africa," the RNS reports, with a threefold increase of seminarians during this period. In Zaire and Ghana seminary students have quintupled; in Kenya the increase was just short of tenfold. In the academic year 1983/84, there were ten minor and four new major seminaries built in Africa and six minor and four major in Asia.

Meanwhile, despite the 25 per cent drop in seminary students between 1967 and 1984, there has, according to the Vatican's central office for statistics, been a steady worldwide increase since a low point of 60,142 in the Holy Year of 1975; by 1984, the figure had climbed to 73,001. It was 102,366 in 1967.

In the United States, after a slight increase in seminarians from 1983 to 1985, the 1985/86 academic year saw a 12% decrease from the previous year at the college level, according to the Center for Applied Research in the Apostolate (CARA). In recent years, enrollments have increased in Spain, Italy, and France.

Puzzled by these unhappy statistics, the United States Catholic Conference (USCC) commissioned a study to determine what the problem might be, conducted by Catholic University of America researchers Dean Hoge, Father Raymond Potvin and Kathleen Ferry, under the direction of Father Eugene Hemrick, director of the USCC's Office of Research; it was released on 23 May 1985. Without saying so directly, the report concluded that Vatican II may be responsible for the drastic decline in U.S. vocations to the priesthood, due to *Presbyterorum ordinis'* stricture that "the more that perfect continence is considered by many people to be impossible in the world today, so much more humbly and persevering in union with the Church ought priests to demand the grace of fidelity, which is never denied to those who ask." In other words, the Catholic U. study thought, the problem was celibacy.[14] Some, however, thought it might be deeper than that.

"Good Pope John sought fresh air when he threw open the windows," wrote regular *New York Daily News* columnist Bill Reel, a Catholic, in a 28 September 1985 diocesan *Brooklyn Tablet* special commentary on the Extraordinary Synod; "but what blew in bears the aroma of the Gowanus Canal. Let's be honest: Vatican II failed."

Reel proceeded to defend the opinion. "Some seventy per cent of baptized Catholics hereabouts attended Mass on Sundays in the years before and during the Second Vatican Council. Fewer than 50% bother to fulfill that Sunday obligation today.

---

[14]That this report was political rather than analytical, however, was suggested by the news that "the full report has a final chapter of interpretive commentary on its meaning," and that, among others, Notre Dame theology department chairman Father Richard McBrien was chosen to provide said "interpretive commentary." In this misnomered book *Catholicism*, McBrien explicitly denies, contra *Dei Verbum*, that Catholics need trust the historical accuracy of the Gospels; and he there also presents the extreme Arian view that Catholics may believe the Mother of God was not really a virgin before her marriage to St. Joseph and the conception of Christ. Accordingly, the Australian bishops' conference issued a *monitum* against *Catholicism* in August 1980. Five years later—on 5 July 1985—at the urging of Cardinal Ratzinger's office according to the *National Catholic Reporter*, the Committee on Doctrine of the National Conference of Catholic Bishops (NCCB), chaired by San Francisco Archbishop John Quinn, also issued a mild rebuke. Though possessed of "many positive features," Quinn's committee said, though McBrien's motivations were "praiseworthy," and though the Committee "appreciates the effort and motivations of theologians such as Father McBrien . . . nevertheless, we think it useful to clarify for the actual and potential readership of the book *Catholicism* its character as one theologian's effort to present such teaching in the light of his understanding of contemporary theological insights, many of which are admittedly of a hypothetical nature, and some of which it seems difficult to reconcile with authoritative Catholic doctrine." Despite these numerous qualifications, Archbishop Quinn further asserted that his committee's statement "should not be used to call into question Father McBrien's authentic Catholic faith or orthodoxy." McBrien himself insisted that from the American episcopacy, "never was there any question of a lack of orthodoxy."

McBrien's "interpretive commentary" on the Catholic U. study concluded that "the vocations crisis is as much qualitative as quantitative." But by that he meant that current recruiting and formation practices too heavily favor the ordination of men who are "more dependent, institutionally oriented, sexually indifferent, and conservative"—or, more succinctly, who do not share McBrien's Modernist opinions.

This hemorrhage began right after the Council concluded. Catholics voted with their feet on the so-called reforms from Rome, apparently."

"Rectories, convents, and seminaries were packed before and during the Council," Reel continued, "as vocations rose to new highs. There were plenty of priests, sisters and brothers to staff parishes, schools, and charitable agencies. But many blithely abandoned their vows during the years right after the Council. Today the harvest is great but the workers have dwindled drastically. Religious orders that thrived a couple of decades ago could be literally extinct by the end of the century. Two or three parishes will have to share a pastor as the priest shortage worsens."

"The Council was supposed to respiritualize the Church. Catholicism had become stale and sterile, a religion of rule and rote—legalistic, pietistic, even pharisaical. Or so some said, anyway. The Council, they were sure, would renew the faith and revitalize the faithful. A spiffy new Church, liberated from reactionary encrustations, surely would capture the allegiance of idealistic young people bent on reforming the world. Heaven on earth was the lofty goal ... so the spirit of Vatican II de-emphasized rules and regulations, and replaced them with a lot of loose talk about peace and love. Hippie priests had their day. Sappy slogans were spoken. We were assured that Jesus was a revolutionary.

"It didn't work. Young people turned away from the Church in massive numbers, turning instead to radical politics, the sexual revolution, and the drug culture. The brave new Church, its self-confidence eroded, its message blurred, its moral authority squandered, lacked the clout to denounce these false gods.... The Council loosed a gusher of vague teaching and ambiguous preaching that diminished the Catholic sense of sin. Too much guilt gave way to too little ... materialism and self-indulgence have betrayed millions of souls in our society...."

And among the U.S. clergy matters are not improving. "U.S. representatives at the synod will bring with them striking statistics that have occurred in the past twenty years of U.S. seminary life," says the Jesuit Brian McDermott in the 28 September 1985 Jesuit publication *America*. "By the year 1990 there will be half as many active priests in this country as there were in 1980. From 1962, when the Council began, until 1984, 76 seminaries either closed or merged with others." In that same issue, the Jesuit

Michael Buckley, while curiously enthusiastic about the sad reality he describes, notes that "membership among women religious in this country, once counted at over 180,000, has decreased to fewer than 120,000, many of whom are elderly and retired. During that same period, the number of religious brothers has been cut almost by half." *Our Sunday Visitor* noted in December 1984 that fully one-third of those 120,000 nuns are retired; and that one third of the income of the female religious congregations goes to supporting the retired nuns. That is, when it can. The crisis in some of the congregations is so extreme that some of these elderly nuns have been forced onto welfare, and dependency on the state. Worldwide, according to *Newsweek*, the number of nuns has decreased by 114,000 since the Council, the number of priests by 28,000. In the United States, there were 5000 fewer nuns in 1984 than 1983.

It is no better in the rest of the West. Vittorio Messori, in his famous interview with Cardinal Ratzinger, noted that up to the Council, Quebec, which had been colonized and evangelized by Catholics who established a Christian regime there, had the highest number of women religious in relation to population in the world. But Quebec has seen a 44% decline in its number of nuns since the Council and a 98.5% decline in new vocations.

The laity, as Reel says, have "voted with their feet." A Gallup poll, according to a September 1985 issue of *Twin Circle*, reports that whereas 65% of the respondents who called themselves Catholic said they attended Mass on a regular basis in 1968, a mere 39% say they do now. Other polls have put that latter figure higher, but none as high as 55%, nor as high as the years before the Council.

There are millions fewer American children attending Catholic schools than in 1965, and thousands fewer Catholic schools as a consequence.

There is, however, in the United States, one statistic that shows an increase since the Council. According to a November 1984 article in the *National Catholic Reporter* there were 338 annulments here in 1968. By 1983, that number had risen to approximately 52,000, an increase of 15,000%.[15]

Pace Marcel Lefebvre, but is it possible that a Council which produced the statements quoted earlier here from its documents could be responsible for this disaster in one part of the world, while producing such great fruit in another?

Or is it time to examine more closely the Modernist resurgence among the clergy of the Western world?

2. Konzils-Ungeist (anti-Spirit)

> *"There is a liberal conspiracy, in the sense John Courtney Murray used the word, of a 'breathing together' (con-spiratio); liberal theologians dominate the public prints, the catechetical training centers, the publishing houses, the professional associations, much of the Catholic bureaucracy. They praise each other's books, award each other contracts, jobs, awards, and perquisites."*
>
> Robert Hoyt, former editor of the *NC Reporter*

> *"While such hopes, be they ever so delusive, live in him, why should the Modernist leave the Church?"*
>
> the Modernist George Tyrrell

---

[15]In the opinion of many, in fact, the annulment or *de facto* divorce scandal in the United States rivals, or—because a sacrament is involved—surpasses the indulgence scandal that so inflamed Martin Luther in the 16th century. Prelates, of course, deny there is any problem now, as they did then.

The implications are manifold, however; for one thing the situation is more complicated for Catholics who never really were married, and thus do deserve an annulment, for they can no longer trust the judgment of the diocesan tribunals. The heart of the matter was nonetheless perhaps best captured in a letter that appeared in a 1985 *St. Anthony Messenger*, the basic thrust of which I have encountered numerous times in the past ten years:

"I don't understand what is missing or invalid about marriages that allows the Church to take away the blessing of marriage given at the Church altar in the marriage rite," its writer appealed. "To personalize, my husband wanted to marry someone else so he divorced me." Thus, an annulment "blesses him for divorcing me. I still feel married even though we have been divorced 16 months. My four children and 35 years with my husband show me that our marriage must have had a few valid moments. By giving him an annulment, his lifestyle becomes officially valid and mine, invalid. I pray someday the Church will look at annulments differently. Annulments erase guidelines Jesus set."

A look at the *periti* of the Second Vatican Council gives reason for pause. Among them: Hans Kueng, who now openly denies the Divinity of Christ; Gregory Baum, who shortly after the Council left the priesthood, and who now publicly advocates the Sacrament of Matrimony for practicing homosexuals; Charles Davis, who has formally apostatized; Bernard Haering, who has since the Council defended sterilization; and Edward Schillebeeckx, a sodomite who has devoted himself since the Council to attacking the Divinity of Christ as understood by the Council of Chalcedon (and thus all Catholics), and whose police record in Holland for public nudity and exposure was recently revealed in the *National Catholic Reporter*.[16] And this list, alas, is by no means exhaustive.

The reality of the Council, however, is that the influence of the Modernist *periti* on the Council documents themselves, was minimal; in effect, non-existent. "Xavier Rynne," the purportedly composite journalist who presented the Modernist polemics and policies for the *New Yorker* during the Council, also occasionally let slip observations that contradicted his general theses; and his book, *The Second Session* openly acknowledges that despite the media lionization of the *periti* as official interpreters of the Council, in its actual conduct "not enough use was made of the Council experts or *periti*, who not infrequently found themselves virtually excluded from any participation in the work." During the private meetings of the Council commissions, as Britain's John Cardinal Heenan notes in his book *A Crown of Thorns*, "the only discord came from the advisors (*periti*) in attendance. A German theologian addressed us in a voice often rising to a scream."

This tonal quality seemed to characterize *periti* conversations with an eager press as well. From the outset men like Michael Novak, Robert Kaiser of *Time* magazine, Rynne, and countless others, presented Vatican II as if it were a running battle between "progressives" and "conservatives," with the "progressives" invariably portrayed as victorious. When the First Session, for example, approved the Introduction and First Chapter of *Sacrosanctum Concilium* (where, among other things, we may recall it is commanded that Latin is to be preserved as the language of the Latin rite, that no priest may change anything in the liturgy on his own authority, and that in the Church "the

---

[16] 10 January 1986.

human is directed toward and subordinated to the divine, the visible to the invisible, action to contemplation, and this present world to that city yet to come"), Robert Kaiser announced that "to the Council's progressives, euphoric over other battles fought and won, this [approval] was a sweet message. True, they would have to vote on other chapters. But they would be mere formalities. 'Within the preface and the first chapter,' a member of the Liturgical Commission told me, 'are the seeds of all the other reforms.' " If Kaiser's analysis was correct, then the progressives were in a strong position indeed given the 1922 to 11 vote. One suspects that even Archbishop Marcel Lefebvre might have been among them.

Kaiser's book *Inside the Council* further reported that "the bishops were learning, too, about the intellectual bankruptcy of the Curialists in Rome. When they held conferences with integralist theologians, they found them a defensive lot, inclined to rely not on reasoned argument but on wild charges." Men like Congar, Schillebeeckx, Karl Rahner, and Hans Kueng, on the other hand, were "theologians on the march, men well equipped with the ideas that dovetailed neatly into the needs of pastors around the world." The journalists thought highly of—and took the time to praise—each other as well. Michael Novak suggested the reason for Kaiser's deep perception was that he "had more sources of information on tap" than any other reporter at the Council. So impressive were these, in fact, that they entered into the very brain of Pope John himself. "In his private apartment," Kaiser wrote, "John XXIII sat watching on closed-circuit television, and he, too, was stirred. 'At last, the Fathers are beginning to understand what this Council is for,' he said."

The real nature of Kaiser's perception can perhaps be better grasped when we consider his view that Pope Pius XII was "a small town aristocrat"—Rome being the small town to which *Time's* American correspondent referred. Accordingly, Pius XII "was simply not listened to by a Church composed of intelligent human beings."

"Like the Mounties from across the border," wrote Bishop G. P. Dwyer of Leeds, England, reviewing *Inside the Council* for the *Catholic Gazette*, Kaiser "always gets his man. And he got him—Cardinal Ottaviani and the Curia. As in the standard T.V. horse opera the cast is divided into 'goodies' and 'baddies'. The former very very good and always rather larger than life, the latter the villains of the piece."

And to be sure, not only Kaiser. Whomever the media approved were as glorious as those they disliked were despicable. Segni Archbishop Carli's "pathetic voice," wrote Father Antoine Wegner in the French *La Croix* and the London *Tablet*, "will again often be heard and his specious arguments in favor of the primacy and against the collegiality of the bishops." This, as opposed to for instance Kaiser's love song to the Jesuit Augustin Cardinal Bea, whom we are told had "rounded blue eyes, observant, penetrating, flickering with sudden, deep intelligence ... a thin, slight, stoop-shouldered frame, bowed but not weighted beneath the burden of thought, and giving the impression of a mind encased in a tenement of clay, bespoke the fire ready to be kindled, the suppleness of restraint, the measured discretion to accept the real, the reserved power to attempt the possible, the air of intellectual dominion and practical conviction that the draught of life's potion given to him was to be tasted to its subtlest fineness, distilled and distinguished as a fine oblation to the Father of all things."

Sort of like Hans Kueng, in short, according to Michael Novak. Yes, consider how much more timid your average timid bishop was likely to prove after reading the account in Novak's *The Open Church* of Father Kueng's American Victory Tour. "The tension in the hall was electric.... In his clear, forceful voice, his blond hair shining in the lights, Father Kueng brought the careful, strong theology of Europe to American audiences caught up in the enthusiasm of Pope John's *aggiornamento.*"

"I do not know whether," commented Father Louis Bouyer, considered a "progressive" at the time of the Council (as was Father Joseph Ratzinger), "as we are told, the Council has freed us from the tyranny of the Roman Curia, but what is sure is that, willy-nilly, it has handed us over to the dictatorship of journalists, and particularly the most incompetent and irresponsible among them." After the Council their authority increased still more, on the principle—elucidated in the Protestant Modernist McAfee Brown's *Ecumenical Revolution*—that "the council documents themselves often implied more in a way of change than the council fathers were aware of when they voted." You may guess who would be allowed to understand their real implications.

Hans Kueng, for example, denounced "the promulgation of the misleading title *Mater Ecclesiae* against the expressed will of the Council majority, which will arouse in non-Catholic Christendom great indignation, and grave doubts as to the genuinely ecumenical sympathies of the Pope." The Protestant uprising failed to materialize, however, except perhaps within the Catholic clergy; for it was by such commentary that they were instructed about the "will of the Council majority."

Some bishops tried to stem the tide. "I fear *periti* when they are left to explain what the bishops meant," cautioned Cardinal Heenan. "It is of no avail to talk about a College of Bishops if *periti* in articles, books, and speeches contradict and pour scorn on what a body of bishops teaches."

But interpret and pour scorn they did. Jesuit Father Peter Hebblethwaite, editor of the influential Jesuit journal *The Month* (until he abandoned the priesthood to get married), insisted that though "it is perfectly possible to read the Council as the reassertion of Vatican I's intransigent teaching on the power of the papacy . . . there is another reading equally possible which stresses that the Pope exercises his office of unity in the context of the world's bishops (collegiality)." The trick here, of course, is to present these two ideas as if they were contradictory, instead of complementary, as taught by Vatican II.

Some bishops, to be sure, thought all this commentary quite helpful, for which their penetrating intelligence was immediately compared to Cardinal Bea's. Cardinal Leo Suenens, in fact, returned the favor dauntingly in the 6 April 1965 *La Croix*, upon observing that "in order to strengthen the awareness of the People of God and for the Christian to assume his adult responsibilities in the Church today, he needs daily enlightenment on events which have to be seen in the light of faith: the Catholic journalist, then, is the theologian of the present day." To help advance this new thesis, Cardinals like Bea and Franz Koenig were publicly praising the clear, forceful voice and blond hair of Hans Kueng, with Koenig "predicting" that Kueng's 1963 book on the Council "and the challenge it presents will be received with understanding and spread far and wide." Koenig was, to be sure, absolutely right; for by then the Modernist apparatus was not only in place, but also capable of what looked like something close to absolute control.

The Council Fathers, alas, were at first stunned, ultimately unable to cope, and finally cowed into submission, at least in public, by these constant and deliberate distortions of the Council documents and events as presented by the media. Pope Paul VI was little better, indecisive one moment, tolerating scandal and disarray the next, though always teaching very deep and Christian truths—which the press and the world utterly ignored, until the storm of abuse provoked by the encyclical *Humanae vitae*, though of course even here its actual contents were rarely published. Nonetheless, it was precisely that encyclical which revealed Paul's greatest strength, or perhaps we should say Peter's. "If the Roman Pontiff had been a politician," as anti-nuclear activist Juli Loesch observed, "he would have OK'ed contraception. Virtually every social, political, scientific, and religious institution on earth was for it. Any politician can tell which way the wind was blowing; and any religious charlatan can get the drift and call it the Holy Spirit. But the Holy Spirit isn't just anything that's blowing in the wind. And Paul VI was not a politician."[17] He would pay for it bitterly, however; before he died, he was speaking of the self-destruction of the Church, and suggesting that perhaps his role had been not so much guiding Her, as suffering for Her. Still, throughout the incredible and unexpected avalanche, he kept at least *proclaiming* Catholic truth for those who would hear it. "Most of the Council fathers," meanwhile, as historian James Hitchcock noted in the November 1985 *Catholicism in Crisis (CinC)*, "seem to have been woefully insensitive to the symbolic and psychological ramifications of their deliberations;" in particular how they were being presented to the world, and how little was being done to correct these distortions.

And so the machinations of Modernism worked. Much of the clergy was already infected with it by the time of the Council. After Vatican II, the bishops seemed weak and in disarray, the Pope confused. The media was constantly denouncing Catholicism and Catholic piety, practice, belief, and devotion, in the name of the Council, in the name of its spirit, while extolling every wild or studied Modernist opinion as the official interpretation of Roman Catholicism and Vatican II. It was made clear that anyone who expected to be heard, move forward, have fun, or be relevant must echo Kueng and the crowd, and in effect repudiate the Faith. In addition, "the Modernists" as St. Pius had noted less than sixty years before in *Pascendi*, "vent all their bitterness and hatred on Catholics who zealously fight the battles of the Church. There is no species of insult they do not heap upon them with ignorance and obstinacy. When an adversary rises up against them with an erudition and force that renders them redoubtable, they seek to make a conspiracy of silence around him to nullify the effects of his attack."

---

[17]In a (for this magazine quite shocking) contribution to the 18 October 1985 *Commonweal* symposium on the Synod.

"This policy," the encyclical continued, "is the more invidious in that they belaud with admiration which knows no bounds the writers who range themselves on their side, hailing their works, exuding novelty on every page, with a chorus of applause. For them the scholarship of a writer is in direct proportion to the recklessness of his attacks on antiquity, and of his efforts to undermine tradition and the ecclesiastical *magisterium*. When one of their number falls under the condemnation of the Church, the rest of them, to the disgust of good Catholics, gather round him, and hold him up in veneration almost as a martyr for the truth. The young, excited and confused by all this clamor of praise and abuse, some of them afraid of being branded as ignorant, others ambitious to rank among the 'learned', and both classes goaded internally by curiosity and pride, not infrequently surrender and give themselves up to Modernism."

In the West, the clergy and the male and female religious orders began to surrender themselves literally by the tens of thousands. The Modernists, in a perfect imitation of their historicist political mentors, took advantage of the very disarray they had provoked to absolutize their power in Catholic organizational structures where they already had a foot in the door; and to seize control and drive out the Catholics where they had not. If a bishop questioned the takeovers, he was simply ignored; if he tried to resist it, he was openly disobeyed and publicly reviled in the press and elsewhere for being "pre-conciliar" and opposing the spirit of Vatican II.

Meanwhile, in going after the very highest and most influential positions within the Church, the Modernists did not ignore the crucial role of apostolic delegate or papal nuncio, who advises the Pope and in effect chooses for him those priests who should be appointed to the bishopric in any particular country. In this manner, open Modernists such as the American apostolic delegate Archbishop Jean Jadot (the only U.S. apostolic delegate in history ever to be denied promotion to the cardinalate), and more subtle if no less overt ones such as Britain's Archbishop Bruno Bernard Heim, were able to subvert entire national hierarchies for the Modernist cause, thus establishing yet another direct analogy to the great Arian seizure in the fourth century. Accordingly, neo-Arian publications such as the *National Catholic Reporter*, *Commonweal*, and the Jesuit *America* (and throughout North America and Europe, literally hundreds of others), went from ridiculing the bishops in the 60's, to praising their authority with tremulous awe in the 70's and 80's. In addition, when the Modernist bishops began to employ methods far more ruthless than the most monarchical of their pre-Conciliar Catholic predecessors, but now in order to suppress and/or punish those priests, religious, and laity who had throughout remained faithful to the teaching of the Council, such bishops were invariably praised as far-seeing, pastoral, and progressive.

Consequently, it was not long before even orthodox prelates, priests, and nuns began to unravel, leave the faith, or go into material schism: though many bore the cross, albeit realizing that for a season anyway, most public resistance was futile. Many more were simply swept up in the frenzy, though more still probably began to go along in order to get along. Apart from everything else, a public defense of actual Vatican II teaching was an implicit, indeed virtually an explicit condemnation and reproach to their brother priests or sister nuns—not to say brother bishops—who had been seduced by the distortion of these teachings. Considering the emotional and as it were professional ties that priests, sisters and bishops inevitably establish among themselves, it became easier to accept the new theories than challenge them, particularly given the ruthlessness of the overt and covert punishments that attended such challenges. As such, it often took very few Modernists—one thinks of Milwaukee Archbishop Rembert Weakland's eerie influence within the NCCB—successfully to corrupt an entire structure, simply because it would be "uncharitable" to challenge the sincerity of their motives, despite the fact that their public actions and statements necessarily implicated the entire body. Thus implicated, many priests soon abandoned even their quiet opposition and uneasiness, and fraternally adopted the views of the interloper. Criminal means once tolerated, as Edmund Burke somewhere observes, are soon preferred.

The Catholic faithful, the laity, were no more prepared for any of this than the nuns had been. The laity were not as such a captive audience, however, and so were only abused; the nuns were systematically and deliberately corrupted, so that many besides the one of three who simply abandoned their vocation became embittered and manipulated Modernist pawns, some willing even to be used to advance the abortion industry, or to openly advocateing witchcraft in "Catholic" workshops and seminars for other nuns and laity. "The sources of revolt," notes Hitchcock, "intellectual, emotional, organizational, lie with the clergy and religious. Most lay people stood by bewildered and disedified as the first spasms of clerical rebellion swept the Church in the late 1960's." Acting like their nuns, one of every three would stop attending Mass altogether as a result, in the United States. Millions more became confused and far more prey to the destructive temptations of the age. Most, after awhile, adjusted as they could, gritted their teeth, and persevered. A tiny minority joined the Modernist frenzy, "almost always as a result of clerical influence," as Hitchcock observes.

"While seldom a thinker," the historian elsewhere remarked, "the liberal social innovator has usually armed himself with a whole catalog of arguments against the status quo. The traditionalist, on the other hand, is usually taken by surprise when his beliefs are challenged. He finds it amazing and incomprehensible when values which to him are so obviously correct are questioned, and his response, at least initially, is indeed likely to be an irritable gesture, a few familiar cliches to ward off the enemy until the forces of tradition can be rallied."

"The virtues of traditionalists are also their vices," he continues. "The classic defense of traditionalism holds that, while good and sufficient reasons can be adduced for most traditions, it is precisely of the nature of tradition not to require philosophical defense, except in extreme situations. A traditional way of life is one which takes its practical authority from custom itself, from the instinctive sense of the rightness of things which a genuinely traditional community inculcates in its members. The tree can grow because its roots are not being constantly yanked out of the ground for examination.

"But this settled way of life is, because of the very conditions which make it possible, highly vulnerable to attack. Skepticism, whatever else it is, is always corrosive. It can dissolve existing bonds with relative ease, even when it is powerless to create new ones. The simple question, 'Why not?' often reduces the traditionalist to an uneasy silence. They are ready-made victims of the predatory intellectuals and of the media, which prefer to allow traditional ideas to be defended by visibly nervous, tongue-tied, seemingly stupid people."[18]

This describes, of course, precisely the failure and predicament of the faithful Catholic in the post-Vatican II era in the United States. As Sobran puts it, "for the civil man, politics is generally a distinctly part-time matter. For the political fanatic,

---

[18]*National Review*, 6 February 1981.

politics is everything." Eventually, when Catholic influence was so devastated in the U.S. that abortion was legalized by Court *fiat* in 1973, the laity began to learn political skills in order to fight this decision, which skills then began to be used to oppose the Modernist clerical takeover of the U.S. Church bureaucracy. Not surprisingly, a horrified clergy responded by turning upon the laity with a vengeance.

Echoing St. Pius, Hitchcock also points out that "although liberal rhetoric officially encourages passionate adherence to one's beliefs, in practice those who set the terms of the public debate make sure that only 'progressive' ideas are accorded respect." Despite this, he argues in the *CinC* piece, "it is the 'conservatives' who have been able to cope with change, precisely in their suspicion of it, because they are the people who insist on maintaining, in the face of great difficulties, the crucial distinction between what is and what is not essential to the faith."

There was also, to be sure, the unfortunate paradox that simply by drawing Catholics into the ecclesial political fray, the historicists achieved a kind of victory by forcing them to abandon some of what might be called life's finer pursuits, whereas the angst-ridden historicist has little interest in these, since he must always keep despair at bay with activity: "Attending meetings, serving on committees, drafting manifestoes, making speeches, lobbying politicians, even filling envelopes, and licking stamps are felt to be meaningful actions," as Hitchcock notes. "Whatever philosophical convictions they may or may not hold, people attracted to such activity are almost always automatically disposed toward further change, if only because it sustains the sense of movement which they crave and provides justification for further activity."

To quote Cardinal Ratzinger, "a theologian who does not love art, poetry, music, and nature can be dangerous. Blindness and deafness toward the beautiful are not incidental; they are necessarily reflected in his theology." And what is most offensive about all this, according to Hitchcock, "is that it encourages wrenching kinds of social change for the sake of titillating bored people who believe they have an undeniable right to lead 'interesting' lives."

There is, finally, a further motivation behind the post-Conciliar Modernist explosion, to which St. Pius drew attention in *Pascendi* before it blew. "It is pride," he wrote, for "pride sits in Modernism as in its own house, finding sustenance everywhere in its doctrines and lurking in its every aspect. It is pride which fills Modernists with that self-assurance by which they consider themselves, and pose as the rule for all. It is pride which puffs them up with that vain-glory which allows them to regard themselves as the sole possessors of knowledge, and makes them say, elated and inflated with presumption, 'We are not as the rest of men,' and which, lest they should seem as other men, leads them to embrace and to devise novelties even of the most absurd kind. It is pride which rouses in them the spirit of disobedience ... it is owing to their pride that they seek to be the reformers of others while they forget to reform themselves."

"Truly," the Saint concludes, "there is no road that leads so directly and so quickly to Modernism as pride."

III. The Dream Of Caiaphas

1. Martin Heidegger's Eager Student

> *"Very often, deceived by the Evil One, men have become vain in their reasonings, have exchanged the truth of God for a lie, and served the world rather than the Creator."*
>
> Lumen gentium, section 16

> *"Every Catholic must have the courage to believe that his faith, in communion with that of the Church, surpasses every 'new magisterium' of the experts, the intellectuals."*
>
> Joseph Cardinal Ratzinger

As Paul Johnson observes, the Jesuit Karl Rahner was fond of dismissing, not without contempt, the popular beliefs of the vast majority of the world's some 850,000,000 Roman Catholics.[19] Johnson contrasts this with the views of John Paul II who, in the words of *New York Times* Rome bureau chief E. J. Dionne, "is an intellectual, but he is dedicated to the intellectually unfashionable symbols of popular Christianity: relics and statues, devotions to the saints, and, above all, to the Blessed Virgin Mary."[20]

From his academic enclave in Germany, Rahner has pronounced such views "naive theism," and "is fond of remarking that such a theist believes in a God as illusory as the one in which atheists refuse to believe," despite, as Johnson remarks, that "Christians have always believed in such a God and always will... Rahner's argument indeed leads him to the absurd paradox that this kind of theism, the demotic theology of the masses, is con-

---

[19]In *John Paul II and the Catholic Restoration.*
[20]*New York Times* Sunday magazine, 12 May 1985.

cealed in atheism and vice versa, 'and in that sense [says Rahner] ultimately no one can say of himself whether he believes in God or not.' "

In short, Karl Rahner is the Gnostic element in Modernism, Gnosticism being one of the earliest heresies in Christianity, the meat of which is essentially that God does not of course reveal Himself to the vulgar faithful, but only to very clever people: such as those, for example, inclined to work in German universities, or (in the 20th century anyway) to join the Jesuit order. It is not surprising that Rahner's view of things flowered at the University of Freiburg in the mid-30's; for not only was Hitler's Germany an historicist hothouse, it was also notably Gnostic on the question of race. Indeed, Martin Heidegger became very popular among philosophers during that period—and remains so in some circles in the sense that the historicist-leader Vladimir Lenin does in some political circles—despite the atheist philosopher's enthusiasm for his Chancellor.

"In the spring of 1934," notes the prominent Heidegger scholar Thomas Sheehan in the 4 February 1982 *New York Review of Books*, "just two years after becoming a Jesuit priest, Rahner registered for a doctorate in philosophy at the University of Freiburg, and over the next four semesters he attended virtually every lecture course and seminar that Heidegger gave. He was in the classroom when Heidegger echoed Neitzsche's condemnation of Christianity as 'Platonism for the masses' and when he asserted that 'a faith that does not constantly expose itself to the possibility of unfaith is no faith at all'. ... The effect," Sheehan observes, "was overwhelming. Thirty years later Rahner would remark that 'although I had many good professors in the classroom, there is only one whom I can revere as my *teacher* [Rahner's emphasis], and he is Martin Heidegger.' "

Nonetheless, "the experience proved to be an academic disaster for Rahner. In the spring of 1936 he presented as his doctoral dissertation a radical new interpretation of Aquinas's theory of knowledge from the viewpoint of Heidegger—and he was promptly flunked" by his Catholic dissertation director, the Thomistic philosopher Martin Honecker. "Rahner withdrew from philosophy and eventually took his Ph.D. in theology," Sheehan adds.

Nonetheless, despite the continuing tension between Catholicism and the Third Reich—let us note in passing that the German edition of this country's oldest national Catholic weekly

The Wanderer was immediately suppressed when Hitler came to power in 1932—the regime allowed Rahner's flunked philosophy dissertation to be published under the title *Geist in Welt (Spirit in the World)* in 1939. It proved, as Sheehan reminds us, "immediately and immensely successful," and, for Modernists, "the book reshaped the foundations of the Thomistic theory of knowledge and being, and it provided the groundwork—as much Heideggerian as Thomistic—for the new theology that Rahner has continued to pour forth since the end of World War II."

Pour forth indeed. "Rahner's published works," Sheehan reveals, "run to over 3500 titles in a dozen languages, including fourteen volumes of collected essays, a score of monographs, and a half-dozen or so dictionaries and encyclopedias," in which—among, as we can imagine, much else—the German Jesuit came up with the novel idea that besides Catholicism's ancient *magisterium*, there is to be considered a second one. This was to be composed of theologians: such as Dr. Rahner, for example.

Rahner's magisterial teaching, however, as Sheehan enthusiastically reveals, is resolutely hostile not only to Catholic teaching, but also to any Catholic unfortunate enough to be excluded from the academic bourgeoisie. He despises prayer, for example; or, as Sheehan puts it, he is a resolute enemy of "Christianity's furtive Platonic fantasy that the soul, in anticipation of its full liberation from the flesh, can occasionally excuse itself from matter and slip out for a brief fling with Ultimate Reality before returning, refreshed and perhaps wiser, to the humdrum (but fortunately temporary) bonds of marriage to the world." According to this view then, the Desert Fathers, St. Francis with his trip to Alverna where he received the stigmata, indeed Christ and his frequent insistence upon solitude even for Himself, but most of all the average Catholic who through the centuries has slipped into a church or closet in order to better orient his heart toward Ultimate Reality—are all to be firmly condemned.

"What then happens in the afterlife?" Sheehan asks. "For Rahner, precisely nothing—for there is no afterlife, no duration beyond experienced time. We may choose to speak of man's salvation by talking of eternity, Rahner says, but that 'does not mean that things continue on after death as though, as Feuerbach put it, we only change horses and then ride on.' " The atheist Ludwig Feuerbach, it should be noted, was not, like Heidegger, a right-wing historicist, but rather in his own estimation a left-wing one:

which is why Karl Marx revered Feuerbach much as Rahner did Heidegger.

Sheehan also exposes a certain quirky pantheism in Rahner's historicism, since the Jesuit believed that "in death one does not leave the material world but enters more deeply into it and becomes what he calls 'all-cosmic', somehow present to and in communication with all material reality, an 'open system towards the world and a real ontological influence on the whole of the universe,' " and "on this hypothesis," Rahner asserts, "certain parapsychological phenomena, now puzzling, might be more readily and more naturally explained." One is reminded of G. K. Chesterton's observation that the problem with atheism is not that atheists believe nothing, but that they will believe anything.

In any event, whether as poltergeists or good German businessmen, Rahner "sees man as bound to *this* world, with no possible escape to some spiritual heaven," as Mr. Sheehan informs us so succinctly. Consequently, "dogmatic theology [Rahner says] must be reformulated as theological anthropology. Thus Rahner carries out Feuerbach's program of transforming theology into anthropology."

"When Rahner considers the specific content of Christian revelation, he *begins* [my emphasis] with the radical principle that the entire world always was within the dispensation of supernatural grace even *before* [Sheehan's] the birth of Jesus, the founding of the Church, and the spreading of the Gospel message." In so doing, he attacks what Mr. Sheehan considers to be "one of the least felicitous formulations of Christian doctrine, traceable in large measure to St. Augustine, namely, that the world and history are divided into two orders: the natural and the supernatural, the fallen and the redeemed, the pagan and the Christian."

"The consequences of this position," Sheehan continues, "which Rahner calls 'anonymous Christianity' are far-reaching" because "if the whole universe [is] already caught up in God's saving grace, then it becomes well-nigh impossible to distinguish a 'merely human' act from a so-called 'supernatural' and salvific act." The consequences of this on moral theology should be readily apparent if we consider for a moment the merely human act of, say, masturbation and the supernatural one of sexual continence—or for that matter, the conquest of any temptation. On the other hand, Sheehan feels, Dr. Rahner's views might help "the problems missionaries would have in evangelizing extraterrestrial intelligences. How much would these beings be obliged to accept—the Virgin Mary? the Pope? the seven sacraments and the rosary?"

The point of course, is how much should terrestrial intelligences be obliged to accept Christianity. "In general, Rahner serves up a demythologized and slimmed down Christianity with none of the Rube Goldberg mechanisms that have kept theologians busy over the centuries. . . . For example, Rahner takes the liberal path that the resurrection of Jesus is not at all a 'historical' event entailing the 'resuscitation of a physical, material body,' but rather is simply the 'definitive salvation of [His] concrete human existence by God."

As such, Mr. Sheehan admits he considers Dr. Rahner to be "the most brilliant Catholic theologian since Thomas Aquinas. During the last forty years this German Jesuit priest has almost singlehandedly revolutionized the way the Church understands its message." That last sentence is, to be sure, a reflection of Mr. Sheehan's hopes rather than of reality, though he was much closer to the mark upon noting that "if the last two decades have witnessed a radical change in the articulation of Church teaching, and if the revolution should survive, the credit must go to this brilliant, controversial, and immensely productive man."

Well, busy anyway. The virtue of Thomas Sheehan, meanwhile, is the ruthlessness by which he reveals what the Modernist theologians are really saying, beneath all the obscurantist verbiage. St. Pius X had that quality too, albeit for different reasons. Since Sheehan, however, completely supports the Modernist agenda, and indeed writes articles attacking Cardinal Ratzinger to advance it for the *New York Times,* his forthrightness has caused more than a little dismay among the Modernist clergy. This was particularly the case with a piece he composed that appeared in the 14 June 1984 issue of *The New York Review of Books,* which, it has been suggested, may have figured in John Paul II's decision to convene an Extraordinary Synod on the Second Vatican Council some seven months later.

As we shall see, the article reveals just how completely the views of such as Karl Rahner have conquered the decimated seminaries of the West: which is to say nothing less than the education of the European and North American priesthood.

2. The Liberal Consensus

> *"Fundamentally, it is a schism between two magisteria, the magisterium of the professors and the magisterium of the pope. . . . This is really what Kueng is calling for: that the academy replace the hierarchy as the teaching magisterium of the Church."*
> Rosemary Ruether, a Kueng supporter

> *"The rhetoric of free procedure is only a cover for a substantive goal . . . They want freedom for certain practices because they want the practices, not the freedom. When the practices are established, the freedom can be dispensed with. The actual goal is always to maximize the practice, first by allowing it, then by encouraging it, and finally by mandating it."*
> Joseph Sobran, *Human Life Review*, fall 1984

Titled *Revolution in the Church*, Sheehan's '84 article told its tale by ostensibly reviewing a then-recent Hans Kueng work called *Eternal Life*? "The dismantling of traditional Roman Catholic theology," it quickly begins, "is by now a *fait accompli*." In what Sheehan considers a "vigorous intellectual renaissance . . . Catholic theologians and exegetes . . . in scarcely two decades have marshaled the most advanced scriptural scholarship—until recently the work mainly of Protestants—and put it at the service of a radical rethinking of their faith. The consequences for the Catholic Church as it approaches its third millennium are," Sheehan adds, "for some, deeply disturbing," though in his own view "immensely promising."

"In Roman Catholic seminaries," he proceeds, "it is now common teaching that Jesus of Nazareth did not assert any of the divine or messianic claims the Gospels attribute to him, and that he died without believing he was Christ or the Son of God, not to mention the founder of a new religion.

"This kind of whittling away at belief in the divinity of Jesus is scarcely new. It reaches back at least to the last century when liberal Protestants like Albrecht Ritschl and Adolph von Harnack tried to strip away what they thought were the Church's divinizing embellishments." It of course also reaches back to George Tyrrell, Alfred Loisy, and St. Pius X, though for political reasons Sheehan considers it wiser to suppress this information, perhaps for fear of reviving interest in *Pascendi*. That he is quite aware of this encyclical became apparent in the article he was to write attacking Ratzinger for the *Times* on 16 September—three months after the *Review of Books* piece—wherein he contradicts himself by adopting the standard Modernist political argument that St. Pius had condemned a "cardboard heresy . . . called 'Modernism'," in which "scores of brilliant and quite orthodox theologians were discredited because of it, and the Church's intellectual life was set back half a century." Sheehan's all-embracing—and of course once again political—view of what constitutes orthodoxy, can be grasped by his assertion in the Rahner piece, that Rahner's theology "is a very orthodox and even conservative Christianity."

"But the surprising thing today," he continues, in *Revolution in the Church*, "is that the scholars who are advancing the reevaluation of Jesus are neither atheists who attack the Church from without nor liberal Protestants of the nineteenth century," but "rather, these scholars are Roman Catholic exegetes and theologians, most of them priests, faithfully ensconced at the heart of their infallible Church"—as, we may remember, the cardboard *Pascendi* had observed.

Though often "circumspect about what they say outside professional·journals . . . the fact remains that a new and revolutionary approach dominates Catholic theology today, even if"—and here we come to the nub of the post-Council crisis in the West—"the folk religion of most practicing Catholics still lives on the pre-revolutionary fare that generally is served up from their local pulpits and especially from the one currently occupied by the conservative Pope John Paul II."

"The new approach that Catholic scholars are taking to Jesus and the scriptures," Sheehan goes on, "I shall call, by way of shorthand, the 'liberal consensus'. By that I mean the scientific methods employed" (earlier, with some coyness, he calls "the new reading of Christianity that Catholic scholars now propose . . . not a rationalist attack on traditionalist doctrine," but rather nothing more than "the result of scientific exegesis of the New Testament"), "and the conclusions generated by Catholic exegetes and theologians internationally recognized in their fields, the ones who hold the chairs, get the grants, publish the books, and define the limits of scientific exegesis and theology in the Catholic Church today. This liberal consensus reflects the presuppositions and procedures that Catholic scholars like Rudolph Schnackenburgh, *Raymond E. Brown*, Roland Murphy, Pierre Benoit, John P. Meier, J. A. Fitzmyer, David M. Stanley, Rudolph Pesch, *Walter Kasper, David Tracy, Edward Schillebeeckx, Hans*

Kueng,"—I have italicized particular names here because of their appearance at other points in this book—"and hundreds of others use when they do their research—as well as the results they publish in their monographs and in such scholarly journals as the *Catholic Biblical Quarterly, New Testament Studies, Revue Biblique,* and *Biblische Zeitschrift.*"[21]

And what might be the presuppositions and procedures that carefully do not "get the grants"? Mr. Sheehan is happy to tell us: "That the liberal consensus has become dominant in Catholic scholarship does not mean that those identified with it embrace all the work of their colleagues. Here, as in other fields of research, scholars have reached a consensus not on a body of dogmas but on the questions to be asked and the methods for answering them. A consensus allows wide-ranging internal dispute, but it draws lines that exclude certain presuppositions and procedures. This does not mean that the old approaches are universally rejected or that they cease to function in certain circles. For example, one can still find seminaries where Ludwig Ott's long summary of traditional theology *Fundamentals of Catholic Dogma,* is required reading. But scholars who continue to employ the older methods find themselves pushed to the margins of scholarly discourse. The gradual triumph of a new approach in a discipline is usually in direct proportion to the retirement of those who held the old one."

James Hitchcock's description of this process is a bit more succinct. "Liberals," he notes, "practice censorship all the time. They have merely learned to call it another name."[22] *Pascendi* elaborates: "in their writings and addresses [Modernists] seem not

---

[21]Sheehan cites Father Walter Kasper's assertion in *Jesus the Christ* that "a divine intervention in the sense of a directly visible action of God is theological nonsense." Nonetheless, Kasper was chosen by John Paul II to be the Special Secretary, or theological consultant, to the Extraordinary Synod; and though one hesitates to join the Modernist analysis of the Pontiff's political manuevers, it may not be wholly unfair to suggest that on occasion he engages in some. The observations of Kasper correspondent Peter Hebblethwaite, in fact, rescued Catholics from despair over the Pope's choice: in the 13 December 1985 *National Catholic Reporter,* Hebblethwaite complained that the content of the Synod's *Final Report* "came about because no theologians were present. True," he added, "Walter Kasper came from [Hans Kueng's] Tuebingen University, but he departed muttering that his theological services had not been called upon." As expected, Kasper later denied his friend's assertion.
[22]24 October 1982 *National Catholic Register.*

infrequently to advocate doctrines which are contrary one to the other, so that one would be disposed to regard their attitudes as double and doubtful. But this is done deliberately and advisedly," for the reality is that when a Modernist "makes any utterance, the others applaud him in chorus, proclaiming that science has made another step forward, while if an outsider should desire to inspect the new discovery for himself, they form a coalition against him. He who denies it is decried as one who is ignorant, while he who embraces and defends it has all their praise. In this way they entrap not a few." Or Cardinal Ratzinger, who in his famous interview with Messori, notes that as a consequence of the presuppositions and procedures Sheehan describes, "Scripture has again become a *closed* book. It has become the object of experts. The layman, but also the specialist in theology who is not an exegete, can no longer hazard to talk about it. It seems almost to have been withdrawn from the reading and reflection of the believer, for what would result from this would be dismissed as 'dilettantish.' The science of the specialists has erected a fence around the garden of Scripture to which the nonexpert now no longer has entry."

Or, to quote again the passage from *Pascendi* that closed Part Two, "it is pride which fills Modernists with that self-assurance by which they consider themselves and pose as the rule for all," and "puffs them up with that vainglory which allows them to regard themselves as the sole possessors of knowledge, and makes them say, elated and inflated with presumption, 'We are not as the rest of men,' and which, lest they should seem as other men, leads them to embrace and to devise novelties even of the most absurd kind."

"Many of the conclusions of the 'liberal consensus,' " Mr. Sheehan meanwhile continues, "conflict sharply with traditional Catholic doctrine. Today, for example, one would be hard pressed to find a Catholic Biblical scholar who maintains that Jesus thought he was the divine Son of God who preexisted from all eternity as the second person of the Trinity before he became a human being. Strictly speaking, the Catholic exegetes say, Jesus knew nothing about the Trinity and never mentioned it in his preaching,"—which seems somewhat ideological given that the penultimate verse in the Gospel of St. Matthew reads: "Go ye therefore, and teach all nations, baptizing them in the name of the Father, and of the Son, and of the Holy Ghost."

The authority Mr. Sheehan cites against St. Matthew in a footnote to the above paragraph is Father Edward Schillebeeckx, from his book *Jesus: An Experiment in Christology.*

"Nor did Jesus know that his mother, Mary," Sheehan perseveres, "had remained a virgin in the very act of conceiving him," because "most likely Mary told Jesus what she herself knew of his origins: that he had a natural father and was born not in Bethlehem but in Nazareth, indeed without the ministrations of angels, shepherds, and late-arriving wise men bearing gifts." And Sts. Matthew and Luke? "She could have told her son the traditional nativity story," Sheehan says, "only if she had managed to read, long before they were written, the inspiring but unhistorical Christmas legends that first appeared in the Gospels of Matthew and Luke some fifty years after her son had died." He cites Father Raymond Brown as his authority for this view, while noting Brown's standard caveat that while "the totality of the scientifically controllable evidence leaves an unresolved problem" about the virginal conception of Jesus, this "calls for ecumenical discussion and, ultimately, resolution within the frame of the teaching authority of the Church." Such as, perhaps, Dr. Rahner's second magisterium?

What neither Brown nor Sheehan are fond of citing is the fourteenth proposition condemned in *Lamentabili* that "in many narrations the Evangelists recorded, not so much things that are true, as things which, even though false, they judged to be more profitable for their readers." Or condemned proposition #24 that, "the exegete who constructs premises from which it follows that dogmas are historically false or doubtful is not to be reproved as long as he does not directly deny the dogmas themselves." Or the *Pascendi* observation of the Modernist tendency to mask "an incredible audacity under a mock semblance of humility. While they make a pretence of bowing their heads, their minds and hands are more boldly intent than ever on carrying out their purposes."

Meanwhile, after noting the Liberal Consensus perspective that Jesus performed no real miracles, instituted no sacraments, ordained no priests, and consecrated no bishops, since "he did not know he was supposed to establish the Holy Roman Catholic and Apostolic Church with St. Peter as the first in a long line of infallible popes," Sheehan then turns his attention to Father Kueng's *Eternal Life?.* "Growing as it does out of the consensus's reinterpretation of the resurrection of Jesus," its "centerpiece ... is a deconstructive analysis of the Biblical idea that Jesus was raised from the dead. Here he says nothing that we cannot find elsewhere in modern Roman Catholic exegesis," and thus Kueng "leaves the corpse of Jesus, corrupted by physical death, in whatever tomb it may now occupy," and makes clear his view that Christ "saw himself not as God or the Messiah, but as a Jewish prophet."

"The next event that can be dated in Christian history," Sheehan proceeds, "is not Jesus' emergence from his tomb but the birth of the disciples' faith in him," and so the question arises, "what happened between Jesus' death and the emergence of Christian faith?" According to the Consensus, "We are thrown back on the claims of his first disciples that they had some kind of revelatory experiences ['appearances'] that convinced them Jesus was alive. Virtually all New Testament exegetes agree that the first such 'appearance' was to Peter. Kueng follows the scholarly opinion that it took place in Galilee, not Jerusalem, and had nothing to do with later stories that Jesus had left the tomb three days after he died. . . . According to Edward Schillebeeckx, with whom Kueng agrees, even if Jesus' body could not be found after he died, that fact 'had a merely negative effect: it did not lead to triumphant hope in resurrection, but to confusion and sorrow.' . . . Only later, when [the disciples] came down to Jerusalem from Galilee, did they make the empty tomb story a vehicle for the faith which had been born independently of it."

"New Testament exegetes argue that the authors of the Gospels used . . . apocalyptic tropes not to describe historical events but to express in imaginative and symbolic language their belief that Jesus was somehow alive with God and would someday reappear." In a footnote, Sheehan adds that "a growing body of Catholic exegetes think the gospel stories of the empty tomb originated in a cult legend."

And so it goes. Still, *Eternal Life?* somewhat sentimentally argues that though Christians have the obligation to follow the reasoning of the second magisterium and thus abandon all belief in Christ's physical resurrection, they should nonetheless "hope that Jesus is somehow with God and therefore that life has an ultimate meaning." Sheehan lacks enthusiasm for this view, but nonetheless praises Kueng for having "done more than his share, in a lifetime of work, to challenge the apocalyptic and mythical content of Catholic folk religion in the name of the best scientific scholarship that can be brought to bear on the Bible

and the theological tradition; and he has consistently risked his
own career in order to unmask the ideological power structures
that inform so much of the Roman ecclesiastical structure."

On the other hand, there have been compensations for
Father Kueng's risks, not excluding the longest op-ed piece the
New York Times has ever allowed to be published. The question is
rather more whose ideological power structure it is that needs to
be unmasked; and one begins better to understand the discomfort
Cardinal Ratzinger's interview provoked upon reading his observation that "one should not forget that for the Church, faith is a
'common good,' a wealth that belongs to everybody, beginning
with the poor who are least protected from distortions.
Consequently, the Church sees in the defense of right belief also
a social work for the benefit of all believers."

"From this viewpoint, in regard to error," His Eminence
continues, "it must not be forgotten that the right of the individual theologian must be protected but that the rights of the community must likewise be protected," for "broad circles in
theology seem to have forgotten that the subject who pursues
theology is not the individual scholar but the Catholic
community as a whole, the entire Church. . . . People sometimes
give the impression that the exegetes, with their historico-critical
methods, have found the 'scientific' and hence the nonpartisan
solution. This is not the case, however; every 'science' unavoidably
depends upon a philosophy, an ideology. There is no neutrality,
here least of all."[23]

Pascendi was more blunt: "The truth is, that their history
and their criticism are saturated with their philosophy, and that
their historico-critical conclusions are the natural outcome of
their philosophical principles."

And while on the subject of Mr. Sheehan's appreciation of
Dr. Kueng, it seems fair to enquire how true it is that "Catholic
folk religion" has been challenged by Kueng "in the name of the
best scientific scholarship that can be brought to bear on the
Bible and the theological tradition."

Not surprisingly, G. K. Chesterton,—whom Sheehan
logically attacked in his Rahner piece—rather captured the
essence of this scientific scholarship in his public controversy on

---

[23]Unless otherwise noted, most of Cardinal Ratzinger's observations in the present work are from *The Ratzinger Report*,
Ignatius Press, 1985, which is based on his August 1984 interview
with Vittorio Messori.

the question of miracles with Robert Blatchford that appeared in *The Clarion* in 1903.

"The historic case against miracles," Chesterton wrote, "is also rather simple. It consists of calling miracles impossible, then saying that no one but a fool believes impossibilities; then declaring that there is no wise evidence on behalf of the miraculous. The whole trick is done by means of leaning alternately on the philosophical and historical objection. If we say miracles are theoretically possible, they say, 'Yes, but there is no evidence for them.' When we take all the records of the human race and say, 'Here is your evidence,' they say, 'But these people were superstitious, they believed in impossible things.' "

"The real question," Mr. Chesterton continued, "is whether our little Oxford Street civilization is certain to be right and the rest of the world certain to be wrong. Mr. Blatchford thinks the materialism of 19th century Westerns one of their noble discoveries. I think it is as dull as their coats, as dirty as their streets, as ugly as their trousers, and as stupid as their industrial system."

"Mr. Blatchford himself," Chesterton pursues, "has summed up perfectly his pathetic faith in modern civilization. He has written a very amusing description of how difficult it would be to persuade an English judge in a modern law court of the truth of the Resurrection. Of course he is quite right; it would be impossible. But it does not seem to occur to him that we Christians may not have such an extravagant reverence for English judges as is felt by Mr. Blatchford himself."

St. Pius X in *Pascendi* is no less relentless than Chesterton. In "that famous method which they describe as historical," the Saint observes, "in the Person of Christ, they say, science and history encounter nothing that is not human. Therefore . . . whatever there is in His history suggestive of the divine must be rejected. Then . . . the historical Person of Christ was *transfigured* by faith; therefore everything that raises it above historical conditions must be removed. Lastly, [they] lay down that the Person of Christ has been *disfigured* by faith, [and thus] require that everything should be excluded, deeds and words and all else, that is not in strict keeping with His character, condition, and education, and with the place and time in which He lived. A method of reasoning that is passing strange, but in it we have the Modernist criticism.

"Hence they delete from His *real* history and transfer to faith all allegories found in His discourses. We may peradventure inquire on what principle they make these divisions?"

St. Pius does. "Their method is to put themselves into the position and person of Christ, and then attribute to Him what they would have done under the circumstances. In this way, absolutely *a priori* and acting on philosophical principles which they hold but which they profess to ignore, they proclaim that Christ, according to what they call His *real* history, was not God and never did anything divine, and that as man He did and said only what they, judging from the time in which He lived, consider that He ought to have said and done."

The best scientific scholarship? "The truth is," *Pascendi* reminds us, "that a whole multitude of Doctors, far superior to them in genius, in erudition, in sanctity, have sifted the Sacred Books in every way, and so far from finding anything in them blameworthy have thanked God more and more heartily the more deeply they have gone into them, for His divine bounty in having vouchsafed to speak thus to men."

And the Second Vatican Council? In *Lumen gentium*, sec. 8, the Council declared: "This is the sole Church of Christ which in the Creed we profess to be one, holy, catholic and apostolic, which our Savior, after His Resurrection, entrusted to Peter's pastoral care, commissioning him and the other apostles to extend and rule it, and which He raised up for all ages as 'the pillar and the mainstay of truth.' " *Dei Verbum* "unhesitatingly affirms" the historical accuracy of the Gospels, as they "faithfully hand on what Jesus, the Son of God, while he lived among men, really did and taught for their eternal salvation, until the day He was taken up." But of course, *all* of the documents of the Second Vatican Council amount to a bitter reproach to these Modernist clerics who have done so much in its name. And to be sure, what they did was not meant for, and "did not confine itself to professional journals of the aulae of graduate schools. It was advocacy in the undergraduate classroom, not a discussion among peers, and the corrupt doctrine soon descended into high school religious instruction"—as Ralph McInerny observed in the December 1985 *Catholicism in Crisis*.

The "immense promise" Sheehan sees in all of this is no less sentimental than Kueng's opinions. Though hostile to the idea of immortality , Sheehan feels that, with the Church's international organization, it could still be used to promote various social positions, such as those advanced in certain aspects of liberation theology. About the fundamental implications of the liberal consensus, however, Sheehan is not sentimental at all.

"If we follow Kueng and the liberal consensus in demythologizing the resurrection of Jesus," he asks, "what does Christianity have to tell us about eternal life? Very little, it would seem, or at least very little that we did not already know." Thus, he concludes, its "major achievement ... seems to be bringing the Church to what can be called the end of Catholicism, that is, to the limits of what it can say about God and the human condition."

"But there is a further possibility," the article concludes, "as the liberal consensus continues to push Catholic theology to and beyond its limits. Could the Church shelve even its purified belief in Jesus' resurrection and still remain itself? The direction of Kueng's reinterpretation of the resurrection has been to move through the traditional apocalyptic legends and beyond them toward a more rational hope in a somewhat vaguely defined immortality. But what would happen if liberal theologians abandoned apocalypse altogether and returned full circle to the pre-apocalyptic faith of the prophets with its intrinsic moral, social, and political concerns? On that hypothesis we might have found Hans Kueng writing, 'As far as one can know, when you're dead, you're dead—and the same holds for Jesus.' "

3. The End Of Catholicism?
The Academy Responds

"Jesus said unto them ... Before Abraham was, I am."
John 8:58

"And he said unto him, if they hear not Moses and the prophets, neither will they be persuaded, though one rose from the dead."
Luke 16:31

"Will the theologians and their followers write to the *New York Review of Books* to disassociate themselves from the conclusions Sheehan so gleefully draws from their work?" asked the edi-

tors of the *National Catholic Register*.[24] "Or will there be a large
and revealing silence?" In a 15 July 1984 *Register* op-ed piece, in
fact, James Hitchcock predicted that such a disassociation was not
"likely to happen" because, "privately, most of those who make
up Sheehan's 'liberal consensus' know he is right. For various
strategic reasons they will not put it as bluntly as he has, but they
cannot accuse him of distortion."

In reality, though no further discussion appeared in the
Review of Books, various Catholic and Modernist journals were not
silent about Sheehan's expose, so let us consider whether those
who addressed the issue provide something as large and revealing
as those—such as Raymond Brown for example—who felt it in
their interests to remain silent.

In the July 1984 *Catholicism in Crisis*, Ralph McInerny agreed
that if Sheehan is right, it would, indeed, mean the end of
Catholicism: "Most Catholics would simply stop being Catholics if
they accepted the liberal consensus as true. . . . At Easter we
would not contemplate the glorious truth of our risen Lord but
rather the psyches of an early generation of Christians who, in
order to express their sense that the influence of Jesus somehow
persisted among them, began to tell a story of an empty tomb, a
risen Christ, appearances and manifestations to hundreds, etc.
Lies, all of it, of course, but Happy Easter and what did the
Bunny bring?" McInerny also noted, however, the growing resistance to Arianism both among the faithful and the priesthood,
not least by observing that "on Sheehan's assumptions, people
like Ratzinger, Laurentin, Fabro, Grisez, Roach, William Smith,
George Kelly and thousands of others simply do not exist."

The 6 July *National Catholic Reporter* was more reverent. Its
regular op-ed columnist Tim Unsworth called Sheehan's piece
"very thoughtful," and also "exciting," in short, an "excellent article." Its contents left Unsworth "honestly relieved to hear that
the virgin conception and birth are highly suspect. And I'm not
terribly troubled to learn that Jesus performed few miracles, ordained no priests, consecrated no bishops and made no plans for
establishing a church." With Sheehan, he felt it was still nice to
have the Church around advocating peace and justice, but
Unsworth's basic conclusion was summed up in a discussion with

[24]A Catholic weekly to be distinguished from its neo-Arian
counterpart, *The National Catholic Reporter*. The *Register* posed this
question, meanwhile, in its 5 August 1984 edition.

Michael Perry, who is a colleague of Sheehan's at the ostensibly Catholic Loyola University at Chicago.

"Perry's view echoed much of my own thinking," Unsworth wrote. "He wasn't disturbed by these new findings. We both agreed that installing stop signs at the crossroads of institutional church and scholarly pursuit has never worked. Perry would be relieved if the church would quietly drop the creed from the Sunday liturgy to make more room for the faithful doubter. Good idea."

The main discussion of the Sheehan piece, however, appeared in the Arian intellectual journal *Commonweal*.[25] "In an editorial in the August 10 issue," Hitchcock wrote for the *Register*, "*Commonweal's* editors expressed fear that Sheehan's claims might lend support to what 'conservatives' in the Church have been saying all along about contemporary theology. Thus one of the main purposes of the *Commonweal* symposium has been to provide a more benign interpretation of what the 'liberal consensus' really stands for." The 13 December 1984 issue of *The Wanderer* was less benevolent in its interpretation of the *Commonweal* symposium, charging that innumerable "letters have since appeared ..., full of minor quibbles, [but] little of the outrage that would have been provoked had Sheehan *attacked* 'the liberal consensus'."

The principal replies in *Commonweal* came from Father Andrew Greeley, whose literary efforts with the popular and somewhat pornographic novel are no less impressive than his sociological contributions; and, more importantly, from University of Chicago theology professor Father David Tracy, whom Sheehan had cited as one of the prime pillars of the liberal consensus. The front-page title introducing this discussion was "The end of Catholicism: Is liberal theology eviscerating the faith? Two Catholic scholars reply to Thomas Sheehan." Its editorial introduction asserted that Sheehan's analysis "merits further discussion," and that accordingly the *Commonweal* editors "hope the discussion will continue."

Father Tracy's response appeared first. He starts by praising "Sheehan's previous articles in the *New York Review* on Catholic theology, especially his extraordinary article on Karl Rahner," as "quite simply, the best articles that journal has published on religion or theology." Still, though "a great admirer of Thomas Sheehan," who "would rather write an article on how good

---

[25]As with most Modernist journals, *Commonweal* will on occasion, if rarely, also publish Catholic writers.

Thomas Sheehan's other *New York Review* articles and his
Heidegger work are," Tracy felt compelled to say that in regard
to the piece in question, "I basically disagree with it."

At the same time, the theology professor was also quick to
note points of agreement. For example, "Sheehan is right, I think,
in his basic description of the liberal consensus for interpreting
the scriptures," though "I wish, however, that he had spent more
time on these scholars' methods and questions than on simply list-
ing their conclusions." In addition, Tracy thinks Sheehan was too
concerned with "rhetorical shock value," such as his assertion
that "one would be hard pressed to find a Catholic biblical
scholar who maintains that Jesus thought he was the divine Son
of God who preexisted from all eternity as the second person of
the Trinity before he became a human being."

"This is true," Tracy is quick to add, but unfair since "on
the scriptural evidence alone as interpreted through historico-
critical methods, the historian as historian can hardly be expected
to know much about what Jesus actually thought. Moreover,
given the nature of the scriptures as confessional documents, the
historian can reach the plausible conclusion that in many cases it
is more likely that statements attributed to Jesus were added by
Christian believers who wrote these texts to affirm their faith in
Jesus Christ rather than made by Jesus himself."

"After this interpretation of the liberal consensus," Tracy
proceeds, "the article heads out to sea," because Sheehan does not
define "proof" or "folk religion" or "supernatural revelation " etc.
The priest agrees, however, that "Kueng is clearly committed to
that consensus and exemplifies it in his new book," and that "the
Catholic theologians to whom Sheehan directs our attention follow Vatican II," but he feels it is theologically "all more complicated than that—as Sheehan's earlier article on Rahner showed."
The reason, he says, is that "there can exist a liberal consensus on
methods of interpretation of scripture side by side with far less
theological consensus on how to use the results of these methods
in Catholic theology ... simply to list 'conclusions' from scriptural
exegesis and ignore how those conclusions are, in fact, related to
theological proposals for the Catholic community by individual
theologians does not help much"—especially given Father Tracy's
view that "what is new in modern Catholic theology is a greater
recognition that the tradition which is fundamentally trusted as
the mediator of this faith is also, like all traditions, ambiguous
and thereby in constant need of correction and self-reform."

In a sidebar, Father Tracy brings a bit more clarity to his objections. "What if these liberals will one day eliminate all belief in the scriptures and tradition, what then? The answer seems obvious: then we will have proposals for a post-Catholic or even post-Christian theology. Until then, we should argue with the theology proposed. In short, we should make our arguments not on the 'what if' basis of what Hans Kueng might someday say if he had said something entirely different from what he does say. We should make them on the basis of what Kueng actually says."

One had thought that is what Sheehan had tried to do. In fact, so he confesses in his 21 September *Commonweal* answer to Father Tracy. "Unlike the faithless historian, the believing Christian supposedly knows that the real Jesus was the ontological Son of God and somehow was aware of that fact. But this solution is illusory, and I am quite sure that, despite appearances, David Tracy cannot possibly be proposing it in his response. . . . I hope that David, whom I prize and admire, will not be offended by my saying that . . . the liberal position which Tracy advocates . . . strikes me as an exercise in polishing brass on the Titanic."

In addition, since "virtually all modern theologians agree" that the Resurrection "is a hermeneutical symbol rather than a historical event," Sheehan thinks they ought to be more honest about the ambiguous tradition to which Tracy admitted they cling. "Home is where Simon is: it is the Bark of Peter," Sheehan concludes. "The only problem is that Simon Peter missed the boat he should have taken and instead signed on as the captain of the Titanic. That is, rather than leaving Jesus dead and then going on to live the Kingdom that Jesus proclaimed, Simon hoped him out of the tomb and identified the Kingdom of God with the prophet who had preached it." As such, doing precisely what Tracy accused him of ignoring, Sheehan proceeds to draw an eminently logical conclusion "on the basis of what Kueng actually says."

This conclusion "is not to salvage Catholicism or Christianity but to let go of them . . . to help people leave the church with a good conscience . . . what we need to do today is not to correct and reform the tradition so much as (in Heidegger's sense of the term) to 'destroy' it and retrieve what it has concealed."

Father Tracy, meanwhile, closes his main article by giving an example of what Sheehan in the original piece called the liberal consensus approach to those outside the liberal circle. "If you demand 'proofs'," Tracy wrote, "then return to Ludwig Ott—or get yourself on Phyllis Schlafly's mailing list. For myself, I would rather stay with all the real Catholics—like Geraldine Ferraro and Thomas Sheehan."

Father Greeley, on the other hand, does not dispute Sheehan's critique of what is taught in Western Catholic seminaries these days, but rather the conclusions he draws from this phenomenon.

"The issue finally in any discussion of religion is not the historical accuracy of a given story, but whether that which the story offers as a model of ultimate reality is true," says the Chicago priest. "The question is not the accuracy of a given account of the resurrection of Jesus in a gospel story, but whether the God whom Jesus preached is in fact a useful model to fit the data of experience. Does a religious story which claims that love is stronger than death is what the universe is about fit the data better than any other story? That is an extremely . . . maybe the only important question." Sheehan's error, Greeley says, is his concern about whether Christ's Resurrection or the Doctrine of the Trinity and Redemption is really true, because neither orthodox Catholicism "nor agnostic secularism is an appropriate criterion for religious model fitting. When both are used, as they are by Professor Sheehan, as alternatives, they violate the rules of the language/model fitting game." He invokes David Tracy to whom he considers himself "heavily indebted" as an authority on this, and concludes that "everyone fashions a model of faith. Some do it openly. Others pretend not to, but still do it in secret. They are no less naive than the rest of us, only less honest."

Sheehan responded contemptuously. "Christianity according to Father Greeley is a useful tale, a nice myth, for getting through the day. I have nothing against this kind of ecumenical Rotarianism, even when it is presented in the guise of modern Catholicism . . . . But we'll leave it to others to decide how much, if at all, this civil-religion-cum-feeling has to do with Catholicism, Christianity, and the message of Jesus of Nazareth."

The letters are no less instructive. Father Peter Chirico, a seminary professor in Archbishop Raymond Hunthausen's Seattle, wrote that though "one can concede that Sheehan is correct in attributing to the 'liberal consensus' [its] disagreement with traditional Roman Catholic theology . . . he fails to show that these elements of disagreement are essential to the faith," when "in fact, a good case can be made that they are not."

Father John Jay Hughes, who heads Archbishop John May's St. Louis *Renew* program[26] took the occasion to proclaim his adherence to the liberal consensus, and announce his fondness for David Tracy's notions: in particular the idea that Catholic tradition should be considered ambiguous. Hughes also cheerfully suggests that though the dismantling of traditional Catholic theology is a *fait accompli*, "it is certain that in time Catholic theology will emerge reconstituted and renewed." To help advance that certainty, Father Hughes denounced "champions of frantic orthodoxy such as Msgr. George Kelly"—an antagonist of Raymond Brown—"and *The Wanderer*," an antagonist not only of the liberal consensus, but also of *Renew*. Father Hughes charged that "it is these zealous defenders of the faith who are the true modernists."

Sister Anne Carr, who had been a special consultant to the Bishop's committee devising an upcoming Pastoral Letter on Women until she signed the Catholics for a Free Choice abortion ad in the *New York Times*, praised Karl Rahner as "the single thinker who was and is probably the most influential of the Vatican II era." In addition, she chided Sheehan for thinking that "most practicing Catholics" still believed in the "folk religion" of "already dismantled traditional Roman Catholic theology," since Rahner's "overarching theological vision has 'trickled down' in distinctive personal and collective ways to the average pulpit and pew."

Sebastian Moore of the Jesuits' Boston College wrote that "the invaluable contribution of biblical criticism is that it deprives us of a Jesus who gave us our church and our faith *in a quite plain and simple way* (his emphasis)." He concludes that "the faith is enriched, not impoverished, by being deprived of such a Jesus," and that accordingly "there is a grounded lack of trust in church authority today, a feeling that it will continue to sell this authority-supporting image of Christ, if it can get away with it, drawing for support on the current wave of Catholic fundamentalism."

Father Gerard Sloyan, a professor of religious studies at Temple University, vice-president of the Association for the Rights of Catholics in the Church (ARCC, which among other

---

[26]To be examined more later, *Renew* is in effect a clerical program developed by Newark Archbishop Peter Gerety for the purpose of winning lay acceptance of the Modernist proposals passed at the 1976 Detroit Call-to-Action Conference.

things opposes Catholic norms against adultery and legal abortion), and former president of the National Liturgical Conference during Vatican II, wrote that "it is a scandal when anyone in authority in the church deals with another person as if the *mythos* [of the Bible] were historically true in all its details or, worse, through failure to read and study, thinks that such is the case."

There were many other contributors to this symposium, not least among them Milwaukee Archbishop Rembert Weakland's auxiliary bishop Richard Sklba, who stated that "although I often find Sheehan provocative and helpful, his review of Kueng proved disappointing," because "the list of exegetes marshalled into a single category combines people who are not united by any 'liberal consensus' but rather by a conviction that the historical evolution of ideas is an essential element in the process by which God reveals truth and salvation to and through the church. The rediscovery of biblical history, indeed of the unfolding of the faith within the context of Scripture itself, is one of the primary contributions of the past forty years of Catholic exegesis. These insights may result in the restatement of commonly held Catholic doctrine in more nuanced and existential terms. The sweeping generalizations of Sheehan, neither nuanced accurately nor contextualized critically, were unfairly projected into classrooms of universities and seminaries."

Bishop Sklba, incidentally, is also a Patron Member of *Commonweal* Associates, a group of people without which, the *Commonweal* editors have said publicly, the magazine's deficit would "put us under quickly." Archbishops Weakland and May are also members of this exclusive association, as are Robert Hoyt, Father Sloyan, Bishops Gumbleton of Detroit and Cummins of Oakland, the openly pro-legal abortion Jesuit Robert Drinan, Msgr. George Higgins, Msgr. John Egan, and numerous others who shall appear in the course of this narrative. Sustaining Members, who give less, include Father James Coriden, ARCC member, and the man chosen by the Canon Law Society of America (CLSA) to co-edit its official Commentary on the Code; Bishop Raymond Lucker of New Ulm, Minnesota, and none other than Bishop James Malone, ordinary of Youngstown, Ohio and President of the National Conference of Catholic Bishops. Archbishop May, incidentally, is that organization's Vice-President. Archbishop Weakland, Bishop Gumbleton, and Gerety auxiliary Joseph Francis are also on *Commonweal's* Anniversary Committee, joined there by formal Catholic apostate Michael

Harrington, Father Theodore Hesburgh, Msgr. Higgins, Father Tracy, Sister Theresa Kane, New York Governor Mario Cuomo, and Rosemary Ruether.

Thomas Sheehan, meanwhile, refused to let his supposed antagonists in *Commonweal* off the semantical hook. "The essay that I published in the *New York Review of Books*," he wrote in his *Commonweal* reply to Tracy, "dealt with this foundational crisis in Christianity. The essay was centered on the question of Jesus' alleged Resurrection from the dead ... and also touched on the discrepancy between what Jesus of Nazareth apparently thought he was, a special but very human prophet, and what orthodox Catholic believers now take him to be, the divine Son of God, eternally consubstantial with the Father and the Holy Spirit."

Sheehan dismissed them all, since "none of the *Commonweal* respondents has chosen to discuss that matter." The silence was large and revealing, after all.

Even so, Bishop Francis Mugavero's *Brooklyn Tablet* editorialized in September 1984 that the *Commonweal* symposium "should be on the lists of those planning school or parish study programs for the months ahead"—whence it doubtless has become a topic of keen interest in catechism classes and *Renew* programs across the land.

"The curriculum in a Catholic seminary or school of theology in 1985," wrote the Jesuit Bryan McDermott in the 28 September 1985 issue of *America* magazine as part of a series on the then upcoming Extraordinary Synod, "eloquently reflects the change of consciousness encouraged by Vatican II. Narrowly defensive apologetics courses and Latin texts have long since given way to courses that take a historical-critical approach to both Scripture and church doctrine."

We have seen what they discuss, and why the winds howl through the empty seminaries of the declining West.

THE BISHOPS

I. What Kind of Shepherds? A Divergence of Opinion

> "*Christ the Lord, Son of the living God, came to redeem his people from their sins that all mankind might be sanctified. Having been sent by the Father, He in turn sent His apostles whom he sanctified by conferring on them the Holy Spirit so that they also might glorify the Father on earth and procure the salvation of men 'for the building up of the Body of Christ,' which is the Church.*"
>
> Vatican II, Decree on the Pastoral Office of Bishops

> "*Woe be unto the pastors that destroy and scatter the sheep of my pasture! saith the Lord.*"
>
> Jeremiah 23:1

"The National Conference of Catholic Bishops," notes the 1980 *Official Catholic Directory*, "is a canonical entity operating in accordance with the Conciliar Decree *Christus Dominus*. Its purpose is to foster the Church's mission to mankind by providing the bishops of this country with an opportunity to exchange views and insights of prudence and experience and to exercise in a joint manner their pastoral office. The NCCB is the successor to the Annual Meeting of the Bishops of the United States, approved in the brief *Communes* issued by Pope Benedict XV, April 10, 1919 and in a special letter of Pius XI issued on August 10, 1927. The present NCCB statutes with some slight amendment are those originally approved by the Sacred Consistorial Congregation in a decree issued on June 22, 1922."

"The National Conference of Catholic Bishops," it continues, "is composed of every Bishop, residential or titular, who serves the Church in the United States, its territories or possessions. Each bishop has an active and passive voice in the Conference. Under certain conditions, enunciated in conciliar legislation, the National Conference of Catholic Bishops can initiate actions that are juridically binding on all the bishops of the country.

"The National Conference of Catholic Bishops is presided over by a president who is elected by the general membership. Other officers of the organization are a vice president, secretary, treasurer and general secretary. The organization functions through forty-two different bishops' committees. The National Conference of Catholic Bishops is a distinct entity from the United States Catholic Conference. Its relationship to the USCC is that of a sponsoring organization.

"The United States Catholic Conference (USCC) is a civil entity of the American Catholic Bishops, incorporated under the laws of the District of Columbia, assisting the Bishops in their service to the Church in this country by uniting the people of God where voluntary, collective action on a broad interdiocesan level is needed. The USCC provides an organizational structure and the resources needed to insure coordination, cooperation, and assistance in the public, educational and social concerns of the Church at the national or interdiocesan level."

One would think the preceding paragraphs simple enough; yet some of what they calmly assert as fact has proved instead to be the source of bitter controversies within the Church in the United States. For example, the idea that the NCCB has the prerogative "to initiate actions that are juridically binding on all the bishops of the country," has no basis in Catholic tradition, any document of Vatican II, or, for that matter, any authoritative Catholic document. There is, in addition, a large body of Catholic opinion which believes that the USCC has primarily subverted, rather than upheld, its purposes as outlined above.

Meanwhile, there are some 300 successors to the Apostles, auxiliaries and ordinaries, that are members of the NCCB, of which according to the *Washington Post,* 174 were chosen when Archbishop Jean Jadot was the apostolic delegate here. That among Catholics, and people who call themselves Catholic, there are such extreme differences of opinion about how faithful the American Bishops have been to the teachings of the Second

Vatican Council is doubtless significant in itself—as it is also doubtless worthwhile here to survey some representative examples of those divergent verdicts.

The view of one side is perhaps best captured by the argument of Kathleen Whalen Fitzgerald in the 30 May 1984 issue of the Protestant journal *The Christian Century*. There she insists that for the Church in the U.S., "the strategic figures are the bishops . . . the only ones who can move to protect that very segment of the people of God who took the words of Vatican II to heart. The future of the Church in America lies with the American Bishops: in their fidelity to collegiality, their loyalty to their sisters in religion, their sense of responsibility to the vision of a renewed church that they shared with John XXIII." Human Life International President Father Paul Marx presents the other side: in the June 1983 edition of *Fidelity* magazine he charged that "in thirty-five years of priesthood I have never known the American Catholic Bishops to have less credibility than now."

The best elaboration of the first viewpoint, I think, appeared in a 1983 *National Catholic Reporter* article by its former editor and still regular columnist Arthur Jones, who, with Peter Hebblethwaite, covered the Synod for *NCR*; the second viewpoint was best developed by Joseph Sobran in the 14 January 1985 issue of *Catholic Eye*.

Jones posed the theory that the U.S. bishops are "collectively the most powerful group of men in the world—capable of overwhelming anything coming out of Washington, Moscow, Latin America—or the Vatican," though "the U.S. bishops do not yet perceive themselves as having the power I refer to." He adds in the next sentence: "Their power is media power. Their power comes not from being Catholic bishops. Rather, it comes from being an Episcopal body in a superpower that also contains the largest and most aggressive national and international press corps of any nation in the world. This corps is at the core of what gives the bishops their clout."

"Nobody pays any attention to what the European bishops say," Jones continues, "because most don't say much. But in Europe they do pay attention to what the *U.S. bishops* say. *Der Spiegel* and German television, for example, assiduously and regularly cover the U.S. Catholic beat—Matthiesen, Hunthausen and the Berrigans are well known to more than just Germany's Green party."

"Does this 'power' matter?" Jones asks. "Heavens, yes. See what takes place: what the U.S. bishops agree to in concert rolls across the oceans and landmasses, juggernaut-like, to influence how the debate takes place on those subjects that do and will concern U.S. bishops: nukes, women, capitalism."

"What is happening therefore," Jones insists, "is that an international debate is conducted 'within' the Catholic Church but outside Vatican control—or, indeed, influence. One could say a 'synod' on nuclear arms has taken place in the world's media; mass communication has removed control of the debate from the Vatican," and thus "mass communications is seen to have consequences for the magisterium." Consequently, "for better or for worse, the U.S. bishops' conference emerges as top dog among equals globally. And that means the U.S. bishops will not run second to the Vatican in determining how the church deals with the issues."

"Understand," Jones concludes, "the U.S. bishops will not go *against* the Pope; they will go *beyond* him."

Before looking at Sobran's view, it should be said that, a year later, another writer for the *Reporter* decided that Jones' thesis had gone unrealized, since "after an initial flurry of media attention, *The Challenge of Peace*, the U.S. Catholic bishops' pastoral letter on war and peace in the nuclear age, has—in terms of influence on the public debate, national policy or even the opinion of most Catholics—sunk into that benign oblivion usually reserved for congressional declarations of National Numismatic Week." Nonetheless, as we shall see, the *Reporter* goes back and forth on the subject of U.S. episcopal influence; as do most Catholics and Modernists who are enthusiastic about the bishops' implementation of Vatican II.

Sobran, meanwhile, argues that though the U.S. episcopate has "said nothing heretical . . . this hardly matters," since by doing so, the bishops "would hurt themselves—by inviting a direct reply from Rome, to the detriment of their authority. "But," he insists, "from the dissident's point of view, in fact, the bishops are most helpful when they act as they are now doing. It is not necessary that the bishops should play the role of Hans Kueng: Father Kueng and his kind handle that role very well, and what they need most is not bishops imitating them in defiance, but bishops shielding them through lax exercise of episcopal authority."

"It is an excellent thing for bishops to seek unity and to speak with one voice," he adds, "but what if they are seeking unity with the secular culture, and speaking with a voice indistinguishable from that culture? Not so long ago the Catholic Church was a stubborn obstacle to modern evils. It wielded extraordinary power and influence even in its American character as a private, voluntary association whose members were legally free to disobey or to leave altogether. . . . Ambitious politicians didn't dare insult the standards that the Church, in general agreement with Protestants and Jews, constantly upheld. Today it is hard to find traces of a Catholic presence in American public life. The bishops seem to be trying to feign an influence simply by echoing the tune of the times and joining the secular chorus.

"Needless to say, the result is more than a Catholic problem. It is a serious problem for all believers in traditional moral standards who lack, and yearn for, the kind of influence that depends on the focus of a major institutional vehicle," because "today the secularist forces control such things as the major television networks, the universities, the leading newspapers and magazines, the movie industry, and the public education system; in addition, the court system, dominated by the same forces, has banished rival forces, especially religion, from important areas. Religious people are left with much less potent institutional footing, and are forbidden to exercise legal restraint against those who insult and attack their beliefs . . . without the support and leadership of the largest church in America, their situation is fairly desperate.

"The secularist communications system . . . is radically changing the way people are related to each other, not just marginally relaxing old restraints. The individual person, formerly presumed even by pluralistic American society to be made in God's image and endowed with an immortal soul, is progressively cheapened and treated by the mass market and the state alike as an interchangeable unit in a soulless collectivity. In one way or another, millions of people have some intimation of the nature and depth of the Transformation. But they no longer possess the needed institutional means of resistance."

"It would be unfair," Sobran concludes, "to assume that the bishops fully realize the nature of the struggle they are involved in . . . but if anyone ought to be critical of fashionable notions, it is the hierarchy of a body rooted in two thousand years of highly developed and systematized doctrine. One can only marvel at the frivolity with which such a patrimony is discarded by its very custodians."

It is perhaps significant that the *NCR* is known as the "cleric's paper," and sells the majority of its copies through churches due to mass subscriptions bought by pastors; by contrast, the Catholic newspaper where the Sobran viewpoint (with Sobran himself) regularly appears—*The Wanderer*—is known as the "laity's paper" precisely because over three-quarters of its sales are due to individual subscriptions. The number of copies that each paper sells weekly is almost identical.

Given Mr. Jones's flattering opinions, it may not be wholly surprising that clerical support for the *NCR* can also be found among the bishops. Indeed, on the occasion of its twentieth anniversary (which arrived but two months after Tim Unsworth's praise of Thomas Sheehan), the paper published a number of episcopal accolades. Among their composers were the immediate past-president of the NCCB, Minneapolis-St. Paul Archbishop John Roach, who was "delighted to join the many who offer congratulation"; the man chosen by the bishops to help best articulate their recent feeling about economic matters, Milwaukee Archbishop Rembert Weakland, who told the *NCR* that "we have come to learn we cannot exist without it"; and the man chosen to head the committee for the upcoming U.S. Bishops' Pastoral about Women, His Excellency Joseph Imesch, of Joliet, Illinois, who wished to "thank you for what you have done and what you will do in the future." Las Cruces, New Mexico Bishop Ricardo Ramirez said, "The *National Catholic Reporter* is one of the finest products of American Catholicism in post-Vatican II times"; Amarillo, Texas Bishop Leroy Matthiesen called it "competent and responsible"; New Ulm, Minnesota Bishop Raymond Lucker praised its "thoughtful editorial stands"; Fresno, California Bishop Joseph Madera spoke of his "joy and satisfaction" at the *NCR's* "great service to our church" which Orlando, Florida Bishop Thomas Grady called "valuable service"; and, along with Detroit Auxiliary Thomas Gumbleton and Seattle Archbishop Raymond Hunthausen, many other prelates forwarded their congratulations.

Finally, in addressing the question "What kind of shepherds?", there is one voice that deserves particular attention. It is that of the current President of the National Conference of Catholic Bishops, the Youngstown ordinary James Malone. In effect speaking for the entire NCCB, His Excellency submitted such an analysis to his brother bishops throughout the world in preparation for the Extraordinary Synod; while acknowledging certain dilemmas, he concluded that, rather than a lack of leadership on the part of the Episcopate, "cultural factors originating outside the Church and the Council account for many recent problems in Catholic life in the United States, as in many other countries. Among these factors," he noted, "are exaggerated individualism, the culturally conditioned disinclination of many persons to make permanent commitments, the breakdown of marriage and family life, the sexual revolution, and exaggerated secular feminism." Despite these influences, however, he insisted "that the state of the Church in this country is basically sound," because "the Church in the United States is fundamentally on the right track in implementing the teachings and decisions of Vatican Council II." That assessment was released to the public on September 16, 1985. On November 19, in an elaboration of his Synod intervention, Bishop Malone further told the public that "for their part, the Catholic bishops of the United States have tried to be faithful to the Council in their efforts to promote an understanding that would ground its 'spirit' in its 'letter.' "

These assertions were not made in a vacuum. In fact, a major portion of the 14-page single-spaced September document was devoted to explaining exactly how the Church is fundamentally on the right track, as well as explaining various measures the bishops have undertaken since Vatican II "to make the Council known, faithfully received, and implemented."

So let us examine His Excellency's claims, and see how they compare both to his conclusions, and to matters of public record regarding Catholic life and Episcopal responsibility in the United States since the Second Vatican Council.

II. Catholic Schools And Universities

> *"The pastors of the Church should not only be assiduous in their care for the spiritual life of students attending Catholic universities but, in their solicitude for the spiritual formation of all their flock, they should provide by joint episcopal action the establishment of Catholic residences and centers even in non-Catholic universities. . . . Catholic universities and faculties . . . should be noteworthy not so much for their numbers as for their high standards."*
>
> Gravissimum Educationis, Section 10

> *"What efforts do they not make to win new recruits. They seize upon professorships in the seminaries and universities, and gradually make of them chairs of pestilence."*
>
> Pope St. Pius X, *Pascendi*, Section 43

1. Father Curran's Contribution

> *"It is simplistic and wrong to defend older Catholic teachings on specific teachings such as contraception and sterilization as the truths of faith as opposed to the evils of the modern world."*
>
> Father Charles Curran

When during the spring 1985 bishops meeting in Collegeville, Minnesota, America's only black ordinary, Bishop Joseph Howze of Biloxi, Mississippi, was indulgent enough to ask my opinion about why the American Episcopate had so little respect, and what might be done about it, I immediately referred to the debacle at Catholic University in the spring of 1967 when the openly Modernist priest Father Charles Curran was granted tenure there.

At the time, Father Curran had not publicly argued against granting legal protection to unborn children, nor disclosed his conviction that sodomy need not always be considered objectively sinful. He had, however, already stated his enthusiasm for chemical contraception; and more importantly, he had established a methodology, known in the parlance of the hour as "situation ethics," wherein his later support for legal abortion and sodomy could—in his case, would—logically follow.

Originally, on 17 April 1967, Father Curran was denied tenure at Catholic University because of his defense of situation ethics in a book titled *Christian Morality Today*. The decision was made in conjunction with the University statutes of the time (later scrapped), which stated that the Chancellor of the University had the obligation to safeguard Catholic teaching there. The vote not to renew Father Curran's contract was made by the school's 44 trustees, eleven of whom were laymen: the remaining 33 were bishops. There was only one dissenting vote, that of Archbishop Paul Hallinan of Atlanta (whom Chicago's Cardinal Joseph Bernardin rates publicly as one of his two episcopal mentors—the other being John Cardinal Dearden of Detroit). Meanwhile, that the theology department of the University had unanimously recommended a promotion for Curran is evidence of the extensive corruption in that department. But it was the reaction of the bishops when their decision was protested, I submitted to Bishop Howze, that has won for the American Episcopate a reputation not unlike the kind reserved for women of easy virtue: which is to say a respect that does not endure the proferring of favors.

In any event, the theology department immediately issued an ultimatum: either the bishops back down or the department would go on strike. The secular and Modernist press rushed to Curran's defense, and indeed a campus-wide strike was mobilized. Though presented with a golden opportunity to teach, in fact to drive home the principles of Vatican II both to the Catholic community and the secular community beyond it, the bishops chose instead, on April 24, to capitulate; and Father Curran was granted tenure.

It does not seem wholly unfair to suggest that whatever hopes the bishops may have had about upholding the Council, or of resisting a wholesale sweep of the Church's bureaucratic organization by proponents of the Council's anti-spirit, may well have come to an end on that crucial day, less than seventeen months after the close of Vatican II. Consequently, I suggested to Bishop Howze that unless the American Episcopate finds within itself a strength of character, not to say faith, that would repudiate the want of fortitude demonstrated at that time, it seems unlikely the bishops will ever achieve any but the sort of superficial respect that is already their lot. Bishop Howze sighed, not without sorrow it seemed, and said he was glad there were no universities that would confront him with such responsibilities in Biloxi.

In his September report, Bishop Malone takes a more optimistic view. Upon detailing what he and his fellow bishops have done to make the Council known, faithfully received and implemented, His Excellency boasts that "the Catholic Church in the United States continues to maintain the world's largest system of Catholic schools at all levels," and is pleased to report that "although Catholic schools experienced a kind of institutional identity crisis in the late 1960's and early 1970's, this has been largely resolved by now," since "Catholic colleges and universities have placed renewed emphasis on their Catholic identity in recent years." He further insisted that "the continued vitality of Catholic school and catechetical efforts in the U.S. speaks eloquently of the skill and dedication" of "teachers and administrators at all levels."

The nature of this eloquence received some attention with the publication in early 1984 of a poll of 1,062 full-time teachers in 45 Catholic high schools that was conducted by the National Catholic Educational Association (NCEA). A little over half supported a Constitutional Amendment affording legal protection to unborn children, 72% felt the Church should endorse abortifacients and chemical contraception, 44% favored homosexualist legislation, and 68% supported the Equal Rights Amendment (ERA)—despite the NCCB's own published report that the pro-abortion Federal judiciary would almost certainly interpret abortion-on-demand to be a constitutional right, should the ERA pass.

There was even more eloquence at the spring 1985 gathering of the NCEA in St. Louis, Missouri. Major speakers included atheist Carl Sagan, self-proclaimed Teilhardian cosmologist Robert Muller, as well as John Goodlad, author of *Schooling for a Global Age*, which argues in favor of extensive "globalist" propaganda campaigns, since "otherwise children and youth enrolled in globally oriented programs may find themselves in conflict with values assumed in the home. And then the educational institution frequently comes under scrutiny and must pull back." All of this, of course, is opposed to the arguments in *Gravissimum educationis* in Section 3 that "As it is the parents who have given life to their children . . . they must therefore be recognized as being primarily and principally responsible for their education."

Still, Mr. Goodlad's historicist view fit in neatly with the NCEA Convention theme, *Gateway to Global Understanding,* as did the "Five Teilhardian Enlightenments," proclaimed in Muller's book *New Genesis: Shaping a Global Understanding.* Muller thinks the Church should be radically restructured and divested of things that stand in the way of his own perspectives, such as, in his words, "dogmatism," and "hierarchialism." According to the 11 May 1985 *Human Events,* "Muller's 'world core curriculum' is now being used, with his blessing, by the School of Ageless Wisdom in Texas. The school is affiliated with the Lucis Trust of New York, the repository of the occult teachings of the now deceased occultist, Alice Bailey. Muller has frequently spoken at Lucis Trust gatherings," *Human Events* notes—despite the Trust's belief in the ancient and dangerous heresy, revived by Bailey, that Satan was a benevolent figure, ill-treated by God.

Muller told *NC Reporter* editor Tom Fox he thinks Catholic education is in a state of transition. "The fact that I would be invited here this year is one sign," he observed. "It would have been unheard of even five years ago."

Other speakers included Archbishops Weakland and Roach, and Father Brian Hehir, from the USCC Committee on Social Development and World Peace.

On the other hand, based upon his own education, the former managing editor of *Catholic Eye,* John Fowler, presents a somewhat less sanguine analysis than Bishop Malone's.[1]

"At Catholic colleges, with few exceptions, traditional Catholic values are not only ignored, but also attacked. This was the last thing I expected from a Catholic education when I decided to attend my now alma-mater, the Jesuit-run College of Holy Cross in Worcester, Massachusetts. How *my* need as a Catholic student—to have my faith strengthened and my religious knowledge broadened—could have been ignored and tam-

---

[1]In the 10 May 1984 *Catholic Eye.*

pered with, *here*, at this school which boasted a reputation for an emphasis on Catholic teaching, I would not at first have believed.

"My professors, priests included, followed the now-patented solution: they took a 'neutral' position towards Catholicism in their classroom lectures . . . many teachers showed that they were not so much 'neutral' toward the faith as prejudiced against it: a prejudice which held Catholicism to be more harmful than meaningless. Some of my professors expressed this prejudice outright . . . these professors, priests included, had little good to say about the Church . . . openly attacking Church dogma in both lectures and conversation, whether or not Catholicism was pertinent to the subject at hand. But then this 'dissent' was said to be valued because it challenged the students to think harder about their faith. From a lack of visible or effective opposition to it by the college, 'dissent' had become *de facto* school policy.

"On the other hand, the Religious Studies department did deal passionately with Catholicism," though "courses on the Church Fathers or Church history were rarely taught, never mind stressed. Instead, I was . . . encouraged to venerate . . . Kueng, Schillebeeckx, Rahner, Teilhard, Father Drinan and the Berrigans. I learned little about Catholic history, dogma, original sin (or any other kind of sin), the Just War theory, or traditional morality. Nor about the early Church Councils, Augustine, Aquinas, Pascal, Dante, the Church Fathers, the Saints, Xavier or Chesterton. . . . Incredibly, a student could graduate from Holy Cross without ever having *heard* most of them mentioned, never mind knowing or reading about them."

"To receive an education at Holy Cross . . . meant being unfamiliar with Catholic doctrine or theology; being told to recognize Catholic traditions as meaningless and superstitious; being taught the dark incidents of Church history, true or alleged; and being cut off from the moorings of 2,000 years of Catholic history and culture."

Mr. Fowler graduated from Holy Cross in May, 1983.

2. Father Curran's Colleagues

*"And Jesus asked him, What is thy name? And he answered, My
name is Legion, for we are many."*   Mark 5:9

Holy Cross is not the only Jesuit school that seems to have
made a career of blocking the implementation of Vatican II.
When Seattle University's Jesuit President Father William
Sullivan calls himself a "post-Vatican II priest," for example, he
does not mean just that he was a priest after 1965; but rather more
"post" in the way Cardinal Lustiger uses the term when
speaking about "post-Christian Europe." Recent articles in the
Catholic press, for instance, have revealed Father Sullivan's pride
in bringing an atmosphere to Seattle University much like the
one described by John Fowler at Holy Cross: though Father
Sullivan has gone beyond merely bringing in a stream of pro-
contraceptive lecturers (such as Father Curran) to ensure that his
students will reject *Humanae vitae* and fit docilely into the
contraceptive culture; he has also instituted regular lectures so
that his students will know how to use contraceptives and
abortifacients, and how to abort their children.

The Jesuits' Fordham University in the Bronx, New
York—whose President, Father Joseph O'Hare, was, until he
came to Fordham in 1984, the editor of *America* magazine for
twelve years—is also notable for its extreme antagonism to the
teaching of Vatican II. Given the relentless Modernism in *America*
magazine since the Council, it is not particularly surprising
O'Hare was hired as President of Fordham: but even the Jesuits
surprised people by their 1982 choice of the polemicist George
Gordon, a non-practicing Jew, to head Fordham's
Communications Department. The surprise was due to Gordon's
bizarre classroom antics as detailed in his book *Erotic
Communications: Studies in Sin and Censorship*. In it, Professor
Gordon details his use of hard-core pornographic films in a
Communications "class of fifty-five students who were more or
less under my control . . . thirty were females and twenty-five,
males," all of whom were single. The median age "of the class
was twenty years; the mean, twenty-one years," and all were
subject to "the requirement that every student attend one x-
rated porno film *in a theatre* [his emphasis] either in Nassau or
New York County and report in writing the entire experience in
detail. . . . I assumed that students could not understand the
problem of eroticism's relationship to its audiences *in vacuo* and

that a trip to a porno grind house, no matter what risks were entailed to their sensitivities, limb or epidermis, was necessary . . . "

"Student resistance to this assignment, then four years old," Professor Gordon continued, "had from the start been quite high," despite his practice of showing pornographic films in class, which he detailed graphically in the book. After showing them, meanwhile, Gordon then "handed out a questionnaire," asking the students to tell him "did any of the explicit sex 'turn you on'—that is, physically produce 'the itch' as you watched? Which scenes were particularly stimulating? For how long and when during the film did you experience an erection? . . . Did you experience any direct vaginal stimulation as a result of the film or the classroom experiences?" The questionnaire then asked the students to inform Professor Gordon of the "dominant sexual activity in your life" and asked them to note "any change in any of your sexual activities that you can fairly ascribe to the film," and if "any of your own personal sexual fantasies [were] enacted in this film? If so, when, where, with whom, etc.?"

Though not required to return the questionnaires, Gordon "pleaded with the students to return them," and "made it my business to find out why" some students were hesitant to do so—"five males and four females were asked to keep their ears to the ground and report to me reasons for the low response if they could discover them."

Professor Gordon also proved something of a contradiction to Bishop Malone's assessment due to numerous columns the Communications Director wrote—prominently noting his Fordham association—for the hard-core pornography magazine *Screw*, which magazine according to the *New York Post* has among other things "published a doctored and obscene picture of Pope John Paul II, and has also editorially rejoiced at news of [New York] Cardinal Cooke's leukemia." Gordon's own contributions to that paper discussed masturbatory techniques, mocked Christ and His mother, and much else. When controversies about Gordon's employment at Fordham broke out in 1985, Father O'Hare announced in a letter to the *National Review* that though "embarrassed" by Gordon, his activities "could and would be defended as an exercise of academic freedom." Curiously, the Jesuit seemed much more irritated with the Episcopal Reverend Lester Kinsolving, who delivered a series of scathing radio commentaries about Gordon's activities at Fordham. Whereas

O'Hare only accused Gordon of being embarrassing, he devoted eight paragraphs in a press release denouncing the Kinsolving commentaries as "vulgar and reckless . . . malicious . . . character assassination . . . cheap . . . of dubious legality . . . anti-Catholic bigotry . . . scurrilous," and so on.

The example of Professor Gordon is not at all extraordinary. At Notre Dame, Frank Reilly, the dean of its College of Business Administration, invited Christie Hefner of *Playboy* Enterprises to the campus, in order to explain the business angle of selling flesh. When asked about this decision, Reilly said of *Playboy* that "Most of what they do, I don't think is terribly inconsistent with the Church. If you look at some of the causes they have given to and worked on and helped with, they have been very consistent. If you look at where they've given money to women's groups, beyond the abortion thing, I think they have been very liberal and very Christian."

A similar attitude doubtless influenced Notre Dame's telephone-tape counseling service, called Counseline, which informed students who called in to ask about lesbianism, that "there are certainly strong anti-homosexual attitudes found in this society in general and in many religions," but "my"—Counseline's—"own viewpoint is that religious and legal authorities have laid down rules against homosexual practices because of their own biases and fears and not because they have more of a direct pipeline to truth than you or I. I strongly think that when two people of the same sex express their love for each other in a sexual way that that expression can be very beautiful and positive. I don't feel that such an experience can be called morally wrong." Students who protested this tape were at first ignored: when their protests began to generate public controversy, Professor Utz, who was responsible for the Counseline tapes, announced he had been planning to redo the lesbian one anyway, though "we don't want to redo it according to Catholic teaching, but according to sound psychology."

The theology faculty at Notre Dame, meanwhile, seem on the whole to be devoted students of Professor Utz: not least the department chairman, Father Richard McBrien. Because of their increasing frustration about their inability to learn anything Catholic from that department, a group of students undertook a survey of its 39 members in the spring semester of 1983. Seventeen of the professors refused to participate, though one wrote a letter to the school paper, *The Observer*, denouncing the students for undermining the unity of the Notre Dame community simply by asking the questions; he said they "would do better to take a course in the study of Scripture than to write letters to *The Observer*." Of the twenty-two who did respond, only eight did so on paper. On the Virginity of Mary, only one professor answered a clear cut yes. The rest either denied it, or said the question was simply too complex to answer. Questions about abortion, contraception, divorce, homosexuality, the teaching authority of the Church, hell, Transubstantiation, the Resurrection, and the Divinity of Christ received similarly vague and/or heretical answers, and were given detailed attention in the June 1984 issue of *Fidelity* magazine. One professor, William Storey, who taught Introduction to Theology and was a member of the liturgy program, admitted not only his hostility to the Church and to parents—"The wishes of parents," he said, "are a menace to academic freedom"—but also that he had lost his faith and become an atheist during the course of his theological professorship at Notre Dame.

More than professors lost their faith, as Notre Dame senior James Rickert made clear upon noting in the *Observer* that though "I was raised in the atmosphere of Catholicism, and I accepted its major tenets," after four years of Notre Dame, "my faith in minor matters, such as the role and status of Mary, the saints and the pope has been transformed, and I thank our theology department for any help they may have given me in this transformation."

That Notre Dame's hostility to Catholic teaching is not restricted to the campus was, alas, revealed in a particular way in the 27 January 1985 *Washington Post*. A Catholic woman who, though married, has masturbated regularly for some 30 years, wrote a letter to the advice columnist saying she felt guilty about this compulsion, but had heard the Church no longer considered it a sin. Could Ann find out for her? She could. Coincidentally, she found a source who was not only in accord with her own views, but was willing to present them as if they were the position of the Church.

Thus, Father Edward Malloy informed Landers' vulnerable readership that "there has been a significant change in the evaluation of masturbation by the Catholic Church," and that "masturbation now is seen as a relatively common form of sexual release. In most cases, individual acts of masturbation do not in-

volve the moral quality of the person in such a way that it constitutes a serious offense."

Fr. Malloy is the associate provost of Notre Dame
University. According to some, he is scheduled to replace Father
Hesburgh as the school's next president.

Meanwhile, a spate of articles in such diverse publications as
the *San Francisco Examiner, Twin Circle* and the *National Catholic
Register* have shown that such approaches have led not only students and professors, but also priests and nuns to lose their faith.
Many are dissatisfied, however, with the bleak postures of secularism, which may account for the growing fascination with
witchcraft and Satanism, topics becoming not only more popular,
but also increasingly a functional part of the curriculum in a
growing number of Catholic universities. The most celebrated of
these is the Institute of Culture and Creation Spirituality run by
the Dominican priest Father Matthew Fox, who is presently under investigation by the Congregation for the Doctrine of the
Faith (as, incidentally, is Father Curran).[2]

"Fox," reports the 28 July 1985 *S. F. Examiner*, "has already
raised a few eyebrows in local Catholic circles by hiring an unusual group of freethinkers to serve on the faculty of the
Institute of Culture and Creation Spirituality," which "runs a
nine-month program at Oakland's Holy Name College"—founded
by the Sisters of Holy Name in 1868—"that awards masters degrees in spirituality to about 50 students a year. Included among
the institute's 14 faculty members are a certified masseuse, a yoga
teacher, an Episcopal vicar turned Zen Buddhist and a self-de-
scribed witch named Starhawk."

"I get a lot of hate mail from Catholics because I hire
witches," Father Fox told the *Examiner*, but dismissed their complaints because "there's a lot of wisdom in witchcraft." In order
to help plumb this wisdom, Starhawk teaches seminars in
"Feminist Theology," and "Creating Rituals," and other faculty
members teach such things as "Drawing on the Right Side of the
Brain," "Women's Quest for Wholeness and Empowerment,"
and "Awakening the Inner Eye with Extrovert Meditation."
Fox himself teaches a course in "Erotic Justice," in which, in the
Resources handbook his Institute distributes, he charges that justice "is not effective and easily degenerates into new moralisms,

---

[2]After writing the above, the Curran case became public in
March 1986; that development will be addressed near the end of
this book.

new orthodoxy or orthopraxis tests and laying of new layers of guilt on people. Why is this? Because eros, the feminine side of justice, has been ignored. We worship thanatos or love of death instead of its counterpart, eros and love of life."

"Fox's message is popular," says the *Examiner*, and notes as evidence that in July "170 people from around the United States and abroad attended a week-long workshop on creation spirituality at Holy Name college. It was one of three such events being held around the nation this summer"—another being at St. Thomas College in St. Paul, Minnesota, whose ordinary, let us recall, is Bishop Malone's immediate predecessor as NCCB President, Archbishop John Roach. "Those in attendance," at the Holy Name event, reports the *Examiner*, included "a number of Catholic nuns, lay activists and Protestant ministers."

The 19 January 1986 *Catholic Twin Circle*, meanwhile, notes that at an October "Women's Spirituality Conference held at Mankato State University ... women from Catholic backgrounds are very much involved in what they refer to as 'The Craft.' More than 500 women, many of them nuns, religious education coordinators, Catholic school teachers and professors from Catholic colleges, took part in the conference," which "emphasized witchcraft." Rosemary Ruether was the keynote speaker.

"Many workshops dealt with 'liberation' from established religion or elements of established religion considered oppressive," reported the 10 November 1985 *National Catholic Register*. "Within the context of the conference, ritual was often seen as synonymous with a form of witchcraft ritual advocated by Starhawk, a witch who has gained credibility within Catholic circles in recent years as a faculty member of Dominican Father Matthew Fox's Center for Creation Spirituality, located at Holy Names College in Oakland, California."

"Workshops dealt with such topics as 'Re-framing Reality,' presented by Lynn Levy, a founder of the Re-formed Congregation of the Goddess; Homophobia: Impact on Spirituality and Gay/Lesbian Liberation, " and "From Convent to Coven—A Journey to the Old Religion of the Goddess," which "drew a large crowd to hear Sister of St. Joseph Joan Keller-Maresh describe her personal journey from the days in which she was a member of a community of women—a convent—to her personal affiliation with a circle of women—a coven."

"Starhawk's 'Dreaming in the Dark' spoke to me," the nun announced. "Here was this woman, a proclaimed witch, saying things that were a part of me," and accordingly Sister Joan decided that "to worship a male God is to worship the oppressor." In discussing the witchcraft rituals outlined by Starhawk, Keller-Maresh noted that "the ritual sounded hokey when I first read about it, but when experienced, it was awesome." An eyewitness account of the Wiccan ceremony (as the witch ritual is called) that ended the Mankato State Conference appeared in the *Register* piece. "In the center of the earth," chanted the priestess, "fire and earth combine to make molten lava and fire . . . feel that healing, transforming fire in the center of the earth . . . bring that energy up, through your roots into your body . . . the energy can handle whatever comes to you, all you need to do is call it up . . . feel yourself a part of the tribe, the tribe of women who are trusting in their own spiritual expression . . . open your eyes and we'll begin casting the circle of the east, the south, the west, the north . . . welcome spirit of the east, blessed be . . ."

"Blessed be," replied the some 250 women in the circle. "Hear me, hear me, Aphrodite,"—a pseudonym for the spirit of the west—they chanted. "Kneeling," the *Register* reports, "with foreheads touching the floor, the circle began calling up the spirit of the north. The women in the circle then silently stood up. Then they cried out in words of pain. They howled. They moaned . . . and the spirit of the north was invoked."

When the circle was chanted to completion, "the women once again joined hands, this time for the spiral dance. As they spiraled, winding, coiling, circling toward the center of the circle, they chanted over and over, 'we all come from the goddess and to her we shall return, like drops of rain falling in the ocean.' " Then "the women sat on the floor, pounding it with their fists, some shouting. others screaming, others yelling 'Freedom!' The energy raising ended, and the energy was grounded by the women putting their hands back into the earth. Then the circle opened with a chant, 'the earth, the water, the fire, the air, returns, returns, returns . . .' "

"The circle is open," the priestess concluded, "but the circle is never broken . . . may the blessings of the goddess go with you."

Two associate professors from the College of St. Catherine—which, with the College of St. Thomas, appears in the *Official Catholic Directory*—were also at the Mankato Conference, and gave a workshop entitled "A Theological Approach to

Teaching Human Sexuality." While doing so Patricia Bartscher and Joan Timmerman, the teachers in question—the latter a professor in theology—upheld the Wiccan position that "if you think something is right, it's right." When questioned whether this ample teaching might present difficulties due to the occasional human proclivity for rape, bestiality and incest, Professor Bartscher answered "at risk of bringing the house down, there might be situations where incest might be OK." Another person asked how the professors got away with advocating such things at a Catholic college, whereupon Professor Timmerman—like Fordham President O'Hare and William Storey before her—replied that "academic freedom protects you from all kinds of things."

Meanwhile, the College of St. Benedict arranges for its students to attend this annual event in women's spirituality.

"Could it be possible that the college's officials are unaware of the emphasis on witchcraft at the annual conferences?" *Twin Circle* inquired. "While one may wish that this were the case, it appears that, far from being unaware of the involvement in witchcraft, college officials have been actively promoting it for some time."

A recent graduate of the college referred to only as Kathy, spoke with *Twin Circle* about this, and "described her introduction to the goddess religion in a telephone interview." "I first encountered witchcraft when, as a sophomore," she said, "I was asked by Father George Werkin"—the Director of Campus Ministry—"and two nuns on the campus to attend the Mankato conference. I attended that one and every year after that until I graduated last spring [1985]. At first, I didn't realize it was witchcraft, but I felt drawn to it. At college, it had been instilled in me that women are oppressed, and here I was dealing with women who felt the way I did." Due to this influence, Kathy added, witchhcraft rituals began to thrive on campus. In the spring of 1985 a formal Wicca ritual was held during the college's annual Women's Week events. According to the graduate, it was arranged by the Associate Director of Campus Ministry, the college's Wellness Coordinator, and a counselor on campus, and was entitled "Womenspirit Rising: A Ritual of Symbol and Movement."

Kathy also wrote a short article for the Campus Ministry bulletin, in which she quoted Starhawk. Uncertain how to describe the witch, Kathy "showed the article to Father George, and he thought it would be best to refer to Starhawk as 'the noted spiritual writer' instead of identifying her as a witch."

Similarly, when St. Thomas College Alumnus Michael Gaworski called his alma mater to protest Starhawk's 1985 summer appearance there under the sponsorship of Father Fox's Institute, "I was told that I needed to be more 'open minded, " and "willing to dialogue," and not "jump to conclusions." In short, he added, in a letter published in *The Wanderer*, it was "the same rhetoric which was used in the theology classes I attended at the same college several years ago."

"The Dominican order is standing behind me," Father Fox told the *NC News*; and his provincial Fr. John Gerlach agreed, noting that the Dominican theologians asked by the Vatican to review his books "supported Fox's work."

3. Panic in Academia (and Episcopalia)

> *"The Catholic University touches the Church Herself and hence it cannot be considered as a purely private institution. It is for this reason that the relationship between the Catholic University and the Church as a whole, and with its Pastors, must be seen as an internal requirement of the University."*
> 1985 *Schema* of the Sacred Congregation for Catholic Education

One reason Bishop Malone may have considered it prudent to pass over these public difficulties in his 16 September Submission is that to acknowledge them would be to acknowledge the obligation the NCCB has to confront this conquest of the Catholic university system by opponents of Vatican II—as outlined by the very Revised Code of Canon Law produced at the behest of Vatican II. He would in short have to announce the intention of the U.S. Episcopate to do now what it was too frightened to do at Catholic University in 1967. And what makes this such an explosive question—one which may well decide whether Pope John Paul II has any hope of seeing that the Council is applied in the United States—is that according to the Council's Canon Law, U.S. bishops do not merely have the right to restore Catholic teaching at universities that call themselves Catholic: they are legally required to do so.

Canon 810 of the Revised Code reads as follows: "In Catholic universities it is the duty of the competent statutory authority to ensure that there be appointed teachers who are not only qualified in scientific and pedagogical expertise, but are also outstanding in their integrity of doctrine and uprightness of life. If these requirements are found to be lacking, it is also that authority's duty to see to it that these teachers are removed from office, in accordance with the procedure determined in the statutes." That is section one of Canon 810, but it is the single sentence that comprises the second and concluding section of the Canon which many believe will determine the future of Vatican II in this country. Canon 810 (2) seems simple enough. It reads: "The Episcopal Conference and the diocesan bishops concerned have the duty and the right of seeing to it that, in these universities, the principles of Catholic doctrine are faithfully observed."

As we can discern from the examples so far provided, contrasting as they do with Bishop Malone's confidence that the "institutional identity crisis" he admits once afflicted Catholic schools has "been largely resolved by now," the U.S. bishops did not especially like this newest expression of the Council—in particular because the Canon Law Society of America (CLSA) insisted at its 1984 annual conference that Canon 810 could not possibly apply to Catholic universities in the United States. But if the American Episcopate found this opinion conclusive, Pope John Paul II did not.

Accordingly, in April of 1985, very soon after the announcement of an Extraordinary Synod, the Sacred Congregation for Catholic Education sent out a *schema* to numerous heads of Catholic universities in this country, and to the NCCB as a preliminary consultative step to the promulgation of a *Pontifical Document on Catholic Universities*—the purpose is the implementation of the disputed Canon.

Among other things, the *schema* criticizes "the temptation of pragmatism, the tendency to secularization, the influence of extraneous ideologies, and the weakening of the Catholic character" of Catholic universities in the United States. It reminds the bishops that Christian education "is not to be considered something added from without, but rather as an internal profound dimension," and that students "must be helped to understand how intellectual research can only be accomplished if the Catholic university be a truly intellectual community in which Catholicity be present and active."

"Religious teaching is not enough," the schema continues, because Faith, "to have a decisive force on human realities in order to elevate them, must become culture," since "a faith that does not become culture is a faith not fully accepted, not wholly thought, not faithfully lived."

"The Catholic university makes it known that ethics have priority over technology, the person has primacy over things; being prevails over having and doing, spirit is superior to matter . . . ."

Meanwhile, the *schema* notes, "if the Catholic character of the university continues to be compromised in a serious way the competent ecclesiastical authority shall declare the university to be no longer Catholic." This means that "in a special way spiritual values in relation to the person and the Christian community must be coherently shared and properly fostered by all members of the university community," and "all teachers . . . are to be distinguished by academic and pedagogic ability as well as by doctrinal integrity and uprightness of life so that they may cooperate effectively to achieve the goals of the university." Thus, "teachers who lack these requirements are to be dismissed, observing the procedures established in the statutes, or equivalent document." In addition, "in view of their accepting appointments to teach in Catholic universities, non-Catholic teachers shall loyally respect the Catholic character of the universities," and the "Catholic students shall be educated in such a way that their learning and general development as well as their continuing formation are always marked by sound Catholic doctrine and practice so that they be evident in their everyday lives."

Predictably, the *schema* provoked some reaction from a number of university representatives across the country. Sister Alice Gallin, the executive director of the Association of Catholic Colleges and Universities immediately announced that "most of the Americans feel the document doesn't serve a useful purpose in this country." The chairman of the Theology Department at Boston College, Jesuit Bob Daly, immediately denounced the document on the grounds that "American Catholic universities have taken up a tradition of academic freedom." Comically—since the head of the Sacred Congregation for Catholic Education is the American Cardinal William Baum—Providence College President Father John Cunningham denounced the document for clearly being written by someone "not totally aware of our pluralistic situation."

When the *schema* was sent out last April, the Vatican asked for comments to be sent to Cardinal Baum's office by November 30; but since many Catholic colleges and universities had not received it by mid-summer, the Cardinal extended the date of return through February 1986. Meanwhile, Catholic University's Jesuit President William Byron, announced that "Rome must let universities be universities," and that the "proposed new Vatican norms would not do that. In the United States, anything which seems to impose outside control on a college or university, as the Vatican's draft document does, is threatening to destroy the university." Of course, what Father Byron meant is a particular *kind* of university, since he—and one suspects most Catholic university presidents in the country—are more than willing to allow outside control if it be exercised by the government; especially if said government threatens to take away financial subsidies should that control be challenged. By way of example one could note the remarkable Jesuit docility when the Washington D.C. government threatened to withdraw aid to the Jesuits' Georgetown University due to the latter's hesitancy about formally recognizing school groups that promote sodomy. Recalling his alarmed reaction to the Baum *schema*, one finds it oddly inconsistent that Father Byron felt no similar compulsion to accuse the city government of trying to destroy the university in the Georgetown case.

But perhaps not so odd. That the U.S. government has at its disposal billions of U.S. taxpayer dollars, while the Vatican has only moral authority, proved to be a matter of obsessive university concern: "If the Church had the power to make and enforce rules like those proposed," remarked the Jesuit Marquette University Vice President Quentin Quade, well then "hell yes, you'd lose your accreditation, and rightly so. You'd lose your federal funding because you'd be seen as an arm of the Church."

Father Charles Curran made a similar point. "The fear," he charged, "is that the new Vatican regulations would deny autonomy, integrity and academic freedom to Catholic colleges or universities. Such institutions would then no longer be accepted as colleges or universities on the wider American scene. Accrediting associations would not give recognition to Catholic institutions regulated in the way the Vatican is now proposing, and funding from government sources and many other private sources—foundations, for example—would be cut off. The very existence of Catholic higher education in the United States is thus in jeopardy."

The Holy See—Cardinal Baum—is collecting more information. Accordingly, Father Hesburgh of Notre Dame, Father O'Hare of Fordham, and numerous others, are holding their fire for the moment. Father Hesburgh did say, however, how much he appreciated the views of Milwaukee Archbishop Rembert Weakland, whose perspectives on this shall be examined shortly. In addition, Notre Dame's president said he felt the key to solving the tension generated was a document issued by the International Federation of Catholic Universities (IFCU) in January 1973, when Father Hesburgh was its president. That document, the priest feels, "gives the *magisterium* everything it needs. It gives the hierarchy everything it needs. And it gives the universities everything we need." It does so, he thinks, because of its attention to the "delicate balance" between the hierarchy and the Catholic university, which recognizes the right of the hierarchy to intervene "when it judges the truth of the Christian message to be at stake." The IFCU recognizes this right, however, only if the hierarchy acknowledges that such an intervention must take second place to academic procedures—which of course absolutely deny the right of the hierarchy to intervene in any way. The IFCU document further insists the hierarchy must admit that "Church authority in doctrinal matters does not of itself imply the right of the hierarchy to intervene in university government."

It is perhaps now easier to grasp why Notre Dame theology professors consider the question of Mary's virginity at Christ's conception to be impossibly complex.

Meanwhile, while during the Extraordinary Synod itself Bishop Malone was understandably hesitant about discussing this matter in detail, the chairman of the USCC's Committee of Bishops and Catholic College and University Presidents—Covington, Kentucky Bishop William Hughes—was more forthright. Reflecting the expressed opinions of numerous bishops during the mid-November U.S. Bishops Conference meeting that took place just prior to the Extraordinary Synod, Bishop Hughes asserted that "the bottom line" on the *schema* is, that "it's bad." Noting a legal brief that a number of college lawyers had thoughtfully provided the Bishop, Hughes said it demonstrated that the *schema* threatened "the very existence" of Catholic universities in the United States.

Consequently, Father Byron told the *NC News* that if the norms of the Vatican *schema* were adopted, American Catholic colleges and universities would refuse to observe them. Rather than do so, he said, "boards of trustees would declare that the institutions do not have a 'Catholic Identity'."

Thus, the key to John Paul II's solicitude for his American flock will perhaps be discovered in watching the fortitude with which he confronts this Modernist demand to call itself Catholic. More bluntly, it has been observed that if the Pontiff chooses not to implement Canon 810, he will in effect have abandoned any serious hope of seeing Vatican II realized in the United States in the course of his Pontificate: and American Catholics faithful to the Council will accordingly be expected to continue to endure their dark night of the soul.

4. The Abortion Industry and the American Catholic University

> *"Yea, they sacrificed their sons and daughters unto devils. And shed innocent blood, even the blood of their sons and their daughters, into the idols of Canaan: and the land was polluted with blood."*
>
> Psalms 106:37-38

One thing is certain: if Pope John Paul does insist that the U.S. hierarchy enforce Canon 810, the antagonism of the surrounding secular culture will be extreme. There are many reasons for this, but not least among them is the increasing cooperation between Catholic universities and the abortion industry.

This cooperation is both direct and indirect. *Penumbra*, or shadows, if I might borrow the Supreme Court's terminology, include such simple gestures as the Catholic University School of Law presentation of its 1985 "First Amendment Defender" award to the furiously pro-abortion *New York Times*, and that same university's presentation of the 1985 Distinguished Award for Government to Iowa's Catholic U.S. Senator Thomas Harkin—who votes consistently pro-abortion. The chairman of the University's Department of Sociology, Father Raymond

Potvin,[3] is on the Board of Trustees of the aggressively pro-abortion Population Research Bureau: his picture, complete with Roman collar, appears regularly in the publicity brochures. And never least, there is the ubiquitous Father Charles Curran, who reminded readers of the 28 September 1985 Jesuit magazine *America* that "the renewed nature of contemporary moral theology is evident"—so renewed, he insisted, that "many moral theologians have an understanding of the nature and role of theology different from that proposed in some contemporary official church documents. . . . In the field of morality, for example, the manualist theologians propose that direct killing or direct abortion is always wrong, but the understanding of direct or indirect is based on one particular philosophical understanding that is not necessarily convincing to many contemporary Catholic moral theologians who would employ a different philosophy."

This brings us to the proposed argument of Milwaukee Archbishop Rembert Weakland that Father Theodore Hesburgh found so impressive—and not only Father Hesburgh. The occasion of Archbishop Weakland's presentation was a lay-sponsored campaign throughout Milwaukee calling upon the Jesuits' Marquette University to dismiss the notoriously pro-abortion laicized priest Professor Daniel Maguire. Maguire—who incidentally was instrumental in organizing the pro-Curran protest at Catholic University in 1967—sits on the board of a pro-abortion organization that calls itself Catholic, and which designed the abortion ad that appeared in the *New York Times*; writes numerous articles not simply defending abortion, as well as abortionists, but also acerbically denouncing the anti-abortion Catholic laity; has written books outlining Curran's thesis above, though suggesting that Catholics as a matter of belief ought not to be allowed to support legal protection for unborn children; and has attended actual abortions, held the destroyed fetus afterward (which he derided contemptuously), and then written about it—in the *National Catholic Reporter* and elsewhere.

The lay campaign against Marquette University's protection of Maguire was called Catholics Concerned for Truth in Labeling. It produced full-page ads in 17 suburban and urban Milwaukee newspapers urging Archbishop Weakland to uphold Vatican II and invoke Canon 810 against Maguire's continued

---

[3]who is also researching the crisis of the priesthood for the USCC—see the Anti-Spirit of Vatican II, Fertile Ground, and the Seed Among Rocks.

exploitation of Roman Catholicism on behalf of the abortion industry. In a 5 April 1985 column in his diocesan paper, the *Catholic Herald*, Archbishop Weakland obliquely, but in the end decidedly, refused to do this.

Indeed, in the opinion of Daniel Maguire, "Weakland's response to all this was a landmark. He gave his view that my teaching on the permissibility of some [*sic*] abortions and my essay 'The Morality of Homosexual Marriage' cannot be reconciled with the views of the Congregation for the Doctrine of the Faith. Then he went on to defend academic freedom for theologians in a way that I believe is without parallel in American church history.... At the very time that the Vatican is trying to intimidate Catholic scholars and crush certain theological debates, an archbishop with a major Catholic university in his archdiocese rises in defense of academic freedom and integrity."[4]

Notre Dame Theology Department chairman and syndicated diocesan paper columnist Father Richard McBrien, meanwhile, has never come out and directly said he supports legal abortion. His role, instead, is to praise the wisdom and excellence of those who do. It thus goes without saying that McBrien would praise the Weakland thesis, though his approach was different from Maguire's. "What is remarkable about

---

[4] From the 21 June 1985 *National Catholic Reporter*. Meanwhile, Archbishop Weakland's defense of free speech is not, however, absolutist. Despite his conviction that academics ought to have complete freedom to promote abortion on Catholic campuses, he does not believe opponents of this position ought to have the freedom to express themselves in diocesan newspapers. In a speech before the Catholic Press Association (CPA) in May 1984, His Excellency opined that "so often the letters to the editors are just sheer gripes, and I don't think that's very helpful," especially because in his view there is a conspiracy involved. "I think you know," he told the CPA, "that these [unnamed] groups are organized, seeking space all over the nation in our secular and our religious press."

The Archbishop said he was unsure what to do about this conspiracy, though he asked the CPA to help him find a solution, as long as its members keep in mind that "in this particular moment of history where the unity question becomes more primary," if a diocesan paper "becomes part of the divisiveness, and continues to carry that on, then the bishop has to find another forum"—which His Excellency feared might "undermine the press." He illuminated this position by adding that "maybe under Paul VI, that was not the great problem. But in the present moment of history,"—under a different Pope—"and I don't think I have to tell press people all the indications of that, I think we are in a new role, and therefore you have to help us with that."

Archbishop Weakland's column," McBrien wrote in an October column of his own, is its "frank, dispassionate manner" which may be why "people in Catholic higher education continue to comment favorably on Archbishop Weakland's thoughtful column."

"One finds a refreshing echo of this attitude," McBrien adds, "in a recent article by Cardinal Joseph Bernardin in the May issue of *St. Anthony Messenger*." Indeed, in the same article McBrien touches upon the real conflict involved, a theme he addresses frequently (he even called for an official pastoral letter on the subject, for which idea Archbishop Weakland immediately announced his support), which is the growing anti-clericalism among Catholic lay supporters of Vatican II.

"By and large," McBrien noted, "theologians don't have trouble with the official [*sic*] magisterium of the bishops, particularly with the kind of teaching authority claimed and exercised by an Archbishop Weakland or a Cardinal Bernardin. The problem is almost always with the unofficial magisterium, the self-appointed defenders of orthodoxy. But the bishops have as much trouble with them as do the theologians—and perhaps more." One wonders where Father McBrien's former enthusiasm for the People of God has gone—or if he has read Vatican II's *Decree on the Laity* which in Section 6 reminds clerics that "at a time when . . . grave errors aiming at undermining religion, the moral order and human society itself are rampant, the Council earnestly exhorts laity to take a more active part . . . in fidelity to the mind of the Church, in the explanation and defense of Christian principles and in the correct applications of them to the problems of our times." You will of course find nowhere in Vatican II or its Revised Code of Canon Law, or in Cardinal Baum's Sacred Congregation for Catholic Education's *schema*, or in fact anywhere in Catholic history as a matter of genuine teaching, the argument that "academic freedom" must take precedence over defending a group of people subject to systematic extermination.

Father McBrien's support for Maguire, however, goes beyond simply defending "academic freedom." In the fall of 1983, his department hired Maguire as the John A. O'Brien visiting Professor of Moral Theology at Notre Dame, which decision McBrien defended in the June 1984 issue of *Fidelity* on the grounds that "I don't think you can say [Maguire] is pro-abortion." A month later, in the 20 July 1984 *National Catholic*

Reporter, Maguire and McBrien appeared side by side in a book review forum, wherein both men made a particular point of praising the work of Notre Dame professor Elizabeth Schuessler Fiorenza—a signer of the *Times* abortion ad. Maguire called Fiorenza's book *In Memory of Her* "the most significant book of recent date for moral theologians seeking biblical bases"; McBrien called it "a work of high scholarship and strong pastoral concern. . . . [Fiorenza's] strength as a New Testament scholar and her commitment to the principle of sexual equality are clearly established. In this book she brings together both lines of interest and has produced what biblical scholars regard as a work of good quality."

In fact, the College Theology Society called it the best book of the year, and in June of 1985, the Catholic Theological Society of America elected Fiorenza president. The nature of the Liberal Consensus' appreciation was further elaborated in a 20 September *Commonweal* piece by the Jesuits' Boston College theology professor Lisa Cahill, who wrote that "in the religious realm, scholars such as Elizabeth Schuessler Fiorenza, Raymond Brown, Elizabeth Carroll, and Elizabeth Johnson have used biblical evidence . . . to challenge Mary the Virgin Mother as a role model for Christian women."[5]

Meanwhile, pro-abortion ideologues like Maguire and Fiorenza are not the only prominent figures for whom Notre Dame's top theologian has admiration. When Governor Mario Cuomo accepted Notre Dame's invitation to defend his public position that abortion should be legal and that Catholics and other opponents of abortion should be forced to finance the extermination with their tax dollars, both Father Hesburgh and Father McBrien introduced the man. Upon the Governor's reiteration of these positions, Father McBrien promptly enthused that

---

[5]McBrien's own attitude toward the Mother of Christ in his compendium *Catholicism* has already been noted: in a column, however, he elaborated this view by asserting "that it makes not a scrap of difference really if theologians accept or qualify the doctrine of the virginal conception of Jesus." Presumably to drive this point home, he has also encouraged a Pastoral Letter on "fundamentalism," which would "encourage dioceses to spare no effort or cost in developing first-rate programs of Biblical education for its religious educators and catechists . . . The bishops could insist," he adds, "that biblical studies occupy a central place in the curriculum of clergy education programs, and that the very best young priests be sent away for Scripture degrees with a view to their teaching in seminaries, colleges, and diocesan institutes."

"Governor Cuomo has more effectively conveyed Catholic teaching than most bishops. You cannot name another politician," he added, "who is as consistent with the moral principles of the bishops. He is more in line with the National Conference of Catholic Bishops than Archbishop O'Connor."

As to Maguire, though because of his growing notoriety some schools have cancelled speaking invitations, the largest U.S. Catholic university, the Jesuits' Boston College, made a particular point of inviting Maguire at the end of 1985. The faculty Senate president of Boston College School of Arts and Sciences, one David Northrup, told the *Boston Globe* that "as the largest faculty body on campus, we wanted to make a statement on behalf of the faculty that was as unambiguous as possible."

The collusion between the Catholic university and the abortion industry, however, is not restricted to praising its promoters and disparaging its opponents. When the Agency for International Development (AID) signed a contract on 13 September 1985 with the Jesuits' Georgetown University for the ostensible purpose of promoting natural family planning, AID first gained assurances from Georgetown's Department of Obstetrics and Gynecology that in spending the $15 million approved, the university would also help promote contraception, masturbation (to obtain donor semen), abortifacients—and also abortion itself, as shown by a 31 July letter wherein department chairman John Queenan assured AID that "women who wish to use contraception will receive complete and impartial orientation in all available family planning methods." There is not a contraceptive dispenser in existence—no organization anyway—that does not include abortion as a "family planning method."

To clear up any doubts on the matter, Georgetown agreed to subcontract with the Los Angeles Family Planning Council (LAFLC), a leading California abortion group headed by Thomas Kring—described by William F. Buckley's *National Review* consultant Jim McFadden in *Lifeletter* as "the abortion czar of

California."[6] The Georgetown contract also calls for cooperation with the Family Planning International Assistance (FPIA), the international arm of the Planned Parenthood Federation of America—that is, the very groups the African bishops and their flocks are united against.

Meanwhile Notre Dame's involvement with the abortion industry goes deeper than the enthusiasm of Father McBrien. Father Theodore Hesburgh, who in the early days of the pro-life movement denounced anti-abortionists as "mindless zealots," has always been more sympathetic with pro-abortion activists. In fact, since 1961 he has been on the board of the Rockefeller Foundation, which throughout those years was a zealous promoter of population control in the Third World. And of course the Rockefeller family itself—to quote the pithy assessment of Chicago pediatrician Eugene Diamond in the February 1985 *Fidelity*—"did for abortion what the Krupps did for munitions." The hope that while on the board Hesburgh had ever made any serious attempt to cool this Rockefeller obsession was laid to rest on 14 January 1977, when the Notre Dame president accepted his election as chairman of the Board of the Rockefeller Foundation—and in the face of the furious protests that followed, promptly announced in the *Observer* that "the Foundation has nothing to do with abortion." In fact, as pro-life Notre Dame professor Charles Rice revealed in the April 1977 *Observer*, the Rockefeller Foundation gave $900,000 to the Planned Parenthood Federation of America in the second quarter of 1974 alone. In 1975 it gave a grant to an American Civil Liberties Union project designed to assist abortionists in understanding

---

[6]Indeed, Kring's involvement in the abortion industry is so extensive he has made seven trips to China, during which he reported in an undated memorandum that he met with "top officials in central government who are responsible for family planning policy," visited "urban and rural hospitals" and "small clinics, including neighborhood clinics in urban areas, and communes or workers' clinics in rural areas." The massive programs of forced abortion and infanticide in precisely the places Kring visited have been documented for over three years now in such diverse sources as the TV show *60 Minutes* (which approved), *The Washington Post, The Wall Street Journal,* and Stephen Mosher's eyewitness account after nine months in China, in his book *Journey Into Forbidden China.* According to Chinese officials there have been more than 53 million abortions in China between 1979 and 1984, and according to Mosher, "90% of the abortions performed in China are forced upon women who, if they were truly free to choose, would bear the children."

their legal prerogatives after *Roe vs. Wade,* and in the last half of 1974 made a $50,000 grant to the James Madison Constitutional Law Institute, the group which "during 1972 had handled the entire appeal for the pro-abortion side in *Roe vs. Wade.*" In the companion case of *Doe vs. Bolton* it also "filed the principal pro-abortion brief and wrote the legal arguments related to the medical aspects of the case"—and thus is, according to Rice, nothing less than "the legal spearhead of the abortion movement."

But that is not all that happened in 1977. During the fall term of that year, Notre Dame graduate John Connaughton was working as an assistant professor at his alma mater's school of Law. In obtaining his Bachelor of Science in 1955, Connaughton had majored in chemistry and minored in biology. Before graduation he'd been accepted at three law schools and six medical schools; after a stint in the armed services, he eventually took his Law Degree at the University of Michigan in 1964. Never having lost his interest in the relation between law and medicine, he enrolled in a ground-breaking legal-medical program at Yale University in 1974, and took courses in embryology on the way to earning his LL.M. degree. While there, Connaughton worked under psychiatrist Jay Katz, whose expose of abuses against poor blacks in the Tuskegee syphillis study led to the regulations implemented by the Department of Health, Education, and Welfare which sought to protect people involved in any kind of program involving experimentation and federal money. Accordingly, since Notre Dame faculty members are expected to devote some time to University committees, Connaughton chose the newly-formed Committee for the Protection of Human Subjects. "For the most part," according to a discussion of the matter in the September 1985 issue of *Fidelity* by its editor Michael Jones, "they handled issues like professors in the psychology department offering students better grades in exchange for cooperation in psychology department experiments."

"Then the experiment of Dr. Subash Chandra Basu came before the committee," Jones adds. Basu had come to Notre Dame from John Hopkins, had done work in Sweden, and was presently doing research on Tay Sachs disease. The proposal he submitted to the committee claimed no human subjects would be involved in his experiments, but then added he would be using "a cell culture from cerebrum of a 20-week old Tay Sachs fetus obtained by prostaglandin E induced abortion."

Dr. Larry Schneck of the Kingsbrook Jewish Medical Center in New York, whom Basu had cited in his proposal, had informed readers of *Pediatrics* magazine how the cultures are obtained. Under the heading "Materials and Methods" Dr. Schneck noted that four abortions had been necessary, by means of hysterotomy. "The tissue from the 22-week fetus obtained by hysterotomy," he wrote, "was immediately frozen at -40 degrees, and was used as the basis for most of the biochemical and morphological studies of prenatal TSD."

"Because of his bioethical background," Jones wrote, "the implications of the proposed experiment at Notre Dame were clear to Connaughton. In order for the experiment to take place, at least four human beings had to die ... furthermore, given the fragile nature of the brain tissue, which does not regenerate itself and is at risk after three minutes of oxygen deprivation, the abortions were most probably performed so that the fetus would be expelled alive and then killed *ex utero.*"

"Hysterotomy," Connaughton remarked, "was chosen over saline infusion or prostaglandin injection almost certainly because the goal was to obtain a live infant. Such a goal was necessary because of the fragility of brain tissue."

In other words, as has happened before in this century, children were killed in such a way that their corpses would still be useful for experimental purposes by the people who killed them.

On 28 September Connaughton recommended to Notre Dame University's Committee for the Protection of Human Subjects that Dr. Basu's experiments be rejected. They depended on abortion, he noted, and a Catholic university could "not approve an experiment that depends upon, and benefits from that procedure." Rather than immediate agreement, a protracted discussion ensued. There was, for one thing, money involved, from the National Institute of Health (NIH). Committee chairman Francis Kobayashi was worried about the Indiana State law that prohibited experimentation on aborted children; though it said nothing about experimenting on fetal remains. He asked the NIH its opinion, and was told that though Indiana law did not specifically mention experimentation on fetal remains, it would be within the "spirit of the law" to prohibit the Basu experiments. A call to the Indiana School of Medicine, however, revealed that experiments on fetal remains did take place there. In an October 11 diary note, Kobayashi wrote: "If the University should approve Dr. Basu's project despite Indiana State Law, NIH would not object. But NIH's acceptance or approval should not be interpreted as condoning violation of state law. Once a decision is made for approval of the project, decisions on subsequent cases comes [sic] more easily. Care must be taken not to become insensitive to the intent of state statutes. In [NIH's] view, high ethical standards in this regard ought to be established because of the University's visibility and the public's expectations. Also pursued the question of NIH review panel reaction if Committee should not approve Dr. Basu's project. This is a very real problem. NIH has no procedures for this situation, but Dr. Marches [of NIH] hoped that there would be other aspects of the project that could be pursued without 'killing' the entire project."

On 4 November the Protection of Human Subjects Committee approved Dr. Basu's experiments by a vote of 7 to 2, Connaughton and Kobayashi voting against. Connaughton did not accept the decision. On 10 November, along with eight other Notre Dame law professors, he sent a letter to Father Hesburgh, asserting that to allow such experiments to take place on the Notre Dame campus was unacceptable because they were "immoral and . . . not a proper enterprise for any researcher connected with this University." The letter concluded: "We respectfully ask that you intervene in this matter and forbid performance of this experiment."

When Hesburgh received the letter, he referred the matter to a theological faculty member who would one day become an associate provost at Notre Dame, and who on yet another would tell the world through Ann Landers that the Roman Catholic Church no longer considered masturbation a serious sin (see, for example, the 27 January 1985 *Washington Post*). In any event, in 1977, Father Edward Malloy took an equally tolerant view of experimenting on the remains of unborn children. He concluded that "as long as there is no presumption that fetal life is worthless or that abortion is part of the experimental process, then I would vote positively on this experiment." He added, "I do not sense that this situation exists in the experiment being proposed." Accordingly, on 12 December, Hesburgh wrote to Connaughton and the others that he would not forbid the experiment.

Connaughton did not give up. He wrote Hesburgh pointing out the open dishonesty of Malloy's argument. "The fact is," he noted, "that abortion *is* part of the Basu experiment: in other words, but for the induced abortion there could be no experiment." He then addressed Malloy's position that "We use cadavers of adults for experimental purposes, and this seems an appropriate analogy in this instance," by charging that "the situations are not analogous. In the case before us, the mother had her unborn infant killed and then consented to the experimentation upon the infant's body. That is certainly not the path an adult cadaver takes to the medical laboratory."

He then made a point that Bishop James Malone representing the National Conference of Catholic Bishops would flee from with no less dispatch in 1985 than Father Hesburgh did in 1977. It was that rather than cultural factors outside the Church being responsible for Her problems, it has increasingly been a depraved clericalism which has vastly contributed instead to the decadence of Western culture.

"When this matter was still pending before this university's Committee for the Protection of Human Subjects," Connaughton wrote, "Dr. Kobayashi telephoned an official at HEW in an attempt to gain information and, perhaps, some guidance. That official told Dr. Kobayashi that the people at HEW were looking into Notre Dame to furnish some standards in this area. It will be sad beyond measure if the standards erected by Notre Dame fail to reflect a deep respect for the life of the unborn child."

On 10 April 1978, Father Hesburgh responded to Connaughton by again referring the case back to Edward Malloy. Malloy reaffirmed his earlier decision. Eight years and presumably dozens, perhaps hundreds of Dr. Basu's experiments later, the 19 April 1985 *Notre Dame Report* announced once again the grants for the coming year. Under the name Basu and the title "Glycolipid Metabolism in Tumor and Transformed Cells" one can read of another $94,130 granted to Notre Dame University by the National Institute of Health. "Once a decision is made for approval of the project," as Dr. Kobayashi had noted, "decisions on subsequent cases come more easily."

Meanwhile, things had come full circle. Though Basu got his money, and Curran has his forum, when John Connaughton's contract came up for renewal in 1978, his professorship at Notre Dame was terminated. This time, there were no protests.

III. The Holy Sacrifice Of The Mass

> *"It is the liturgy through which, especially in the Divine Sacrifice of the Eucharist, 'the work of our redemption is accomplished,' and it is through the liturgy, especially, that the faithful are enabled to express in their lives and manifest to others the mystery of Christ and the real nature of the true Church.... No other action of the Church can equal its efficacy by the same title and to the same degree."*
>
> Sacrosanctum Concilium, sections 2 & 7

> *"It is strange that the post-conciliar pluralism has created uniformity in one respect at least: it will not tolerate a high standard of expression. We need to counter this by reinstating the whole range of possibilities within the unity of the Catholic liturgy."*
>
> Joseph Cardinal Ratzinger

The remainder of Bishop Malone's 16 September statement was no less optimistic. As noted, there were a few clouds midst the optimism, however; and at one point His Excellency even went so far as to admit that "inadequate preparation and insufficient interiorization of the Council's authentic teaching and spirit ... to some extent ... were rooted in the attitudes of persons in positions of leadership and opinion formation, who either resisted the Vatican II reforms or advanced personal agendas in the name of renewal."

For example, Malone acknowledges the enormous decline in conversions to Catholicism since 1950, when "there were 4.3 adult converts per year per 1000 active Catholics," whereas "now there are 1.8," and adds "that while entry into the Church is now more time-consuming and difficult for adults, the specific challenges and demands after entry are fewer than they once were. These circumstances," he then adds, however, "do not constitute an 'abuse' so much as they reflect the results of many complex realities," which he declines to name; nor does he note that there were still 4.1 conversions per thousand as late as 1960.

Indeed, throughout, the Youngstown ordinary continues to praise the very things that are responsible for the problems he admits. "While there are far fewer candidates in seminaries and religious formation today than twenty years ago," he says, "the programs offered them are better in a number of ways." Despite the scandal of pro-abortion nuns and the incredible decline in female religious from 180,000 to 120,000 since 1965, His Excellency blithely praises the "new programs of education and formation," that had not a little to do with this "extremely energetic post-conciliar" renewal of religious communities, not to say "the fine work being done by a special commission chaired by Archbishop John R. Quinn," who has from the beginning and throughout his investigation insisted the religious orders are essentially free of serious problems, with the exception of criticism they receive from the laity.

While noting that "there have been declines in Mass attendance and reception of the Sacrament of Penance," the Bishop does not discuss how extreme those declines have been, but instead cheerfully remarks that "however, over half the Catholics in the United States attend Mass regularly, an encouragingly high percentage by comparison with the situation in many other countries." He adds that "Church leadership continues to seek ways to raise the figure even higher," and gives by way of example the "several national and many local structures specifically committed to the implementation of the liturgical reform generated by the Council." Indeed, Bishop Malone asserts that "Vatican II liturgical reforms were introduced expeditiously and for the most part successfully," and though he acknowledges some "problems" and "difficulties," from "those who resisted change and ... those who felt at liberty to introduce innovations of their own," he ignores the reality that said innovations came from precisely the national and local structures he then proceeds to praise.

Cardinal Ratzinger, by contrast, pointed out in the Messori interview that systematic abuse of the Catholic Mass as defined by *Sacrosanctum Concilium* is "one of the clearest examples of contrast between what the authentic text of Vatican II says and the way in which it has been understood and applied."

In 1978 a Gallup poll sponsored by the Catholic Press Association revealed the disturbing news that 64% of the Catholic population still favored the Tridentine Mass over the Rite of Paul VI, nine years after the Pope forbade the former's licit celebration, and thirteen years after Latin had literally been driven out of the American Catholic liturgical service. One suspects it was not the Tridentine as such that Catholics yearned for, and perhaps not even Latin as such; but rather some at least minimal expression of beauty and dignity.[7] Another such Gallup poll in 1984 indicated a drop from the '78 figure; 56% of the women and 51% of the men who responded said they would attend a Tridentine Mass if it were made available at convenient times and locations. But even in this second poll, there were indications of deep lay resentment against clericalism and its "Yuppie Masses" (as they have been called), for it was precisely the groups that are least fashionable, and have the least political power, that want the Latin Mass Vatican II says is their right to have. As noted, 56% of women; but also 65% of those over 50 years of age; and perhaps most significantly, 66% of those with incomes under $25,000 annually, as compared to 46% who make more than $25,000. Thus if you want to know how serious is the priest who continually tells the press about his concern for women and the poor, you might ask how often he celebrates a Latin Mass.

It is, of course, exactly such garrulous priests (not to mention those national liturgical reform structures Bishop Malone cites as the means of attracting Catholics back to church) who are instead determined to fight women and the poor and the elderly (and others) about the Mass and much else, with all the considerable clerical means at their disposal. Interested parties who might once have thought this assertion an exaggeration were rudely awakened by the extraordinary reaction of U.S. and European "liturgy experts" to Pope John Paul II's announcement (just two months short of *Sacrosanctum Concilium's* 21st anniversary), of an

---

[7] On a personal note, I have never attended a Tridentine Mass, and have attended very few Latin Masses, since my reception into the Church in 1973: although having lived in Rome and Assisi throughout most of the '70's, I attended many very beautiful Masses in Italian.

indult allowing the Tridentine Mass, or Mass of St. Pius V, to be said once again under liberal, but limited circumstances.[8]

"I see it as a terrible move!" cried Father Gerard Austin, who is no less than the chairman of the theology department at Catholic University. "This will bring more confusion than enrichment. It will confuse people by giving the impression that the liturgical reforms can be discarded." He further dissembled that "it's not a question of the Latin. It's a question of using the revised liturgy of the Church which was done after years of study and consideration. And now they've gone back to point zero on this."

Father John Gurrieri, the executive director of the liturgy committee of National Conference of Catholic Bishops, was even more furious. "I don't see any need for this at all," he told the Religious News Service, "other than to give into pressure from the right wing. I don't see any need for this concession. It has been nearly 15 years since we've been using the missal of 1970. The number of people who have wanted to use the old missal have diminished." Father Gurrieri was also upset because "the American church had no input whatsoever in this decision. The Vatican conducted a survey of every bishop in the world four years ago, which said there was no need or desire to restore the Latin Tridentine Mass, and where was a need to celebrate the new Mass in Latin, that was already being taken care of."

But then Father Gurrieri hit on the real problem. "Most people in liturgical renewal are going to be upset. Parish priests are going to be upset by this. For one thing, it's confusing as to why it has come out."

One of those involved in liturgical renewal who is likely to be upset is Benedictine Father Daniel Ward, who was chosen by the Canon Law Society of America to give a formal address at its

---

[8]Celebrants had to acknowledge Pope Paul's juridical authority to institute a new rite, for example. Even Archbishop Lefebrve acknowledges the *validity* of Pope Paul's Mass, however, but argues that it is theologically deficient, and so has never celebrated it. Meanwhile, though it is arguable that the French Archbishop has helped provide a *contretemps* to the liturgical "experts" and their Modernist supporters, his role has clearly been injurious in that he has managed to tie up what I imagine is the beauty and glory of St. Pius V's Mass with the absurd position that Vatican II was not a legitimate Ecumenical Council. Accordingly, His Excellency has also unhappily succeeded in making it almost impossible to discuss the Tridentine Mass without discussing him—which has proved an inestimable service to clerical philistines who continue to thwart the wishes of the laity in this matter.

1982 annual convention, on the subject of "Liturgy and Law." It is perhaps no exaggeration to say Father Ward's attitude toward the Mass reflects the ideological underpinning of the entire Modernist and historicist approach to Vatican II.

"It may be argued," he said, "that the context of the liturgy cannot ignore the general norm of *Sacrosanctum Concilium* that 'no other person, not even a priest, may add, remove, or change anything in the liturgy on his own authority.' Yet this norm cannot be isolated from the rest of the Constitution," which means that "if one adapts a liturgy according to the age, condition, way of life, and standards of religious culture of the participants, is not that person adapting on the authority of the Council rather than on his or her own?" Father Ward then gets specific about the latitude allowed these omnipotent interpreters of religious culture. "A prescription to use only bread and wine and no other materials to celebrate the Eucharist," he opines, "does not seem to me to be liturgical law per se," since such law "must be understood, adapted, and applied within the theological context that follows and flows from theology, especially as taught by the Second Vatican Council."[9]

The *St. Anthony Messenger* has also provided us a glimpse of the kind of thing Father Gurrieri and his associates apparently fear we will lose: "Most of the congregation expected to see a clown," it revealed. "The bulletin a week before had carried an announcement about 'Shamrock' appearing. But a few worshippers stirred uneasily as the fanciful figure came into the church at the time scheduled for the homily. Dressed in a green outfit with a detachable red heart fastened in front, Shamrock walked joyfully but with dignity down the aisle, carrying a beautifully wrapped package. . . . Just then, a sister arrived. . . . 'My, that's a beautiful package!' she exclaimed. Shamrock nodded in agreement, clutching at the box as if it were about to be yanked away. 'Who is the package for . . . is it for me?' The clown's yellow-wigged head shook an emphatic 'No!' and, with a wide sweep of the arm, indicated the entire congregation. The sister quickly understood: 'It's for everyone!'

"Then, taking off the large red heart, Shamrock extended it to the sister and to the congregation in a gesture of love. The two

---

[9](Pontifical Council for the Family President Eduoard Cardinal Gagnon remarked upon one example of Father Ward's principle, by telling me in 1983 of priests who like to "consecrate" Coca-Cola and Oreo cookies.)

embraced and marked each other with 'the sign of the clown'—a bright red dot of greasepaint (makeup) on the cheek—one more symbol of love ... finally, the congregation learned what was inside: the bread for Communion.... [A] nun is behind the whiteface: Sister Patricia Jean Garver. Sister Pat as she is affectionately known by the people she serves as director of pastoral services...."

The liturgical experts have never expressed any concern about these abuses. Like Bishop Malone, they have ever been enthusiastic about post-Council liturgical "reform." About the Pope's Tridentine indult, however, it was not only Fathers Austin and Gurrieri who were horrified. It happened that just three weeks after the Pope's announcement through the Congregation for the Sacraments and Divine Worship, there was a 23-27 October 1984 gathering in Rome of representatives of more than 100 liturgical commissions. According to a report from Sister Ann Walsh to the *NC News*, they expressed "grave concern, regret and dismay" because permitting the Tridentine Mass seemed to be moving away "from the ecclesiology of the Second Vatican Council" [sic]; to give support to those who have resisted liturgical renewal; to demonstrate a lack of consideration for all who, at great personal cost and with great difficulty, did in fact accept liturgical reform; and to violate "the collegial sense of the worldwide episcopate."

According to officials of the Congregation for the Sacraments and Divine Worship, however, most episcopal conferences failed to poll their faithful about the old and new rites as the Vatican had asked, simply sending in their own impressions. The Congregation's concern for the laity, however, made the *National Catholic Reporter*'s (and *London Tablet*'s) Rome correspondent Peter Hebblethwaite furious. Referring to an interview that Clergy Prefect Silvio Cardinal Oddi granted me in 1983 that was later published in *The Wanderer*, Hebblethwaite noted that His Eminence had "predicted the restoration of the Tridentine Mass 'when the people want it enough,' ... The indult contains a hint that Oddi's general appeal to 'popular demand' did the trick. He used the same technique on the catechism question, encouraging

unrepresentative right-wing groups to write to Roman congregations."[10]

Meanwhile, Sacraments and Divine Worship Prefect
Archbishop Augustin Mayer sought to encourage sensitivity to
the desire of Catholics to hear the Mass of St. Pius V. The indult
stated that it was only to be celebrated in parishes on a regular,
daily basis, in "extraordinary cases". There was at first some hope
on the part of those who prefer this Mass that due to the liberal
interpretation in so many American dioceses of the word
"extraordinary" in the case of "extraordinary ministers" (who in
limited circumstances may assist the priest in distributing the
Eucharist), there might be an equally liberal interpretation of the
word applied to the celebration of the Tridentine Mass.
Archbishop Mayer assisted this broad interpretation (about the
Mass in any case) when he told the 19 October 1984 *Catholic
Telegraph* that though "it would be up to the bishops to decide
whether to approve the Tridentine Mass on a regular basis in
parish churches . . . 'extraordinary cases' could include groups of
parishioners who want the Tridentine Mass celebrated regularly
in their parish churches." But it was not to be. Father Frederick
McManus, a chief post-Conciliar liturgical architect, consultant to
three Vatican commissions which developed innovations, both
the successor and predecessor to Father Gerard Sloyan as head of
the National Liturgical Conference, and now the academic vice-
president of the Catholic University of America—Father
McManus did *not* think as liberal an interpretation should be
given to the celebration of the Tridentine Mass as under his
tutelage had been given to virtually any other kind of Mass (as
long as it was not in Latin). "The limitations on this appear to be
extremely drawn," he quickly announced. "If that is the case, so
few people will be involved in it that it would not have much
effect."

---

[10]Though Hebblethwaite (and most Modernists) are fond of
vilifying Catholics with the appellation "right-wing" it should
nonetheless be observed that *The Wanderer* is one of the foremost
opponents of the Lefebvre schism in the United States. When the
Mass of Paul VI was authorized, *The Wanderer* gave full support to
the Pope in this matter, and in consequence lost more than 15,000
subscribers who were devoted to the Tridentine Mass. The only attempt *The Wanderer* ever made to recover these subscriptions was
to encourage their adherence to the successor of St. Peter; though
after the indult, *The Wanderer* editorialized "Give the Tridentine
Mass a chance" on 10 June 1985.

"The people who will seek the permission are a very small minority," he then charged. "The people who would be interested in this are those of the fanatical group that holds that the Vatican Council and Pope Paul VI's missal are heretical. There is also a group that is nostalgic about the Mass prior to Vatican II . . . but the numbers are so small that it could be controlled."

Of course, it is possible Father McManus is not as confident as his remarks suggest. To be sure, the *New York Times* cooperatively headlined its story, "Latin Mass Is Not Expected to Have Major Impact," which line was repeated in doubtless hundreds of diocesan and secular newspapers across the country. But then headlines like "Tridentine Mass Draws Overflow Louisville Crowd" began to appear (in the *Register* for one), followed by others such as "No Tridentine Mass For Denver Catholics." Bishop Joseph Ferrario of Hawaii, who allows a "Disco Mass" every Sunday at his cathedral replete with special disco lighting effects and popular love songs, "decided against granting permission" for the Tridentine, saying that "I prefer not to complicate this with my reasoning for the decision." His collegial approach was adopted in dozens of dioceses across the United States.

Even in those dioceses where the Tridentine was not strictly forbidden, the liberal attitude of Archbishop Mayer was nowhere employed. A *Wanderer* survey[11] that covered dioceses responsible for some 18 million Catholics (of an estimated 52 to 72 million baptized in the United States) concluded that "chancery officials have been excessively legalistic in interpreting the Vatican authorization, and have been almost secretive in permitting the faithful to know that they may write to their bishops to request permission to participate in a Tridentine Rite Mass. The survey further found that only three dioceses permit the Mass on a weekly basis. None—in the United States, unlike Canada—permitted it on a daily basis." Former NCCB President Archbishop John Roach of Minneapolis, St. Paul, captured a common attitude when he told former *Wanderer* editor Walter Matt that he "wasn't comfortable with the indult," and was "being made very uncomfortable by my presbytery" for having allowed even one Tridentine Mass. *The Wanderer* survey was taken a year after the Pope's indult was promulgated.

This struggle over the Tridentine revival is of course more a reflection of clericalism than anything; but it throws Bishop

---

[11]published on October 17, 1985.

Malone's September 16 claim that "liturgical renewal remains a high priority for the bishops of the United States" into interesting relief. Meanwhile, one arguable side benefit of the controversy is the statement drawn up by the NCCB Committee on the Liturgy thirteen months after the indult, and two weeks prior to the Extraordinary Synod. "Clown ministry has a legitimate role elsewhere, but not in the liturgy," it said. "The clown is not to be understood as a liturgical minister." Even in children's liturgies, it added, "it is not appropriate to use clowns," although "pastoral reasons may sometimes suggest the use of clowns or mimes in certain celebrations for small children." Unlike denunciations of those who prefer St. Pius V's Mass as right-wing fanatics, however, "the sincerity of those involved in 'clown ministry' is not to be questioned," the statement insisted. Father Gurrieri was particularly concerned about this point, and said he "hoped the statement would not be misinterpreted as a condemnation of all forms of clown ministry," inasmuch as "outside the realm of liturgical worship the statement is actually very supportive of such a ministry."

Meantime, Father McManus touched on other aspects of the Tridentine indult that have crossed many people's minds. "I do fear," he told the *Religious News Service*, "that this may be a signal for change in other reforms—such as ecumenism, Church structures, theological developments involving Bible study, religious freedom, the role of national bishops' conferences, lay participation." Authoritatively, he concludes that "there are people who are steadfastly against all this."

IV. Instructing the Faithful

"Bishops should be especially concerned about catechetical instruction. Its function is to develop in men a living, explicit and active faith, enlightened by doctrine."

Vatican II, On the Pastoral Office of Bishops

"What is most amazing is that there are Catholics and priests, who, we would fain believe, abhor such enormities, and yet act as if they fully approved of them. For they lavish such praise and bestow such public honor on the teachers of these errors as to convey the belief that their admiration is not meant merely for persons ... but rather for the sake of the errors which these persons openly profess and which they do all in their power to propagate."

Pascendi, section 19

1. Promiscuous Imprimaturs

"How then comfort ye me in vain, seeing in your answers there remaineth falsehood."

Job 21:34

"One major goal" of the NCCB, Bishop Malone notes, "should be to clarify and reinforce Catholic identity for contemporary Catholics in the United States. Particular attention should be given to the young," he adds, "and for efforts to dispel the widespread popular confusion about moral issues and the moral doctrine of the Church," though "new instruments must be

129

developed for the presentation of authentic Catholic doctrine at all levels and to all groups."

"Priority in this catechetical effort," he continues, "ought also to be given to moral doctrine and moral issues: e.g. conscience formation, the role of conscience, sexual morality and new and emerging bioethical questions. Considerable attention ought also to be given to the sacramentality of marriage and the permanence and indissolubility of sacramental marriages."

All these suggestions appeared under the question "what new needs, associated with change, emerged in the implementation of the Council?" in the 16 September Submission. Under the question "were there any errors or abuses in the interpretation and application of the Council? Why?," and "What was done or should be done to correct the situation?," His Excellency observed that "how to strike the right balance between 'content' and 'experience' in catechetical methodology has often been debated in the post-conciliar years, but a working consensus in which appropriate emphasis is given to each has begun to emerge." Oddly, given the implied inadequacy of post-Council catechetical programs in these observations, the Bishop replied to the question "What was done to make the Council known, faithfully received, and implemented?," by noting that "major changes were undertaken in priestly formation and catechetics. Lending impetus to these efforts at the national level were, respectively, the NCCB Program of Priestly Formation and the National Catechetical Directory, *Sharing the Light of Faith.*"

Both of these documents are quite Catholic. However, as Section 23 of the Apostolic Exhortation *Reconciliatio et paenitentiae* from the 1983 Synod of Bishops points out, "the specific mission of the Church ... is not a mission which consists merely of a few theoretical statements and putting forward of an ethical ideal unaccompanied by the energy with which to carry it out. Rather it seeks to express itself in precise ministerial functions, directed towards a concrete practice of penance and reconciliation."

The Catholic universities, the Liberal Consensus, *Commonweal* and *America* magazines, and so much else, have shown us how much energy the U.S. bishops have applied to the fundamental matter of priestly formation. The episcopal record in the matter of catechetics, in particular a promiscuous use of the *imprimatur* to advance positions antithetical to Catholic belief, has shown no less energy, and indeed, demonstrates that the Modernism afflicting the U.S. clergy seeks converts. It also indicates that if a working consensus has begun to emerge, that consensus is diametrically opposed to all the "new needs" Bishop Malone publicly considers urgent for the future of the Church in the United States.

"For reasons which remain mysterious," James Hitchcock observed in the 10 November 1985 *National Catholic Register*, "many American bishops have set their faces firmly against any criticism directed at religious education programs, or programs for the 'renewal' of religious life, even when the dubious content of those programs can be amply documented." In fact, the Modernism in such programs is so widespread, the examples so numerous, that it would take an entire book or two to recount them all—particularly if one were to include commonly used texts that did not have an *imprimatur* as such. But let us consider some of the more notorious examples.

It began early. Kalt & Wilkins's "To Live in Christ" series informed students in *Developing Human Community* (1967) that "The Mass is a dinner at which revolutionaries gather in the presence of their leader to celebrate what has been accomplished and to commit themselves to the completion of what has begun." *The Mystery of Christ* in that same series denied the physical reality of Christ's ascension as early as 1966: and having thus dispensed with dogmas of the faith, the series by 1968 was teaching in *Mankind's Search for Meaning* that "a significant number of young people have learned enough psychology to have become acutely sensitive to some to their parents' emotional, sexual and psychological hangups. They wonder if it would not be better to experience sexual freedom before marriage so that they might work these things out before the knot is tied," as well as asserting that "some drugs can be (for stable people) a helpful part of serious exploration of enhanced experiences," and that "where the public concept of morality and immorality has changed, the law must sometimes change accordingly." The series gave as a friendly example: "State laws forbidding abortion."

Kalt & Wilkins were not alone. In the heady days of marijuana and LSD, the Sadlier "Light and Life Series" argued in its 1969 *Growth in Christ* that "on a stable, well-adjusted person, drugs may have almost no effect at all." The same book whispered in the Teacher's manual that "while condemning abortion on the whole, Catholic theologians admit to the exceptional case where expelling a fetus may be the better thing."

The Jesuit James DiGiacomo, who is a trustee of Fordham University and sits on the National Catholic Education Association's Religious Education advisory board, was also a favorite at that time. In the 1969 Conscience and Concern series, he insists "that man *cannot* (his emphasis) accept the ethical teachings of Jesus as laws of conduct which are always obliging in similar circumstances," and thus concludes that: "Catholic morality is in fact situation ethics." DiGiacomo also wants students to ask themselves "Have your parents brainwashed you into accepting their ideas about clothing styles? Have you been indoctrinated into agreeing with them. . . . Have your parents prejudiced you against long hair?"

Has Father DiGiacomo read *Gravissimum educationis,* or for that matter the Fourth Commandment? Have the bishops, who have allowed this to be taught?

These early books were not liberal on all subjects, however. The Teacher's manual of Paulist Press's 1968 *Come to Father* series is firm in warning pedagogues of their obligation to "absolutely avoid all allusions to mortal sin, the devil and Hell."

Another illustration of the state of the catechetical establishment in the United States was given in a recent *St. Anthony Messenger* piece about the Synod by Father Alfred McBride. He argued that "earlier Church councils met to condemn heresy or repulse an attack on the Church," and "were an example of institution stifling charisma." Noting that *Pascendi* was yet a further example of this awful institutional smothering, Father McBride concluded that "Raymond Brown . . . and others did correctly for biblical scholarship what Loisy did poorly in the early part of the century," and wondered "will the World Synod of Bishops continue the dialogue or retreat to the past?" At the close of the piece the *Messenger* noted that Father McBride "directed the religious education department of the National Catholic Education Association for many years."

More recent examples include Rochester Bishop Matthew Clark's *imprimatur* on the Paulist Press book *Parents Talk Love,* which calls itself the "Catholic Family Handbook about Sexuality." In discussing the "sexual expression of intimacy through close sexual contact or intercourse," as "a real concern for Catholic singles," the book asserts that "The clergy . . . need to offer healing, forgiveness, and help instead of moralizing and condemnation. Singles can find intimacy in friends, in the community, and, if needed, in lovers if the Church is willing to be supportive."

But no discussion of catechetics would be complete without looking at the role of Newark Archbishop Peter Gerety. In 1981 he gave the *imprimatur* to Edward Steven's *Making Moral Decisions*, which asserts that "religion doesn't have the answer to moral questions," and that "there are no absolute answers." It accordingly justifies abortion since "there is no magic moment in which human life begins." On page 50 it justifies active euthanasia; on page 55 test-tube fertilization (including masturbation, as well as surrogate motherhood and Notre-Dame like experiments on aborted infants); on page 70 divorce; on pages 78-79 the morality of sodomy; then artificial contraception, and so on for 110 pages, at the end of which he recommends Garrett Hardin for further reading, which is interesting because Garrett Hardin has publicly called for coercive abortion in the United States.

But of course Archbishop Gerety's biggest success was the Paulist Press compendium *Christ Among Us*, which sold nearly two million copies, and not, it should be pointed out, to a laity hungry for Arian theology; but rather to the religious education bureaucrats in dioceses across the country. Rather than detail the errors of this book, however, it should be sufficient to note that after Cardinal Ratzinger told Gerety to renounce the *imprimatur*, even Bishop Malone admitted this was a wise decision.

Unfortunately, Bishop Malone has yet to comment upon another catechism to which Archbishop Gerety gave his *imprimatur* in 1975. Yet another Paulist-press offering by yet another Paulist priest, the misnomer this time was *The Faith of Catholics*, by Father Richard Chilson. The book begins with the very strange analogy equating Vatican II with the serpent's apple. In order for Adam and Eve to return to Eden, Chilson writes, "they would have to rid themselves of the knowledge of good and evil. It is doubtful they would pay so great a price. And what about us Catholics? If we are to regain our Eden, we must also rebuild the defenses and walls. Our defense was our dogma, our Catholic faith . . . could we not say that we American Catholics had to leave Eden in order to find Jesus Christ?"

The book builds from this theoretical base, to attack the truth of the Gospels (and thus *Dei Verbum*) in favor of the Liberal Consensus, and strikingly concludes at one point that "it is time to abandon the old concept of grace for the more modern one of power." Nonetheless, (doubtless among others) Conventual

Franciscan pastor Father Philip Schneider chose to impose *The Faith of Catholics* on an RCIA program at St. Rocco Church in Chicago Heights, Illinois, despite the opposition of his orthodox lay Catholic Advisory Council. Accordingly, the latter protested to Father Schneider's Minister Provincial—the former Censor of Books in the Archdiocese of St. Paul—one Father Juniper Cummings.

Father Cummings reviewed the book in a five-page single-spaced letter to an Advisory Council member, the Chicago attorney Peter Coppa, on 3 December 1984. While acknowledging that *The Faith of Catholics* "is poorly composed ... poorly written," gives "the impression that to accept the cross is something neurotic," and "the impression that because some [priests and nuns] disobediently married or attempted marriage that they have freed us all," that "Vatican II was a sort of sin that expelled us from Eden," and that Chilson takes "an anti-intellectual approach which is part of his negative approach of sort of putting down the past to enhance the future," still, Father Cummings argues that Chilson does "admit on page 301 that in spite of the changes it is by and large the same faith we knew before. I am glad he said that; it's a redeeming factor to the book."

Indeed, despite Father Cummings's view that the book "leaves something to be desired in its clarity," portrays an "unbalanced damning of the past," contains "sexist language " is "not too clear on original sin," might give "the impression that the establishment of the Church was a mishap," Father Cummings "should think that whoever was reading this book or using it as a reference would clarify [certain of] those matters." In summation, he concludes that "it's very difficult to find a suitable text that explains in an effective way what the Church has and is teaching. While I find weakness in this text ... I wouldn't say that the work is unorthodox," and indeed "on the whole, I found the book very good."

Consequently, on 17 January 1985, Father Schneider wrote Coppa that Cumming's analysis demonstrates the book is "well within the right to have an imprimatur," and that as such, "for the rest of the year I find no need to ask those concerned to put out more money for a different book. The fact that ultimately concerns us right now is that the book in question has an imprimatur. As a point of information I here note that I have taking [*sic*] this concern to the proper authorities in the Archdiocese of Chicago, namely: Most Rev. Wilton D. Gregory, DD, and Rev.

Jeremiah J. Rodell, Dean. They saw no problem with using the work in question."

But Coppa did not give up, and so forwarded the various correspondence to Joseph Cardinal Bernardin; whose answer was most educational. On 17 April 1985, exactly 366 days after the news that Gerety had been forced to lift his *imprimatur* from *Christ Among Us* became public, the Archbishop of Chicago wrote: "The responsibility of selecting instructional material for RCIA or religious education programs ultimately belongs to the pastor of the parish. To insure that the pastor will select wisely, the Church provides a process whereby books are reviewed and granted an *imprimatur*. The prudent pastor will be correct in assuming that if work carries an *imprimatur*, it can be safely used in his parish.

"In reviewing the documentation you have provided, it seems to me that your pastor, Father Philip Schneider, OFM Conv., has acted in a responsible way. The text carried an *imprimatur*. He was open to the review of the text by his religious supervisor, who found the book to have weaknesses but to be acceptable. Father Schneider's letter of January 17, 1985, also suggests that he conferred with his Dean and Vicar. Personally, I am appreciative of Father Schneider's diligence in this matter. I also am indebted to Father Juniper for his extensive review of your comments and the content of the book.

"That being said, I also wish to acknowledge the right of the Christian faithful to express their opinions and to question their pastors. It is imperative that all Catholics exercise their responsibility to assist in the proclamation of the Good News and in the building up of the Church.

"However, there is a difference between raising questions or offering advice and assuming responsibility that belongs to others....

"After a careful review of the book, it would seem that it met the criteria for the granting of an *imprimatur* in 1975. However, subsequent to that time the regulations on *imprimatur* have changed, and these changes have been incorporated in the revised Code of Canon Law. Consequently, the question at hand is whether this particular book meets the current criteria. Because of the ambiguity of this situation and because it is a problem that is larger than just this one diocese, I am asking the guidance of the Committee on Doctrine of the National Conference of Catholic Bishops.

"In the meantime, I leave it to Father Schneider to decide what text he will use in the RCIA program at St. Rocco's. I hope this puts your mind at ease. I am sure that Father Schneider is as concerned as you are about passing on the true and authentic faith of the Church."

2. Catholic Media? Human Sexuality?

"Ye are forgers of lies, ye are physicians of no value."
Job 13:4

Of course, many if not most Americans (Catholics included) derive their understanding of the Faith from sources other than catechetical texts, especially from the mass media. Here Bishop Malone makes a valid point: "Of great though sometimes unacknowledged importance in shaping Catholic attitudes toward the Council," Bishop Malone's Synodal Submission notes under the subheading *Media*, "were the secular and religious communication media. Undoubtedly they helped to make Vatican II widely known among U.S. Catholics." He adds: "Undoubtedly, too, their interpretations were sometimes subjective ones."

Yes, sometimes they were. The depth and extent of the secular bias, however, was not subjected to public scrutiny until publication of the famous Rothman/Lichter study (conducted in the early 1980's under the auspices of the Research Institute on International Change at Columbia University) of 240 of the most powerful journalists, executives, and broadcasters in the most influential media outlets in the United States. That is, the very group from whom Arthur Jones of the *Reporter* thinks the post-Council American bishop derives his power and authority.

Just over 12% of this group identified themselves as Catholic, but only 8% attend a church or synagogue weekly: 86% said they never or rarely attended services. On human rights issues, a full nine out of ten were adamantly opposed to granting unborn children legal protection. On issues of sexual morality, three of four expressed no doubts about the morality of sodomy and only half believe that adultery is wrong (only 15% strongly agree that it is wrong). Eighty-five per cent oppose protecting children from announced and practicing homosexuals teaching them in the public schools.

One may also notice a certain symmetry between the views—both expressed and implied—of the media elite, and numerous journals such as *Commonweal, America, The Reporter, The St. Anthony Messenger,* etc., although it should be noted that these journals never take an explicitly pro-abortion stand, preferring to follow the example of Father McBrien of simply praising those who do. Indeed, *America* called Daniel Maguire's pro-abortion and pro-euthanasia compendium *Death by Choice* "an attractive mixture of solid principles"; the Claretian congregation's *U.S. Catholic* not only praised the book's "quiet lucidity and . . . great conviction" but also gave its Catholic Lay Person of the Year award in 1983 to the pro-abortion ideologue Rosemary Ruether. Even the bishops' own *National Catholic News Service*, which distributes news releases to diocesan papers across the country, claimed nothing less than that the book "demonstrates the profoundest respect for life."

There has never been any firm or public reproach of the manner by which these publications "helped to make Vatican II widely known among U.S. Catholics." Indeed, as we have seen, leading American bishops go out of their way to praise papers like the *Reporter*, which may be why each week it has from three to five pages of closely-spaced want ads for all the major bureaucratic positions in Catholic dioceses across the country, such as directors of pastoral care, religious education, Catholic Evangelization, Worship, School Superintendents, Liturgists, Music, Justice and Peace, and School Principals; for despite, and maybe because of, its regular publication of the Ruethers, Maguires, Hebblethwaites, and so on, the *Reporter* serves as the *de facto* recruiting agency for the bureaucracies of a significant minority, and perhaps the majority, of the U.S. Catholic bishops.[12] No other paper has even a full page of such advertisements.

Consequently, it should prove no surprise that the Catholic Television Network of America (CTNA), which is a satellite broadcasting network under the direct control of the bishops of the United States, chose in 1984 to sponsor a series of Lenten

---

[12]The 1985 "Catholic Press Association" convention meantime gave the *National Catholic Reporter* six awards, including the "best editorial" for the paper's defense of Mario Cuomo against Archbishop O'Connor, and the "best regular column" on culture, arts and leisure to Tim Unsworth, not to say first place for "General excellence."

television interview programs wherein such gentlemen as Hans Kueng and Edward Schillebeeckx explained their "faith experiences" and views about the impact of Christian spirituality on contemporary life.

Equally unsurprising were the results of a 1983 survey conducted by the Catholic Communications Network (CNN, which is a lay-sponsored news agency of sorts) in conjunction with the *National Catholic Register*. They sent out 247 ballots with numerous questions to the editors of every diocesan paper in the country, as well as to 39 national publications that identify themselves as Catholic. The response rate, as the *Register* noted, "was unusually high"—just short of 75%. Only 40% of the respondents stood by the teaching of *Humanae Vitae*; only 55% thought Detroit "Archbishop Edmund Szoka was correct in asking Sister Agnes Mary Mansour to resign from Michigan's Department of Social Services," even though her job included dispensing tax monies to pay for the extermination of unborn children. Thirty-six per cent favored the present juridical ban on married priests. Just short of 40% supported the ancient Catholic prohibition of priestesses. And though just short of 72% of the editors thought Pope John Paul II was exercising his office worthily, only 41.8% felt "the present Pope adequately understands the needs and problems of the American Church."

Yet as the accompanying *Register* editorial noted, "the autonomy of every editor is limited by the amount of freedom he gets from his publisher. On diocesan newspapers, the title of publisher is almost always held by the local ordinary."

Further contradictions in the NCCB President's September 16 report could be found under the subheading "Cathechesis and conscience formation." It notes that "confusion over moral issues has also been a recurring reality since Vatican II in the U.S., as elsewhere. This includes general questions like the role of conscience, the Church's teaching authority with regard to morality, and the limits of dissent, as well as issues pertaining to specific moral norms," but then concludes by proclaiming that "the bishop's conference continues to address such matters through its Committee on Doctrine and other bodies." The problem with this solution is not simply Committee chairman Archbishop John Quinn's pathetic reaction to Father McBrien's *Catholicism*: there is also a moral problem.

In May 1981 the United States Catholic Conference Department of Education published a set of guidelines for teaching entitled *Education in Human Sexuality for Christians*. It was put together by a group called the National Committee for Human Sexuality Education, upon which Committee sat the present ordinary of Memphis, Tennessee, one Francis Stafford, and Cardinal Bernardin's replacement as the Archbishop of Cincinnati (as well as a firm opponent of the idea that Vatican II has any application to universities that like to call themselves Catholic), the Most Reverend Daniel Pilarczyk. Their role, however, was minimal in the actual development of the guidelines. This devolved more to the Committee chairman, Dr. Daniel Dolesh.

Dr. Dolesh is no less an expert about sex than say, Father Frederick McManus is about the beauty of the English language or the Catholic liturgy. Those who doubt it may note Dolesh's membership in the pro-abortion American Association of Sex Educators, (AASECT), the United States Council of the International Council of Sex Education and Parenthood, and not least, the Metropolitan Sex Education Coalition, a group formed with the cooperation of Planned Parenthood in October 1965.

Also on Dolesh's USCC Sex Committee were Dr. David Thomas of St. Meinrad's School of Theology, who is a public defender of chemical contraception, and was chosen to write the two opening chapters of the guidelines; and Archbishop Rembert Weakland's Youth Consultant, Ms. Nancy Hennessy Cooney, whose book *Sex, Sexuality and You* (*imprimatur*: former Dubuque Iowa ordinary James Byrne) aptly reflects the strange obsession the educators had with sex throughout the 70's. Among other things, Cooney's book insists that rather than defining man by his spiritual struggles, everything must be called an expression of his sexuality. For Cooney, "although sexuality includes genital acts, its much more than that. Sexuality is the way we live as men and women in the world . . . the priest who tries to bring no life to a sleepy congregation by the words he says and by the life he offers, is living out his call to be a sexual person . . . you and I are sexual people all the time." Accordingly, Cooney seeks to inform her young readers "How to be a sexy Christian," which is the title of Chapter 12 of her book. She further informs us that "during the Easter vigil, the service opens with the lighting of the Pascal Candle, which symbolizes Jesus' passage from death to life. After all the other candles in Church are lit, the large candle is plunged into the just-blessed baptismal water. This is the symbol of the act of sexual intercourse, and serves to remind us how close Christ (the light) is united with His people in the Church (symbolized by the water) . . . the fact that the Church uses this symbolism on the holiest night of the year shows us how much it respects our sexuality," despite Cooney's odd view that "it's only been in the past 50 years or so that Catholic Christians have come to realize that sexuality is a gift from God and that it should be celebrated as such."

The USCC Sex Education Guidelines highly recommend the Cooney book to Catholic educators across the land, or rather to "professional educators" which the Guidelines cite as their "primary audience". Betraying the hostility that such experts invariably seem to have toward parents—not to say toward the explicit teachings of *Gravissimum educationis*—the Guidelines note that "if parents do not want their children to attend a prudently planned program based on these guidelines, they should remember that they have the responsibility to seek alternative forms of *formal* instruction in human sexuality for their children" (my emphasis).

And on the Guidelines gallop. Rather than discussing original sin, the meaning and application of natural law, marriage as a vocation and Sacrament, the importance of the family in the education of children, the need for a life of prayer, penance, and recourse to the Sacraments, or any subject that the AASECT frowns upon, Dr. Thomas instead opens the book by arguing the necessity "to learn every one of life's skills." In fact, in his opening paragraphs he does not even mention the word "family" though the word "community" of the kind run by experts one suspects, pops up five times. So do such Cooney phrases as "sexual persons" and "sexual creatures" and such interesting ideas as "human relating entails sexual existence renewed by the Christ experience."

In the Guidelines' second chapter, titled "The Christian Home and Education for Sexuality," Thomas's opening section, with thirteen paragraphs and over a thousand words, uses the word "love" only twice; once as an adverb—the importance of loving relationships—and once in a laundry list of parental obligations. The words "sex", "sexuality", and/or "sexual" appear 13 times. He also reflects the wisdom of the pro-abortion sex education ideologue Mary Calderone by insisting in the opening paragraph that due to the importance of the home in "psychosexual development," sex education must begin from the moment of birth.

When Dolesh's chapters appear, he notes that by the time children are 12, "sex is becoming an important preoccupation" and that accordingly they should quickly be taught about "not only such aspects of sexuality as love, intercourse, family planning, responsibility, chastity, Christ, joy, and procreation, but also such subjects as homosexuality, abortion, divorce, rape, prostitution, venereal disease, and pornography," including "information regarding . . . contraception . . . transvestism, masturbation, the psycho-emotional and physical processes of intercourse," and not least, "harmful sex role stereotyping."

These were the guidelines that the moral theologian Father William Smith, attacked as "a dangerous perversion of true Christian education," whose "roots and design and inspiration are pure secular humanism," that "would accomplish no more than instill a Planned Parenthood mentality in children at an age earlier than Planned Parenthood now succeeds in doing."

Since then NCCB President Archbishop John Roach was enthusiastic about the guidelines, I wrote him and asked who had authorized them. USCC General Secretary Monsignor Daniel Hoye answered in the Archbishop's stead on November 3, 1982:

"Concerning the authority under which the Guidelines for Education in Human Sexuality were published by the USCC," the Monsignor said, "they were approved for publication by the President of the USCC—at that time, Archbishop John R. Quinn of San Francisco—who had been authorized to do so by the USCC Administrative Board . . . in other words, although it is true that the Administrative Board did not review the Guidelines as such (although it could have done so had it wished), the Board specifically reviewed and approved the procedure for publishing them."

In other words, they were authorized on the authority of John R. Quinn alone, who now heads the Committee on Doctrine for the National Conference of Catholic Bishops.

3. Call-to-Action and Renew

"But there were false prophets also among the people, even as there shall be false teachers among you, who privily shall bring in damnable heresies, denying the Lord that bought them . . . and

> *many shall follow their pernicious ways, and speak evil of the way of truth."*
>
> II Peter 2:1-2

Despite the competition, arguably the most dangerous discrepancy in Bishop Malone's September 16 report can be found in his pride over the NCCB's promulgation of the 1977 National Catechetical Directory, strangely coupled with praise not two paragraphs later of a national parish program which had been designed by the leading episcopal opponent of what that Directory finally acknowledged. I refer to Newark Archbishop Peter Gerety, who also led the fight against the reaffirmation of Catholic sexual morality as presented in the NCCB's 1976 pastoral letter *To Live in Christ Jesus*, and who was also, of course, the principal organizer of the 1976 uprising known as the Detroit Call-to-Action Conference, or CAC. As Bishop Malone hints, however, though Gerety's efforts in '76 and '77 were firmly repudiated by his brother bishops, the Newark Archbishop may yet see them triumph for a season, due to his shrewdness in overseeing the development of a parish program, in 1978, called *Renew*.

Though *Renew* employs numerous group-therapy, values clarification and other screening devices and techniques, and though it rather feebly claims to be not a catechetical, but rather a spiritual formation program, the most striking thing about the hundreds of pages that comprise *Renew* (which I have read), is that it contains none of the moral or theological principles the U.S. Episcopate endorsed and Bishop Gerety opposed during the struggle over the 1976 pastoral and the National Catechetical Directory—and that it does contain virtually everything, directly or implicitly, from the rejected Call-to-Action Conference. Meanwhile, recalling John Paul II's admonition in *Reconciliatio et paenitentiae* that the promulgation of theoretical pleasantries are of little use when "unaccompanied by the energy to carry [them] out," it seems also relevant that the USCC and local diocesan agencies have done virtually nothing to implement or even make known the Directory or the 1976 pastoral; whereas literally millions of dollars have been spent—Paulist Press is the publisher and distributor—promoting *Renew*.

To begin with, the 1976 U.S. Bishop's pastoral *To Live in Christ Jesus*, which Pope John Paul II cited with particular praise during his 1979 trip to the United States, was approved by the American bishops during their annual November conference meeting in

1976—three weeks after the end of the Call-to-Action Conference in Detroit. It is the opinion of some, in fact, that this pastoral (which had been languishing for quite some time), might never have passed, except that the bishops felt they had to do *something* Catholic to recover from the scorn and ridicule provoked by the CAC meeting; this time even from the secular press. And indeed, the pastoral represents one of the U.S. Episcopate's finest post-Conciliar efforts.

"We must recognize the brutal reality of sin," it proclaims, which "is different from unavoidable failure or limitation," and is rather "a spirit of selfishness rooted in our hearts and wills which wages war against God's plans for our fulfillment." Nor does it hide from unpopular positions. "An act of contraceptive intercourse," it notes, "is wrong because it severs the link between the meanings of marital intercourse and rejects one of them . . . sexual intercourse is a human good only within marriage; outside marriage it is wrong . . . homosexuality . . . is morally wrong. Like heterosexuals, homosexuals are called to give witness to chastity, avoiding, with God's grace, behavior which is wrong for them, just as non-marital sexual relationships are wrong for heterosexuals." And not least: "Every human life is inviolable from its very beginning . . . the unborn child . . . is a human entity, a human being with potential, not a potential human being . . . to destroy these innocent unborn children is an unspeakable crime, a crime which subordinates the weaker members of the human community to the interests of the stronger."

Meanwhile, according to *Catholic New York* editor Anne Buckley "fresh from the experience of listening to the concerns of the Detroit delegates," Archbishop Gerety "made a strong attempt to return to committee the document on moral values." He charged that the pastoral "would be most unfortunate" since "it is not sufficiently pastoral", and, worst of all, would force Catholics and bishops "into sharply defined positions." His efforts to table were defeated 162-65, whereupon the pastoral itself was brought to a vote, but Gerety did not give up, still urging his brother bishops to repudiate the document straight out.

"Calling its tone 'apodictic', rather than pastoral," Buckley notes in the Seton University Press compendium *The Bishops of Newark 1853-1978*, "Gerety said the document would do more harm than good. He saw it as inattentive to widespread pastoral practice, insensitive to the position of many sincere Catholics, an obstacle to the Bishops' dialogue with theologians and scholars,

and the product of an ecclesiology which would isolate the hierarchy from 'other significant components of the People of God in
the Church community.'" Despite this plea, the bishops went
ahead and approved the pastoral by a vote of 172-25. Gerety's own
diocesan paper, the *Advocate*, however, promptly and formally
repudiated this consensus by announcing its "support" for "those
bishops, including our own, who spoke out against this [since] as
Archbishop Gerety said, the document is 'insensitive to where
people are.'"

More sensitive, presumably, was the report by the Catholic
Theological Society of America published—by Paulist Press—in
May 1977, and entitled *New Directions in American Catholic Thought*.
Immediately condemned by both the Vatican and the NCCB, this
rather frantic book justified, among other things, not merely contraception, sterilization, pornography, masturbation, sodomy and
adultery, but also group sex, wife-swapping, promiscuity, and, not
least, sex with animals under certain conditions. Archbishop
Gerety's *Advocate*, on the contrary, praised the book throughout
the summer of 1977, calling it such things as "scholarly, consequently serious, and fully integrated . . . a serious, important
work," indeed, one whose "strongest virtue is that it makes
sense."

At the end of that year, during the annual NCCB meeting
in Washington D.C., the Newark Archbishop was defeated on
amendment after amendment that he either introduced or
opposed, to the National Catechetical Directory. These included
such subjects as the reality of sin, the reality of the devil, and his
attempt to replace the words "to offer the sacrifice of His Body
and Blood" from amendment 143 with "to celebrate the
Eucharist,"—which of course could mean anything, and in the
Renew program it does. On moral issues, the Archbishop unsuccessfully but consistently sought to delete specific condemnations
of artificial contraception, sterilization, and abortion, and a ver-
batim reaffirmation of *Lumen Gentium*'s dogmatic teaching on the
teaching authority of the Pope.

In early 1975, meanwhile, John Cardinal Dearden of Detroit
had appointed Gerety to in effect organize the entire Call-to-
Action Conference, which the USCC had decided should be the
means of celebrating the bicentennial anniversary of America's
Declaration of Independence from Great Britain. Gerety's first
responsibility was to arrange and chair six preparatory meetings
in Newark and other American cities, in what his *Advocate*

solemnly called "a two-year nationwide consultation . . . the broadest consultation of the laity that the U.S. Bishops have ever engaged in." From these, he gathered "working papers" which delegates to CAC would use to form proposals and recommendations for the Church to apply to Catholic and secular life in the United States. According to the official USCC booklet on the subject, these working papers were to be composed by "writing committees" who would compose the "wording of the resolutions and recommendations." These writers were selected by the USCC staff. The bishops, however, were directly responsible for the choice of delegates, though they usually left this responsibility to their diocesan staffs.

In fact, as Monsignor George Kelly points out in his 1979 study of U.S. ecclesial politics called *The Battle for the American Church*, "the diocesan delegates were given a preset list of topics for buzz-groups discussions. The main topics were to be the ordination of women, the marriage of priests, use of contraceptives, divorce and remarriage, the role of the hierarchy, amnesty, disarmament, and criticism of the capitalistic system. These were alleged to be the major questions gleaned from the parish consultations over two years. While some knowledgeable delegates never heard these items discussed anywhere in their dioceses, the prescribed agenda could not be broken. In addition, the personal reflections of the buzz-word groups were passed on to the national office through previously chosen discussion leaders."

Despite claims of consultation with the laity by Gerety's *Advocate*, however, some 40% of the CAC delegates were parish priests, close to an equal percentage religious brothers and nuns, and, according to Martin's *The Final Conclave* "special groups present and very active were ex-priests, ex-nuns, homosexuals, pro-abortionists, Christian Marxists, Christian socialists, and Christian pacifists." The vast majority of those who attended listed themselves as actually employed by the Church. Archbishop Gerety himself was chairman of the Rules Committee, from where, according to the *Advocate*, "Newark's delegation wound up in the prime seating area, directly facing the podium, practically on top of seven microphones," helping to "shape conference proposals."

"Cheering and clapping like George McGovern's zealots routing Mayor Daley's helots at the 1972 [Democratic Party] convention," as even the *New York Times* admitted, "they rammed through resolutions for the open election of bishops and pastors, the ordination of women, married priests, the acceptability of divorce and contraception, and equal rights for homosexuals even when teaching in the schools."[13]

Because CAC had so badly exposed how thoroughly corrupted the bureaucracy of the American Church had become, as well as the methods used to achieve that conquest and the culpable flaccidity of the episcopal response, "it was no secret that a number of bishops would have liked to sweep the whole thing under the rug," as Ms. Buckley pointed out. Cincinnati Archbishop Joseph Bernardin was given the broom, in fact; and the CAC resolutions as such, were relegated to the limbo of committeedom.

Not every bishop was unhappy, however. "As mixed reactions to the Detroit Call-to-Action Conference were registered by members of the hierarchy," the *Advocate* informs, "the voice of Newark Archbishop Gerety was most positive."

Indeed. "This was one of the greatest days of the Church," he told the *New York Times*, while adding that though "most of the recommendations are supportive of what the bishops have been teaching, we do have a large educating task ahead of us to help the generality of our people to that consciousness."

Not under the name of Call-to-Action, though. Under the name of *Renew*, which Bishop Malone would in 1986 introduce into his Youngstown diocese, and which in his report to the Extraordinary Synod he would praise by name, for having "helped many persons acquire new attitudes and insights."

4. The Lure of Perversion

> *"When they knew God, they glorified Him not as God, neither were they thankful: but became vain in their imaginations, and their foolish hearts were darkened ... For this cause God gave them up unto their vile affections."*
> Romans 1:21 and 26

There was a further aspect of Archbishop Gerety's influence at the Call-to-Action Conference that would have far-reaching consequence.

---

[13]16 January 1977, *New York Times* Sunday magazine.

"The first thing Archbishop Gerety did as chairman of the rules committee," according to the Newark *Advocate*, "was to rule in favor of seating delegates that had previously been turned down" during that broad-based input from the laity. One of the organizations His Excellency at "the last minute" chose to recognize—for the first time—was the explicitly pro-homosexual lobbying group that calls itself Dignity. His Excellency also "subsequently got into the conference recommendations, a call for support of its work by the Bishops."

Of course, in the chaos of the post-Council era, the problem of active homosexual priests would likely have raised its head in any case. There is an obvious difference between that, however, and a formal recognition, indeed a call for support, of a body that did not hide its intention of defending and encouraging such activity. And so as the 7 January 1986 *National Catholic Reporter* proclaimed, "gay religious men and women are organizing as never before."

"When a bishop learns that a priest under his jurisdiction is sexually active," reports the homosexual pornography magazine *The Advocate*[14]—not to be confused with Archbishop Gerety's diocesan paper—"he tends to be lenient." *The Reporter* backs this analysis in its coverage of a January 1986 symposium on homosexuality in San Francisco. "Few of the dozens of men and women religious who attended," it pointed out, "view homosexuality negatively ... Many said their superiors know and support their efforts to integrate their sexuality positively," while adding that "the only problem is if you go public ... that puts him in a corner, and then he might dismiss you." The San Francisco symposium was endorsed by the National Conference of Religious Vocation Directors, the National Sisters Vocations Conference, and the Religious Formation Conference. Rosemary Ruether was the keynote speaker.

"Dignity should be the prophetic voice of the Church," reads the New York chapter's June 1984 newsletter. The chapter had been founded in 1973 by the Jesuit Father Robert Carter, who held a press conference to announce that he often felt sexually attracted to males. "I got a lot of support from my provincial and my own community," Father Carter told the June 1984 Franciscan publication *The St. Anthony Messenger*, where he also disparaged Catholic teaching on chastity.

---

[14] 4 February 1986.

The *Messenger's* coverage of the topic and Cincinnati Archbishop Pilarczyk's recent praise of the *Messenger* as "balanced" and "professionally very competent" reflects a common episcopal approach. The cover of the issue mentioned above was all black, with a shadowy orange figure in the background, and "Gay and Catholic" emblazoned across the front. Inside, a full nine pages were devoted to praising Dignity and what is euphemistically known as "the gay life-style," beginning with a tale of how cruelly a homosexual named Michael Dillinger suffered due to the Church's condemnation of sodomy. The *Messenger* called this attitude "understandable when one looks at the controversy surrounding the issue of homosexuality and the Church's stand towards it."

In fact, 31 of the article's first 40 paragraphs quote people or organizations who either want the Church's teaching on sodomy to be changed, or think it can be, or have been in trouble with the Church because of their ambiguity in the matter. Six of the paragraphs provide neutral information within the barrage of propaganda: and four paragraphs present variations of Church teaching, or else quote people who support it. But even of those paragraphs, two include: an ambiguous bishop's interpretation of an NCCB document encouraging charity towards people who find themselves tempted by homosexual desire; and an orthodox Catholic priest quoted as saying how difficult it is for such people to reverse their inclination after they reach their mid-twenties. The other two quotes that reflected Church teaching were immediately followed by rejoinders. With the exception of two paragraphs disclosing pastoral initiatives, the next 37 paragraphs all praise or quote people who explicitly oppose Church teaching, or are ambiguous at best: and many of these praise the fine efforts of Dignity/New York. Then nine paragraphs about a New York group called Courage, an organization that seeks to help people inclined towards homosexuality within a context of chastity and orthodoxy; but these are followed by six explaining that Courage doesn't work, doesn't appeal to the young, that its members aren't really chaste and don't think others should be, and that because they even desire to be chaste, "to many Catholic gays, Courage is an organization of fanatics, and is the butt of much humor." Consequently, the *Messenger* reassures its readers, Courage is bound to die out, especially because "younger priests in the New York area tend to shy away from Courage and all it stands for." The last six paragraphs of the article report the happy return of Michael Dillinger to the Church, due to his discovery that through Dignity, he could, so to speak, have his cake and eat it too.

As the *Messenger* observes, "a great many religious in the area applaud Dignity's aims, and there is no shortage of priests eager to celebrate liturgies for Dignity/New York." Given the simmering national scandals that finally received national attention in the spring of 1985, what is perhaps most unsettling about priestly and episcopal support for Dignity—among others, Baltimore Archbishop William Borders and St. Louis Archbishop John May have appeared at Dignity masses and prayer services—is the homosexual group's increasing moral and juridical support for the North American Man-Boy Love Association, or NAMBLA. NAMBLA is a pedophile organization that promotes sodomy between older men and young boys, and with the umbrella National Coalition of Gay Organizations and the International Gay Association, it lobbies for an end to all laws governing age-of-consent in sexual behavior.

Despite the fact that NAMBLA has been continually implicated in kidnappings and the disappearance of children every year in this country, and is logically assumed to be involved in the burgeoning child pornography industry (estimated to be worth over a billion dollars annually), Dignity has marched arm-in-arm with NAMBLA in gay pride parades for nearly a decade. When admission of NAMBLA into New York's political umbrella organization, the Community Council of Lesbian/Gay Organizations, became a hot topic in the summer of 1983, Dignity's lobbying and vote to seat NAMBLA made the decisive difference: for the final vote was 15-13, and had Dignity voted against NAMBLA, the child-molesting group would have been rejected.

This public support of pedophilia, it should be remembered, took place before the promotion of Dignity in the *Messenger*, before Dignity celebrated its annual convention Mass in Seattle Archbishop Raymond Hunthausen's St. James Cathedral, and before Sister Theresa Kane addressed the 1985 Dignity convention in New York during which she called for "bonding and solidarity" between homosexuals and feminists. It also took place before the growing frequency of priests raping young boys under their care received national attention on *CBS News* and in *Time* magazine in July of 1985.

"In cases throughout the nation," the 7 June *National Catholic Reporter* announced, "the Catholic church is facing scandals and being forced to pay millions of dollars in claims to families whose sons have been molested by Catholic priests," adding that an even "broader scandal seemingly rests with local bishops and a national episcopal leadership that has, as yet, no set policy on how to respond to these cases"—or how to respond to Dignity, or indeed newspapers like the *Reporter*, which has consistently supported Dignity and most of its goals.

"All too often," the *Reporter* noted nonetheless, "complaints against the priest involved are disregarded by the bishops, or the priest is given the benefit of the doubt. Frequently, local bishops exhibit little concern for the traumatic effects these molestations have on the boys and their families—even though mental disturbances and, in one recent case, suicide, have followed such molestations. Only legal threats and lawsuits seem capable of provoking some local bishops into taking firm action against the priests." *Time* magazine said there were at least 15 cases across the country that had come to public attention—and there have been more since that July 1985 report.

Among the crucial elements which the *Reporter* chose to ignore in its study, however, is the regularity in which Modernism and moral relativism are systematically promoted in those dioceses where it seems the pedophile priests had been listening all too closely.

Some examples:

—The priest originally authorized to be the chief celebrant of the Seattle Dignity Mass—after Archbishop Hunthausen had been called to Rome to prevent him from serving that role—was Father Thomas Oddo, President of the University of Portland, Oregon in the diocese of Portland. In 1983, the former President of the Portland diocesan Priest's Senate, Father Thomas Laughlin, was convicted in court of sexually abusing young boys. When arrested, the 57-year-old priest said he had been molesting children for some fifteen years. Meanwhile, Portland Bishop Cornelius Power had been informed as far back as 1979 of Laughlin's activities by a laywoman: but His Excellency denounced her for "maligning a good and honest man by saying things like that." Other similar warnings went unheeded.

—Boise, Idaho Bishop Sylvester Treinen, who as recently as 10 January 1986 was implicitly denouncing the Vatican for the "incalculable pain" caused by its investigation of the "great archbishop" Raymond Hunthausen, also has a notorious reputation for opposing the rights of the laity. In a 3 February 1984 column in his diocesan paper, the *Idaho Register*, Bishop Treinen called such people "terrorists," since "priests right here at home are often terrorized by threats of being reported to the bishop. Bishops are terrorized by threats of being reported to the Apostolic Delegate or to the Holy See.

"Or said in another way, one negative letter is one negative letter, while one positive letter is equal to several hundred positive letters ... for me, the 25 negative letters added up to 25 negatives, sincere as they might have been. The ten positives added up to a thousand positives. Unsigned lettters count for nothing."

Thus, when Father Mel Baltazaar was sentenced to seven years in the state penitentiary in January 1985 after pleading guilty to a reduced charge of lewd behavior with a minor, we learn that Bishop Treinen had always refused to investigate Baltazaar's past record, despite letters, unsigned and otherwise. Yet the sentencing judge's own investigation revealed Baltazaar's history of illegal sexual abuse of young people going back to just after the Second Vatican Council, and including his being dismissed as a naval chaplain in 1979 "for his involvement with a dying youth on a dialysis machine," after having "plied him with liquor and drugs and pornography."

—In Milwaukee, Father Richard Nichols surrendered his license to the state psychology examining board after admitting he had sexually abused a minor male patient. Meanwhile, his Archbishop, Rembert Weakland, has a reputation as a kind of theoretical patron of priests and religious interested in children's sexual activity, due to the strange methods of sex education in his Archdiocese. Apart from Youth Consultant Nancy Hennessey Cooney the Religious Education Department of the Milwaukee Archdiocese published a Leader's Resource Manual in 1980 entitled *Valuing Your Sexuality*. Its most stunning feature is the game of "charades" in which a child is to act out without "words, letters, or numbers" such terms as clitoris, copulation, ejaculation, erection, homosexual, masturbation, menstruation, pubic hair, rape, sanitary pad, penis, vagina, and so forth, before a mixed classroom of adolescent and often pre-adolescent boys and girls. The child or group from the classroom who "shouts" the correct answer "first and loudest" of the sexual term or activity being simulated, "gets a point." Archbishop Weakland, meanwhile, has frequently (I know of at least three occasions, one as recent as the beginning of 1985) feigned shock and surprise when presented with the material by his flock. He has promised to investigate the matter, but of course it continues; and the Archbishop's professional perplexity became extremely untenable when an enthusiastic teacher allowed the Public Broadcasting System to film her giving a little religious education to some children in the Milwaukee Catholic schools, which was aired in the spring of 1985. "Vagina!" the camera captures her shouting at one pretty little girl who looked about ten.

—It is not known whether Franciscan Brother Robert Coakley, or "Brother Edmund" attended the lectures Archbishop Peter Gerety had arranged for Father Charles Curran to give Newark priests and religious in 1974 about the licitness of sodomy in some circumstances. Or how influenced Coakley was by the enthusiasm Archbishop Gerety displayed for Dignity at the Detroit Call-to-Action Conference in 1976. Or if he knew of the growing support Dignity was giving to groups that advocated sex between grown men and young boys. Nonetheless, according to the *Newark Star-Ledger*, "when Christopher Schultz attended a Boy Scout camp" in the summer of 1978, one under the jurisdiction of the Archdiocese of Newark, Brother Edmund "forced Schultz to engage in sexual activities while attending the camp, and then used threats to keep the boy silent." According to the *Reporter*, Coakley "afterward forced the boy to perform sexual acts in the basement of the parish church in Emerson, [New Jersey]." When this became known, the Archdiocese at first offered to pay the boy's medical bills, but then changed its mind, on the grounds that this might indicate Archdiocesan legal culpability. The Schultz's sued, but their case was dismissed on 9 May 1981, as the *Reporter* notes, "because the church and other charitable organizations were exempt from such litigation under a 1958 state law." The New Jersey Supreme Court vote on this matter was 4 to 3. Meanwhile, after months of despondency following his trip to the Franciscan summer camp, on 29 May 1979, Christopher Schultz drank a bottle of liniment, and died a few hours later. He was 12 years old.

—Finally, one case at greater length. In Lafayette, Louisiana, Bishop Gerard Frey chose to ignore numerous complaints against the Modernist takeover of his diocesan bureaucracy, in particular as represented in the somewhat sneering question/answer columns by one Monsignor James Songy in the diocesan paper, the *Morning Star*. Among Msgr. Songy's published opinions is that "if any of us, be we bishops, priests, religious, or laity, have by our theological training or faith experience the ability to see a statement from Rome in a clearer and more advantageous light, then we have by Christian charity and some of us by our state in life (bishops and priests) the responsibility to share this insight with our sisters and brothers." About whether "heaven, hell and the devil really exist," Songy writes, "I really don't think it would be wise for me or anyone else to base our lives on their existence or lack thereof." Was Msgr. Songy's confrere, Father Gilbert Gauthe, reading such ideas? Did he accept Songy's view that "It is not the unfaithfulness to his promise of celibacy as such which makes this law [of being obliged to go to Confession] applicable to the priest who judges himself guilty of fornication or adultery, it is the GRAVITY [Songy's emphasis] of his SINFULNESS (which can be judged only by HIM) which makes the law applicable. . . . if a priest (or anyone!) has 'AFFAIRS,' with all the connotations of that word, and 'HE BELIEVES this to be GRAVELY SINFUL,' he would be required by church law to 'seek the sacrament of reconciliation' before celebrating Mass. But the key words in your question are those I have emphasized by capitalizing them . . ."

"Between 1972 and 1983," the *Reporter* reveals, "Father Gilbert Gauthe committed hundreds of sexual acts with dozens of boys in four south Louisiana Catholic parishes . . . he drew most of his victims from ranks of the altar boys. While they were trained in rituals of the mass at ages seven, eight, and nine, the priest drew them into acts of sex. . . . Gauthe sodomized some boys in early hours before mass, introduced oral sex in the confessional and in the sacristy, and showed them video pornography," and "during sexual encounters, he also took hundreds of instant snapshots," that is, "pornographic photographs," and also "instigated sex games and threatened at least one child he would kill his parents if the boy spoke."

Gauthe admits he began molesting children during his first assignment as an assistant priest in 1972. In fact, he admitted it then, when confronted by the parishioners, who in response paid for some psychiatric sessions over a period of several months. When Bishop Frey was appointed to Lafayette in 1973, he quickly moved Father Gauthe to a different parish. By then, the Lafayette clergy were already troubled, though according to a nun, "when they became suspicious, they were afraid to falsely accuse. I noticed how [Gauthe] would have little boys spend

Friday and Saturday nights in the rectory"—where he lived alone—"and I thought, how inappropriate—but also how sad, that a man would depend on the companionship of children. The more I worried about it, I felt caught between my growing suspicion and the need to bring the matter to others."

The first time Bishop Frey says he learned Gauthe had been molesting children was when informed of such by a State Correctional official who had been counseling one of the priest's victims. In a legal deposition, Bishop Frey said the counselor "seemed to be disturbed by the thing, and I didn't want to pursue it with him." He did ask Father Gauthe about it, however; the priest admitted it, but said it was a mistake, an isolated incident, solely a matter of imprudent touching, and would never happen again. So Bishop Frey reports. There is no record of his having contacted Gauthe's victim for a more complete picture of the incident.

Bishop Frey also found Father Gauthe's defense impressively persuasive, as shown by His Excellency's decision in 1975 to appoint him chaplain of the diocesan Boy Scouts.

In 1976, the priest was assigned to yet another parish. Immediately parents began complaining to the pastor, Monsignor Richard Mouton, who in consequence asked Lafayette's vicar general, Monsignor Henri Larroque, what should be done. Larroque said Gauthe should have treatment, and so six psychiatric sessions took place with Dr. David Rees. Meanwhile, Gauthe continued camping trips with young boys as chaplain of the Boy Scouts. Msgr. Mouton did take the prudent steps of forbidding Gauthe to have youngsters in the rectory, and his bedroom was moved to an upper floor. But the Monsignor never asked either Gauthe or Dr. Rees anything about the treatment, which example was followed by Bishop Frey. Only after Gauthe's 12-year record of systematic abuse became public knowledge did his ordinary confer with Dr. Rees.

Indeed, despite two formal counseling sessions for sexual abuse of children in some six years of priesthood, Father Gauthe was promoted to pastor of St. John's parish in Henry, Louisiana on December 23, 1977. St. John's parishioners began making complaints shortly thereafter; on April 5, 1980 they did so formally in a letter to Bishop Frey, in which they noted that "Father's house became a second home to a bunch of Abbeville boys, who are often left unsupervised." Bishop Frey referred the letter to Msgr. Jude Speyrer, who reported, as clerics so often have since Vatican

II, that the laity's "complaints were superficial." As Mr. Berry points out, despite Gauthe's history, "no action was taken to determine what Abbeville boys were doing at the rectory. According to depositions, Frey did not meet with Gauthe about the letter. Neither did Larroque."

Upon learning in June 1983 that Gauthe had raped all three of his sons—all three altar boys—a Henry parishioner apparently knew better than to go to his bishop. Accordingly he went to a Catholic lawyer instead, one Paul Hebert. Hebert called Bishop Frey, who was out of town; but on this occasion Msgr. Larroque was very cooperative, very interested to get to the bottom of these indiscretions that had been going on for twelve years. He met with Hebert he even met with the parents. He was very sympathetic. On the very next day he drove to Bishop Frey's vacationing spot. Two days later Larroque—not Frey, who chose to continue his vacation—called Gauthe in and said "Gil, we have a big problem. It's with the little boys."

The leniency which both the homosexualist *Advocate* and the *National Catholic Reporter* have cited as virtual episcopal policy in the United States, had, in this case, finally come to an end. Father Gauthe began to weep. Larroque allowed him to say one final Mass the following morning to keep up appearances, but otherwise suspended Gauthe from further exercising his priestly faculties. The suspended priest wandered about the diocese largely unsupervised for the next three months, before being sent to a home for troubled priests in Massachusetts, where he stayed for a year. In October 1984 Gauthe "was indicted on 11 counts of aggravated crimes against nature, 11 counts of committing sexually immoral acts with minors, one count of aggravated rape (sodomizing a boy under 12) and 11 counts of crimes of pornography involving juveniles," according to the 9 June 1985 *Washington Post*. These "11 counts" represent those who have so far been willing to come forward and testify. Gauthe was sentenced to 20 years in prison.

In seducing the children, a Monsignor from Lafayette wrote and told me, Father Gauthe often employed an argument which his brother priests have used frequently in dealing with the laity over the past twenty years. He told the boys that their new "ritual" had been authorized by Vatican II.

Two final points about the episcopal response. In July 1983, attorney Hebert asked Larroque to contact all the families whose children had been altar boys under Gauthe. Despite repeated requests, this did not happen. On August 12, 1983, Bishop Frey agreed to meet with Hebert and "a core group of families." The *Washington Post* reports that the Lafayette diocese and its seven insurance companies, including Lloyd's of London, agreed to $4.2 million worth of settlements with the nine core group families originally represented by Hebert. One of those families, however, disagreed that the affair should remain secret. They hired attorney Miles Simon, who made it public, and who said there may well be grounds for a nationwide class action suit against the entire Catholic church in this country, since it has known of homosexuality among many priests, and yet failed to prevent them from preying on children. "Eleven additional damage suits are pending" in Lafayette, reports the *Post*, "with claims said to total more than $100 million."

"Last summer," the same article adds, "families of victims who had agreed to settle out of court asked to meet with Bishop Gerard Frey to talk about the situation and receive counseling. Their request was denied." The reason, according to the diocesan attorney, is that "my clients are inhibited by contractual insurance arrangements to do nothing which might jeopardize the insurers' rights of defense."

"If you are a bishop," the *Reporter* observed, "and legal recourse seems likely, then consult your attorney, call in the priest, but never, under any circumstances write or communicate with the parents. Whatever you say or do may be held against you. The same holds true for religious superiors. What is needed is legal defense, not moral intervention. All this may sound cynical, but in case after case of priests' molesting children, many pastors, bishops and religious superiors have responded precisely in this way."

One final observation concerns the bishops' refusal to see the connection between these scandals,—and all the others that stem from an episcopal fear of implementing Vatican II. During a press conference held at Collegeville, Minnesota on 15 June 1985, Archbishop Quinn was explaining to the media the importance of "new definitions" of obedience, authority, and discipline in regard to his investigation of the religious orders. Bishop Malone sat next to him. "The recent scandal of various priests molesting children," I said, "and apparently their bishops doing very little about it, would seem to indicate certain shortcomings about a hesitancy to impose discipline or to exercise the obligations of episcopal authority. So—Bishop Malone—do you think this scan-

dal might encourage American bishops to begin seeing some utility in exercising a bit more authority and discipline in the future,
even in other arenas? And do you see any connection between
this scandal and other examples of lax discipline in matters of
Catholic faith and morals?"

The Bishop frowned. He said the matter was "under study
by one of our committees," and that information on
"psychological profiles" was being gathered, as well as the
"sociological setting" in which child molestation takes place, "so
that we can give the bishops the information needed to understand these aberrations and to deal with them in an effective,
pastoral way."

I asked the question again. "Do you see any connection
between this scandal and other examples of lax discipline in
matters of faith and morals?"

"No," he said, and turned for the next question.

V. The U.S. Episcopate at Work

> *"For a bishop must be blameless, as the steward of God . . . holding fast the faithful word as he hath been taught, that he may be able by sound doctrine both to exhort and to convince the gainsayers, for there are many unruly and vain talkers and deceivers . . . whose mouths must be stopped, who subvert whole houses, teaching things which they ought not."*
> The Epistle of St. Paul to St. Titus

> *"NCCB and USCC have become effective instruments for collaboration among the bishops."*
> NCCB President James Malone

1. The USCC, the NCCB

> *"He made a pit, and he digged it, and is fallen into the ditch which he make."*
> Psalms 7:15

In the 16-page single-spaced November 29 Elaboration distributed at the U.S. Bishop's first press conference during the Extraordinary Synod, there is clearly a more plaintive, even more humble, tone than in the more complacent September 16 document. Referring to the years immediately following Vatican II, when the authority of the Council collapsed like a promising souffle at Catholic University, Bishop Malone drew attention to some earnest efforts the bishops had in fact made at that time to uphold Council teaching. Noting particularly the U.S. bishops' 1967 pastoral letter on *Lumen gentium* called *The Church in Our Day*,

His Excellency pleaded the case that "clearly the bishops were trying to keep faith with the Council and its concern for evangelization. They sought to see to it that Vatican II would not be misinterpreted. But their efforts," he sighed, "did not succeed in putting an end to polarization in the everyday life of the Church during the two decades since Vatican II. Historians will surely call attention to the fact."

"At times," he adds a bit later in the Elaboration, "pluralism makes it very difficult to preach the Gospel effectively. It is the obligation of bishops to preserve and strengthen the unity of faith and discipline in this context. The bishops of the Episcopal Conference of the United States have not found this easy to accomplish."

No, they have not. With the post-Council American bishops, however, especially with the arrival of Archbishop Jadot, one has the impression of a certain longing at the root of episcopal policy—the very human longing for a little social approval. And since orthodox priests would be willing to follow their bishop almost regardless of what he did, wouldn't it be better to—what was the word?—to be pastoral? Perhaps the bishops could shift their attention to subjects at least nominally Christian, but in any case subjects that would be more likely to win the approval from those responsible for the means of social communication. Well, perhaps there would be some inadequacies in this approach, but it could hardly be worse than what was already happening; and there were all these young Jesuits and others like them and educated by them, so eager to help if one . . . if one adopted this "pastoral" attitude they talked so much about.

Thus, after a series of episcopal interviews in 1985, the Indian Catholic editor of *Policy Review* Dinesh D'Souza concludes that the bishops' more recent activities are "rooted in their discontent with previous, largely unsuccessful battles to uphold orthodox Catholic teaching." In addition, he continues, "In the late 60's . . . the newly-formed USCC began to hire an increasingly militant set of officials who were not content with what they considered . . . a narrow emphasis on individual and family behavior. The USCC staff urged the bishops to . . . place more emphasis on collective sins and collective (i.e. governmental) solutions." In the 1970's the USCC sought to enhance the tattered prestige of the American episcopate by issuing public policy papers with which the media elite were sure to be pleased. These included, among others: support for the Panama Canal treaty, despite public complaints from prominent American Cardinals that they knew nothing about Panama; public support of the SALT treaties with the Soviet Union; opposition to an anti-ballistic missile system for the United States; a demand for increased aid to the fledging Marxist governments of Angola and Mozambique; along with a demand for cutting off all military aid to the government of El Salvador, though it was under siege from Marxist guerrillas.

"The reason the bishops boldly press ahead in their political activism," D'Souza thinks, "is their abiding trust in the people who write their pastorals—the policy staff of the United States Catholic Conference. Although most have no formal training as defense strategists or economists, the USCC staffers enjoy tackling public policy matters, and submitting lengthy analyses that the bishops assume is a correct application of Catholic principles."

Russell Shaw of the Public Affairs Department of the United States Catholic Conference told D'Souza that his colleagues are "probably more liberal" than the bishops, and "unrepresentative of the Catholic population," which D'Souza "confirmed by conversation with the three senior USCC officials who, by common agreement and their own admission, had the greatest influence on the two [most recent] pastoral letters . . . by the hierarchy—Edward Doherty, Fr. Brian Hehir, and Ronald Krietemeyer. . . ."

"Doherty wants the Bishops to advocate immediate unilateral disarmament by the United States in favor of a conventional weapons deterrent. He does not think this will be exploited by the Soviet Union . . . Even if the Soviets do take advantage, Doherty asked what was so bad about America being in a situation like that of Poland—subject to Soviet domination, but free in the heart?"

"Father Hehir is secretary of the Office of Social Development and World Peace, the umbrella group which coordinates both domestic and foreign policy statements by the USCC. . . . It takes a moment to realize that Father Hehir has convinced himself that every approach to deterring war is either strategically foolish or immoral or both. . . ."

"Ronald Krietemeyer, the youthful director of the USCC's Office of Domestic Social Development, is supervising the pastoral letter on the economy. He wants an expansion of social spending which he admits will cost 'in the tens of billions of dollars.' . . . [W]here will all the money come from to pay for all the bishops' proposed programs? Krietemeyer doesn't want a bigger deficit, and he doesn't want significantly higher taxes. He finds his revenue in national defense."

But D'Souza asks, "didn't the bishops in their war and peace pastoral call for a shift from nuclear to conventional deterrence"—they did—"a shift that is by its nature more expensive? 'That's out of my field,' Krietemeyer says. 'I'm not into the conventional arms issue.' "

Meanwhile D'Souza interviews with some of the bishops who depend upon these men provoked much commentary in the closing months of 1985. "Interviews with these bishops," D'Souza wrote, "suggest that they know little or nothing about the ideas and proposals to which they are putting their signature and lending their religious authority. The bishops are unfamiliar with existing defense and economic programs, unable to identify even in general terms the Soviet military capability, ignorant to roughly how much of the budget currently goes to defense, unclear about how much should be reallocated to social programs, and innocent of the most basic concepts underlying the intelligent laymen's discussion of these questions," and this despite the fact that "in their pastoral letters the bishops do not confine themselves to . . . moral assertions. Indeed the reader is struck by the depth and specificity with which the bishops seek to dissect concrete policies and propose remedial action."

All of this is in stark contrast to the generous citations of contemporary expert sources that mark the pastorals, which has prompted Michael Novak to wonder "if the bishops have ever read the many volumes cited in the notes." D'Souza wondered too, but he questioned some of them. Bishop Edward O'Donnell, who supports the weapons pastoral but did not sign it because he was chosen after its release as an auxiliary to NCCB Vice-President and St. Louis Archbishop John May, "is perplexed about terms such as 'frictional unemployment' and 'hard target kill capability' which appear in the pastoral letters . . . he has no idea what per cent of our budget is spent on defense . . . he wants an 'adequate non-nuclear defense' to protect Europe against a possible Soviet invasion, but is alarmed at the information that conventional weapons cost more than nuclear weapons. . . . How many troops does the United States have in Europe? Bishop O'Donnell 'just can't say.' " Among those who not only support it, but signed it, Detroit auxiliary Patrick Cooney hasn't "looked very deeply into our military situation," has "no idea" how much of the military budget goes for nuclear weapons, but is convinced "the West uses 80 to 90 per cent of the wealth of the world," though he was unable to cite sources for this opinion. Des Moines ordinary Maurice Dingman, who presents himself as something of an authority on the suffering of the Midwestern farmer—he opines that the basis of U.S. economic policy is to help the "rich get richer, the poor get poorer, and the rich start working with the military"—nonetheless did not know who Maynard Keynes was, nor anything about his economic theories; His Excellency did not even know the word "Keynesian", or what cutting marginal tax rates meant. He did, however, wonder "why we can't win wars without ever lifting a gun," and when asked about the massive Soviet military build-up over the past twenty years, confidently noted that the best-selling futurist book *"Megatrends* gives me the answer. Both we and the Soviets have hierarchical systems that are outdated. We have to move into networking." The interviews with other bishops revealed equal depth and intelligence.

Meanwhile, "the enlightened bishop," as Phyllis Zagano observes in the January 1986 *Catholicism in Crisis,* "may have hired a deacon or two to do staff research, but he dare not show up at an NCCB meeting with a nonclerical aide. It's just not done; it would look as if he could not attract qualified men to his presbytery. So he is left to the mercy of the 'insider' clerics whose political agendas are mercilessly complicated and simply put."

"Insulated by clericalism," Zagano continues, "the American bishops . . . haven't a clue as to what is going on in the Church, let alone in the technical specifics of pastoral letters. The black wall around them won't let in the least bit of light to shed on, say, questions of declining church attendance, declining vocations to the clerical state, declining donations, declining influence in areas of moral concern, and declining interest in general."

2. Fighting Abortion?

> *"There are two kinds of injustice: the first is found in those who do an injury. The second in those who fail to protect another from injury when they can."*
>
> Cicero

Still, to repeat, there were certain advantages to all this after the humiliations of the late 60's timidity. "One immediate result of the two pastorals," as D'Souza notes, "has been a switch of
constituencies for the bishops. The people who once ridiculed and
caricatured the theology of the bishops and their pronouncements on settled Catholic teaching on abortion and artificial birth control, now speak their names solemnly, almost rever-
entially, invoking of all things the bishop's Authority. Even
groups such as People for the American Way (PAW), which
greeted the activism of evangelicals and Archbishop John
O'Connor's comments about abortion last year with apocalyptic
warnings about mixing God and politics, now throw confetti at
the Catholic clerics as they march ... into the public policy arena.
John Buchanan, president of PAW, calls the bishops' recent poli-
ticking 'valuable' and 'encouraging.' " There were many other
such reverential reversals, from such as New York Governor
Cuomo, or Newark Episcopal Chief Minister John Spong, whose
otherwise bitter anti-Catholicism is so extreme, it was publicly
rebuked by the Catholic League for Religious and Civil Rights in
1984. In 1982, *Time* magazine put Cardinal Bernardin and the
weapons pastoral on its cover.

The result, in Joseph Sobran's view, is that "the liberal
clergy see no tension between the sacred and the trendy; they virtually identify the two, hailing their own leftist protest as
'prophetic'—as if they were defying contemporary currents of
power, rather than being swept up in them. They are embarrassed
by dogma; they adapt their theology to politics," but "there is a
core of timidity in all this 'speaking out,' a spirit of abdication in
all this activism."

This insight was unhappily borne out by the bishops' choice
of Cardinal Bernardin as chairman of the NCCB's Pro-Life
Committee, upon the death of New York's Terence Cardinal
Cooke in 1983. The move sent shock-waves through the pro-life
movement in the U.S., since one of Bernardin's first actions when
he became Archbishop of Chicago was to encourage Catholic
support for a group called the Crusade for Mercy, despite that
organization's direct contributions to Planned Parenthood and
thus the extermination of unborn children. At the end of 1983,
His Eminence then gave the famous "seamless garment" speech
at Fordham University, which asserted that in order to be
"credible", it was not enough for pro-lifers to oppose abortion;
but that they must be "equally visible"—and equally was his

word—in opposition to a long list of evils such as unemployment, nuclear arms, and the conditions of illegal immigrants. The *New York Times* gave the speech front-page coverage.

"On its face, the 'seamless garment' argument seems to be consistent and evenhanded," Joseph Sobran observed in the 14 January 1985 *Catholic Eye.* "In fact, it is neither. It is, considering the Cardinal's office, a virtual pro-abortion position. It is recognized as such on all sides. It is applauded by liberals who favor abortion and who have no intention of achieving the 'consistency' the Cardinal asks on that issue. . . . his list of 'life issues' is, apart from abortion, completely congruent with the fashionable liberal agenda," though his implied solutions "have no official standing as *Catholic* teachings."

Meanwhile, "Cardinal Bernardin doesn't address his demand for a 'consistent ethic' to liberals. If he meant it seriously, however, he . . . would certainly warn them that they could not (credibly) oppose war and poverty unless they also opposed abortion. He said not a single word to this effect; and until he does so, his whole metaphor will deserve to be regarded, as it already is, as a rhetorical stratagem," which "serves precisely to 'dilute' the anti-abortion position. It has no other effect whatsoever," which is why it "has left Catholic politicians like Edward Kennedy, Tip O'Neill, and Mario Cuomo completely unaffected. It would be an ambitious goal to want to convert the unbelievers; but the bishops can't even convert a single Catholic! Seen in this light, the recent progressive statements and strategies of the bishops represent not an assertion of authority but the nearly complete loss of authority. The 'seamless garment' refrain is merely the ecclesiastical equivalent of the 'personally opposed, but' evasion so dear to the liberal Catholic politician."

Those who doubt Sobran's analysis may wish to consider Daniel Maguire's praise of Bernardin's "seamless garment" in the 20 July 1984 *Reporter* for its contribution to the "new moral theology." Or Father Richard McBrien's view that "one of the most positive of recent developments in the U.S. Catholic Church has been the succession of Chicago's Cardinal Joseph Bernardin to the chairmanship of the National Conference of Catholic Bishops' Committee for Pro-Life Activities." Or that the NCCB's poverty program, called the Campaign for Human Development, has contributed tens of thousands of dollars to explicitly pro-abortion organizations like the Center for Constitutional Rights (CCR), which has even filed pro-abortion *amicus curiae* briefs before the Supreme Court. Or that Mrs. Ellen Christiansen was invited to give a lecture at the October 1985 National Catholic Youth Conference, though she runs a birth control clinic in Buffalo that also helps women to get abortions. Her talk was called "Sexuality and Spirituality."

This list, alas, is far from exhaustive. As an example of the NCCB's "firm commitment to Vatican II," however, Bishop Malone's September 16 statement notes that after *Roe vs. Wade* the bishops launched "a major pro-life program intended to educate and sensitize Catholics and other persons of good will on abortion and many other issues pertaining to the dignity and sanctity of innocent life." Unfortunately, as Liz Armstrong of the *NC News* revealed at its meeting before the Synod in November 1985, "the National Conference of Catholic Bishops has approved a revised 'Pastoral Plan for Pro-Life Activities' which links the fight against abortion to opposition to capital punishment, nuclear war, and other such attacks on life.... the plan follows a previous one, approved 10 years ago, which was limited almost entirely to fighting abortion."

Because the new plan calls for cooperation and creation of non-church congressional district pro-life action committees, Mario Cuomo's friend Bishop Joseph Sullivan of Brooklyn was critical, on the grounds that such committees are "almost totally geared to the abortion question," and "I think it's inconsistent with the consistent ethic." Archbishop Weakland agreed, arguing that such committees in practice only emphasize the "old pro-life" concept. Accordingly, the bishops passed a measure authorizing Bernardin to include in the new plan a section insisting that cooperation with the district committees must be underscored by their acceptance of the entire "new" pro-life concept.

Indeed, over the summer of '85, the USCC's legal counsel Wilfred Caron apparently got so carried away, or perhaps confused, by the new and the old concepts, that he filed a brief with the Supreme Court which effectively accepted the premises of *Roe vs. Wade* that abortion is a constitutional right. This seemed not least significant because Caron's bitter opposition to the Helms Human Life Bill in 1981 had killed that bill's chances of passing, and in effect broke much of the pro-life momentum that had been achieved with the election of an anti-abortion President and an astounding twelve new anti-abortion men and women to the United States Senate at the end of 1980. Caron said his opposition was based solely on his conviction the bill was unconstitutional: but the passion with which he fought it—in the name of the U.S. Bishops, remember—led many to suspect the real issue was USCC hatred of Rightist North Carolina Senator Jesse Helms (the bill's sponsor), and the largely Catholic staff who managed Helms' political agenda.

In addition to opposing that bill, Caron induced the NCCB to endorse a controversial Constitutional Amendment that would not have outlawed abortion, but only allowed individual states to do so, and which for various other reasons provoked opposition from large segments of the pro-life movement. The effect was an abortionist's dream, with pro-lifers fighting among themselves instead of against the industry; but the very strange thing was that no matter how you counted, there was no possibility of winning the 67 Senatorial votes necessary to move out an Amendment. As a pro-life measure, it was absolutely futile at the time, though it did prevent unity and unravel momentum, so that pro-abortion Republican Majority Leader Howard Baker was able to stall efforts to have the Helms Bill voted on in 1981, indeed stalled them until September of 1982. By then, to no small extent because of Caron's contributions, pro-life political power had dissipated considerably; three separate votes seeking to break a filibuster on the Helms bill gathered steam with each vote, but only got as high as 54, before a fatigued Senate voted 47-46 to end debate. A later vote on Caron's favored Amendment was unable to muster even 50 of the 67 votes needed.

So despite explanations, one might recall that Caron has a history. Accordingly, one of the things the secular press—Aaron Epstein in the 4 September *Philadelphia Inquirer* for example—immediately picked up about Caron's 1985 Supreme Court brief (still in the name of the bishops) was that "Ironically, the Reagan administration went further in its opposition to abortion than the Catholic Church did."

In fact, considerably further. The case in question was a Supreme Court review of state laws passed in Illinois and Pennsylvania that sought to monitor the unrestricted practice of abortion-on-demand. The Reagan Administration took advantage of this to do what the Federal government had not done for over three decades, the last occasion over the moral issue of racism: it urged the court to reverse one of its own decisions, in this case *Roe vs. Wade.* Immediately thereafter, 82 Congressmen from both the House and Senate filed another brief, again calling for reversal of *Roe vs. Wade.* Then came the Caron brief, which not only refused to join in the call for a formal repudiation of *Roe vs. Wade*, but chose extremely dangerous language when it at least defended the state restrictions. It said, for example, that the restrictions did not "unduly" burden the "constitutional protection" of a woman's "right" to abortion.

This time, a number of bishops decided not to be their normally docile selves. The USCC would not say how many, but it did admit that "several" bishops had called to express their fury: New Orleans Archbishop Philip Hannan in a virtually unprecedented gesture, charged publicly in his diocesan paper, the *Clarion Herald*, that the brief "admits that we accept as a constitutional right a woman's decision to have an abortion," when "that's precisely the point we're opposing." Since "the Church is and must be inexorably opposed to abortion," His Excellency added, "we need a clear and convincing explanation from the legal counsel of the United States Catholic Conference of his *amicus* brief which did not support the brief of the Administration calling on the Supreme Court to reverse the 1973 *Roe vs. Wade* which legalized abortion."

Numerous explanations followed, to be sure, though none of them very clear or convincing. The veiled pro-*Roe* language within the context of the otherwise anti-abortion brief was overlooked by most of the secular press, with the result, according to the *National Catholic Reporter*, that the USCC had room to effect some quick damage control. Accordingly, it "changed an internal policy," that "put its general counsel on a shorter leash. . . . A USCC spokesperson said Caron's department, like other USCC offices must now obtain approval in principle from three other USCC offices—public affairs, government liaison and the general secretary—before releasing statements."

One of the most striking results of all this, however, was the public embarrassment it caused syndicated diocesan columnist, Weakland consultant, and longtime USCC functionary Msgr. George Higgins. Higgins had been growing increasingly vituperative in his attacks against Cardinal Ratzinger, and was particularly upset by His Eminence's cold critiques of bishops' conferences, not impossibly because of the considerable sway the Monsignor has for years exercised, as he still does, over what those conferences have to say.

In August of 1985, Msgr. Higgins was railing against Cardinal Ratzinger's attacks on the national episcopal conferences. Cardinal Ratzinger had complained, in the Messori inter-

view, that the truths of *Lumem gentium* about the role of the apostles' successors, are "in reality restrained or actually risk being
smothered by the insertion of bishops into episcopal conferences
that are ever more organized, often with burdensome bureaucratic structures. We must not forget," he added, "that episcopal
conferences have no theological basis, they do not belong to the
structure of the Church, as willed by Christ, that cannot be eliminated; they have only a practical, concrete function," and that
thus "no episcopal conference, as such, has a teaching mission; its
documents have no weight of their own save that of the consent
given to them by the individual bishops."

In addition, he noted, "with some bishops there is a certain
lack of individual responsibility, and the delegation of his inalienable powers as shepherd and teacher to the structures of the
local conference leads to letting what should remain very personal lapse into anonymity. The group of bishops united in the
conference depends in their decisions upon other groups, upon
commissions that have been established to prepare draft proposals. It happens then that the search for agreement between
the different tendencies and the effort at mediation often yield
flattened documents in which decisive positions, where they
might be necessary, are weakened."

"This seems to be open season on bishops' conferences,"
Higgins charged in an early August column, adding that most
American criticisms, such as those from *Catholicism in Crisis* editor
Ralph McInerny "would hardly merit a response were it not that
the same complaint is being voiced by others, including Cardinal
Joseph Ratzinger, prefect of the Vatican's Congregation for the
Doctrine of the Faith." Though quickly dismissing the published
Messori interview as "this pessimistic book," Higgins gives a fair
outline of the Ratzinger quotes above, and contrasts their distaste
"for a watered-down consensus," with McInerny's fear "that the
bishops are being manipulated by their staff into rubber-stamp-
ing left-wing statements." He concludes that "both Ratzinger and
McInerny have it wrong, at least in the case of the USCC, because they are not well-informed about the conference's inner
workings."

Then came the Caron scandal. One of the USCC's explanations as demanded by Archbishop Hannan, was that "although
the bishops on the NCCB Committee for Pro-Life Activities did
not review the brief, the staff office did so at the last moment."

Perhaps a pause is merited here. Because we're not talking about some routine piece of daily business, but rather a legal brief, to the Supreme Court of the United States, on the subject of *Roe vs. Wade*: and no bishop ever read it before its delivery. And thus, though that brief would undermine (yet again) a united attack on the abortion industry, and indeed contained extremely dangerous language that later had to be explained away, not one bishop, not even Pro-Life Committee Chairman Joseph Bernardin himself, even glanced at the thing, unless somebody is lying.

What does that say about matters of lesser concern to the NCCB? "The really powerful documents against National Socialism," Cardinal Ratzinger pointed out to Messori, "were those that came from individual courageous bishops. The documents of the [German] conference, on the contrary, were often rather wan and too weak with respect to what the tragedy called for."

Meanwhile, if Msgr. Higgins felt it wise to ignore the subject of bishops' conferences until memories faded a little, NCCB President Bishop James Malone did not have that luxury. He thus brought up the subject of episcopal conferences—albeit rather modestly—on September 16, and went on to make them the central focus of both his Intervention and Elaboration during the Extraordinary Synod, an event which by then seemed to be closing in on so much that had taken place since 1965.

3. The American Bishops
and the Mystery of the Church

> *"Then said Paul unto him, 'God shall smite thee, thou whited wall, for sittest thou to judge me after the law, and commandest me to be smitten contrary to the law?'*
> *And they that stood by said, 'Revilest thou God's high priest?'*
> *Then said Paul, 'I wist not, brethren, that he was the high priest . . .'"*
>
> The Acts of the Apostles 23:3-5

Since the mystery of the Church proved to be a question of some importance during the Synod—as it had been during the Council—one does not wish to address the subject too soon. Still, upon arriving in Collegeville on the Feast of the Sacred Heart in June 1985 and seeing over two hundred bishops gathered together (as I had never done before), I confess to feeling a strange sense of awe. The mood was not cheerful, to be sure, for the pederasty scandal had just been exposed in the *Reporter* and CBS news, there was much insecurity about the upcoming Synod, and, not least, Archbishop Weakland was speaking, who does not have a cheerful voice. Still, for all their blandness and even malevolence, despite the arguable thesis that these men are more responsible than any for depriving the American faithful of the fruits of Vatican II, it is nonetheless through them that the struggle for truth finds particular expression—if even only through the hope that their successors will be braver.

The toll, however, has been severe, for without the virtue of courage the practice of any other virtue remains but a theoretical possibility; and the American episcopate has not only lacked courage, it has sought to elevate cowardice itself into a virtue, by calling it compassionate or prophetic, or whatever word was handy. Yet as Father Bruce Ritter (the priest who since Vatican II has fought in Times Square and across the country to rescue sexually abused and abandoned teen-agers) recently pointed out, in 1968 the drug trade had not yet left the American inner city, and "the first massage parlor and the first porno book store hadn't opened in Times Square yet," though "a multi-billion dollar industry was waiting to be born."

Today, he continued, "in 1986, our society is totally permeated and saturated by a huge illegal drug and sex-for-sale commercial enterprise that has profoundly affected the lifestyle, the quality of life, the marriage and the families of almost every man, woman and child in the United States." And while this happened, this and so much more, the American bishops talked about academic freedom, and the Panama Canal, and the scourge of sexist language in the liturgy, because they feared their Christian mandate to *lead*, to fight bravely and perhaps even die protecting the real victims—who are an ever-expanding list before secularism's ever-expanding appetite.

The world had the power to make them look bad, it seems they feared; and so some of their bravest would on occasion whisper about reality, the post-Council U.S. Episcopate has with but few exceptions (and these only with qualifications) discussed what the secular powers have told them was, in the vernacular, relevant. Having been presented with the very real opportunity of resurrecting the tradition of the Colosseum, the bishops understandably, but not very admirably, chose instead to join Nero in playing the fiddle, while Rome burned.

"I have understood that a certain 'contestation' of some theologians," Cardinal Ratzinger told Messori, "is stamped by the typical mentality of the opulent bourgeoise of the West." Reading such lines, one is hardly surprised at the hatred this man has provoked among the Modernist elite. It is perhaps not too much of an exaggeration to note that Christ's words, though less gentle, provoked a similar fury amid the clergy of His day; and that He predicted no less enthusiasm for those who would uphold His words in the generations to follow.

And yet, there remains the Mystery. However ineffective the bishops have been in comparison to what the situation demanded, however many have lost their faith or come to hate it, or are simply conformists or scared, or maybe just dumb, despite all this, there is a Mystery involved, for without the prestige of the American bishops (no matter how much they obstructed or whined or insisted it was impossible to oppose abortion unless one was "equally" opposed to everything else), without the Grace of God mediated through the bishops by the Sacrament of Ordination and Confession and Confirmation and the Eucharist Itself, without the Teaching Authority they symbolized even if they were afraid to teach, without the Mystery of their *succession*, in short, it is very unlikely there would have been *any* resistance to the abortion culture, because there would have been no Catholic laity to draw their inspiration from the Sacraments and their faith in order to resist it. Episcopalians have not been conspicuous for holding opinions contrary to those found on the pages of the *New York Times* in recent years, and when you consider how far the abortion culture has come since 1965, consider too how far it could have come had there been no resistance, consider indeed the secular enthusiasm for euthanasia, infanticide, sterilization of the poor, or consider that, in her farewell speech before her term ended with the election of Reagan, Jimmy Carter's Secretary for Health and Human Services Patricia Harris suggested that perhaps we should make it illegal for certain classes of people to give birth without state permission. "Coercion is a dirty word to most liberals now," the population expert Garret Hardin wrote in 1968, "but it need not be forever so." And then added: "the only way we can preserve and nurture other and more precious freedoms is by relinquishing the freedom to breed, and that very soon."

"In a world in which, at bottom, many ... are gripped by scepticism," says Ratzinger, "the conviction of the Church that there is one truth, and that this one truth can as such be recognized, expressed and also clearly defined within certain bounds, appears scandalous ... real reform presupposes an unequivocal turning away from the erroneous paths whose catastrophic consequences are already incontestable." Unequivocal, he says; but if a tall order, the Cardinal makes clear he understands its implications upon acknowledging the "pressure that every moment weighs heavily upon a man such as today's priest, who is so often called to swim against the current. Such a man, in the end, can grow weary of resisting, with his words and even more with his manner of life, the seemingly so reasonable realities that are accepted as a matter of course and that characterize our [Western] culture." Still, he insists, "it is time to find again the courage of nonconformism, the capacity to oppose many of the trends of the surrounding culture."

His Eminence continues: "Catholic priests of my generation have been habituated to avoiding oppositions among colleagues and to trying always to achieve agreement and not to drawing too much attention to ourselves by taking eccentric positions. Thus, in many episcopal conferences, the group spirit and perhaps even the wish for a quiet, peaceful life or conformism lead the majority to accept the positions of active minorities bent upon pursuing clear goals. I know bishops who privately confess that they would have decided differently than they did at a conference if they had had to decide by themselves. Accepting the group spirit, they shied away from the odium of being viewed as a 'spoil-sport', as 'backward', as 'not open.' It seems very nice always to decide *together*. This way, however, entails the risk of losing the scandal and the folly of the Gospel, that salt and leaven that today are more indispensable than ever for a Christian—above all when he is a bishop, hence invested with precise responsibility for the faithful—in the face of the gravity of the crisis."

"Thus the 'good' priest," as James Hitchcock points out in the December 1985 *Catholicism in Crisis*, "is now one who rarely alludes to matters of doctrine or morals in any very specific way ... who possesses certain kinds of therapeutic skills, and who is regarded by his parishioners as warm, compassionate and 'open',"—and who finds that "acting charitably towards 'conservative' Catholics, that is, those who insist on raising inconvenient doctrinal questions, tests his patience more than any other single thing."

As with priests, so with their shepherds—as exemplified by the bishops' 1985 meeting in Collegeville, Minnesota. "During two days in June," *National Catholic Reporter*[15] editor Thomas Fox writes of Rembert Weakland and the Collegeville Conference gathering, "the Milwaukee prelate solidified his leadership within the conference, and the bishops appeared to continue on a course likely to keep them out of step with the Vatican for some time to come. The conflicts—real and potential—center on ways the church should conduct its affairs and stem from different understandings about the nature of the church." Archbishop Roach, who appointed Weakland to draft the economic pastoral when the former was President of the NCCB[16] , told Fox that though the Collegeville meeting "started off slowly . . . by the second day, Weakland had grabbed the reins and it went remarkably well."

"But on the minds of many bishops during the gathering," Fox continued—and this was my impression as well—"were broader church questions . . . key U.S. Bishops admit they see conflicts growing with Rome. This disturbs them . . . several bishops mentioned their particular alarm with the way Rome has investigated the orthodoxy of local bishops and their seminaries . . . some U.S. bishops express their serious concern for the direction the Pope is taking the church. These bishops see recent papal moves as already demoralizing many priests . . . one detects among some of the bishops a sense they are being dragged into conflicts they would prefer to—but probably cannot—avoid."

"Central to these concerns," Fox opined, "is the meaning of collegiality, or the way bishops together with the bishop of Rome collectively involve themselves in decision-making within the church. Reflecting these concerns, one high-ranking prelate recently remarked that collegiality is 'the fundamental issue' to be discussed at the extraordinary synod set for November. He said it will revolve around the question of who gets to write the document(s) that will come out of the two-week session."

" 'Will the gathered bishops write it . . . or will it be left to the holy father and a few of his aides?' asked the bishop. Clearly, he thought that, given the limited time of the gathering, the latter is more likely to be the case. This upset him.

---

[15]July 5 issue.
[16]And, as later revealed, at the time a severe alcoholic.

"Looking toward the extraordinary November synod, many U.S. bishops' attitudes range from quiet alarm to a nearly total dismissal of the importance of the event. They point to the impossible task of discussing the full spectrum of church-related issues in two weeks of ceremony-laced activities. Some contended the synod will be a platform for the pope, during talks at the beginning and end of the meeting, to place his personal stamp of approval or disapproval on the range of post-conciliar concerns and, in the process, determining church direction for years to come."

"These shifts within the church," Fox concludes, "very much on the minds of the bishops, unsettled many, but did not appear to deter them from their work."

THE POPE

I. The Education
of Karol Wojtyla

"I like John Paul II because ... he's an intellectual, an athlete, a skier and a phenomenologist. Most importantly, he's a whole man, a mensch."

Walker Percy

"John Paul II may be the third Pope in history to be called 'The Great.'"

Paris-Match

In the *Pensees*, Pascal says that one of the most convincing arguments for the truth of the Catholic faith is the manner in which throughout history the Church's demise has appeared imminent on so many occasions, even to the detached observer. And indeed, time after time, beginning with the crucifixion of Her Founder, attacks on the Church from within and without have seemed for awhile so overwhelming and comprehensive that the Pharisees, the pagans, the Roman emperors, the Arians, the Moslems, the Lutherans, the deists, the Communists—and by the death of Pope Paul VI in 1978 the citizens of North America and Europe's abortion culture—had come to relax, in the conviction that they, finally, had discovered the one truth sufficient to render Roman Catholicism but a curious artifact of history.

Still, when Pope Paul died on the Feast of the Transfiguration, it had been some time since Catholics in the West had been subject to the kind of savage onslaught that characterized the period of his reign. Though it came from many sources, doubtless the most disheartening aspect for American Catholics—the aspect which would drive a third of them out of the Church altogether—was the constant, growing, and vitriolic hatred for the Church and Her people on the part of so many priests and nuns. That the U.S. Episcopate seemed to collapse before all this venom and that the Pontiff himself chose (as had other Pontiffs in other crises) the prudential role of refusing to discipline, expose, or excommunicate those who used their clerical or episcopal authority to attack the faithful, arguably contributed to the grim condition in which the Church seemed to find Herself, when the Cardinals gathered in Rome to elect yet another successor to Peter at the end of August in 1978.

The gentleness, the kindly Italian smile of the man they chose, gave a moment of respite to the Church; though it was short-lived, for the Venice Patriarch Albino Cardinal Luciani died within a few weeks of his election to the Papacy.

Nonetheless, if history is not likely to give the man who may prove to have been the last Italian Pope much credit, there are at least two significant effects of his Pontificate. One is simply that he broke the strain of the great sorrow and administrative incompetence that hung like a pall around Pope Paul in his final years; and Papa Luciani was in that sense a harbinger of things to come. The other effect was equally simple: it was his choice of the name John Paul I, which as it were defiantly asserted the authority of Vatican II, despite what had been done to destroy its fruits—and despite the mendacious claim that this destruction was by mandate of the Council itself. As Cardinal Ratzinger was to observe almost six years to the day after Cardinal Luciani's election, "the true time of Vatican II has not yet come, its authentic reception has not yet begun." Albino Luciani knew this: when his Papal name was announced to the gathered throngs in St. Peter's Square, however, he made it clear there would be no retreat, that the Church would yet proclaim this Council.

Meanwhile, with Luciani's death, Pascal was about to have his thesis vindicated again; though one wonders if even he would not have been surprised to see it happen so dramatically. Karol Wojtyla was born on 18 May 1920, in Wadowice, Poland, about thirty miles from the city of Kracow, which latter he would one day serve as its Archbishop. The date is also significant, for until 1918, Poland had not even been recognized as a nation for some hundred and fifty years; and it was not until three months after Wojtyla's birth that the Polish people finally secured the independence of their new state, upon defeating Leninist Russia in the Battle of Warsaw on the Feast of the Assumption. The Poles call it The Miracle of the Vistula. Between the wars, Poland was at first a parliamentary democracy, then—after Hitler and Stalin began their longing gazes—a military dictatorship. The Nazis swept in and conquered it in 1939, dividing some of the spoils in the East with the Soviets as a tribute to the Hitler/Stalin pact signed that year. For the next six years, Hitler's men proceeded to slaughter as many Poles as Jews, and it is thus not without the authority of experience that John Paul II calls Auschwitz "the Golgotha of the modern age." After the war, with Europe finished as a serious world power (and the United States having not yet grasped its new role), the leftist historicists moved quickly, and soon brought all of Eastern Europe, including Poland, under Stalinist domination.

It was clear, as the historian Paul Johnson notes, that "in 1945, the architects of the new Communist regime intended to destroy Catholicism completely and believed it was possible to do so. During the war 30 per cent of the clergy had been murdered. The church had lost nearly all its property. It was now deprived of its schools, and of the opportunity to conduct any religious instruction within the framework of the public system of education. Many of its churches had been destroyed or damaged. It was almost impossible to get permits to rebuild or repair them, let alone build new churches made necessary by the vast upheavals in population. Laws specifically framed to entrap clerical opponents were applied with rigor."[1]

When Father Karol Wojtyla began work on his philosophical thesis in the early fifties, Polish prisons held over 900 priests and eight bishops, among them Wojtyla's predecessor in the Archdiocese of Kracow. The priest's first lecture course on ethics to the seminarians of Kracow was conducted underground, as in wartime with the Nazis. Them in 1949 a man named Stefan Wyszynski became Archbishop of Warsaw, Primate of Poland, and Father Wojtyla's episcopal mentor—and things began to change.

Wojtyla's youth in free Poland was vigorous but marked by much personal sorrow: first his sister died, then his mother when he was nine, then his elder brother Edward of scarlet fever, when

---

[1] *John Paul II and the Catholic Restoration.*

Karol was thirteen. His father died eight years later. Nonetheless, Wojtyla became a brilliant student as well as a passionate skier, hiker and swimmer. He loved dance and the theatre; above all, with his baritone voice, he loved to sing. On the eve of the Nazi invasion, he and his father moved to Kracow, so that the son could attend the pride of Polish culture, Jagiellonian University.

Then the Nazis arrived, determined to destroy the Polish *untermenschen*. All public expression of Polish culture was forbidden. Universities and schools ceased to function legally; most Jagiellonian professors were deposited in the concentration camps, whence few emerged alive. Underground, however, the culture lived, perhaps even thrived. Wojtyla was able to continue his studies: he even helped to form an underground theatrical club, defiantly called Rhapsody Theatre, and "it was a matter of pride," says Johnson, "that they contrived to stage twenty-two performances of Polish classics in private houses and apartments."

It did not last. "In 1940 an able-bodied Polish male caught by Nazi patrols without a work-card," Johnson reports, "was liable to instant deportation as a slave labourer. Hence, in the winter Wojtyla found himself a labouring job in a stonequarry at Zakrzowek. The conditions were atrocious. The quarrymen worked in the open in inadequate clothing; to avoid frostbite they smeared grease or vaseline on their hands and faces." But the young Pole did not just chatter his teeth. He gained some practical experience of what it meant to be a modern industrial worker; and Zakrzowek also provided the theme for many of his poems about alienation, as well as the theme for Wojtyla's longest—and in Johnson's view "most striking"—poem, *The Quarry*.

The winter after his father's death, Karol was knocked down by a tram, and then run over by a truck as he lay on the road unconscious. His skull was fractured, and the slight stoop in his shoulders dates from this accident. Distant relations took him in and nursed him to recovery, and meanwhile life in his beloved Poland became ever more desperate and grim. While recuperating, Wojtyla started reading St. John of the Cross, and *Dark Night of the Soul*. Shortly thereafter, he decided to become a priest.

Upon beginning clandestine studies for the priesthood, the seminarian at first hoped to become a Carmelite, as John of the Cross had been. The Polish ecclesiastical authorities thought differently, however, and Wojtyla eventually began training for the

secular priesthood. Throughout, of course, his existence as a seminarian in Poland was only slightly less dangerous than if he had
pursued the same course in Elizabethan England; and indeed he
lived in a series of priest's "hiding holes" in private houses
through most of this period. More dangerous still, he joined an
underground group which took Jewish families out of the ghet-
tos, gave them new identity papers and, according to testimony of
the Anti-Defamation League of B'nai Brith, found them hiding
places when necessary and possible. On 6 August 1944, after the
Warsaw uprising, the Nazis rounded up all males in Kracow between the ages of fifteen and fifty—and had them summarily
shot. Wojtyla escaped the deathnet, and was thereafter hidden
with four other seminarians in the crumbling palace of Kracow's
Prince-Archbishop, Monsignor Adam Sapieha. Prince Sapieha
then personally ordained Father Wojtyla on All Saints Day,
November 1, 1946. The new priest celebrated his first Masses in
memory of his father, mother, and brother in the crypt of St.
Leonard in Wawel Castle, among the tombs of Polish kings.

Archbishop Sapieha recognized the talent in the new priest
he had ordained, and thus, Father Wojtyla was sent to study in
Rome, at the Dominican Angelicum. At that time, unlike the
Jesuit Gregorian, the Angelicum was a temple of Catholic ortho-
doxy. Among many of Father Wojtyla's outstanding professors
are to be counted Luigi Cardinal Ciappi, later Master of the
Apostolic Palace, and the great French Thomist Father Reginald
Garrigou-Lagrange.

Meanwhile, Archbishop Sapieha funded the (in those days)
relatively inexpensive vacations of his young protege: and Father
Wojtyla began what would some day be considered his celebrated
pastoral travels, though in these early, uncelebrated days, they
were confined to Western Europe. Throughout his studies, the
priest also kept in touch both with the Carmelites and Carmelite
spirituality: his doctoral thesis dealt with the doctrinal concept of
faith in the work of St. John of the Cross. In April 1948, he obtained his doctorate, *magnum cum laude*; doubtless with special joy,
the former underground student saw his degree confirmed at the
Jagiellonian the following December.

Back in Poland, his first three years were as a parish priest,
during which time he began what would prove many contests
with the Soviet-sponsored regime, nearly all of which have seen
the priest victorious in the long run. In particular, Father

Wojtyla established at this time his affinity both for and with the Catholic laity: and he even managed to get a church built by out-witting the Communist authorities with the enthusiastic support of volunteer labor. His administrative talent was also admired, and before the priest was granted sabbatical to continue his stud-ies, Wojtyla had established strong parochial institutions and Catholic societies, despite the disarray in Polish society on the heels of the Nazi and Communist invasions.

Back at the Jagiellonian, Wojtyla's interest first with exis-tentialism, then the phenomenology of Edmund Husserl led to the priest's philosophical thesis, *On the Possibility of Grounding Catholic Ethics on the System of Max Scheler.* Eventually, he began lecturing in social ethics at the Kracow Theological Seminary and in 1956 he was appointed Professor of Ethics at the prestigious Lublin University—which remains the only Catholic center of higher education in the entire Communist world. Formally, that Lublin chair of ethics still belongs to Pope John Paul II.

Father Wojtyla quickly established himself as one of Poland's leading ethical philosophers; in Johnson's words "with a reputation throughout the Catholic Church on the Continent, and indeed even beyond Catholic circles. His name became well known at international gatherings of phenomenologists. In Lublin he also established himself as an academic administrator, creating a new department of patristic studies."[2]

Despite his immersion in the academic world, however, the energetic young priest continued his involvement with the pas-toral life of the Kracow Archdiocese Primate and on 28 September 1958, as an auxiliary in Kracow, he became Poland's youngest bishop.

The immense figure of Primate Stefan Wyszynski continued to grow throughout this period. Central to Wyszynski's success

---

[2]Ken Woodward quoted Jefferson City Bishop Michael McAuliffe in the 10 October *Newsweek* to the effect that the Pontiff had never had experience with women religious who were theologians or who "went out into communities" but rather only with the sort restricted to menial tasks, like "maybe cooking." To the contrary, however—without wishing to disparage the ines-timable value of cooking I suspect—the Institute for Religious Education, a major branch of the Pontifical Department of Theology in Kracow, was headed by a nun when Archbishop Wojtyla was in charge of it. In Poland, nuns are involved in Catholic Religious Education at every level, including professor-ships, in catechetics, philosophical ethics, pedagogy, the history of ancient philosophy, the philosophy of religion, modern languages, Holy Scripture, etc. Polish nuns, however, tend to be Catholic.

with the Polish government, however, was the ruthlessness by which he refused to have any truck with the Communist supported pseudo-Catholic *Pax* movement under Boleslaw Piasecki. "In fact," as Farley Clinton observes in the 25 December 1981 *National Review* "what appeared to hamstring the Polish bishops in the 1950's actually became an asset" under Wyszynski. Since "the Communists had given Piasecki a profitable monopoly on all religious publishing, while the bishops had almost nothing ... their poverty made it impossible for them, even if they had wanted to, to play [establishment] games." Accordingly, "the Polish Church survived on the free offerings of the masses who saw their bishops as the real leaders of the nation."

The government jailed Wyszynski in 1953, and the imprisonment continued until the worker's uprising in 1956. "The Catholic bishops were gradually released from gaol," writes Johnson, "as the 1950's progressed," for "the sheer weight of Polish Catholicism began to tell against a regime which, from the start, was narrowly based and unsuccessful. Each time the government aroused the open anger of the population by its economic failures, it was forced to turn to the Catholic hierarchy for assistance ... the first unofficial agreement between the church and government came during the 1956 crisis; thereafter the church gradually strengthened its institutional position, working through informal deals, through Catholic deputies in the Sejm, the Polish parliament, and opposition groupings, which invariably took on a Catholic colouration."

As a result, the church kept Lublin University, expanded its seminaries, and increased its numbers of full-time workers. By the 1960's, the Catholic clergy was back to its pre-war strength, the percentage of vocations became even higher, the number of religious, chiefly nuns, grew from about 22,000 in 1939 to over 36,500 in 1960. By the end of the 1960's there were over 50 per cent more monastic foundations, priories and convents than before the war. As Johnson concludes, "These developments not only reversed the pattern of Catholicism in every country behind the Iron Curtain: they run counter to the secularizing trend in every country in Western Europe." Wyszynski was made a cardinal in 1956.

Meanwhile, due to his youth, and the extreme age of Kracow Archbishop Baziak (Sapieha's successor), Karol Wojtyla began to shoulder many of the routine operations within that Archdiocese. When the Archbishop died in 1962, his auxiliary was first made chief administrator, or Vicar Capitular; and then after

two years at the Second Vatican Council, he was appointed
Archbishop of Kracow by Pope Paul VI on 30 December 1963. In
that capacity, of course, as Johnson notes, "Wojtyla became, inevitably, the chief lieutenant to the embattled Polish primate."

Time has demonstrated rather clearly that if Cardinal
Wyszynski taught Bishop Wojtyla to be a great popular leader,
the student learned his lesson well. In fact, the combination of
the Bishop's charismatic gifts with the Cardinal's shrewd wisdom
proved formidable indeed. After Vatican II, Johnson observes,
though "there is some evidence the regime initially saw Wojtyla
as a liberal alternative to Wyszynski . . . the government soon
learnt to fear the skill with which [Wojtyla] used the changes introduced by the Council to reinforce the traditional populism of
the Polish church. They were dismayed also by the rapid growth
of his own personal popularity, the expertise he quickly developed in handling crowds and the enthusiastic response he evoked
from them. . . . Wojtyla showed notable energy and enthusiasm in
putting through the administrative reforms laid down by the
Council to promote lay participation at every level of church activity and even government. In 1971-72, for instance, he triumphantly organized an archdiocesan synod, following meticulous preparations, including detailed consultations with junior
clergy and laity [which showed] a vigorous belief in the Council's
notion of the church acting as a community."

Prior to the Council, Bishop Wojtyla's ideas on
"personalism," in particular his ruminations on the Sacrament of
Matrimony, were taking both pastoral and intellectual form. In
Kracow, he created the Family Institute, and put a female psychiatrist in charge of it who had survived the horrors of the
Ravensbrueck concentration camp. His thirty years pastoral and
episcopal experience prior to becoming the Bishop of
Rome—reinforced by his understanding of heroic Polish resistance to totalitarianism, as well as doubtless the sorrow of the
losses in his youth—gave him profound insights into the importance of the family as a check to the rapacious appetite of the
modern state. Yet if he learned how the Catholic family upholds
the dignity of man, neither was he ignorant of the devastating
toll when social forces worked against the family: the impact of
poverty, desertion, wife-beating, alcoholism, illegitimacy, and so
on, were the specific problems the Family Institute was designed
to confront.

In 1960 he produced two works on the Marriage Sacrament: his play *The Goldsmith's Shop*, which was performed before enthusiastic audiences and to good reviews throughout Western Europe as late as 1985, and his book, *Love and Responsibility*, a pastoral and ethical treatise on marriage, parenthood, abortion, birth control, and sex, whose impact on the universal Church would later prove definitive.

As Mr. Johnson explains: "The masterly style in which Wojtyla produced what might be termed a unified theory of sex and procreation seen through Christian eyes, made the book a notable success and it was translated into Italian, French, and Spanish. Paul VI read it while awaiting the report of the technical commission and doctors which John XXIII had appointed to study the birth-control issue. The intellectual rigour with which Wojtyla's book demolished the case for artificial contraception stiffened Pope Paul in his resolve to reject the majority findings of the commission ... when [Paul] came to write his own encyclical *Humanae Vitae* on the subject, much of Wojtyla's thinking reappeared in the argument and gave the document an original and positive content which a simple reiteration of traditional Catholic teaching would have lacked."[3]

At the Council itself, Archbishop Wojtyla was one of the some 10 per cent of the bishops who actually made oral interventions; a total of nine over the four sessions. Indeed, one of the more ironic—not to say comic—aspects of the Modernist campaign that accused the Pope of intending to invalidate the Council by means of the Extraordinary Synod, was that his Council interventions were on the side of precisely those documents the Modernists most frequently invoke as their justification for attacking the faith of Catholics: i.e., *On the Dignity of the Human Person, Gaudium Et Spes*, and also the order of *Lumen Gentium*, which put the hierarchy, the laity, and the religious of the Church within the context of Her Mystery as the People of God. Council Father Cardinal Gabriel-Marie Garrone, who

---

[3]Though John Paul II has yet to formalize the teaching of *Humanae vitae* in an *ex cathedra* statement, he did in fact proclaim it part of Divine Revelation and thus infallible near the end of his four-year series of Wednesday homilies on human sexuality. His precise words, on 18 July 1984, were that the prohibition of artificial contraception "is in accordance with the sum total of revealed doctrine contained in Biblical sources . . . precisely against the background of this full context, it becomes evident that the above-mentioned moral norm belongs not only to the natural moral law, but also to the moral order itself."

opened the Synod's First General Congregation with nostalgic recollections of Vatican II, told the Italian journal *30 Giorni* that Archbishop Wojtyla had in fact written one of the chapters in *Gaudium Et Spes.*[4]

In fact, during the period immediately following the Council, Archbishop Wojtyla showed considerable skill in applying the underlying principles in *Gaudium et spes*, by playing a major role in effecting genuine reconciliation between Germany and Poland against considerable odds, including the initial opposition of the Polish government. As a result, his diplomatic skills began to rival his reputation for pastoral zeal and theological and philosophical depth, which skills were often tested, since Wojtyla both supported and became deeply involved in Pope Paul VI's general policy of *Ostpolitik* with the Communist regimes of Eastern Europe. This, indeed, demanded particular delicacy not only due to Paul's clumsy and in fact shabby treatment of Hungary's Cardinal Mindszenty, but because of Cardinal Wyszynski's ill-concealed contempt for Pope Paul's approach. In fact, the Primate openly complained that the Polish Church would prove the chief victim of what he considered Paul's naivete, which embittered the Cardinal particularly because his warnings and protests went unheeded, and because he was generally kept in the dark about the process of negotiations. If the Polish Church represented the Church of silence, Wyszynski publicly remarked, then the Vatican was "the Church of the deaf."

Partly because of his moral impact on the matter of contraception, it was Wojtyla, as Johnson points out, "who, by virtue of his growing status and reputation in Rome, was best placed to put the Polish case privately. He did so with great skill and persistence, and by 1972 he had got the Pope to accept it. Thereafter the policies of the Vatican and the Polish episcopate were much

---

[4]The Pontiff's personal feelings about the Council were perhaps best captured on 29 September 1985, when during an Angelus gathering on the Feast of St. Michael and the Archangels, the Pope with some passion noted that "Providence disposed that, when the hour struck for the Council, I was just beginning my episcopate, having received episcopal ordination on 28 September 1958. Therefore I had the singular grace of participating in this great work and giving of my contributions to its labors. In this way, from its preparatory steps, through the various stages of its development, and then in the phase of the application of its commitments, Vatican II constituted the basis, climate, and inspirational center of my thoughts and activities as pastor of that beloved particular Church to which the goodness of the Lord had called me."

more closely coordinated, and the Poles were given, in effect, a veto on Vatican initiatives in the East,"—albeit with distinct exceptions, as the Mindszenty case demonstrates.

Archbishop Wojtyla also helped shape the Polish episcopate's policy of determined presence at various Catholic international gatherings—such as the 1976 Eucharistic Congress in Philadelphia for example—and he became Poland's most frequent representative. Moreover, his impact at the post-Council synods was such that in 1971 and 1974 he was elected to the Secretariat of the Synodal Council; was chosen to act as the *rapporteur* to the full Synod for the study group on *The Gospel in the Modern World*; and was elected chairman of the Secretariat for the 1977 Synod on Catechesis, about which, as Pope, he would later write an Apostolic Exhortation presenting the Synod's major themes. When Pope Paul appointed him to the Cardinalate on 29 May 1967, Father Wojtyla presaged his election to the Papacy and proved himself very much one of Cardinal Wyszynski's priests, by arriving in Rome the following month without the money to buy his Cardinal's robes.

Finally, in 1976, Pope Paul honored Cardinal Wojtyla by inviting him to give a traditional series of sermons to His Holiness and the Pontifical household during the penitential season of Lent. Twenty-two sermons in all, these were received with great acclaim, and later published under the title *Sign of Contradiction.*

Meanwhile, despite the seemingly grim position of the Catholic Church at the death of Pope Paul VI, the seeds of his work and of the Council itself could be seen in the unprecedented international character of the 111 Cardinals who arrived in Rome to elect Cardinal Luciani as Pope John Paul I. A clean one hundred of them had been elevated by Paul, and were thus Princes of the Council at their first Conclave. Only twenty-seven were Italian; twenty-nine came from Eastern and Western Europe, eleven from North America, nineteen from Latin America, thirteen from Asia and Oceania, and twelve from Africa. Most were diocesan bishops, but there were three Jesuits, three Franciscans, two Dominicans, a Benedictine, a Salesian, a Redemptorist, and an Oblate of Mary. Upon the new Pope's death, Karol Wojtyla returned to Italy once again, as well as to a small sanctuary in Mentorella, where he had made many retreats, beginning from his days at the Angelicum in the late 1940's. It was on a mountain, some twelve and one-half miles of winding roads up from Palestrina, itself 25 miles from Rome. On October 14, 1978, his latest retreat completed, Cardinal Wojtyla got into his borrowed car, but the car wouldn't start. Thus, as in days past, His Eminence began to hike down the mountain, then to hitchhike; finally, he waved down Christendom's secret hero, one Candido Nardi, who understood the situation and got the Cardinal to Palestrina in seventeen minutes flat. There His Grace took a bus to Rome, and arrived just in time to don vestments and join the procession of Cardinals into the Sistine Chapel.

Two days later the Archbishop of Kracow was elected Bishop of Rome. He was the youngest Vicar of Christ in 132 years, the first Prince of the Apostles to come from outside Italy in 456 years, and the first Slavic Successor of St. Peter ever. He was also, according to his titles, the Supreme Pontiff of the Universal Church, the Patriarch of the West, Primate of Italy, Archbishop and Metropolitan of the Roman Province, and Sovereign of the city-state known as the Vatican. Before accepting these titles, Cardinal Wojtyla's last act was to seek and receive the personal approval of his primate, Stefan Cardinal Wyszynski. He then chose the name John Paul II, went out to the balcony overlooking St. Peter's Square and said in perfect Italian, but with a Polish accent:

"The cardinals have summoned a new Bishop of Rome. They have called him from a far-away country, far away, yet close, because of our communion in the traditions of the Church . . . though I was afraid to accept this responsibility, yet I do so in a spirit of obedience to the Lord, and total faithfulness to Mary, our most holy Mother."

II. Clericalism, Abortion, and the Revolt of the Laity

> *"In the village of Chelmo the local police watched several times a week as a boy of 13, his ankles in chains, shuffled through the village to get grass for the [rabbits of the] SS. 'Everyone in Chelmo knew him.' Four hundred thousand Jews were murdered in the village of Chelmo. The Nazis burned 2000 people every day, said the survivor. 'No one (local people) shouted. Everyone went about his work. It was silent. Peaceful.'"*
>
> Father Henry Fehren, columnist for *U. S. Catholic*

> *"They say they want to dialogue. They want to dialogue about abortion. There's nothing to dialogue about. You don't dialogue with murder."*
>
> Walker Percy

Chesterton points out somewhere that great literature never originates in a vacuum, that only a rich cultural soil can produce a Dante, a Shakespeare, a Dostoevski. The same, perhaps, can be said about the origins of good bishops, good priests, or, for that matter, a great liturgy. When Stefan Cardinal Wyszynski became Primate of Poland in 1949, for example, a superficial or worldly view of the Church might have suggested that the Poles were no more ready for a Catholic renaissance then, than Africa was in 1965.

And yet, the speed by which the historicist clerics in the West were able to dismantle most functional as well as real expressions of Catholic belief, devotions, spirituality and so on, with so little effective resistance, and in such a short time, is daunting. For all the pain and misery this as it were Rahnerian *blitzkrieg* has wrought these past twenty years, for all the jackboot tactics and arrogant gnosticism, one cannot escape the sense that the Catholics of the West, if not exactly ready for all this, had nonetheless long since lost the virility necessary to fight against it. We all bought televisions, accepted the soulless suburban architecture, became obsessed with comfort and convenience, and abandoned any pretence of an even vague aspiration to cultural depth. Pope John Paul II has labeled and condemned the underlying tendency in all this with the painfully appropriate word, Consumerism.

Nonetheless, for all their debility in the face of a cultural and clerical onslaught, the Catholic laity in the United States would prove not altogether as dead as everyone had thought. For too long, no doubt, it kept expecting the clergy to somehow right itself, for the forces of Tradition to rally, as James Hitchcock put it, for *something* to happen; and yet, for too long, nothing did. Still, there was, as Ralph McInerny observed about Thomas Sheehan's *New York Review of Books* piece about the End of Catholicism, "a tremulo in the triumphant voice. On the one hand, Sheehan purports to speak for the winners in a battle for the soul of the Church; on the other, he is profoundly worried about Popes and prelates and other folk, who, strangely enough, make up the vast body of the Church."

Sheehan had reason to tremble, as the social forces in the United States were to discover when the Supreme Court legalized abortion-on-demand on 22 January 1973. For though, as Sobran says, "the secularist forces control such things as the major television networks, the universities, the leading newspapers and magazines, the movie industry, and the public education system," though "the court system, dominated by these same forces, has banished rival forces, especially religion, from important areas," though these forces even gained essential control of the bureaucracy of the Catholic Church, and though together they used all the formidable means at their disposal to dismiss, ridicule, in fact to silence opposition to abortion-on-demand—despite it all, they did not succeed.

And they did not succeed because of the Catholic laity. Finally, gruesome as the provocation was, American Catholics were able to focus on a specific evil, were able even to agree on a specific goal—a Constitutional Amendment—and not least were able to begin recognizing the fatuity at the heart of the previous decade's enthusiasms. And there was more, for the abortion battle forced Catholics to learn political skills; indeed, the pro-life movement has been fueled primarily by women who would never otherwise have wasted their time with the superficial pleasures of the political arena.

These skills were not learned quickly, however. It began with bake sales and emotionally naive complaints. Then one Nellie Gray organized a protest demonstration in the dead of winter, the first anniversary of *Roe vs. Wade*, and over 50,000 came, the vast majority Catholics. She called it the March for Life, and to be sure, the television stations refused to cover it, as did the *New York Times*; the *Washington Post* put the story in a back section describing local events. But the protesters came the following year, more of them, still mostly Catholics, so that the media finally gave some begrudging attention; and the official pro-abortion line revived formal anti-Catholic bigotry, charging that a few fanatics wished to impose their morality on the good, free folks who had no qualms about imposing their morality on the life of an unborn child. Still the right-to-lifers came, all the while organizing in their local communities, whereupon the politicians began to take note, laws began to pass in Congress, were challenged, fought, usually overthrown in the Courts, but the fight went on, the skills increased, as did the bigotry and the ridicule. By the 1980's, the March for Life was drawing well over a hundred thousand (as I have witnessed), though Dan Rather was still reporting that it could gather together only some "4000, mostly parochial schoolchildren." And no matter how many tens of thousands turned out to support the rights of the unborn child, the pro-abortionists would need but a dozen to win equal coverage in the major outlets of the media.

Nonetheless, though persistent, the movement grew slowly. Both major parties wished the issue to go away, which is to say they hoped Americans would quietly accept abortion-on-demand, and that Catholic opposition would fade. But it did not. In 1975 Republican President Gerald Ford appointed abortion-mogul Nelson Rockefeller Vice President, and he was confirmed by Congress, as was the pro-abortion Supreme Court Justice John Paul Stevens, whom Ford chose to replace William Douglas. In 1976 Jimmy Carter announced he was against abortion, won Iowa that way, then clarified his position by pointing out that he was personally opposed. The sophistication of the anti-abortion forces by that time, however, had gained enough, with other forces, to drive Rockefeller off Ford's ticket, and replace him with the pro-life Senator Robert Dole. They had also gained enough to force decisions: the Democratic Party, despite the opinions of the majority of all too passive Democrats, forcefully affirmed the glories of *Roe vs. Wade* in its 1976 Platform, and then again in 1980 and 1984. The Republicans, meanwhile, after a half century in the American political swamp, stayed there in 1976 with but a tepid opposition to *Roe vs. Wade*. During the years of the Carter Administration, however, the Republicans began to see that antagonism to *Roe* would not go away; and people began to speak of analogies to the Supreme Court's pro-slavery decision of 1857 called *Dred Scott*, which preceded the American Civil War by four years.

The Catholics had proved the leaven, had kept the issue alive when no one else would. By 1978 the Evangelical Protestants began to rise from their 50-year political slumber, as rose, without precedent, the Orthodox Jews—and '78 was the year it became clear that a pro-life position at worst did no harm, unlike the pro-abortion position which in election after election proved fatal in both the House and Senate. In 1980 Ronald Reagan was riding the populist crest[5] and 12 pro-abortion Senators—one-third of those standing for office—were repudiated at the polls, among them some of the biggest names in Democratic Party politics, such as Magnagson, Talmadge, Bayh, Nelson, and the 1972 Presidential standard-bearer McGovern.[6] Meanwhile, most pro-life Senators were re-elected, and the Republican Party, whose 1980 Platform was aggressively pro-life (though it got even more aggressive in 1984), took control of the Senate for the first time since 1952, and in 1982 kept control for the first time in 54 years. It kept control again in 1984. That was the year that Reagan—who, despite criticism of some of his tactics (and despite such assistance as was continually offered by Will Caron and the USCC), had not wavered in his commitment to the pro-life cause—was re-elected by one of the largest electoral and popular vote landslides in history; and indeed won more states that year than any presidential candidate

[5]And publicly apologized for the liberalized abortion bill he'd signed as governor of California in 1967 (for rape and incest only, everyone said at the time).

[6]The winners were no less surprising, and included a Mormon woman in Florida—the three pro-abortion women who ran for Senate were all defeated—a Catholic in Oklahoma and even *Alabama*, as well as the first pro-life Italian Al D'Amato, who beat the pro-abortion Jacob Javits in the New York Republican primary, despite Javits's 24 years in the Senate.

ever, losing only his pro-abortion opponent's home state, and that by but a few thousand votes.

Abortion was not the only factor in all this, but it was a critical factor, and arguably the *central* factor, in that it undermined the moral superiority upon which so many Democrats and liberals had sought to base their reputations. This also, of course, went beyond mere electoral politics, which is why the pro-life movement provoked such hatred from the Modernist establishment and why figures such as Andrew Greeley promptly began to denounce pro-lifers with shrillness and regularity in, for example, his widely distributed column among diocesan Catholic newspapers. In fact, the battle for human rights of the unborn soon became a lay resistance against Modernist clericalism as well, and the two struggles are now intimately intertwined. As early as 1970, the Catholic convert Robert Pearson began organizing pregnancy counseling centers to show women the reality of abortion and to provide practical assistance to those with crisis pregnancies. By 1986, there were thousands of these Pearson-inspired centers throughout the United States, saving perhaps millions of lives, and poised to become a powerful source of social assistance if *Roe vs. Wade* is overturned. In addition, because of the cooperation engendered between Catholics and Evangelicals, these centers and the pro-life movement in general have probably done more than any single factor to promote the serious ecumenism called for by Vatican II. Accordingly, the pro-life movement has also provoked an unprecedented outbreak of anti-Evangelical bigotry from the Modernist establishment, such as you will never hear directed against pro-abortion Protestants who dutifully pay their obedience to the secular agenda.

Also by 1986, the abortion clinics themselves were being confronted daily by thousands of demonstrators; and perhaps another million children have been saved—indeed who knows how many?—by the thousands of sidewalk counselors who each day stand outside the aboratoriums offering assistance and urging mothers not to abort. Two bishops that I know of, Thomas Welsh of Allentown and John McGann of Rockville Center on Long Island, have joined the laity in this Christian work, though hundreds of priests and nuns have also done so. Meanwhile, in yet another analogy to the American Civil War, Catholics and Protestants have increasingly begun to engage in civil disobedience against the clinics, and occasionally to invoke the ancient

Catholic doctrine of the necessity defense by demolishing them with fire.

Still, perhaps the most profound contribution of the anti-abortion movement is that inevitably it began to expose those flaws in modern culture which go deeper even than abortion itself. In the early days, reacting defensively to the bigotry, Catholics sought to downplay the religious motivation at the root of their struggle. In fact, there is every indication that in the early '70's, they naively hoped the parliamentary procedures of a decaying West would be sufficient to turn the tide; progressively, however, the connection between abortion and the entire fevered emptiness of the modern era began to emerge, so that pornography, state-mandated sex education, feminism, contraception, population control, materialism, utilitarianism, and ultimately the consumerist ethic itself began to come under attack.[7]

Thus inevitably, strains over strategy began to appear. In 1978, a major split took place when Judie Brown broke from the moderate line of the National Right-to-Life Committee (NRLC) that dealt strictly with abortion, and formed the American Life

---

[7] "Human beings are mysteries," Joe Sobran writes for example in the 31 December 1985 *National Review*. "They deserve to be treated as mysteries, not stripped open like a cellophane package . . . people do fail in love, all the time. That is why the essential kinds of love need social support. The problem is that we are currently giving our support not so much to the wrong people as to the wrong side of our nature, the side that wants love on the cheap. . . . The price is high, but the rewards of loyalty and fidelity are priceless. To be a parent is more than a joy: it is to be related to the world in a radically different way from the way of youth, to see another who is not 'wholly other,' but a strangely free part of yourself."

"Socialist utopianism," on the other hand he continues, "has gone hand in hand with sexual utopianism . . . The feminist movement, with its bitterness against men, is at least an understandable reaction against all the lies of sexual 'liberation,' which has been particularly injurious and insulting to women; there was no such movement or general mood in the days when marriage was the norm. A woman was expected to be chaste; and though this was derided as a double standard, it gave women a special protection against male aggression. There was no confusion about what a lecherous man was asking of her. She had the right not only to refuse, but to take offense at improper advances. If women could be virgins again, there would be no feminism. Women are now fair game for the men who prize them least, and they know it, and they resent it, and they are right; but they also know that to speak of a woman's 'honor' is to sound ridiculously quaint. By the same token, a man's honor used to consist largely in respect for women's; that has changed too. Is everybody happy?"

League (originally called American Life Lobby), which focused not less on abortion, but also on these deeper roots of the abortion culture. In its early days, the League had some trouble attracting support because of its radical image; by 1983, it was clearly the organizational leader of the right-to-life movement, whereas the NRLC had come to be regarded as something of a kindly, if occasionally troublesome old uncle that was utterly ineffectual in addressing the militant new mood.

In fact, by 1984, groups that had once been considered slight embarrassments, proved instead to have been prophetic, and are now as it were the cutting edge of the movement. Among others, these include Catholics United for Life,[8] which from the mid-70's has advocated those originally embarrassing positions that within a decade would be at the heart of the movement: the need for sidewalk counseling, militant confrontation, the umbilical connection between abortion and contraception, and not least the insistence that, rather than incidental, Roman Catholicism was indeed not only fundamental to the pro-life struggle, but also the solution to the historicist domination that made the abortion industry inevitable. Of equal, and perhaps ultimately even greater impact, were the confrontational tactics of the six-foot four-inch bullhorn-toting former Benedictine novice Joseph Scheidler, and his Chicago-based Pro-Life Action League. Scheidler did not mince words: the abortionists and their allies were no better than Nazis, and history would some day regard the pro-life movement as it now does the resistance movements against Hitler during the Second World War. At the beginning of 1985, *Newsweek* magazine reluctantly acknowledged what the movement had known for some time, which was that Scheidler had become their philosophical and tactical general. Meanwhile, despite some differences, both the structural and political cooperation between Catholics and Evangelicals continued to grow daily.

In addition, as Catholics began to notice the similarity in both tactics and perspective between the abortion establishment and the Modernist clerics, they began to give the documents of

---

[8]Which, interestingly, was originally a kind of hippie commune. Composed mostly of Jews, the commune began searching for truth in a more earnest matter upon witnessing, and doubtless to some extent suffering, the dissolution that struck the communes in the '70's. The group resisted Catholicism, however, until *Roe vs. Wade*; whereupon the horror of that decision broke their resistance and they converted to the Faith *en masse*. They are now a Third Order Dominican community.

Vatican II greater scrutiny, in particular that call in *Apostolicam actuositatem* (On the Apostolate of the Laity) which "earnestly exhorts the laity to take a more active part ... in the explanation and defense of Christian principles and in the correct application of them to the problems of our time." Clearly, neo-Modernism had become one of the acute problems of the time; and by the 1980's Catholics were not only saying so in increasing numbers, they had organized to fight it by employing the same political skills that had been learned in the fight against abortion.

By the time Pope John Paul II announced the Extraordinary Synod, this organizing had already resulted in the creation of many effective new national and local groups and journals, and the strengthening of older ones which had resisted the Modernist tide of the 1960's and 1970's. Some of these, to be sure, were tinged with a certain Modernist nationalism (such as had been condemned, among others, by Pope Leo XIII), as a reactive means of battling against the dominance of left-wing historicism in the USCC; but the majority of these journals and organizations were Catholic across the board; and even those tinged with nationalism have carried on *serious* debate with Catholic orthodoxy, something the Modernists have always been careful to avoid.

Despite the significant contributions of numerous smaller groups, within the Church as such "the largest, best-organized, and apparently most influential ... is Catholics United for the Faith (CUF)"—as admitted by the 8 June 1984 *National Catholic Reporter*.[9] "In its declaration of purpose, CUF quotes profusely from the council documents, stressing two great principles: the urgent need for the laity to take a more active role in the mission of the church, and the necessity of every Catholic to accept the ordinary teaching of the church as binding in conscience." In fact, according to its own literature "the first task of CUF members is actively to seek after holiness, in accordance with the teaching of the Second Vatican Council that 'all in the Church, whether they belong to the hierarchy or are cared for by it, are called to holiness.' "

Founded in 1968 by Catholic converts, CUF has had considerable influence right along, but especially so after the lay challenge to Modernist clericalism found its voice. There was a time, in fact, when the U.S. Catholic Bishops were not so hostile toward

---

[9]Which otherwise almost always denounces CUF as "right-wing."

CUF as they presently seem to be. In 1977, for example, when Archbishop Gerety was leading his charge against Vatican II during the formation of the National Catechetical Directory (NCD), CUF submitted nearly a tenth of the total input into the NCD, more than any other single organization in the United States; and its influence was even given credit by USCC Education Secretary Msgr. Wilfred Paradis, who wrote a letter to the organization saying, "You can, I am sure, see the mark of CUF in many of the passages of the [NCD] document."

CUF also conducts retreats, publishes numerous local newsletters and one international circulation, sponsors a speaker's bureau and a publications service; it boasts 130 chapters worldwide, including branches in Australia, New Zealand, Southeast Asia, Africa, Europe, and the United States. But the organization's two chief claims to notoriety are its extensive catechetical analyses and its exhaustive research files. Apart from devastating critiques of the heretical catechisms the bishops have allowed to flourish since Vatican II, CUF also supplies lists of orthodox catechisms as well as supplementary religious education programs for parents. Meanwhile, a simple phone call or letter to the national office in New Rochelle, New York will usually provide the inquirer with whatever she wants to know about the public statements of various bishops, theologians, priests, nuns, Modernist or orthodox—which doubtless explains why CUF is so loathed and feared in certain quarters. An additional explanation could be its extensive contacts at the Vatican, even though CUF officials refuse to lobby Rome without first addressing their concerns to the diocesan bishops involved, as encouraged by Vatican II and the Revised Code of Canon Law. There is, however, considerable evidence that CUF played a key role in Cardinal Ratzinger's decision to order the removal of Archbishop Gerety's *imprimatur* from *Christ Among Us*.

Among the formidable new Catholic periodicals, meanwhile, are *Catholicism in Crisis*, despite its tension between Ralph McInerny's orthodoxy and Michael Novak's neo-conservatism;[10] the *New Oxford Review*, a sharply anti-consumerist journal that attacks neo-conservatism as forcibly as it does Arianism;[11] and doubtless the most brilliant, Michael Jones' *Fidelity*, the logo of

---

[10]Though still a Modernist, Novak has repudiated the political liberalism of the '80's, and is reportedly less enthusiastic about Hans Kueng than he used to be.

[11]NOR is also unique because it started as an Anglican publication until its editor, Dale Vree, converted to Catholicism in 1983.

which bears the exhortation in Nehemiah 2:17 : "You see the trouble we are in: Jerusalem is in ruins, its gates have been burnt down. Come, let us rebuild the walls of Jerusalem and suffer this indignity no longer."

Older examples of aggressive and orthodox Catholic journalism include *The Wanderer*, the *National Catholic Register* (both news weeklies) and *Triumph* magazine. Founded by the convert Brent Bozell in 1966, *Triumph* lasted only nine years before folding just as the message it preached began to take hold in 1975; but few will disagree that it provided the theoretical foundation for an entire generation of Catholic intellectuals. The *Register*, meanwhile, has been around for most of the century, but has become more formidable as the alternative to the *Reporter* under Fran Maier, who took over as editor in 1981 while in his early 30's. *The Wanderer*, successfully dismissed by the Modernists in the 1970's, grew in the 1980's to be easily the most influential Catholic paper in the country, as demonstrated by increasing secular and episcopal attacks against it. Its unapologetically aggressive approach was perhaps best captured by a 1985-86 advertising campaign, in which *The Wanderer* claimed to be a paper for Catholics who "think the important thing about Pope John Paul II is not that he's photogenic, but that he tells the truth," as well as one for those "looking for a journal that isn't shy about naming names and exposing those who distort Church teaching, especially when they try to do it in the name of the Church."

And thus the beat goes on, with Modernist clericalism being challenged at virtually every front. Perhaps the most recent example is a group of Catholic women who at the beginning of 1985 formed Women for Faith and Family in response to the ominous tone of yet another proposed Episcopal pastoral letter—this one on women—under the chairmanship of Joliet Bishop Joseph Imesch. The direction this pastoral was likely to take was quickly revealed when media reported that one of the nuns chosen to help organize the preliminary hearings had signed the pro-abortion ad in the *New York Times*. The nun, Anne Carr—one of the *Commonweal* respondents to Sheehan's piece in *The New York Review of Books*—diplomatically resigned, but the increasingly stacked and frantic tone of the hearings even after her resignation showed that her views remained influential. Indeed, the potential for open schism inherent in this new pastoral—particularly in light of the disparity between Bishop Malone's September 16 report to the Synod Secretariat and the reality of Modernist power within Catholic bureaucratic structures—was given some attention by Rosemary Ruether's claim, as noted by James Hitchcock in the 4 August 1985 *Register*, that "she and other feminists, in formal dialogue with American bishops, have found some of the latter basically sympathetic to their position," though Ruether "laments that they do not translate this into public action."

Taking a somewhat different view, Women for Faith and Family decided to help their bishops by issuing an Affirmation of Catholic Women, which asserts that "because of the assaults against the Christian faith and family by elements within contemporary society," and also because, "we adhere to the Catholic Christian faith as expressed in Holy Scripture, the Nicene, Apostolic and Athanasian Creeds ... we wish to affirm our desire to realize our vocations and our duty as Christians and as women in accordance with these authentic teachings, following the example and instruction of Our Savior Jesus Christ, and the example of Mary, His Mother."

In doing so, the Affirmation notes that "through God's grace our female nature affords us distinct physical and spiritual capabilities with which to participate in the Divine Plan for creation. Specifically our natural function of childbearing endows us with the spiritual capacity for nurture, instruction, compassion and selflessness, which qualities are necessary to the establishment of families ... and to the establishment of a Christian social order ...

"Accordingly, we reject all ideologies which seek to eradicate the natural and essential distinction between the sexes, which debase and devalue womanhood, family life and the nurturing role of women in society ... we affirm the intrinsic sacredness of all human life and we reject the notion that abortion ... is the 'right' of any human being, male or female. Furthermore, we recognize that the specific role of ordained priesthood is intrinsically connected with and representative of the begetting creativity of God in which only human males can participate. Human females ... have a different and distinct role within the Church and in society from that accorded to men," and "can no more be priests than men can be mothers."

In conclusion, the Affirmation states that "we stand with the Second Vatican Council which took for granted the distinct roles for men and women in the family and in society and affirmed that Christian education must impart knowledge of this distinction," and "we pledge our wholehearted support to Pope

John Paul II. We adhere to his apostolic teaching concerning all aspects of family life and roles for men and women in the Church and in society, especially as contained in the Apostolic Exhortation *Familiaris consortio*"—with its explicit condemnation of contraception—"and we resolve to apply the principles contained therein to our own lives, our families, and our communities, God being our aid."

It may not be too harsh to say that more and more Catholics yearn for an episcopate capable of publishing a statement, not to say a pastoral, with the quiet and noble clarity of this document.

If that day is nonetheless in the distant future, it is perhaps less distant because of things like the Affirmation of Catholic Women, which itself has already garnered tens of thousands of signatures of support, and this with virtually no money, and very little publicity, since most diocesan papers have proved reluctant to publish, much less promote it.

Indeed, there is liable to be some question as to whether the bishops' new pastoral or the Affirmation ought to be considered the authentically Catholic document, not only because of the doubts Cardinal Ratzinger has raised about bishops conferences, but also because in January 1986 Women for Faith and Family revealed their Affirmation had been signed by the 1979 winner of the Nobel Peace Prize, Mother Teresa of Calcutta. The bishops may find it difficult to convince Catholics they should repudiate Mother Teresa in favor of Rosemary Ruether.

Therein, in fact, may lie the nub of the deepening crisis within Roman Catholicism in the United States: the declining ability of the bishops to convince people of their good faith. A chief hope, indeed goal, of the Catholic laity, as called for by Vatican II, is to help their bishops proclaim Catholic truth without apology or equivocation in union with the successor of Peter. Another is to remind bishops of their obligation to protect Catholics from enemies of the Faith, especially when these enemies wear a Roman collar. Lay activists of the early 1970's generally staunchly maintained that bishops were all sound men who were badly advised and that the main fault lay with their middle management; later, the orthodox hope was that the bishops were pretty much victimized by their staffs. The problem now, however, as in the days of Arianism in the 4th century, is that the faithful are beginning to suspect that many of the bishops themselves, for all their judicial authority, are the principal ecclesial

enemy—and the chief obstacle to the Council's call for an authentic Catholic renewal.

Curiously, Archbishop Edouard Gagnon made similar spec-
ulations to me when discussing the American bishops shortly after his appointment to the Roman Curia in 1983, in an interview
that was subsequently published in *The Wanderer*. Cardinal
Bernardin was rumored to have been upset by the contents of
that interview; what is certain is that he lodged a formal protest
against it with the Vatican Secretary of State, Agostino Cardinal
Casaroli. The protest did not, however, prevent John Paul II from
honoring Gagnon by promoting him to the College of Cardinals
in 1985.

III. To the Holy Year:
The Pontificate of John Paul II
through June of 1983

"The people accept this Pope of 'hard sayings'. They welcome him, cheer his tough message, and accept him as their spiritual leader. In an era when some voices have pleaded for a Church of accommodation, perhaps the 'common' people in every country and culture are reminding us it is not true that 'hard sayings' alienate; what alienates is when the Church says nothing at all."
Our Sunday Visitor, 18 May 1980

"I have seen a lot of heads of state in my life since I was 13 years old. I have seen many leaders, including President Franklin D. Roosevelt and others, that I found impressive. But I find the Pope to be one of the most remarkable men I have ever met."
King Hassan II of the Maghreb and Morocco

"When he assumed command," the 12 February 1985 *Catholic Eye* observed about John Paul II, "his forces were disorganized, some mutinous; morale was low. As with Washington at Valley Forge, a bitter winter had to be endured while the core of the army was hardened for battle. This required steady determination, unflinching willpower, and, most of all, the cardinal virtue of fortitude. Plus getting out and visiting the troops: good soldiers love and serve best the leaders they *know.*"

And visit the troops he did. Not three months went by before the former Karol Wojtyla set foot in the Western Hemisphere, in anticlerical Mexico no less, there to begin his challenge to the certain aspects of liberation theology that were in fact nothing more than undisguised historicist Marxism. Six months later he returned to Poland, and a little more than a year after that a very interesting strike broke out in the town of Gdansk, led by a man named Lech Walesa. Before a year of his papacy was finished, the Pontiff had visited Ireland and the United States; his second year began with a trip to Istanbul, known once as Constantinople, where John Paul shifted the ecumenical focus of the Church to Eastern Orthodoxy and—despite protestations to the contrary—away from increasingly secularized Protestantism.

With his first encyclical in the spring of 1979, the Pastor of the Universal Church launched what would in a very real sense define the entire challenge of his Papacy. Entitled *Redemptor hominis*, The Redeemer of Man, it charged into the very teeth of the historicist heresy by proclaiming the dignity of man over all the institutions that man creates—in particular the State. This was not, however, merely a humanist document, for it pointed out that man's dignity was firmly grounded in the Incarnation, Resurrection, and Redemption of Christ, indeed in the awesome Mystery that God should assume our human state for the sake of our salvation.

In hardening the troops for battle, the Pontiff also quickly made clear that the era of anxiety and self-pity among priests was at an end. Between the period 1940 and 1965, according to data released by Fichter in 1968, less than one of every thousand ordained priests in the United States abandoned his calling prior to death. Such resolution was common throughout the rest of the world as well, until the post-Council Modernist onslaught; during the reign of Paul VI tens of thousands of priests were released from their vows. John Paul at first simply refused to give any dispensations at all. On the anniversary of Christ's founding of the priesthood, His Vicar released a Holy Thursday Letter to All Priests which gently but firmly pointed out that henceforth "since the priesthood is given to us so that we can unceasingly serve others, after the example of Christ the Lord, the priesthood cannot be renounced because of the difficulties that we meet and the sacrifices asked of us. Like the apostles, we have left everything to follow Christ; therefore we must persevere beside Him also through the Cross."

Then, upon his return from Ireland and the United States and on the first anniversary of his Papacy, His Holiness released the Apostolic Exhortation *Catechesi tradendae*, expressing the mind of the 1977 Synod of Bishops. *On Catechetics in Our Time,* as it was called in English, also zeroed in on themes that would be central to the Wojtylan Papacy: "the person who becomes a disciple of Christ," it insisted, "has the right to receive the word of faith not in mutilated, falsified or diminished form, but whole and entire, in all its rigor and vigor." Instead, it charged, "language today is being misused for ideological mystification, for mass conformity in thought and for reducing man to the level of an object," and consequently "the desire to . . . keep up with fashions . . . has often resulted in certain catechetical works which bewilder the young and even adults . . . by deliberately or unconsciously omitting elements essential to the Church's faith," and therefore "care should be taken not to reduce Christ to His humanity alone or His message to a no more earthly dimension," but ". . . He should be recognized as the Son of God." Under the subheading "Bishops," *Catechesi tradendae* sought to remind then that "needless to say, although your zeal must sometimes impose upon you the thankless task of denouncing deviations and correcting errors, it will much more often win for you the joy and consolations of seeing your Churches flourishing because catechesis is given them as the Lord wishes."

In April 1979 the Congregation for the Doctrine of the Faith, then headed by 74-year-old Franjo Cardinal Seper, condemned the work of the French Dominican Jacques Pohiers, whose "reformulations" of Christian doctrine were understood to be nothing more than an explicit denial of the resurrection of Christ. Indeed, the Congregation also kept up its conversations with Edward Schillebeeckx, and coincidentally completed one of those on 15 December 1979, while His Holiness was giving a lecture about the irreformable nature of defined doctrine as well as the importance of the *magisterium,* at the Jesuit Gregorian University. Later that afternoon, after nearly a decade and a half of conversations with Hans Kueng, the Congregation formally condemned his work. Shortly thereafter, the German bishops announced that Father Kueng was no longer qualified to teach Catholic theology due to his apparent inability to grasp the subject. This decision was not impossibly influenced by the Cardinal Archbishop of Munich, who would succeed Cardinal Seper as head of the Congregation for the Doctrine of the Faith in 1982.

Meanwhile, the material schism of the Church in Holland had reached scandalous proportions. In March 1979 the Pontiff began a series of conversations with each of Holland's bishops individually, and then announced a Synod of the Dutch Episcopate, which took place from January 14 to 31, 1980. It closed with 46 propositions upholding the traditional teachings of the Faith, in particular priestly celibacy, as well as a condemnation of unauthorized liturgical experimentation, intercommunion with non-Catholics, and the employment of defrocked priests—licitly or otherwise—as teachers of theology. By the Pope's pastoral visit to Holland in May 1985—one of the seminal events of his Papacy to date—virtually the entire Dutch episcopate had become solidly orthodox.

In 1980, John Paul released his second major encyclical, *Dives in misericordia* (Rich in Mercy), which pointed out that justice without mercy is not, in fact, justice at all. In February of that year, he also released an Apostolic Letter to the world's bishops, and through them to its Catholic priests, called *Dominicae cenae*. Building on the Council's liturgical document *Sacrosanctum Concilium* as well as Pope Paul's encyclical *Mysterium Fidei*, the letter was remarkable, and perhaps unprecedented, in that it contained a public apology to the laity for the gross sacrilege to which the Eucharist had been subject in so many places since the Council. "I would like to ask forgiveness," the Pontiff wrote, "in my own name, and in the name of all of you, venerable and dear brothers in the Episcopate, for everything which ... through the at times partial, one-sided and erroneous applications of the directives of the Second Vatican Council, may have caused scandal and disturbance concerning the interpretation of the doctrine and the veneration due to this great Sacrament."

In May that year, the Pope commenced the first of what by 1985 would prove three apostolic visits to the thriving Church in Africa. In the same month he also visited the devastated Church in France, whose episcopate was as schismatic in tendency as the one in Holland had been. Shortly after that, he appointed the brilliant Jewish convert Jean-Marie Lustiger as Archbishop of Paris; in 1983 Lustiger was made a Cardinal.

In July the Pope went to Brazil, in November to West Germany. The Jesuit Robert Drinan, a consistent opponent of human rights for unborn children, was forced to leave his post in the United States House of Representatives. Archbishop Jadot was replaced as Apostolic Delegate to the United States by Archbishop Pio Laghi, who later became Papal Nuncio when the Vatican and the United States established diplomatic relations in 1984. In August (1980), Solidarity was founded in Poland. And this was also the year the Pope began his weekly discussions on human sexuality. At the end of 1980, the bishops gathered in Rome for a Synod on the family; a year later, John Paul expressed its will through the Apostolic Exhortation *Familiaris consortio*.

On 14 January 1981 His Holiness granted personal prelature status to *Opus Dei*, whether to keep an eye on some of its disputed recruiting techniques, or as a counterpoint to the Jesuits, or both, remains to be seen. In addition, he ordered the investigations of seminaries in the United States that year, and later of its religious orders. In February, he visited Japan and the Philippines, during which he publicly rebuked Philippine head-of-state Fernando Marcos for his wanting record on human rights. On this same subject, the Pontiff served as a vigorous figurehead in the Italian referendum designed to secure human rights for unborn children. Three days before the vote, on the anniversary of the apparitions of the Mother of God at Fatima in Portugal, John Paul was shot down by Mehmet Ali Aqca in St. Peter's Square. Far more painful, he was later to observe, was the Italian vote that followed, which weakened legal protection for the unborn.

His recovery was slow and painful, but still he kept up attempts at reform. When the Jesuit General Pedro Arrupe was felled by a heart-attack in August, John Paul intervened in an unprecedented move and took direct control of the Jesuits, refusing to allow either a general chapter meeting, or for temporary replacement of Arrupe as General by the notorious Modernist U.S. Jesuit, Vincent O'Keefe. The Pope instead appointed a personal delegate, Father Paola Dezza, to run the order until the convening of a general chapter, "to be called in due time." Two years later, in fact, it took place, during which the unknown Lebanese missionary Hans Kolvenbach was elected to run the order. Kolvenbach's efforts at reform, alas, have at least publicly appeared to be comparable to those employed so far by the U.S. Episcopate. Nonetheless—one sensed at the direct behest of John Paul—Father Kolvenbach did dismiss one of the heads of the Nicaraguan government from the Jesuits at the end of 1984, for his refusal to abide by the dictum of the Revised Code of Canon Law that priests may not hold public office.

In April of 1981, meanwhile, Archbishop Laghi wrote a letter to all the episcopal ordinaries in the United States noting that "with increasing frequency the Holy See receives letters from the United States complaining about articles appearing in Catholic newspapers, including diocesan publications, which cause harm to the Faith of the people because of lack of respect for the teaching and decisions of the *magisterium* ... the impact of such criticism is heightened when columns are syndicated and widely circulated ... and ordinaries are encouraged to consider their responsibilities in governing those publications over which they have control." As far as can be discerned, the only impact of this letter was that Father Andrew Greeley was soon replaced as the most widely published diocesan columnist by Father Richard McBrien. One significant aspect of the Archbishop's letter, however, is that it revealed for the first time the growing Vatican sensitivity to lay frustration with Modernist clericalism; for complaints about heresy in the diocesan paper would prove neither the first nor the last subject about which Catholics would feel compelled to appeal directly to the Universal Pastor of the Church because of the contempt they encountered—contra Vatican II—from their diocesan bishops.

Doubtless the most remarkable achievement of Pope John Paul II in 1981, however, was the publication of his third encyclical on a subject that would also be intimately identified with his Papacy—human work. His Holiness had originally intended to publish *Laborem exercens* on the ninetieth anniversary of Pope Leo XIII's seminal encyclical *Rerum novarum*—which in effect defined the Catholic approach to social organization in the modern age—but could not due to Aqca's bullet. With the *Solidarity* union at the height of its power in Poland, John Paul instead proclaimed for the world in *Laborem exercens* on September 14 that "the value of human work is not primarily the kind of work being done but the fact that the one who is doing it is a person," since "the primary basis of the value of work is man himself ... work is 'for man,' and not man 'for work.' " and work itself, "though it bears the mark of *bonum arduum* ... this does not take away the fact that, as such, it is a good thing for man," and "not only good in the sense that it is useful or something to enjoy; it is also good as being something worthy, that is to say, something that corresponds to man's dignity, that expresses this dignity and increases it." Accordingly, the encyclical asserts the Catholic "principle of the priority of labor over capital" as opposed to any consideration of "human labor solely according to its economic purpose. This fundamental error of thought can and must be called *an error of materialism* [the Pontiff's emphasis], in that economism directly or indirectly includes a conviction of the primacy and superiority of the material, and directly or indirectly places the spiritual and the personal in a position of subordination to material reality."

In December 1981 martial law was declared in Poland, Lech Walesa was put under house arrest, and the *Solidarity* union was crushed—for a season.

In the opinion of many, the Pontiff's gloomiest year was 1982, due both to the debilitating after-effects of the bullet wound, and the depression he suffered because of the injustice to which his homeland was being subjected once again. And yet there was not much public evidence of his gloom, with the possible exception of his appointment in August of Cincinnati Archbishop Joseph Bernardin to head the Archdiocese of Chicago. Many American Catholics feared this meant the Pope had. in effect abandoned any hope of seeing Vatican II implemented in the United States, due to Bernardin's established reputation for skilfully circumventing its precepts (apart from everything else, Father Andrew Greeley had led an open lobbying campaign to win the Chicago See for the Cincinnati prelate). That the *National Catholic Reporter* celebrated the appointment with unconcealed jubilation was another gloomy sign, one which was not alleviated when the Archbishop promptly encouraged Catholics to give their money to the Crusade for Mercy, despite that crusade's donations to Planned Parenthood. Bernardin justified it on the grounds that the Crusade also gave money to organizations that didn't kill unborn children. The gloom increased when Bernardin was made a Cardinal the following January.

Still, calmer heads suggested the appointment was a necessary practical move, precisely because by giving the Modernists their own man in such a major See, the Pope had seriously undercut the possibility of U.S. Episcopal schism, rumors about which by 1982 had become rife in the United States. Everyone knew that Bernardin would never go so far as to support a schism himself—and without his support, especially given his new status, it was argued that a move of this kind from lesser bishops must inevitably fail.

Regardless of the reasoning, the Pontiff began to pick up steam again in 1982. In February he returned to Africa. Cardinal Ratzinger was appointed to head the Congregation for the Doctrine of Faith. On the first anniversary of the assassination attempt, John Paul journeyed to Fatima to give thanks to the Virgin, during which trip another assassination attempt failed. At the end of that month, His Holiness then went both to England

and Argentina in vain efforts to stop the war between those nations over the Malvinas Islands. He also visited Switzerland in June, San Marino in August, and Spain at the end of the year, where a newly elected Socialist government had promised to "liberalize" divorce and abortion laws, perhaps as a complement to the enormous flow of pornography that had inundated the country since the death of Franco. It was here the Pope began driving home a theme which he has not since abandoned, that Europe had lost its soul, and that Christians had to help her retrieve it once again.

Meanwhile, back in the United States, a remarkable interview appeared in the 26 September 1982 *National Catholic Register* with Luigi Cardinal Ciappi. This presaged a series of Curial interviews which would prove to have a major impact on the Church in the United States and indeed throughout the West, culminating in Messori's extensive conversations with Cardinal Ratzinger in 1984.

In the *Register* interview, Cardinal Ciappi revealed, among other things, that "Pius XII, without using Teilhard's name, nonetheless was referring to him in the encyclical *Humani generis*," and further suggested that the discredited French Jesuit Teilhard de Chardin was in fact guilty of formal heresy in his views about original sin. Pressed about the nature of heresy in regard to various Modernist tenets, Ciappi acknowledged that "anybody who doesn't obey the Pope in these areas commits a grave sin. Look," he elaborated, "I know these priests and nuns who oppose the teachings of Vatican II. They are clearly not Catholics. They excommunicate themselves. Not in a juridical sense, but in the moral, theological sense. They are not in communion in thought, or in communion in their lives, with the Catholic Church."

Asked what the faithful ought to do about such clerics, His Eminence observed that "the faithful have a right to appeal to their pastors, their bishops, and also the apostolic delegate to express their difficulties in these areas. If that doesn't work, they can write to the Holy See, to the competent authorities. They can also write to the Holy Father directly. Vatican II made it clear that the faithful have a duty to collaborate in assuring the truth of the Catholic faith."

And so collaborate they did. Letters began to pour into the Vatican from all over the United States by the tens of thousands, and apart from revealing the potentially explosive split between the orthodox laity and the increasingly Arian clergy, these letters did something else: they revealed that if the Pope did start to initiate aggressive measures in defense of the Council in the United States, he would have a solid core of support from the faithful themselves.

In fact, with the Holy Year in 1983—which the Pontiff announced in the closing months of 1982—a discernible shift took place in the course of the Wojtylan Papacy. Until that time, as far as the crisis in the West was concerned, the Prince of the Apostles had to a great extent been gathering data, visiting his flock, establishing themes, proclaiming the truth. The moves against Kueng, Pohiers and Schillebeeckx only finished the work that had begun under Paul VI (though in the case of Schillebeeckx the work has yet to be completed). The Pontiff's intercession with the Dutch bishops and with the Jesuits had been provoked by crisis situations—more easily handled in the case of the Dutch because of the small number of bishops there. In addition, as Henri Cardinal de Lubac observed in an interview in the July 1985 Italian journal *30 Giorni*, the media had done "little to make known—no doubt it would be impossible for them to do any better than they do—the real work of the [Pope's extensive pastoral] trips: the very solid exchanges between the Pope and the bishops, priests, Religious, and lay people of the country; the homilies and public addresses full of instruction; the stimulating encounters with the young.... As a consequence, the media more or less leave out the essentials."

"It was at the beginning of that year," as *The Wanderer* observed, that "the name of Joseph Cardinal Ratzinger began to provoke a trembling of knees in certain quarters throughout the world." In January of the Holy Year, (though it was not formally inaugurated until 25 March), His Eminence directly intervened in the composition of the U.S. Bishops' pastoral on weapons, not a little because its second draft was at best theologically facile, and at worst riddled with the heresy of consequentialism, which had been popularized by Charles Curran over the matter of abortion and contraception. It was during these conversations with Cardinal Bernardin, Archbishop Roach, and others involved with the pastoral, that Ratzinger first pointed out "a bishop's conference as such does not have a *mandatum docendi*," a mandate to teach, since "this belongs only to the individual bishops or to the college of bishops with the Pope." Over the next three years, this point was to become a matter of keen importance to the Church, and, as previously noted, during the Extraordinary Synod of Bishops disputing it was to be the major thrust of Bishop Malone's intervention.

Of equal and perhaps even more importance, was a trip Cardinal Ratzinger took that same month to France. In Lyons, he brilliantly dissected the Arian tendencies of the Liberal Consensus in the French catechisms, and invoked the name of St. Pius—who had composed an international catechism after the Council of Trent—as the solution. In so doing, His Eminence reflected the view of Pope John Paul, who in *Catechesi tradendae* had noted that "the ministry of catechesis draws ever fresh energy from the Councils. The Council of Trent is a noteworthy example of this," because "it gave catechesis priority in its constitutions and decrees."

"For several months after the Cardinal's visit," Thomas Molnar wrote in the November 1983 *Catholicism in Crisis*, "the controversy was raging in French Church circles and outside. Many religion editors of progressive papers were indignant that Rome should want to interfere with the management of the Church of France," and "some accused John Paul of wanting to re-establish 'authoritarian' manners. . . . In fact, right after the Cardinal's departure, indications were given that no changes would occur in the area of catechetics."

"The winds began to change," however, as Molnar observed, "according to all appearances as a result of talks between Rome and the French hierarchy. The latest news has it that 'the bishops of France welcome the advice and cooperation offered by the Vatican' and will issue new instructions and revised texts." They did so, and in late 1983 Peter Hebblethwaite was lamenting in the *National Catholic Reporter* that the *imprimatur* was withdrawn from a popular French catechism. That it was only popular with certain French clerics, Mr. Hebblethwaite thought it helpful not to stress.

The hand of Jean-Marie Lustiger was observed in this seachange, for the Cardinal Archbishop of Paris quickly established himself as the chief spokesman for a revitalized Catholicism throughout France. Socialist head-of-state Francois Mitterand, indeed, failed to notice the extent of this impact when he sought to bring Catholic education in France under the direct control of the state—for his actual attempts to do so provoked the largest anti-government demonstrations in the post-war era, in fact nearly brought the government down, whereupon Mr. Mitterand felt it prudent to abandon his totalitarian plans.

"For those who could read the signs," Hebblethwaite later informed readers of the *Reporter*, "the attack on the U.S. text was bound to come. French Catholics believed the bans came because so many ... Catholics wrote to [Silvio Cardinal] Oddi complaining about the modern catechisms. Oddi then 'had to react' in response to these complaints, so he handed over the files to Ratzinger, who likewise 'had to react' by his bans and condemnations." Whatever the reasons, Ratzinger ordered Gerety to remove his *imprimatur* from the heretical *Christ Among Us* in February 1984, and shortly thereafter ordered Seattle Archbishop Raymond Hunthausen to remove his from the immoral compendium *Sexual Morality* by Father Philip Keane. Before that spring had ended, Richmond, Virginia Bishop Walter Sullivan was told to remove his name from a book compiled by the openly homosexualist quiverer Father Robert Nugent, which book to be sure contained numerous assurances that God really rather approves of sodomy, despite St. Paul's views on the matter. All the books in question had been published by the distributors of Peter Gerety's *Renew*, Paulist Press. Meantime, discussions about other U.S. *imprimaturs* are reportedly still in progress.

Another very uncharacteristic development was the decision of the U.S. bishops at their November 1985 meeting in Washington to launch a study investigating the possibility of issuing a national catechism. What made this a particular surprise is that *The Wanderer* editorially called for such an initiative in the summer of 1985, right after the idea was furiously denounced in the pages of the normally bland *Our Sunday Visitor* (OSV) by those ubiquitous Catholic experts: "Catholic experts look upon this idea with abhorrence," the *OSV* announced, while assuring us this was "not because they don't want Catholic students to master a knowledge of their Faith."

There are other major developments that took place in 1983, which shall be discussed shortly. Nonetheless, two of the most stunning that year were the Pontiff's pastoral visits, in March to Central America, and in June to Poland a second time.

The Central American trip clearly changed the tenor and history of that part of the world; before huge crowds the Pope condemned the brutality of both the extreme right and the extreme left. On the eve of John Paul's visit, the anti-Catholic apostate President of Guatemala, Efren Rios Montt, made a point of executing six political enemies, despite a direct Papal appeal for clemency: Montt's regime collapsed shortly thereafter, as has recently the regime of Jean-Claude Duvalier in Haiti, whose record on human rights also came under sharp papal criticism in 1983. Neither did John Paul hesitate to blast the assault on Catholic sexual morality throughout Central America, financed by the imperialist population control outfits in the United States. On the positive side, by his appointment of Archbishop Oscar Romero's aide Arturo Rivera y Damas as Archbishop of San Salvador at the beginning of the trip—as well as John Paul's own conversations with El Salvadoran officials—a fundamental contribution was made to the political stability that has since come to that country after years of civil war.

But doubtless the most memorable aspect of the Pontiff's pastoral visit was the manner by which it exposed the fanaticism of the Marxist "Sandinista" junta in Nicaragua. For his part, the Pope was blunt: apart from publicly reproaching priests in the regime for abandoning their vows for the thrill of politics, John Paul also reminded Catholics in one Nicaraguan speech that "you do not need ideology outside our Christian tradition to love and defend man: indeed, if you forget it, you will have revealed to all your willingness to compromise your own dignity."

Furious, the junta responded with a gratuitous desecration of the Mass which John Paul celebrated before the entire world. Giant murals of Karl Marx and other historicists were hung behind the altar, but no crucifix was allowed. Accordingly, His Holiness held his own staff with its crucifix high above junta officials seated on the platform to the cheers of the crowd. Junta supporters retaliated by choosing to shout and heckle the Pope not only during his homily, but right through the Consecration of the Host, the most sacred moment in Catholic worship; the successor to Peter finally cried "silence!" several times, but they would not cease. The vast throngs then took courage and began to drown out the blasphemies with cries of "El Papa! El Papa!"—whereupon junta officials supplied their allies with microphones, and the desecration continued. While it did, John Paul quietly finished the Mass—but the world had seen it all, and the Sandinista regime has had little real support ever since, except from overt Communists, Jesuits, and the denizens of Modernist radical chic.

In June, the Pope returned to Poland. As martial law was still in effect at that point, virtually the entire media predicted before the Pontiff's return that it would be a "low-key" visit, for diplomatic reasons. Then John Paul arrived in Warsaw. He went directly to the principal Cathedral to say a Mass in honor of Cardinal Wyszynski, where he promptly denounced martial law in bitter terms.

"To all my compatriots," he cried, "especially those who are most acutely tasting the bitterness of disappointment, humiliation, suffering, of being deprived of their freedom, of being wronged, of having their dignity trampled on, I stand with you all, beneath the Cross of Christ!"

And with that, one of the most remarkable events in modern history was launched. "From the beginning," a surprised media suddenly noted, "the Pope's behavior was not at all what the regime had hoped for and counted on—even the faithful were startled by the Pope's swift attack on everything [Polish head-of-state General Wojciech] Jaruzelski stands for." In fact, John Paul met with the General the following morning, during which visit the latter openly trembled, and the successor to Peter openly challenged him to end the brutality of martial law, and restore the legitimate agreements established between Solidarity and the government at Gdansk in August 1980.

And then, like an embodied affirmation of human dignity, and in the teeth of all the suffering this land has endured, John Paul II swept through Poland, from Warsaw to Niepokalanow to Czestochowa and Poznan and Katowice and Nowa Huta, and finally to his own beloved See of Kracow, to tumultuous crowds, the largest in the history of Poland, perhaps in the history of the world. It was said more than eighteen of Poland's thirty-six million people saw the Pope in the course of the visit. Throughout, he never let up, constantly proclaiming the dignity of man, the necessity of freedom, the obligation of human rights, with Solidarity banners flying everywhere. "Propaganda Disaster Seen for Communists," the *New York Times* announced, whereupon the junta panicked, claimed the visit was hurting Polish stability, but John Paul proclaimed his vision all the same, "not only despite government warnings," as one paper noted, "but almost as if he ignored the government's presence altogether"; and indeed, the French weekly *L'Express* seemed to capture it all with the cover headline "Pope John Paul II: King of Poland."

Eventually it ended, and the King was gone. Martial law ended shortly thereafter, Lech Walesa was awarded the Nobel Prize for Peace, but the Gdansk accords have yet to be revived, the economy has not improved, the tension remains ever near to the breaking point, though it has not broken, not even with the murder of Father Jerzy Popieluszko, though the junta felt compelled to bring his murderers to justice. And the shadow of the Soviet Army, to be sure, is ever present. But as John Paul told his brethren during this epic voyage, "perhaps at times we envy the French, the Germans, the Americans, because they are so easily free, while our Polish freedom comes so very dear. And yet," he added, "let us not wish for a Poland that would cost us nothing."

IV. Two Interviews and an Exhortation: The Holy Year Continues

"Catholic doctrine tells us that the prime duty of charity does not lie in the toleration of false ideas . . . nor in the theoretical of practiced indifference towards the errors and vices in which we see our brethren plunged."

Saint Pius X

"When the shepherd turns into a wolf, the first duty of the flock is to defend itself. As a general rule, doctrine comes from the bishops to the faithful, and it is not for the faithful, who are subjects in the order of the faith, to pass judgement on their superiors. But every Christian by virtue of his title to the name Christian, has not only the necessary knowledge of the essentials of the treasures of Revelation, but also the duty of safeguarding them."

Dom Prosper Gueranger, on Nestorianism

Poland, however, was not the only country in need of recapturing a minimal sense of dignity either.

No, the summer of 1983 was not over. In July, the Prefect for the Sacred Congregation of the Clergy, Cardinal Oddi,[12] took a short tour of the United States, and gave a number of addresses, before Catholics United for the Faith and other groups, and doubtless gathered much information for Vatican plans to come to the aid of beleagured Catholics in this country. At one point

---

[12]Described by the 4 February 1985 *Time* magazine as "affable" and "a friend of John Paul's; the Pope enjoys his dry humor and no-nonsense."

during the trip, he granted me an interview for publication in *The Wanderer*.

"It went well, didn't it," Cardinal Oddi later said to me of the 1983 interview during the Extraordinary Synod. In any event, it shook things up. His Eminence began by praising Catholics United for the Faith as "an apostolate with excellent intentions; indeed I would add that the most important intentions in the world are those which seek to protect and defend and present the purity of Catholic truth, of the Catholic Faith."

"I think that is an urgent apostolate here in the United States," he added.

In addition, the Clergy Prefect seconded Cardinal Ciappi's observation that "Teilhard was the occasion" for the Encyclical *Humani generis,* and then revealed "a certain faith . . . that the Mass of St. Pius V, the Tridentine Mass, will not be obstructed, as it is nowadays . . . I believe a reform will be adopted, and permission will be granted throughout the Church. It will be for all the world" and "will be authorized when the people want it badly enough." After that successful prediction, he acknowledged that while it was unlikely the Jesuits would formally be suppressed as they had been—for bad reasons—in 1773, their "power in the schools and the press and the esteem they enjoy" seems "to have diminished" their "loyalty to the Holy See." His Eminence thought this odd given that it is "the Pope from whom the Jesuit order directly derives its authority."

Things were just getting started. When asked why the catechism *Christ Among Us* was not formally condemned, Oddi said it was "because the examination of the book in Rome has not yet been finished"—implying, accurately, that it would be soon. In discussing the Cardinal's Hat given the previous January to the controversial French theologian Henri de Lubac—which had raised eyebrows in certain quarters—Oddi revealed that "we know that Father de Lubac, years ago, many years ago, in a certain moment, had some sympathy for certain movements, which he then abandoned, and truly returned to the profundity of Catholic doctrine. Today, he is a theologian who respects and defends the doctrine of the Church." Doubtless due to de Lubac's acquaintance with Teilhard, and the Cardinal-to-be's occasional tortured attempt to squeeze his follow Jesuit's pantheism into some possible expression of Christianity, Cardinal Oddi felt it prudent to insist—twice—that "de Lubac's elevation had nothing to do with Teilhard de Chardin."

I then asked why the Holy See did not more aggressively protect the faithful from Archbishops "Peter Gerety or Rembert Weakland" and various other notorious figures, to which His Eminence replied that "the Church has not publicly corrected these people because perhaps She doesn't know, or doesn't believe it is opportune to take energetic measures, possibly not to create an even greater scandal in the face of disobedience," and "perhaps the Church thinks it is better to tolerate certain errors, in the hope that by overlooking certain difficulties, the offender will eventually abandon the errors and return to the Church." Oddi nonetheless rebuked "the proud of heart, who pretend to know more than the Church, more than the successor to Peter," when "they know that the infallibility of theological teaching is entrusted to the Pope, and that when speaking of faith and morals, as is the case with *Humanae vitae*, he has the charism of infallibility."

"The same applies to the bishops," he added. "The bishops are sons of Adam, are they not?. . . . unfortunately priests and nuns, Catholics and bishops are not exempt from these grave weaknesses. There are many who have been seduced by a false science, a false discovery of pretensions—doctors, psychologists, and also some bishops, who have come to believe in their own infallibility. They are wrong, and far from the teaching of God. They are condemned. They are condemned most of all before the Church, particularly those in authority who authorize [immoral and/or heretical teaching in their dioceses.]"

Accordingly, I asked His Eminence if the arguments of Aquinas and Cardinal Newman were correct, that—in the words of Aquinas—"if the faith be in imminent peril, prelates ought to be accused by their subjects, even in public."

The Pope's friend and colleague answered, "Absolutely. Without question."

The interview ended with the Clergy Prefect making a distinction between the sins of a confused or weak laity, and the public preaching of heresy by an ordained priest. A Catholic couple, for example, who poison the Sacrament of Matrimony with chemicalized sex, in Oddi's view, should try to remember that "the Mercy of God is great. And married couples who fall short of their responsibilities as Christians, should put themselves before this Mercy, in the struggle to overcome their weakness by eventually surrendering to the teachings of Christ and His Church." A priest who publicly opposes "a central tenet of the

Catholic faith" on the other hand, has a different status. Such priests, remarked the Prefect (whose chief juridical responsibility in the Church *is* the world's priests), are simply "out of the Church. They put themselves out of the Church."

"Are their absolutions in Confession valid," was my penultimate question, to which His Eminence replied, "of course they are valid, but because the layman doesn't know the priest is out of the Church. If they know, then they musn't go to such a priest for confession, precisely because he is out of the Church."

"And this applies to *Humanae vitae* as well?," I asked. As he rose to leave, he gave his final answer almost incidentally. "Oh yes," he said, "also to *Humanae vitae.*"

The explicitly Modernist religion editor of *Newsweek* magazine, Kenneth Woodward (who once quipped that "Christ was a great preacher, but a lousy theologian"), denounced Oddi in that magazine the following November, as the impact of the Cardinal's remarks seemed to be reaching a crescendo. It should be remembered, as discussed in a previous chapter, that 1983 was the year in which John Paul II followed the mandate of John XXIII and the Second Vatican Council by promulgating the Revised Code of Canon Law—which formally took effect that November. Accordingly, the *Reporter* and various other Modernist tabloids joined the secular papers in blasting Oddi, for 1983 was also the year during which the Vatican had moved against the Mercy Sisters for the sterilization programs in their hospitals, and in which a nun by the name of Mary Mansour had been dismissed from her order because she oversaw the extermination of thousands of unborn children in an agency she ran for the state of Michigan. And yet, every diocesan paper in the country was careful not to publish—to censor, if you prefer—the contents of the interview with the man John Paul II has made directly responsible for the care of priests throughout the world.

This policy was repeated in regard to the interview with Archbishop Edouard Gagnon that appeared in the 29 September *Wanderer*, and which picked up where Cardinal Oddi had left off. When asked about the sex education programs approved by Archbishops Gerety and Weakland, for example, Gagnon cut instead to the Liberal Consensus, and the heart of the problem.

"I think the greatest scandal," he remarked, "is that they only allow people to teach that Christ is not God, and that there was no real, physical Resurrection. The rest comes from there. Teaching sexual perversion has, I think, resulted as a consequence of this fear of the nature and calling of Our Lord. If Christ is not God, then His Church has no authority to teach morality. So that is the main scandal, and it is what has been happening. Of course, though the teaching of sexual perversion is a consequence, it is often by working on the consequences that you bring people to see and work on the source," but "ultimately, it is not until the bishops and the laity return to Christ and His truth, that a solution can be found."

About the condition of the U.S. Episcopate, His Excellency observed that "I do think that like in the most difficult periods of the Church, much of the fight has to be fought by the lay people in the places, the diocese and parishes, where the particular distortions have taken hold . . . and I encourage associations of parents and other groups to fight and be ready to work at the parish and diocesan level," since often the efforts of the Holy Father "are disobeyed, and they will not *be* obeyed, in too many cases, until such time as the local people make their bishops understand that they *have* to be obeyed, that the bishops have to obey them." He said this could prove of particular importance because "oftentimes, I think some would like to obey, except they are surrounded by people who implement things contrary to the will of the Church, and perhaps such bishops are afraid to discipline, or make the necessary changes."

Given that John Paul made Gagnon a Cardinal at the first consistory held after the appearance of this interview, and particularly given all the controversy it provoked, one could perhaps do worse in speculating about the Pope's intentions for the United States than to note how insistent Gagnon was that "it is within the laity's competence to insist that the bishops obey the Pope." A large part of the interview was devoted to giving specific details about how the laity should approach this competence, and how to present the evidence they gather to the Holy See if a bishop repudiates Vatican II, or tries to punish those who seek to implement it. In light of all this, one can also perhaps better understand why Archbishop Weakland appealed to the Catholic Press Association to censor Catholic opinion, which appeal came but a few months after Gagnon's opinions were publicly aired in *The Wanderer*.[13]

"At one time a great number of bishops fell into Arianism," the French Canadian Archbishop in fact observed, "and it was

---

[13]See footnote 4 in "The Abortion Industry and the American Catholic University."

the lay people who brought them back, and through the centuries it has been like that. Two or three centuries ago, the bishops of France were quite involved in the life of the court in France and other countries," he added, "and it was the lay people, working with some good priests, who had the courage and grace to change the situation."

In addition, for the first time in a public forum since the close of the Council, a Curial official discussed the possibility of a formal schism in the United States. Pope Paul VI, Gagnon asserted, "had been afraid of schism, and did not want to deprive the faithful of the grace of the Sacraments because of the shortcomings of their pastors. I think in a great measure it was a matter of charity. But this is a very prudential judgment, and a very difficult one, which the leaders of the Church have to make, and this is why we have to pray for them every day."

Then *Wanderer* editor Al Matt asked directly: "Could one say that the Church is tolerating a material schism in the United States?"

"Yes," he answered, initially without elaboration. Later he added, "it's an ancient problem. You know, much of the reason for the whole schism with the Oriental Church was for political reasons—to follow the leaders of their own country against that of a stranger because they do not understand his authority."

"How worried do you think the present Pontiff is," I inquired, "about a formal schism being initiated by the American bishops?"

"I would not be able to comment on that," His Excellency responded. "The Holy Father takes time before making judgments, and little by little he is making decisions, but I don't think he wants to act in a hasty manner."

In fact, John Paul's prudential approach was forcefully revealed during a speech to a group of some twenty-five American bishops, among them Archbishop Weakland himself, on 5 September 1983. By speaking just after publication of the Oddi interview and just before Archbishop Gagnon's, the Pope's collegial message gave particular weight to the views of these two prelates. The *New York Times* considered the Pontiff's talk striking enough to give it front-page coverage.

"The bishop," His Holiness observed, "precisely because he is compassionate and understands the weakness of humanity and the fact that its needs and aspirations can only be satisfied by the full truth of creation and redemption, will proclaim without fear or ambiguity the many controverted truths of our age. He will proclaim them with pastoral love, in terms that will never unnecessarily offend or alienate his hearers, but he will proclaim them clearly, because he knows the liberating quality of truth...."

"Hence the compassionate bishop ... will proclaim the incompatibility of premarital sex and homosexual activity with God's plan for human love ... with equal compassion he will proclaim the doctrine on *Humanae vitae* and *Familiaris consortio* in its full beauty, not passing over in silence the unpopular truth that artificial birth control is against God's law. He will speak out for the unborn, the weak, the handicapped, the poor and the aged, no matter how current popular opinion views these issues, [and will] oppose any and all discrimination of women by reason of sex. In this regard he must likewise endeavor to explain as cogently as he can that the Church's teaching on the exclusion of women from priestly ordination is extraneous to the issue of discrimination and that it is linked rather to Christ's own design for his priesthood. The bishop must give proof of his pastoral ability and leadership by withdrawing all support from individuals and groups who in the name of progress, justice, or compassion, or for any other alleged reason, promote the ordination of women to the priesthood, [for] in so doing, such individuals or groups are in effect damaging the very dignity of women that they profess to promote and advance.

"All efforts made against the truth are destined to produce not only failure, but also acute personal frustration. Whatever the bishop can do to prevent this failure and frustration by explaining the truth is an act not only of pastoral charity, but of prophetic leadership. In a word, the bishop as a sign of compassion is at the same time a sign of fidelity to the doctrine of the church....

"Finally, it is evident in all this that the bishop, as a living sign of Jesus Christ, must vindicate to himself the title and accept the consequences of the fact that he is, with Jesus Christ, a sign of contradiction. Despite every dutiful effort to pursue the dialogue of salvation, the bishop must announce to the young and the old, to the rich and the poor, to the powerful and the weak the fullness of truth, which sometimes irritates and offends, even if it always liberates....

"Precisely because he cannot renounce the preaching of the cross the bishop will be called upon over and over again to accept criticism and to admit failure in obtaining a consensus of doctrine acceptable to everyone. As a living sign of Christ he must be with Christ a sign of fidelity and therefore a sign of contradiction.

"Venerable and dear brothers, these reflections, partial though they be, speak to us of the reality of the episcopate of our Lord Jesus Christ in which we share. I offer them to you as an expression of our common strivings and perhaps to some extent of our common failings. As your brother in the See of Peter, humbled and repentant, I offer them as a challenge of grace in a moment of grace, a moment of collegiality and a moment of fraternal love. I offer them to your apostolic responsibility and to your pastoral accountability to Jesus Christ, the chief Shepherd, and to me, His servant vicar. I offer them as a manifestation of deep gratitude for what you are and intend with God's grace ever more to become: in Christ, a sign of hope for the people of God as strong and unbreakable as the Sign of the Cross, becoming a living sign of the risen Christ."

V. The Clerical Backlash

"[It is regarded as a] duty to tolerate, without even voicing an objection, people who want to destroy his way of life, prey on his children, and desecrate everything he used to hold sacred."
Joseph Sobran

"A collegial style of pastoral practice, rooted in dialogue, sharing of responsibility and sensitivity to the multiple charisms within the Body of Christ, is one of the distinguishing marks of the Church since Vatican II."
Bishop James Malone

The year closed with a swirl of activity. In Rome, a synod of bishops was held on the subject of Sacramental Confession, Reconciliation and Penance,[15] the fruits of which would be harvested a year later in the Apostolic Exhortation *Reconciliatio et paenitentiae.* In the United States, Seattle Archbishop Raymond Hunthausen and Washington D.C. Archbishop James Hickey held a joint press conference, during which it was announced that the latter had been appointed apostolic investigator of the Seattle Archdiocese, an unusual move since such investigations are usually done confidentially. Hunthausen's reign had, however, become a point of particular scandal; but unlike Archbishop Gerety, who would soon be retiring, and Archbishop Weakland, who was protected because Archbishop Roach had, so to speak, chosen him to represent the entire U.S. Episcopate in the composition of the economic pastoral, Hunthausen was both young and had no particular status in the NCCB as such.

At the time, Hunthausen charged that "reactionary elements within the Church," were responsible for the investigation, but in fact, when its results were published two years later while the world's bishops were gathered for the Extraordinary Synod,

---

[15]Shortly after its conclusion, on 27 December 1983, the Pontiff visited Ali Aqca in prison.

the complaints of these slandered elements were fully vindicated. Though couched in terms of priestly charity, the 14 November 1985 letter from Papal Nuncio Archbishop Pio Laghi to Hunthausen (who released the letter of November 26), in effect publicly reproached His Excellency for failing "to bring into clear focus certain teachings of the Church ... in particular, the need to present more clearly the Church's teachings concerning the permanence and indissolubility of marriage," to uphold with "greater vigilance ... the Church's teachings with regard to contraceptive sterilization and homosexuality ... the need to ensure that pastoral practice regarding the liturgical and sacramental ministry of the Archdiocese is in accord with the Church's universal norms especially in the celebration of the Eucharist and Reconciliation," and not least, "the need to review the ongoing education of the clergy and the selection and formation of candidates for the priesthood." The 13 December 1985 *National Catholic Reporter* promptly editorialized that Hunthausen had "been dealt with in a grossly unjust manner," and "is one of the most impressive bishops ever to head a U.S. diocese."

There was, to be sure, a certain embarrassment in citing Hunthausen alone for these abuses, since they were widespread throughout many dioceses in the United States. Nonetheless, the reform had to begin somewhere, and it was hoped that if the Pontiff's fraternal exhortations from Rome were insufficient motivation, then the experience of Archbishop Hunthausen in tandem with those exhortations might prove more effective.

There were some further twists to the Hunthausen investigation, which touched upon additional remarks John Paul II had made to the American bishops in the 5 September 1983 address.

"The choice of bishops," he said, perhaps with the name Jadot in mind, "is as important today for the Church as was the choice of the Twelve Apostles for Jesus. The recommendation and selection of every new bishop deserves the greatest prayerful reflection on the part of all those associated with the process of the selection of candidates. In this regard the bishops themselves have a special role in proposing ... priests who have already proven themselves as teachers of the faith as it is proclaimed by the *magisterium* of the Church and who, in the words of Paul's pastoral advice to Titus, 'hold fast to the authentic message.'"

Accordingly, on 3 December 1985, a week after Hunthausen had released Laghi's letter, the Papal Nuncio made the surprise announcement that Father Donald Wuerl would be sent to Seattle as an Auxiliary Bishop upon his consecration at the hands of Pope John Paul himself, at St. Peter's Basilica on 7 January 1986. Wuerl's background made this appointment particularly striking. Now 45 years old, the priest took his bachelor's and master's degrees from Catholic University in the pre-Curran days, and then served as secretary in Rome to John Cardinal Wright, who was Cardinal Oddi's predecessor at the Congregation for the Clergy, from 1969 to 1979. During that time, Wuerl took his doctorate at the Angelicum, where he taught theology for the last four years of his stay in Rome. When he returned to the diocese of Pittsburgh where he had been ordained, the priest served until 1981 as vice rector, and from then until his appointment to Seattle, as rector of the Pittsburgh seminary. In 1982, Burlington Bishop John Marshall, who was leading the investigation of U.S. Seminaries, chose Wuerl as his executive secretary. And not least significant was the active priest's co-authorship of an orthodox Catholic catechism called *The Teaching of Christ*, which has been translated into seven languages. One reason some considered this appointment particularly noteworthy had to do with the very forthright observations made in the June 1985 *Catholicism in Crisis* by one of the catechism's co-authors, the Capuchin friar Father Ronald Lawler. Among other things, Lawler noted at the time that "the Catholic Church today is in as great a crisis as was the Church in the days of Arianism."

There was at least one other investigation in 1983 that became a matter of public knowledge; St. Louis Archbishop John May was sent out to inquire about the activities of Richmond, Virginia Bishop Walter Sullivan, (who'd written the introduction to Father Nugent's homosexualist book before Cardinal Ratzinger's intervention). Nothing further has been heard about that investigation, however; though admittedly not a great deal from Bishop Sullivan either.

Meanwhile, at the NCCB Washington meeting of November 1983, Archbishop Roach ended his tenure as President by publicly acknowledging "tensions in the relationship" between Pope John Paul II and the U.S. Episcopate, while adding that the majority of these tensions were based on "misperceptions and misinformation," which many considered an allusion to the enormous amount of mail the Vatican had been receiving from Catholics in the United States. And so the clerical backlash began.

Newsweek's Kenneth Woodward, whom neither Archbishop Roach nor any other prelate sought publicly to correct (privately, there are indications Woodward was asked to do the piece), got very explicit about this. In an editorial disguised as an article, Woodward charged that "the American bishops have good cause for complaint," since "much of the misunderstanding between the Curia and the American bishops may be traced to *The Wanderer*."

"It's as if the conservative zealots had launched their own communications satellite called 'Tell the Pope,'" Woodward was told by Saginaw, Michigan Bishop Kenneth Untener—who had himself been subject to heated criticism in *The Wanderer* for showing some pornographic films to seminarians as part of a new, or perhaps by now old, approach to sex education.

Coincidentally, the syndicated columnist Lester Kinsolving—who often politically disagrees with *The Wanderer*—was present while *Newsweek* shot photographs of editor Al Matt for the Woodward piece: and he promptly wrote a column about it. Estimating that over 75 photographs were taken, to the point of disrupting the episcopal press conference that was going on at the same time, Kinsolving "leaned over and whispered [to Matt] 'What have you done to offend Ken Woodward?'" According to Kinsolving, "What really drives Woodward up the wall is the apparent fact that a number of significant clergy in the Curia in Rome put far more credence in *The Wanderer* than they do in mighty *Newsweek*." Accordingly, in the photograph *Newsweek* finally used, "Matt was caught either as he was about to be overcome with a yawn or as he was wrestling with the temptation to tell this photographic tormentor to go take a flying leap. *Newsweek* flanked this dreadful picture with Minnesota Archbishop John Roach looking heavenward . . . on the other side, there was Seattle's Raymond Hunthausen, smiling beneficiently, as he stands next to a crucifix."

"What upsets the American bishops most," Woodward said in *Newsweek*, "is the seeming willingness of some conservatives in the Curia Romana to accept what they read without first checking into the complaints or the complainers. . . . In September, for example, Cardinal Silvio Oddi, head of the Congregation for the Clergy, used a workshop with 90 visiting U.S. bishops to criticize some religious textbooks that have been endorsed by the American hierarchy and condemned by various right-wing groups."

The backlash against such "right-wing groups" has taken various forms. One is the approach of the Catholic Library Association. The CLA is very careful to include such publications as

America, Commonweal, the *National Catholic Reporter*, etc., in its Catholic Periodical and Literature Index—which, as the *Reporter* once noted, "for many religious researchers is simply the only game in town." It adamantly refused, however, to index either *The Wanderer* or the *National Catholic Register* until a major controversy about this censorship broke out whereupon the CLA accepted the *Register*, in 1983, but still refused *The Wanderer*.

By its spring 1984 annual meeting, the heat on the CLA was still great enough that it felt compelled to invite leading Modernist Father Gerard Sloyan to, in the words of James Hitchcock, "make a plea for censorship." Not indiscriminate censorship, to be sure, since in his keynote speech, Father Sloyan was most insistent about the CLA's obligation to stock "the great classical departures from Catholic orthodoxy," as opposed to more "ephemeral" things, like "papal writings." Nonetheless "Sloyan saved for the end the heart of his advice about what not to make available to Catholic readers," as Hitchcock reveals in the 18 November 1984 *Register*; namely, "works of the past 20 years in which 'some Catholics accuse other Catholics of a betrayal of the faith.'"

"To be sure," Hitchcock continued, Sloyan insisted that his "reasons for this were not the censorship of ideas. Rather, you see, it is that such people are guilty of uncharity, and hence are not real followers of Christ. Like most of those who denounce the 'stridency' of the 'right,' Sloyan ends up sounding pretty strident himself, using terms like 'garbage! garbage! garbage!' and 'splenetic defenders of Jesus Christ whose orthodoxy is a hatred!' to describe those whose ideas he rejects. If we attend to his claims very strictly ... libraries would have to jettison ... a good part of theological writing over the centuries, [which] has been characterized by a sharp tone and often by bitter attacks on opponents . . . . Indeed, some of Sloyan's own writings would have to be removed from the shelves if his advice were taken literally"—such as his 1984 CCA keynote speech, for example.

Nonetheless, deeply moved by Father Sloyan's view of charity, CLA officials renewed their decision to censor *The Wanderer*, though they were perhaps also influenced by CLA executive director Matthew Wilt, who, as Hitchcock notes, "has expressed his extreme personal distaste for *The Wanderer*, including among its many sins that it publishes advertisements for communities of nuns who wear habits." Such advertisements, Wilt wrote *The*

Wanderer in rejecting its application, "only promote divisiveness within our Catholic community."

Indeed, by 1984 a pale fear of divisiveness seemed to permeate the Modernist establishment. "During the CLA convention, two officials"—including Wilt—"refused to discuss the matter with the *Register*," though everyone knew it had been the subject of Sloyan's speech. Accordingly, or perhaps one should say naively, *Register* editor Fran Maier sought to resolve this scandal through the Catholic Press Association. On 16 May 1984 he wrote all its members, stating that "whatever your opinion of *The Wanderer*, we hope you'll see how truly unconstructive this [CLA] censorship is . . . we believe that this should be a cause for concern to the Catholic Press Association, and we hope that the CPA will fully support *The Wanderer* in its bid to be indexed. If *The Wanderer* can, in effect, be blacklisted, then so can any other publication."

Maier wanted the CPA to pass a resolution to this effect (during the CPA convention when Rembert Weakland was urging exactly the opposite approach) but "in the end," he told me, "we decided against pushing that resolution because we ran out of time due to extended debate over *Christ Among Us*." He also said not only that he expected such a measure would have been defeated, but that top CPA officials had urged him not to introduce it on the grounds that the debate it would provoke might prove "divisive."

The blacklist of *The Wanderer* continues to this day.

And it very clearly reflects the approach of numerous American bishops. Apart from his appeal to the nationwide diocesan press, Archbishop Weakland manifested a particularly ugly repudiation of both the Revised Code of Canon Law and Vatican II in the spring of 1984, when one of his parishioners requested the right to review the sex education program wherein Weakland has children play charades before each other with sexually explicit terms. On 25 April Mrs. Nancy Evers wrote "requesting your permission for a group of concerned parents to review all the materials which will be used for this program, including the manuals. I have previously been denied this request by Maureen Gallagher," of Weakland's Adult and Family Ministry Office, who "stated in her letter to me that I must go through the 'training process' as 'the process of the VYS [Valuing Your Sexuality] Program must be experienced to be understood.

Reading a manual without the training will only lead to misunderstanding and confusion."

The remainder of the Evers letter quoted some remarks form a 1983 document on sex education from the Congregation for Catholic Education, all of which contradicted the policies of Rembert Weakland in the Archdiocese of Milwaukee. Surprisingly, Mrs. Evers neglected to quote from *Familiaris consortio* which in the name of the world's bishops teaches that, *contra* Weakland, "sex education is a basic right and duty of parents, must always be carried out under their attentive guidance, whether at home or in educational centers chosen and controlled by them." This in turn, of course, only reflects the Council teaching of *Gravissimum educationis*, which among numerous similar passages quoted earlier, notes that "above all" teachers "should work in close cooperation with the parents."

But Archbishop Weakland thinks both the Pope and the Ecumenical Council, not to say parents, are wrong on all these points, and proceeds to repudiate them, along with Canon Law.[16] On 8 May 1984 His Excellency wrote Mrs. Evers: "I am informing all of the agencies of the Archdiocese not to reply to your letters anymore. After much prayer and reflection I have come to the conclusion that you are simply one of those people who cannot listen because they are so preoccupied with searching out in a legalistic and unchristian way whatever they can find wrong within the Catholic Church. You do not even hesitate to judge and condemn in the public forum . . . the institution I hold sacred."

So sacred, in fact, that though willing to let Daniel Maguire attack it with not only impunity but with specific episcopal protection, His Excellency decided to threaten Mrs. Evers with excommunication. "I will begin now to respond to your public statements taking whatever processes are necessary, legal or ecclesiastical, to protect the good name of this Archdiocese and the people who work for it."

Helena, Montana Bishop Elden Curtiss was even more specific. When some parishioners wrote to say that because of Curtiss's promotion of Peter Gerety's *Renew* program and the "catechism" *Christ Among Us* they could no longer contribute to

---

[16]Canon 212 states that the laity "have the right, indeed at times the duty . . . to manifest to the sacred pastors their views on matters which concern the good of the Church," as well "the right also to make their views known to others of Christ's faithful."

the diocesan collection fund, Curtiss wrote back on 12 July 1984 charging that "it seems clear to me that you do not agree with the renewal of the church as mandated by the Second Vatican Council and the policies of this diocese. . . . I regret that the Church has changed in ways you do not like . . . The fact is that you do not really understand the nature of the Church . . . It probably has something to do with the fact that you are converts and that you bought the Church as it was before the Council. You want the Church to be what it was 30 years ago, not what it is today, and what it is becoming."

"I do not accept your refusal to support the mission of the diocese," he concludes. "If you do not accept the mission, then you really must question whether you are really a Catholic or not." As for Curtiss's Helena diocese, its ordinary asserts that "we do not consider you a member of our diocesan family."

To other parishioners who criticized *Renew*—which Curtiss admitted on 16 June 1983 was "to help you to understand some of the new theologies that are being emphasized"—His Excellency invoked a very pre-Vatican II approach in order to bring the glories of the post-Council era to Montana. "For you to say that *Renew* misrepresents the beliefs of the Catholic Church," he wrote on 18 July 1984 "is to say that your opinion about what the Catholic Church teaches is correct and that mine is not," whereas "as bishop of this diocese . . . my interpretation of the documents of the Vatican Council is the official interpretation."

Cardinal de Lubac disagrees. "The truth is," he told *30 Giorni*, "the universal church is on the contrary neither an abstraction, nor the sum of the originally independent Churches. There is nothing, either in the origins of Christianity or in the Tradition of the Church or in Vatican II, which could even suggest such a thing . . . each particular Church exists fully only in the 'one and unique catholic' Church." Thus each bishop is not a little tyrant whose "interpretations of the documents of the Vatican Council is the official interpretation," albeit a different one from town to town, or diocese to diocese. That does, in fact, seem to be very much the case in the United States: but the bishops' "interpretations" are valid only to the extent that they are in union with the rest of the Church, which means in union with the teaching of John Paul II. Otherwise, as Cardinal Gagnon pointed out, you have material schism; something that is not really Catholic at all.

Despite these countermeasures, the letters kept pouring into the Vatican, and so the Modernists kept getting more and more upset. Jesuit Richard McCormick wrote an April 1984 piece for *America* called "The Chill Factor: Recent Roman Interventions" in which he denounces "archconservatives" for writing directly to Rome about "those they consider 'dissenting,' 'dissident,' 'deviant,' 'unorthodox,' as if these words were all synonyms." ("Gosh, who'd think *that*?" *Catholic Eye* observed). Being chilled, McCormick suggested, were such eminent figures as Raymond Brown, Avery Dulles, Bryan Hehir, and Richard McBrien, and their episcopal allies such as John Dearden, Raymond Hunthausen, Thomas Gumbleton, Walter Sullivan, Rembert Weakland, and Joseph Bernardin.

Attacks against the laity for exercising their rights as defined by the Council and Canon Law began to appear in diocesan papers as well, especially after the *imprimatur* was removed from *Christ Among Us* (CAU). The "methodology" of "conservative" Catholics United for the Faith (CUF), and its many "smirky insinuations" were denounced in Bishop Ernest Unterkoefler's Charleston *Catholic Banner*. Brooklyn Bishop Francis Mugavero's top diocesan spokesman and columnist Father Howard Basler—who was also at the Extraordinary Synod, and who once admitted to me that he had lied on behalf of Mario Cuomo due to pressure from the Governor's office, accused CUF's criticism of CAU's explicit repudiation of the sacraments of "nitpicking" and "arbitrary charges." Basler also denounced "the direct-mail game," and was strangely frank in insisting that only those laity who have clerical approval—say, through *Renew*—should be entitled to the rights defined by Vatican II. "*If*," Father Basler grumbled (though my emphasis) "CUF is to receive a hearing, let it be alongside the voice of more informed and representative Catholics."

The *National Catholic Reporter* fulminated against "CUFism" and "these stupid little men," and "narrow-minded bookburners," which it made sure no one would confuse with the CLA or Archbishop Weakland by also charging them with being "a Roman thought patrol."

Perhaps the most radical suggestion—of dealing with CUF by formally repudiating Vatican II altogether—was published in Bishop James "Jim" Niedergeses's Nashville *Tennessee Register*. "If the American Catholic Church at large tolerates this sort of CUF activity, there arises the real question of who is going to be determining the pastoral worth of catechetical resources . . . in a word, these people are going to have to learn to accept the teaching authority of the processes and agencies provided by the Bishops," because "a doctrinal issue in the United States that is to be presented to a Vatican congregation should depend wholly on the discretion of the Bishops of the United States."

By the summer, the attacks reached a kind of hysterical peak. "All of us," Father John Healey wrote in the 18 August *Brooklyn Tablet*, "ought to disassociate ourselves from religious fundamentals of every kind, including the Catholic brand, who acquire their 'certainty' (and intransigence) from 'Church teaching' just as other fundamentalists get it from the Bible." The cleric felt this "disassociation" was particularly important, since, as he opined in another column, "most Catholics, and others, are really like children in matters of religion." This is presumably unlike Father Healey himself, who claims to have achieved that "maturity which is attainable only through responsible decision-making."

In 1985, Father McBrien picked up on similar themes in column after column, employing an intellectual dishonesty that was at least daunting for its audacity. Though he invariably spits out the word "far right-wing" and other epithets at anyone who disagrees with him, the cleric took to lecturing Catholics for "mean-spirited criticism, saturated with sarcasm and even loathing," which, when they do it, he insisted, is "out of place." The priest was also consistently critical of the political cooperation between Catholics and Evangelicals in fighting abortion. "Where does that leave us?" he asked as recently as a February 1986 column. "Are politics and social philosophy, in the end, more important than theology and doctrine?"

In fact, McBrien wrote close to a dozen columns in 1985 that used an ostensibly critical view of Evangelical Protestantism as the club with which to attack his real target—Catholics who were serious about implementing Vatican II. In a column titled "Lust for Certitude" the head of Notre Dame's theology department begins by noting that millions of Catholics have left the Church "because of fundamentalism," by which he appears to mean—since it is the case—various branches of Evangelicalism. He then immediately asserts, however, that "fundamentalism is of two kinds, biblical and doctrinal," and suggests the U.S. bishops should write a pastoral letter, which "would have to address both." From then on, whenever McBrien uses the term "fundamentalism," it is rarely clear whether he is denouncing Evangelicalism or Catholicism. "Fundamentalism," he writes, "stems from what one theologian once called a 'lust for certitude,'" and "just as physical lust, which seeks total possession of the other, so the lust for certitude ... destroys the bond of faith." Accordingly, "the serious pastoral problem posed by Catholic fundamentalism cannot be solved by education alone." Presumably some excommunications might also prove helpful.

In the 28 September 1985 *America* Charles Curran picked up on McBrien's theme by blasting the bishops for refusing formally to acknowledge "the diversity and pluralism available to those who must confront the many complex questions that touch upon controversies regarding abortion laws. In sensitive areas that relate to what is sometimes called 'private morality,' the hierarchical church teaching office might offer a notable service to the faithful if it were to articulate clearly the recognition that one cannot always attain an absolute moral certitude about the existence of specific universal norms."

According to the 20 October 1985 *Our Sunday Visitor* (OSV), Milwaukee Archbishop Rembert Weakland was deeply impressed by this argument. "Churches must avoid attitudes that contain easy, fundamentalist answers," *OSV* reports he told a Lutheran congregation in York, Pennsylvania; for these try "to eliminate religious doubt and the struggles that result when religious values clash with those of the secular world." In addition, *OSV* said the Archbishop darkly warned "that fundamentalism has become part of many congregations, including Catholic parishes."

Meanwhile, Father McBrien was not the only priest seeking to provide a theoretical structure for excommunicating Catholics loyal to Vatican II and willing to exercise the rights it defined. Among others, Father Charles Irvin also made contributions to that approach in Bishop Kenneth Povish's diocesan paper (Lansing, Michigan), which efforts eventually won Irvin an appointment to the advisory council that would help Bishop Malone prepare his Spetember 16 Submission to the world's bishops on the condition of the Church in the United States.

Father Irvin first tried his hand at, as it were, irony, by titling a piece "How to Destroy Your Church," which he said could be done by subscribing to a: "newspaper run by laymen, such as *The Wanderer*. Then join an organization like CUF. ... Begin by going to work on your local priest and parish ... after all, as everyone knows our seminaries have been infested with heterodox

teachers due to lack of adequate supervision by our laxist bishops
... note how often your priest fails to directly attack any form of
abortion ... note down any latent forms of secular humanism you
find creeping into your priest's homilies or talks to parish groups
... withhold dollars. That's where your power will exert the
most control. Only don't merely withhold dollars, be sure and tell
as many people as you can exactly why you are discontinuing
your contributions and call upon them to do the same, [and] if
you would be polite, be sure to inform your priest, [and] then begin all over again with your bishop. Remember that your bishop
is a captive of his staff and middle management. ... If he has
been to any 'theological updating' seminars or workshops then
you would be correct in assuming that the orthodoxy of your
bishop has been diluted by the teachings of modern secular humanist theologians. Perhaps even the cancer of disobedience has
been infectiously transmitted from the thinking of modern, dis-
obedient theologians into the thinking of your bishops. ... Which
brings me to my final point. The way to gain power and control
over your priest and our bishops is to write to Rome. But mind
you, it's good form to first write the Pope's Nuncio in Washington
D.C."

Yes, the Modernist clergy were upset. Accordingly, Irvin
later charged in the same paper that *The Wanderer* and CUF were
guilty of ultramontanism, "a deviant belief, an error," which
"leads to the idea that local bishops can't be trusted, that the
fullness of the teaching office (the Magisterium) can't be found
in them, and that local bishops must constantly be tested for their
loyalty and orthodoxy. ... Ultramontanists are forever talking
about ... unswerving adherence to orthodoxy," and "they speak
in terms that erode your confidence in your local bishops and
priests. They are busily about the task of eroding the full authority of our bishops' Pastoral letters, particularly the one on nuclear
armaments and peace, and the forthcoming Pastoral Letter on
Christianity and economic policies."

This theological ploy reached its peak, however, in the 13
October 1984 *America* where Ken Woodward's confidante Bishop
Kenneth Untener went public with an embarrassingly transpar-
ent example of intellectual deceit. The whole point of the piece,
again, was to denounce the laity for exercising their rights as defined by Canon Law and Vatican II. Before making that point,
however, Bishop Untener sought to stress the reality that in each
diocesan Church, in Cardinal de Lubac's words, "is present, essen-

tially, 'mystically,' the entire universal Church, since Christ is there, through the Eucharist celebrated by the bishop,"—while ignoring as de Lubac does not, that "equally, each particular Church exists fully only in the 'one and unique catholic' Church."

Claiming to "communicate a more accurate (and traditional) ecclesiology," Untener argues that "another helpful approach is to examine the titles 'Vicar of Christ' and 'Vicar of Peter.' People tend to think that the title 'Vicar of Christ' belongs exclusively to the Pope," but "Vatican II points out that the term 'Vicar of Christ' applies to every bishop who leads a diocese. The distinctive title of the Pope is 'Vicar of Peter.' The opening prayer of the Mass for a deceased Pope reads: 'May your servant, our Pope, Vicar of Peter. . . . ' The prayer after Communion of the same Mass describes his Petrine role: 'You made him the center of unity of your church on earth.' There is a significant difference between the Pope's relating to the bishops of the world as sole Vicar of Christ (and therefore source of all power and authority) or as Vicar of Peter (and therefore the center of unity). The above clarification of titles touches on the heart of the Vatican II teaching on collegiality."

Doubtless it does in the minds of those materially schismatic bishops to which Cardinal Gagnon referred, but precisely because there is a significant difference between the Pope's relating to the bishops of the world as Vicar of Christ or as Vicar of Peter, it should be mentioned that nowhere in the documents of Vatican II does the expression "Vicar of Peter" ever appear—though "successor to Peter" appears more than a dozen times. *Lumen gentium* does teach the reality that the "bishops, as vicars and legates of Christ, govern the particular Churches assigned to them," but as this is the only time Vatican II refers to the bishops as vicars of Christ, it should perhaps also be noted that the vicars are in this case described with a lower case "v" (sec. 27)—that is, in contrast to *the* Vicar of Christ.

This citation also follows the information in *Lumen gentium*, sec. 18, where we learn that "bishops, successors of the apostles, who together with Peter's successor, the Vicar of Christ and the visible head of the whole Church, direct the house of the living God." It follows too the rather straightforward passage in section 22, which reveals that "the college of bishops has for all that no authority unless united with the Roman Pontiff, Peter's successor, as its head, whose primatial authority, let it be added, whether pastors or faithful, remains in its integrity. For the Roman

Pontiff, by reason of his office as the Vicar of Christ, namely, as pastor of the entire Church, has full, supreme, and universal power over the whole Church, a power which he can always exercise unhindered."

As for the title Vicar of Peter, Bishop Untener neglects to tell us that he unearthed the only instance where it formally occurs: in prayers for the soul of a deceased Pontiff, where as Father Robert Bradley points out, we are reminded that "each of some two hundred and sixty-five Popes in historical succession has had two roles: two 'vicariates' held simultaneously, yet with a wholly different refence to time. In one role he fills a certain limited and fixed role in history: it is mortal Hildebrand (Gregory VII) or Sarto (Pius X) or Montini (Paul VI) who is standing in *for* the mortal Simon Bar-Jona (Peter): he is *Peter's* vicar. In the other role he transcends all limits of time, for now it is the identical person standing in *with* all his predecessors beginning with Peter, for the one immortal Risen Christ; he is *Christ's* vicar . . . in a word, the 'vicar of Peter' dies, the 'Vicar of Christ does not."[17]

Despite this, Bishop Untener concludes that for the laity to write the universal pastor of the Church "distorts the nature of the church," and "is not only contrary to proper ecclesiology; it is contrary to the Gospel."

Bishop Untener's reputation suffered a further blow when he refused to challenge the interpretation of his *America* piece offered in two panegyric columns published in November 1984 by Richard McBrien. McBrien called Untener's contribution "excellent" and "one of the best popular-level articles on collegiality I've seen," in particular because it revealed, according to the columnist, that St. Peter—and to be sure his successor—"was not over and above the other Apostles. He was an Apostle among Apostles . . . what pertains to the unity of the local church, however, belongs to the authority of the local bishop, not the Pope. The Roman Curia exceeds the limits of legitimate authority, therefore, when it tries to impose (or restrict) pastoral practices which have nothing essential to do with the unity of the universal church."

Father McBrien followed his praise of Untener with a series of articles about how John Paul II—McBrien employed the euphemism "some Church officials"—had not "received," as the cleric put it, Vatican II's doctrine of collegiality. The examples he cited as proof of this conjecture were the removal of the *impri-*

---

[17]From the April 1985 *Lay Witness.*

matur from Wilhelm's *Christ Among Us* and Keane's *Sexual Morality,* the investigation of U.S. seminaries and religious orders; the Dutch Synod; and the exercise of Canon Law in requiring the nuns and priests who signed the pro-abortion *New York Times* ad either to repudiate that action or leave the religious life, which "blunder," McBrien felt, "made it more difficult for Catholic liberals and feminists to part company with the ad's signers and the pro-choice lobby." All this, and "even the structure and style of papal trips has raised questions about the reception of collegiality." Indeed, for arguably the most widely published columnist in diocesan newspapers across the country, "the apparent non-reception of the doctrine of collegiality at certain official levels remains one of the most disturbing features of post-Vatican II Catholicism."

Meanwhile, the *St. Anthony Messenger* launched a counter-campaign in 1984 called "If You're Happy and You Know It Write the Pope." Peter Hebblethwaite encouraged his readers in the *National Catholic Reporter* to write Cardinal Oddi praising catechisms such as *Christ Among Us.* In the summer of 1985 National Federation of Priest's Councils President Father Richard Hynes urged U.S. Catholics to go on the "offensive," by informing the Vatican how delighted they are with their bishops.

None of these campaigns caught fire, however.

VI. Curial Reform and the 1984 Condemnations of Historicism

"For some of our contemporaries, modernity really began only with the exclusive application of the scientific spirit to the study of man himself, taken as a laboratory object—i.e., with the rise of the 'human sciences' and their achieving a monopoly of thought and the expulsion of all metaphysical reflection and all religion. Such will be the last and definitive conquest: the refusal to see in man any transcendent aspiration or to admit that 'man surpasses man infinitely.' For these people, modernity is thus the triumph—the regretful triumph—of finitude, and the full certitude that man at last knows how to destroy himself."

Henri Cardinal de Lubac

"The enemy, for socialism, is any permanent authority, whether it is a long-standing church or a holy scripture, whose tendency is to put a brake on political power. In fact power and authority are often confused nowadays: the thoroughly politicized man who seeks power can only experience and interpret authority as a rival form of power, because it impedes his ambition for a thoroughly politicized society. But authority is more nearly the opposite of power. It offers a standard of truth or morality that is indifferent and therefore often opposed to current desires and forces, standing in judgment over them."

Joseph Sobran

"Impressed with the efficiency of the college of cardinals after the deaths in quick succession of Pope Paul VI and Pope John Paul I," Desmond O'Grady observed in the 24 November 1985 *Our Sunday Visitor*, "Pope John Paul II decided it should not meet only to elect Pontiffs. He wanted the Cardinals to be his collaborators. He also allowed older cardinals, those over 80 (31 at

238

present) who had been excluded by Pope Paul VI from papal elections, to participate in ... plenary sessions."

The first formally constituted plenary session of the College took place on 6 November 1979, shortly after the Pontiff's return from the United States and Ireland, and the publication of *Cate-chesi tradendae.* "In addition to the task of electing the Bishop of Rome," John Paul told the Cardinals at that time, they "also have the task of sustaining him in a particular way in his pastoral solicitude for the Church in Her universal dimensions." It is "precisely in this singular bond," he added, wherein "lies the reason for which the Bishop of Rome wishes to meet with you more frequently, in order to profit from your advice and your wide experience. In addition, the meeting of the members of the College of Cardinals is one form in which we see exercised pastoral and episcopal collegiality, a form which has been in effect for more than a thousand years, and which it is fitting for us to use in modern times as well."

The pastoral and episcopal collegiality employed in that first session addressed some very concrete problems, among which were the annual financial deficits of the Holy See; the relationship of the Holy See to culture with regard to various Pontifical Academies; the apostolate of the family and the need to institute a special department for the family, which was eventually put under the direct supervision of Cardinal Gagnon; and not least, a restructuring of the Roman Curia, as originally called for in Vatican II (*Christus Dominus*), and begun in 1967 by Paul VI with the Apostolic Constitution *Regimini Ecclesiae Universae.*

By the second plenary session of the world Cardinalate, in November 1982, the Holy See's financial problems had grown worse, not least because of naive priestly trust in those who were involved in the scandalous collapse of *Banco Ambrosiano.*[17] However, both the Pontifical Commission for the Family and the Pontifical Council for Culture were established by then, and there had also been much progress on the restructuring of the Curial departments. This latter effort, in fact, was the central concern of the 1982 session, particularly notable because, in O'Grady's words "Pope John Paul II is the first Pope to involve a worldwide cardinalate commission in curial reform."

---

[17]Prior to Vatican II, the Vatican's financial affairs were always handled by Italian priests; Paul VI put these under the charge of Americans.

The third plenary session of the Cardinalate was held from 21-23 November 1985, that is, the three days immediately preceding the opening of the Extraordinary Synod. In fact, the Pontiff gave particular weight to this session by announcing that "the assembly of Cardinals will be an authoritative introduction to the great celebration"—the Synod—"that will soon begin."

Accordingly, it is of some moment that the successor to St. Peter used this meeting to help stress the authoritative character of the Roman Curia, as defined by Vatican II, and against the enemies of Vatican II.

"In exercising his supreme, full and immediate authority over the universal Church," the Pontiff said in his opening address to the Cardinals, quoting *Christus Dominus*, "the Roman Pontiff employs the various departments of the Roman Curia, *which act in his name and by his authority* [my emphasis] for the good of the churches and in the service of the sacred pastors."

"From this definition," John Paul said of *Christus Dominus*, "the Curia is seen as an instrument and a service to the Roman Pontiff. It therefore ... is relative to the Pope, and from him receives its power: and in its identity of views with him resides its strength, its limits, its deontological code.... Its power is that of a vicar, and as such it must continuously measure itself to the will of him *cuius vices agit*—in whose place it acts—in seeking an absolutely faithful interpretation. From this perspective, one sees how aberrant are those conceptions which pretend to oppose the Curia to the Pope, as if it were a question of another parallel power."

The Patriarch of the West's vindication of Cardinals Oddi and Gagnon continued. "The cooperation of the Curia with the Roman Pontiff is essentially incorporated into this service of unity," he said. "It is first of all a matter of unity of faith, which remains its irreplaceable foundation; of charity, but also of discipline; unity that does not fear diversity, which indeed continually enriches itself with the immense variety of gifts that the Holy Spirit grants to the Church—provided that they do not become isolationist and centrifugal tendencies, and that they are brought into harmony with the fundamental unity of the universal Church."

"Peter's task," the Pope added, "is also to *confirmare fratres*—strengthen his brethren—and this involves continual care in guarding, teaching, and declaring the right Faith, as well as supporting his brother bishops in their service as masters and teachers of the Faith—a service which may at times require particular measures and interventions."

Indeed. "In these relations between the universal Church and the particular Churches, between the Roman Curia and diocesan bishops, tensions may perhaps arise," His Holiness observed, "at times due to the lack of a precise and sufficient understanding of the respective areas of competence." But "because the Bishop of Rome is *totius Ecclesiae Pastor,*" or pastor of the entire Church, as *Lumen Gentium* pointed out, "his supreme ministry is eminently pastoral; thus the activity of the Curia must be a clear expression of his pastoral service." Accordingly, "in the light of these principles and particularly that regarding the pastoral dimension, the Curia must carry out all those tasks of the Church in our day that have come into evidence bit by bit in the light of Vatican II." Among these, the Pontiff noted Cardinal's Gagnon's "Council for the Family," which "against the setting of the complex and multiple problems aroused by the current situation regarding marriage and the family—as was manifested, for example, on the occasion of the 1980 Synod—was to become its own 'specialized' organism."

In view of these remarks as the "authoritative introduction" to the Extraordinary Synod on the Second Vatican Council, it is further interesting to note that Cardinal Gagnon in collaboration with Aurelio Cardinal Sabattini devised the official *Schema* for the Restructure of the Curia, which the Cardinals reviewed during the pre-Synodal session, and which is expected to go into effect sometime in 1986. The remarks were also, of course, directly applicable to the growing conflict between the laity and the Modernist clergy in the United States, particularly in light of the frequent and unapologetic Curial insistence upon the right and sometimes duty of the laity to communicate with, in Paul Johnson's words, "Rome, the ultimate court of appeal," especially when writing to the diocesan ordinary has proved futile.

Of equal significance, however, was that John Paul II finally put his own men into the top Curial posts on 9 April 1984. "There is so much good news here," *The Wanderer* opined in its 10 May 1984 issue, "that it is hard to know which is best. Perhaps the most important aspect is that it took place at all. Until now, once a prelate got into the Curia, he never left. In 1967 Pope Paul VI established the policy that Curial officials had to tender their resignation every five years, but that policy was never enacted.

From here on out, derelict officials will be responsible for their decisions."

The *National Catholic Reporter* also understood the momentous nature of the change. "The Pope has taken the Roman Curia into his hands and shaken it in a fashion unprecedented in modern church history," it editorialized. "He has done what Pope Paul VI wished to do but failed to achieve in the latter—and weaker—years of his papacy: free himself from those most determined to distract him from the course he wants set for the church. It is as if John Paul had begun to feel the growing weight of the chains of office and, mustering his considerable strength, cast them aside. Alone, he begins again. His is a very personal papacy."

Still, the *Reporter* also sought to denigrate what had happened as "a new tune called 'Vatican Musical Chairs.' 'Out,'" the editorial continued, "is retiring Archbishop Jean Jadot, apostolic delegate in the United States from 1973 to 1980"—which the *Reporter* lamented because "U.S. Catholics owe him much," since "more than any other person, he shaped the face of today's U.S. Episcopate." Indeed, it noted further that "after Jadot returned to Rome as propresident of the Secretariat for Non-Christians, the insights he gained during his U.S. stay were not sought out."

"'Out too," the *Reporter* continued, "is Cardinal Eduardo Pironio, who has left his position as head of the Vatican Congregation for Religious and Secular Institutes" despite that, in the *Reporter*'s view, "he provided a sympathetic ear to those U.S. religious who travelled to Rome to argue their cases," and though "his influence in recent years has been limited."

"Further cause for celebration," according to *The Wanderer*, "is the appointment of Archbishop Jerome Hamer, a Dominican, to the Congregation for Religious and Secular Institutes. To be blunt, Archbishop Hamer will be in charge of confronting the massive de facto apostasy among both men and women Religious; and all reports say that, unlike his predecessor Eduardo Cardinal Pironio, Archbishop Hamer will not blink." Peter Hebblethwaite took a similar if not identical view, calling Archbishop Hamer "a hard man," who, "although a religious himself ... is out of sympathy with his fellow Dominicans and could not understand why, at their last chapter in 1983, they went out of their way to praise the theology of Fathers Edward Schillebeeckx, Yves Congar, and Marie-Dominique Chenu. He may be expected to be tough on U.S. religious women."

Though not on all religious women, as *The Wanderer* pointed out, since Hamer is in sympathy with the views of Archbishop Augustin Mayer, "a longtime supporter of *Consortium Perfectae Caritatis*, and other groups in vocal and solid union with the Holy See . . . who, though it was expected he would get the job that went to Archbishop Hamer, was instead made head of Sacraments and Divine Worship; not to worry," *The Wanderer* added in its emblematic manner, "for there is reason to hope Archbishop Mayer will firmly confront the widespread and despicable abuse of the liturgy that has driven so many out of the Church altogether, and has otherwise created so much grief."

"No one seems able to understand," Mr. Hebblethwaite meanwhile opined, "why Cardinals Silvio Oddi at Clergy and Pietro Palazzini [kept as head of the Sacred Congregation for the Causes of Saints] have both been retained despite their age."

Some outside the former Jesuit's circle, however, felt they understood the implications of these decisions rather keenly. "Sebastiano Cardinal Baggio is, finally, gone from the crucial Congregation for Bishops," *The Wanderer* noted. "His replacement is Benin's Benardin Cardinal Gantin, whose name means 'Tree of Iron,' and whom [*Wanderer*] sources describe as 'solid and reliable.' Leftist sources grumble that the man who will now be in charge of bishops' appointments 'is not known for his independent thinking,' which means, of course, that he will expect new bishops to be in union with the *magisterium* of the Church."

"Not least," the weekly added, "was the appointment of Philadelphia's own Msgr. John P. Foley to be in charge of [the Pontifical Commission for] Social Communications. Among other things, this ought to delight Catholic pro-lifers, since Msgr. Foley did not hesitate to write an editorial in the *Catholic Standard and Times*"—the Philadelphia diocesan paper of which Foley had until his appointment been editor—"attacking a theory put forth by the Cardinal Archbishop of Chicago that was once known as 'the seamless garment' but has since come to resemble something closer to the emperor's new clothes.

"Even the bad news isn't so bad," *The Wanderer* concluded. "Marseilles Cardinal Roger Etchegaray, appointed head of Justice and Peace, unfortunately means we can expect the release of many unimaginative platitudes that no one will ever read; but it also means that Marseilles is now open for the appointment of a bishop more in line with the perspectives of the eminent Cardinal Archbishop of Paris, Jean-Marie Lustiger."

In tribute to the Irish missionaries throughout the world, Dublin Archbishop Dermot Ryan was made head of the Congregation for the Evangelization of Peoples; but he died a year later, and was replaced by Eastern Europe's Jozef Cardinal Tomko. Finally, one of the most notable aspects of the Curial shakeup, as the *Reporter* pointed out, is that "in the wake of the Vatican shuffle, 16 of the 22 key Vatican positions are now held by non-Italians. At the time of the Vatican council, only four of 16 key positions were in non-Italian hands. . . . These appointments, meanwhile, indicate the papal importance given to Africa, the church's fastest-growing region."

All this was not the only major development in 1984; for earlier in the year, as may be recalled, the *imprimaturs* were lifted from various heretical catechisms in the United States; and in October, Archbishop Mayer introduced the indult for the Tridentine Mass. In addition, on 13 June, with the approval of the Pope, Cardinal Ratzinger wrote to Edward Schillebeeckx insisting that he must publicly repudiate the false argument in his book *Ministry of the Church*, which maintained that a validly ordained priest was not always necessary for the celebration of the Mass. Schillebeeckx promised to do this in a later work.

Arguably the most significant events of that year, however, were two major documents attacking the historicist heresy: the Apostolic Exhortation *Reconciliatio et paenitentiae* in December, and Cardinal Ratzinger's *Instruction on Certain Aspects of the Theology of Liberation* on 6 August.

Though the Apostolic Exhortation was broader in tone, the two documents were similar in thrust. The impact of the *Instruction* can perhaps best be discerned by noting the frantic attack it inspired on the 16 September 1984 *New York Times* op-ed page, from none other than Thomas Sheehan.

"Breathlessly alarmist in tone and ill-conceived," Sheehan opined, "this document was one of the most insidious to emerge from Rome in recent years," such as "was the last used at the turn of the century: in those days the cardboard heresy was called 'Modernism,'" which Sheehan says caused "scores of brilliant and quite orthodox theologians [to be] discredited because of it, and the Church's intellectual life was set back a half a century. Pope John Paul II and Cardinal Ratzinger seem intent today on creating much the same kind of scare to crush liberation theology."

The *Instruction* was in fact calculated to give little cause for comfort "in certain parts of Latin America," as it pointed out, where "seizure of the vast majority of the wealth by an oligarchy of owners bereft of social consciousness, the practical absence or the shortcomings of a rule of law, military dictators making a mockery of elementary human rights, the corruption of certain powerful officials, and the savage practices of some foreign capital interests constitute factors which nourish a passion for revolt among those who consider themselves the powerless victims of a new colonialism in the technological, financial, monetary, or economic order."

Indeed, because "faithfulness to the covenant cannot be conceived of without the practice of justice," the *Instruction*'s "warning against the serious deviations of some 'theologies of liberation' must not at all be taken as some kind of approval, even indirect, of those who keep the poor in misery, who profit from that misery, who notice it while doing nothing about it, or who remain indifferent to it," and "should in no way be interpreted as a disavowal of all those who want to respond generously and with an authentic evangelical spirit to the 'preferential option for the poor,'" since "the Church, guided by the Gospel of mercy and by the love for mankind, hears the cry for justice and wants to respond to it with all Her might." Accordingly, he concludes, "more than ever, it is important that numerous Christians, whose faith is clear and who are committed to live the Christian life in its fullness, become involved in the struggle for justice, freedom, and human dignity because of their love for their disinherited, oppressed, and persecuted brothers and sisters."

So why the alarm from Sheehan and company? It could be that the *Instruction* also exposes the fraudulent claims of historicist concern for justice.

"For there are many political and social movements," Ratzinger continues, which though they "present themselves as authentic spokesmen for the aspirations of the poor," instead cause "the aspiration for justice [to find] itself the captive of ideologies which hide or pervert its meaning, and which propose to people struggling for their liberation goals which are contrary to the true purpose of human life."

Mr. Sheehan's discomfort can be further understood upon noting that His Eminence gets specific by revealing that "concepts uncritically borrowed from Marxist ideology and recourse to theses of biblical hermeneutic marked by rationalism, are at the basis of the new interpretation which is corrupting whatever was authentic in the generous initial commitment on behalf of the poor," wherein "there is no truth, they pretend, except in and through the partisan *praxis.*" He continues:

"Along these lines, some go so far as to identify God Himself with history and to define faith as 'fidelity to history,' which means adhering to a political policy . . . conceived of as a purely temporal messianism. As a consequence, faith, hope, and charity are given a new content: they become 'fidelity to history,' 'confidence in the future' [and so] a radical politicization of faith's affirmations and of theological judgments follows inevitably from this new conception. The question no longer has to do with simply drawing attention to the consequences and political implications of the truths of Faith, which are respected beforehand for their transcendent value. In this new system, every affirmation of faith or of theology is subordinated to a political criterion which in turn depends on the class struggle, [or] the driving force of history."

But "the class struggle," John Paul insists in *Reconciliatio et poenitentiae,* "whoever the person who leads it or on occasion seeks to give it a theoretical justification, is a *social evil*" (the Pontiff's emphasis). Ratzinger agrees. "The class struggle as a road toward a classless society," he points out, "is a myth which slows reform and aggravates poverty and injustice . . . Those who allow themselves to be caught up in fascination with this myth should reflect on the bitter example history has to offer about where it leads. . . . millions of our own contemporaries yearn to recover those basic freedoms of which they were deprived by totalitarian and atheistic regimes which came to power by violent and revolutionary means, precisely in the name of the liberation of the people. This shame of our time cannot be ignored. . . . Those who, perhaps inadvertently, make themselves accomplices of similar enslavements betray the very poor they mean to help."

His Eminence then zooms in on the source of the historicist brutality, by noting that one cannot "localize evil principally or uniquely in bad social, political, or economic 'structures' as though all other evils came from them so that the creation of the 'new man' would depend on the establishment of different economic and sociopolitical structures. To be sure, there are structures that are evil and which we must have the courage to change," but "structures, whether good or bad, are the result of man's actions and so are consequences more than causes." Accordingly, "to demand first of all a radical revolution in social relations and then to criticize the search for personal revelation is to set out on a road which leads to the denial of the meaning of the person—and his transcendence, and to destroy ethics and its foundation which is the absolute character of the distinction between good evil."

"It is only by a careful examination that one can detect [the] root," of evil, according to the Prince of the Apostles, in *Reconciliatio et poenitentiae.* "It is to be found in a *wound* in man's inmost self ... we call it sin, beginning with original sin, which all of us bear from birth as an inheritance from our first parents, to the sin which each one of us commits when we abuse our own freedom."

"But reconciliation cannot be less profound than the division itself. The longing for reconciliation, and reconciliation itself, will be complete and effective only to the extent that they reach—in order to heal—that original wound which is the root of all the other wounds: namely sin. ... [I]t is a truth of faith, also confirmed by our experience and reason, that the human person is free. This truth cannot be disregarded, in order to place the blame for the individual's sins on external factors such as structures, systems or other people."

And yet, "there is no sin, not even the most intimate and secret one, the most strictly individual one, that exclusively concerns the person committing it. With greater or lesser violence, with greater or lesser harm, every sin has repercussions on the entire ecclesial body and the whole human family."

Thus, says Ratzinger, "Liberation is first and foremost liberation from the radical slavery of sin"—which may be what Sheehan and the Modernists hate most of all, for as John Paul points out, "to *acknowledge* one's sin, indeed—penetrating still more deeply into the consideration of one's own personhood—*to recognize oneself as being a sinner,* capable of sin, is the essential first step in returning to God."

Finally, since we are dealing with the resurgence of neo-Arianism, let us note the Pope's commentary on it in *Reconciliatio et paenitentiae.* "Saint John," the Pontiff there points out, "speaks of a sin which leads to death (pros thanaton), as opposed to a sin which does not lead to death (me pros thanaton)" and "by this distinction of concepts seems to want to emphasize the incalculable seriousness of what constitutes the very essence of sin, namely, the rejection of God. This is manifested above all in *apostasy* and *idolatry* (the Pontiff's emphasis): repudiating faith in revealed truth and making certain created realities equal to God."

Meanwhile, it is arguable that one of the most profound expressions of the Catholic understanding of liberation can be found in Pope Paul VI's *Credo*, which may be why Cardinal Ratzinger released his *Instruction* on the sixth anniversary of the Pontiff's death. And closed it with Paul's moving words:

"We profess our faith that the Kingdom of God, begun here below in the Church of Christ, is not of this world, whose form is passing away, and that its own growth cannot be confused with the progress of civilization, of science, of human technology, but that it consists in knowing ever more deeply the unfathomable riches of Christ, to hope ever more strongly in things eternal, to respond ever more ardently to the love of God, to spread ever more widely grace and holiness among men. But it is this very same love which makes the Church constantly concerned for the true temporal good of mankind as well. Never ceasing to recall to Her children that they have no lasting dwelling here on earth, She urges them also to contribute, each according to his own vocation and means, to the welfare of their earthly city, to promote justice, peace and brotherhood among men, to lavish their assistance on their brothers, especially on the poor and the most dispirited. The intense concern of the Church, the Bride of Christ, for the needs of mankind, their joys and their hopes, their pains and their struggles, is nothing other than the great desire to be present to them in order to enlighten them with the Light of Christ, and join them all to Him, their only Savior." But it "can never mean that the Church is conforming to the things of this world, nor that She is lessening the earnestness with which She awaits Her Lord and the Eternal Kingdom."

VII. Restoring Catholicism in the U.S. Episcopate: A Beginning

> *"It is the task of the Church to reaffirm that abortion is death. It is the killing of an innocent creature. Consequently, the Church considers all legislation in favor of abortion as a very serious offense against primary human rights and the divine Commandment: Thou shalt not kill."*
>
> Pope John Paul II

> *"The power to appoint is the power to rule, and the Pope has used this power extensively, and usually effectively."*
>
> E.J. Dionne, Rome correspondent, *The New York Times*

Upon publicly acknowledging the growing tension between the U.S. Episcopate and the successor to St. Peter—or as the *New York Times* more obligingly put it, "the considerable strain between the Vatican and the Catholic Church in the United States"—Minneapolis-St. Paul Archbishop John Roach ended his term, on schedule, as President of the National Conference of Catholic Bishops in November 1983, and was replaced by his NCCB Vice President, Youngstown Bishop James Malone. It is, in fact, the general practice for the NCCB Vice President to assume the Presidency, which makes the 1983 Vice Presidential choice of St. Louis Archbishop John May an interesting one. If, as expected, May succeeds to the Presidency in November 1986, there should prove an engaging tension between His Excellency's short temper and committed clericalism on the one hand, and on the other his desire for the Red Hat, which though normally awarded to the ordinary in St. Louis, has so far eluded its present occupant.

It was also at the November 1983 meeting when the U.S. bishops chose Joseph Cardinal Bernardin, despite his support for Planned Parenthood benefactor "Crusade for Mercy" in Chicago, to replace the recently deceased New York Archbishop Terence Cardinal Cooke as Chairman of the Bishops' Committee for Pro-Life Activities. Within a month, Bernardin gave his famous "seamless garment" speech at Fordham University, questioning the integrity of opponents to abortion who were not "equally" involved with various other social issues; and which made the front page of the *New York Times*.

The impact of Pope John Paul II's episcopal appointments to New York and Boston the following month (January 1984) cannot easily be exaggerated. To put it into relief, one need only consider that when Bernardin made his Fordham speech in December 1983, there was simply no American bishop in the country capable of challenging his thesis. Those who might have had the courage to try did not have either the Chicago prelate's power or prestige. Since January 1984, on the other hand, there is no question but that the Chicago Cardinal's national influence has steadily declined.

Meanwhile, despite Cardinal Bernardin's and New York Archbishop John O'Connor's felt need to make frequent episcopal assurances that they agree on all subjects, such were not heard until almost a year after O'Connor's appointment to New York. Three days after his appointment, to the contrary, O'Connor flew to the Archdiocese and gave interviews which amounted to a direct assault on the Bernardin thesis, an assault which, in tandem with Archbishop Bernard Law in Boston, did not let up until that thesis was quite dead as a Catholic approach in the public mind.

"There is a linkage of pro-life issues," O'Connor observed on 3 February 1984, "but it must be very carefully defined. If one is speaking of the potential use of nuclear weapons to deliberately attack innocent human life and the life of non-combatants, this is condemned. But on the same basis that abortion is condemned, and that is where the analogy begins and ends," because "in the case of an unborn infant, you're never talking about an aggressor," whereas though "there may be many reasons never to use nuclear weapons," the Church at the same time "teaches very explicitly that the state has a right and a duty to defend its citizens against unjust aggression."

Having already observed that "lots of people in the pro-life movement are uneasy with Bernardin's [Fordham] statement," O'Connor added on 3 February that "many in the pro-life movement are concerned that if the appropriate distinctions aren't made, and a heavy emphasis is placed on the *possible* deaths that will happen in the horrible event of a nuclear war, there'll be a tendency to ignore or de-emphasize the *actual* deaths that are taking place through abortion."

And then, in what most understood as a direct challenge to Bernardin, Bishop O'Connor quietly observed that "the anti-nuclear movement is a relatively popular movement in a number of quarters. Some, I feel, would be happy to see the abortion issue smothered by the anti-nuclear issue."

Shortly after this, the Chicago Cardinal made a speech at the Jesuit's St. Louis University defending his Fordham thesis. Making it clear that he had understood O'Connor's challenge, Bernardin used the New York Archbishop's word, when he insisted that the "seamless garment" would not "smother our . . . public opposition to abortion."

"I intend to do everything I can in New York," O'Connor meanwhile promised, "to help the poor, the homeless, the hungry, single parents—everyone who is weak and vulnerable. But it will be done with the emphasis on the unborn. It's an old cliche, but the life you save may be your own. It won't be many years before the Supreme Court will tell us we can kill the handicapped, the retarded, and the elderly. This isn't a scare tactic: it happened, in Nazi Germany."

The Archbishop was as good as his promise. He and Archbishop Law soon appeared on ABC's *Niteline*, explaining the Catholic position. A week before formally assuming the New York Archbishopric on 18 March, he went on the city's most probing interview program with Gabe Pressman, and charged that "the abortion mentality that has swept the country, that has simply declared the unborn to be nonhuman; this is what I compare to the Holocaust." This mentality, he added, "does not differ in essence from that mentality that legalized putting Jews to death in Nazi Germany."

In response to this observation, a horrified *New York Times* published an editorial implying that O'Connor was an anti-semite; but the public outrage against the *Times* for this tactic was so compelling, that it later published an unprecedented six letters in defense of O'Connor, including one from former Supreme Court Justice Arthur Goldberg. "Any inference in your editorial that Bishop O'Connor in any way minimized the tragedy of the Holocaust," Goldberg charged, is "without foundation and constitutes an unwarranted aspersion on Bishop O'Connor's total dedication to human rights and his total abhorrence of anti-semitism in any form."

Archbishop Law was no less forceful; and he was even more eloquent. "Pope John Paul II," Law said at his installation in Boston a week after O'Connor's in New York, "has movingly written that if we hold Jesus Christ in our hearts, we can see Him in the face of every person. To come from darkness into the marvelous light of God's love is to see the dawn of a new creation in Christ Jesus. It is to see Him in everyone—and in that vision to hold out a hope for healing, for reconciliation, for peace. The vision of Isaiah is fulfilled in Christ and the Church: upon us the Lord shines, over us appears His glory."

"But the darkness covering Isaiah's earth, the dark clouds covering the peoples, are with us yet. Jesus tells us quite simply that we are to meet that darkness with the light of holiness, with the goodness of our acts." And yet since "darkness, death, and sin take many forms, to be the light is to name the darkness," for "the father of darkness disguises himself as light—he holds out death in the guise of life, misery in the guise of fulfillment, evil in the guise of good. . . ."

"Nowhere is the shroud of darkness heavier in the contemporary world than in the sin of abortion. . . . Jesus came that we might have life and have it more abundantly, yet we deal out death through abortion to the most innocent of human beings. This is the primordial darkness of our time, this is the cloud that shrouds the conscience of our world. Having made our peace with the death of the most innocent among us, it is small wonder that we are so ineffective in dealing with hunger, with injustice, with the threat of nuclear war."

The two Archbishops were not only eloquent, however; they also launched a practical effort against defenders of the abortion Holocaust.

"You show me the politician," O'Connor told Gabe Pressman, "who is prepared to say 'I am personally opposed to bombing cities with nuclear weapons, but we have to have free choice,' or 'I am personally opposed to killing blacks or Jewish people or Methodists or Lutherans or Catholics, but we have to have a choice.' That's, you know, that's to me, sheer absurdity." Two weeks later he refused to allow photographs to be taken of a private meeting he held with the pro-abortion Democratic Party Presidential candidate Walter Mondale. Afterwards, His Excellency publicly announced he hoped Mondale "would think through the inconsistency of his 'pro-choice' position with his other expressed concerns for human life." Bernardin's seamless garment had clearly been unraveled and rewoven.

That same month the New York State Catholic Conference issued a public statement calling "upon all in public office and positions of authority to oppose legalized abortion, by support of a constitutional amendment." In addition, in what many considered a hopeless gesture at the time, the Catholic Conference in May attacked New York Governor Mario Cuomo's bid for a state ERA as "not an economic equity measure but a pro-abortion funding tool." Nonetheless to everyone's amazement, "the measure was sidetracked," as the *Times* noted, "mainly through pressure from . . . anti-abortion groups." The *New York Daily News* called it "a blow for Governor Cuomo, who made passage of the state ERA a cornerstone of his State of the State message." Cuomo himself blamed the defeat on O'Connor.

On June 24, His Excellency upped the stakes even higher during a live press conference, by leaving open the possibility that Cuomo's pro-abortion position might eventually lead to excommunication. Further, in response to the question of whether a Catholic can "vote for a pro-abortion political candidate," O'Connor answered, "as far as I can see there is no way, I don't see how it can be justified. I've read that you must take the totality of an individual's voting record . . . but I think that no matter what your record on other things, I can't see how a Catholic can support anyone who supports abortion or takes the position, 'I personally oppose abortion, but . . . '. Abortion is a life and death matter and I don't see how anyone can ever deliberately endorse it."

"Leaving the press conference," Bill Reel wrote two days later in the *Daily News*, "someone remarked that Archbishop O'Connor is the Pope's man, the Pope's surrogate, the Pope's spokesman. Others nodded in agreement. Because O'Connor is articulate and unafraid, the Pope put him in New York to turn America around on abortion. . . . The Pope is sure to thank the Archbishop for taking a strong pro-life stand. Catholic politicians will have to take on the two of them."

And not only Catholic politicians. By "defending traditional Church teaching on abortion, homosexuality, birth control and all the issues that, up to now, seemed open to debate in some corners of the American Catholic Church," sometime *National Catholic Reporter* contributor Dick Ryan penned in the *New York Post*,

Archbishop John O'Connor had provoked "anonymous rumblings from certain corners of the Church that other American bishops and Church officials are being shunted aside with their ideas and input about the moral issues of the day. By emphasizing abortion as an issue in the election, he has diffused the 'seamless garment' premise of Chicago's Cardinal Joseph Bernardin." *Our Sunday Visitor's* Jim Castelli, in fact, said that "O'Connor has shredded the seamless garment."

Cutting still closer to the nub, New York Auxiliary Bishop Patrick Ahern told Joe Klein of *New York* magazine that "John O'Connor upped the ante on abortion all by himself. He started the ball rolling and the other bishops have been forced to follow along. I think, too, that it is an act of great courage, because they're going to *flay* him over this before he's finished." Klein himself came to the defensible conclusion that "O'Connor's position may be more a challenge to Bernardin than to Mario Cuomo or Geraldine Ferraro. The real struggle here may be over who's going to be the main spokesman for American Catholics. I think it's significant that you haven't heard much from Bernardin since all this started."

USCC bureaucrats apparently understood the real struggle too; but the first NCCB attempt to undermine O'Connor—in August 1984—fell as flat as the *Times* attempt to portray His Excellency as a racist. On this occasion the *Times* covered, but refuse to publish what O'Connor said at the June press conference, until Mario Cuomo attacked those statements five weeks later; whereupon the *Times* gave it front-page coverage for three days running. The paper then leaked a mid-August statement from Bishop Malone that attacked O'Connor's position, but the original *Times* story was based on only a partial text, which the paper used to imply a complete vindication of Cuomo against O'Connor by the NCCB. Since the full statement (released the following day ahead of schedule because of the leak) also implicitly criticized Cuomo's position, it was this that got most of the attention; and the public was left with the not wholly accurate impression that the NCCB was behind O'Connor a hundred percent.

Closer to the truth was Jerry Filteau's observation in the bishops' own *National Catholic News* wire service, that "properly understood, [pro-abortion Democratic Vice Presidential candidate Geraldine] Ferraro's arguments form the basic philosophy behind the quadrennial USCC statements on political responsibility."

That being the case, as Kenneth Briggs wrote for the *Times*, "the broader moral context put forth by Bishop Malone and his leadership role among the bishops, seemed to some bishops largely obscured by the attention surrounding the actions of the Archbishops in Boston and New York."

Whereupon Archbishop Law picked up the ball. In August he dryly told the Knights of Columbus that "when the USCC ... makes specific proposals directed to the realization by our people of their right to liberty and the pursuit of happiness, it faithfully follows the Declaration of Independence in the assertion that it is the right to life without which no other human rights can possibly be realized. One cannot pluck the right to life from the seamless fabric of our declaration without unraveling its texture by removing its glowing primary strand."

"The right to life is not a 'one issue' tenet of our institutions," he added. "It is *the* issue—primary and predominant."

His Excellency followed through with this on 5 September, the first week of the formal presidential campaign, with a press conference in Boston. There, he read a statement signed by 18 bishops from the Northeastern United States, which asserted that abortion was "the crucial issue in this campaign," and though "we are not saying how you must vote ... we are saying that when you make up your mind, this is the critical issue." Asked why he sought to elevate its importance at the beginning of a political campaign, Archbishop Law answered, "I can explain my own timing. I have been Archbishop of Boston for six months. On March 24 in my homily of installation, which was prior to the political conventions, prior to the formulation of platforms, prior to any of that, I said I think abortion is a primordial evil. And I have been consistent in teaching that. And I will be consistent after November as well."

Three days later Archbishop O'Connor told a reporter that "Geraldine Ferraro has said some things about abortion relative to Catholic teaching which are not true. She has given the impression ... that there is a solid foundation for a variance in Catholic teaching about abortion. But there is no variance, there is no leeway as far as the Catholic Church is concerned in regard to the question of abortion ... so Geraldine Ferraro doesn't have a problem with me. If she had a problem, it's with the Pope."

Mrs. Ferraro denied having tried to distort Catholic teaching. Whereupon His Excellency reminded her of a letter she'd signed as a Congresswoman encouraging people to attend a briefing which "will show us that the Catholic position on abortion is not monolithic and that there can be a range of personal and political responses to the issue. This breakfast has been assembled by Catholics for a Free Choice and is a most impressive one. Our speakers are"—among others—"Daniel C. Maguire, a professor of theology and ethics at Marquette University who has written a highly regarded book on the religious right-wing," and "Jim Castelli, Washington correspondent for *Our Sunday Visitor* and *Gannet News Service* columnist on religion."

But, O'Connor pointed out, "the teaching is monolithic."

On 11 September, the day the Archbishop released Ferraro's letter, "the bishops were deeply divided at the 50-member Administrative Board meeting over whether the situation had become so confused as to warrant a second statement by Bishop Malone," according to Briggs at the *Times*. "One Archbishop," he added, "called the meeting of the highly influential committee, the 'most tense' he had ever attended. At first, the bishops voted against the idea. The next day they reversed themselves."

The meeting closed on 13 September. A month later Bishop Malone issued, as the *New York Times* editorial titled "The Right Tone for Bishops" observed, "a wholesome statement . . . obviously chiding some Catholic bishops and non-Catholic preachers who have recently taken to rating office seekers for their doctrinal fidelity." The *National Catholic Reporter*, equally pleased, agreed that Malone's statement "can easily be read as a rebuke to those bishops who gave the church an increasingly partisan image by singling out abortion as the most important campaign issue."

The pleasure was premature, however, for despite the *Time*'s admiration, Malone's statement was rather tepid and had little impact. This was in contrast to the major policy address Archbishop O'Connor gave on 15 October refuting every defense of abortion that had been put forth over the preceding months. It gained further authority in that His Excellency delivered it with Nobel Laureate Mother Teresa of Calcutta standing at his side.

Meanwhile, on 7 October, Catholics for a Free Choice (an organization kept alive solely by grants from major pro-abortion outfits such as the Playboy Foundation), spent some $35,000 for a full page ad in the *New York Times*, which ad insisted that Catholics and other opponents of abortion should be forced to finance the carnage with their tax dollars, and asserted falsely that it is "a mistaken belief" that "the direct termination of prenatal life as morally wrong in all instances . . . is the only legitimate

Catholic position." It was signed by, among others, twenty-four nuns, a religious brother, three priests, including the vocations director for the Cincinnati province of the Franciscans (which province publishes the *St. Anthony Messenger*, Liz Fiorenza of Notre Dame, Rosemary Ruether, Mary Mansour, Daniel Maguire and his wife Marjorie, who said the advertisement "wouldn't have appeared at all if Archbishop O'Connor hadn't taken such a forceful stand."

Shortly after that Detroit Auxiliary Thomas Gumbleton told Patricia Lefevere of the *Reporter* that Mario Cuomo's position, as outlined in a mid-September speech at Notre Dame, was right. "If you don't have a general consensus on an issue, you can hurt the common good more by trying to put one position into law than by trying to develop a consensus," Gumbleton asserted. Instead of trying to develop such a consensus, however, the Detroit bishop organized a press conference on October 22 during which he denounced Archbishop Law's contention that abortion was the crucial issue of the campaign. Twenty-two other bishops joined Gumbleton in this exercise—among them, Joseph Imesch, who heads the committee presently drafting the pastoral letter on women.

"If now is not the time to emphasize this enormous evil of abortion," Bernard Law inquired of his brother bishops the following day, "when will be the time?"

On 25 October Cardinal Bernardin spoke at the Jesuits' Georgetown University, and, according to Briggs, "called on Roman Catholics to make a broad Catholic attack on social ills that separates itself from both the fundamentalist right wing and a focus on such single issues as abortion." The speech, Briggs added, "implicitly criticized fellow bishops closely associated with waging an anti-abortion campaign," and "was the latest move in jockeying over the hierarchy's long-term approach to public policy.... Many see Cardinal Bernardin's 'seamless garment' appeal as contrasting with Archbishop O'Connor's principal stress on abortion, and believe this divergence signals much deeper differences."

Meanwhile, in a straightforward attack against O'Connor that appeared in the predominately pro-abortion *Village Voice* on 25 December 1984, the *Voice* asked Cardinal Bernardin if he "had ever or would ever do what O'Connor had done—attack a candidate by name."

His Eminence replied: "I try to be very scrupulous about not becoming involved in politics in a partisan way. I try not to personalize these issues. As a teacher, it is better for me to address the moral perspectives and let the people decide who to vote for. I was asked everywhere I would go, one reporter tried four times at one press event to get me to comment about a candidate," but "finally the reporter gave up."

"I am not naive," the Cardinal dryly added. "I want to keep the moral dimension."

On 29 October Bishop Malone spoke at a Christian-Jewish Workshop that devoted itself, according to the *Washington Post*, to attacking various anti-abortion leaders within Protestantism. "Speaking at an opening press conference," the *Post* notes, "Malone said that on the abortion question, 'the value that is attached to the unborn child is a value that is viewed differently by the participants in our dialogue. We acknowledge that, and we don't seek to make converts from Jews and Protestants.' Malone said candidates for public office 'should be expected to articulate' their views on controversial issues. On abortion, he said, 'we are not asking every candidate to agree (with the bishops), but we think they should say where they stand.' "

On 26 October the *National Catholic Reporter* admitted O'Connor's triumph, by noting that "most of the nation's Catholics will go to the polls November 6th convinced the hierarchy singled out abortion as the only critical issue in the 1984 election," which the paper said "was unfortunate." In addition, the *Reporter* charged that "O'Connor, Law, and a few other bishops are undermining the authority of the U.S. Bishops and their national conference." Richard McBrien elaborated on this in a *Reporter* interview that "What I find so unacceptable about Archbishop Law's approach, and to only a slightly lesser extent Archbishop O'Connor's approach, is that they are inconsistent with the stated policies of the National Conference of Catholic Bishops . . . you have an internal conflict in the U.S. hierarchy which religion writers have completely missed: much more interesting than the story of Archbishop O'Connor against Governor Cuomo or Congresswoman Ferraro is the story of Archbishops O'Connor and Law against Archbishops Bernardin and Malone."

In the 18 November *National Catholic Register*, Philip Lawler pointed out that "only rarely do bishops allow their debates to become public, and when they do, something very serious is happening within the Church." But after the election, at the mid-

November NCCB meeting in Washington, Bishop Malone invoked the McBrien/*Reporter* argument to launch what amounted to a major attack on O'Connor and Law.

"Roman Catholic bishops should follow the lead of their national conference in shaping efforts to change pubic policy, the head of that group said today," according to Kenneth Briggs on the front page of the 12 November *New York Times.* "Malone's speech put him and the conference leadership squarely on the side of what has been called the 'consistent ethic of life,' led by Joseph Cardinal Bernardin of Chicago" according to UPI, "and opposed to other influential prelates who stress abortion as the primary public policy issue for Catholics."

"The conference," Malone said, "does not substitute for the voice of individual bishops, but it provides a framework within which a coherent theological, moral, and social vision can be articulated, and a sense of direction for the Church can be determined. The conference is a unique structure, ecclesially and socially, for shaping a consensus on public issues and expressing it," and the "public role of the Church in this country is enhanced and expanded by the episcopal conference," since "the ability to speak corporately on national level has a social significance often recognized by other religious organizations and observers of the Church."

"By Canon Law," Briggs wrote in the 15 November *New York Times,* "bishops are accountable directly to Rome, but since the Second Vatican Council mandated the founding of regional and national conferences of bishops, the individual bishop has become answerable to the conference as well."

Meanwhile, in August 1984, Cardinal Ratzinger began his series of conversations with Vittorio Messori, during which he would repudiate the idea that any bishop anywhere is responsible to a national conference.

On 30 November, the Pope's new man Archbishop Jerome Hamer, head of the Sacred Congregation for Religious and Secular Institutes, wrote to the head of the congregations of the religious who had signed the pro-abortion *New York Times* ad, informing them that said religious must make a "public retraction" of their "scandalous" pro-abortion position; resign; or be prepared for canonical efforts to dismiss them from their congregations. The three priests who signed the ad promptly made the retraction (secular priests in response to admonitions from their bishops instead of Hamer), as did the religious brother; four nuns did

so in the course of the following year. Because of these developments, a nervous Richard McBrien wrote in January 1985 that
"many Catholics are beginning to wonder if the unthinkable is
happening. Are we returning to the anti-Modernist days?"

Archbishop O'Connor, meanwhile, according to a 17
February 1986 profile in the *New York Times*, "has brought a fresh
assertiveness to the role of Archbishop of New York, and has expanded the influence of the Roman Catholic Church on the life
and politics of the city, government, and church. . . . In his less
than two years as Archbishop . . . the Cardinal has reversed the
image of reticence the church had acquired during the previous
15 years, and has heightened its political impact. . . . he attributed
his success to his outspokenness on the moral teachings of the
Roman Catholic Church." And, of course, as O'Connor's auxiliary
Bishop Joseph O'Keefe observed, "what happens in New York has
an influence far beyond New York."

Nonetheless, though the bishops are unlikely ever publicly
to admit this except in elliptical terms, "the American hierarchy," as the *Village Voice* article unhappily concluded, "is now
gravely divided in two camps. Bernardin leads all but a handful,
but his is a wounded . . . voice," whereas "the other camp is small,
but . . . vigorous. It made itself seem to be the national church in
the spotlight of a presidential campaign. It may have Rome in its
corner. It can be charitable when confronted with the homeless,
liberal when championing the hungry. And it knows when to
lyrically transform an unspoken political understanding with the
President . . . into a cry for the dying unborn. At its center is the
fresh face from New York . . . and his effect on America's largest
church may change the face of a nation."

In May 1985, only two American prelates were awarded the
Cardinal's Hat: John O'Connor of New York and Bernard Law of
Boston. Meanwhile, as the *New York Times* Rome correspondent
E.J. Dionne pointed out, "during his six and a half years as
Pontiff, John Paul II has accomplished what many in 1978 would
not have thought possible: the restoration of authority to the pa-
pacy and a clear sense of what the Church stands for."

Having done so, it was time to confront the question of
what Vatican II stands for.

THE CARDINAL

I. An Athanasius for Our Time

> *"Athanasius was the greatest champion of Catholic belief on the subject of the Incarnation that the Church has ever known, and in his lifetime earned the characteristic title of 'Father of Orthodoxy' by which he has been distinguished ever since . . . it is his peculiar merit that he not only saw the drift of things from the very beginning, but was confident of the issue down to the last. His insight and courage proved almost as efficient a bulwark to the Christian Church in the world as did his singularly lucid grasp of traditional Catholic belief."*
>
> The Catholic Encyclopedia

> *"Roughly speaking, three main opinions are competing. To one group, most dramatically represented by the suspended Archbishop Marcel Lefebvre, Vatican II itself is to blame . . . A second group agrees that the council represented . . . a break, but they greet it as long over due . . . Cardinal Ratzinger represents a third view . . ."*
>
> The *New York Times*

"Alongside the overwhelmingly favourable response John Paul evoked among millions of American Catholics," Paul Johnson wrote in 1982, "there was a steady stream of critical venom of a type which no previous pope had ever received from any section of the American Catholic community. John Paul was compared to Jim Jones, leader of the mass-suicidal Jonestown cult. He was accused of 'lack of sensitivity,' of 'pious and moralistic reassertions' of traditional doctrine which 'shocked' and 'perplexed' the faithful. He was called a 'pious, pharisaical, autocratic, woman-hating white,' supporting the 'injustice, phony trials, machinations, hypocrisy and witch-hunts' of the Vatican, allowing Rome to become 'dominated by an atmosphere of bullying and secretiveness and ecclesiastical power plays.' He was told to 'take off his long dress,' and 'assimilate Kueng's masterpiece, *On Being a Christian*.' He was 'a new Torquemada of the Tiber,' determined to force the church into a 'Procrustean bed modelled after the conservative Polish church.' He should 'listen and learn,' show 'more sensitivity and less dogma.' He had 'set the ecumenical movement back a hundred years,' . . . turned the church into 'a giant hypocrisy,'" was "a 'wizard of Castel Gondolfo,' a 'paid star in show-business,' a man whose greatest failure was 'a lack of sympathy and understanding of human problems.'"

Such impartial analyses did not cease after 1982, nor were they unique to the United States; nonetheless, it should be noted that though the atheists and Protestants were saying remarkably similar things, the above quotes come "from sections of the Catholic press, Catholic authors, priests in good standing, and . . . teachers at Catholic universities."[1] Thus it was no surprise that when the Pontiff made his 1979 trip to the United States, CBS news quickly hired the American version of Wyszynski's Boleslaw Piasecki, Father Richard McBrien; there, in Ralph McInerny's words, McBrien "nightly undercut the papal message," with such dutiful observations as that "you can be *too* loyal to the Pope! You can be *too* emphatic about the Divinity of Christ!"

From 25 January 1985, however, the decibels increased considerably. That date, of course, is the 26th anniversary of Pope John XXIII's announcement at St. Paul's Outside-the-Walls that he would convene an Ecumenical Council, on which occasion, and from which place, John Paul II announced there would be an Extraordinary Synod on the Second Vatican Council at the end of 1985, designed to coincide with the 20th anniversary of the Council's Final Session. The enemies of the Council were not pleased. This was understandable since in the course of the announcement, the Pontiff noted again that "Vatican II has always been, and especially during these years of my pontificate, the constant reference point of my every pastoral action, in the conscious commitment to implement its directives concretely and faithfully at the level of each Church and the whole Church."

The Vicar of Christ evidently thought a Synod might help others in this process as well, and thus "the purpose of this initiative," he noted, "is not only to commemorate the Second Vatican Council," but also to "exchange and examine experiences and information about the application of the Council at the level of the

---

[1]*John Paul II and the Catholic Restoration.*

universal Church and the particular Churches, to promote the
further study and the constant incorporation of Vatican II into
the life of the Church, in the light of new exigencies as well,"
and—not least, though it seemed so at the time—"to revive in
some way the extraordinary atmosphere of ecclesial communion,
which characterized the Ecumenical Council." Nor was it insignificant that he was calling an Extraordinary (as opposed to
Ordinary) Synod, since according to Canon Law the former is to
be convened only for "dealing with matters which require speedy
resolution."

Indeed. The Modernist counter-attack was swift, but neither
imaginative nor effective. The *London Tablet*[2] charged in a 2
February 1985 piece called "A Challenge to Bishops" that
"whereas Vatican II laid the emphasis on the team, Pope John
Paul lays it on the captain ... a striking instance was the recent
grant of permission ... to return to the celebration of the Tridentine Mass," which was of course something only the laity wanted.
The *Tablet* also pointed out that non-Catholics were "closely
watching how Rome is exercising its authority," and "do not like
what they see," but argued that "the bishops can change this," by
imitating "the bishops who attended Vatican II," who had been
"strong enough to repudiate the agenda that had been prepackaged by the Curia, and start again. Those who attend the Synod
will not be able to do that: there will not be time. So the Bishops
must begin now ... it is up to the bishops." It is a theme the *Tablet*
would sound throughout the year.

Six days later, on 8 February, Peter Hebblethwaite—who
also writes for the *Tablet*—got more specific in the *National
Catholic Reporter*. Noting that the Synod was scheduled to last but
two weeks, from November 24 to the Feast of the Immaculate
Conception, Hebblethwaite charged that" so brief a synod "can
do no more than rubber-stamp the prepackaged conclusions the
pope has in mind. The synod is designed to permit the world's
bishops to advise the pope on matters of common interest. But
Pope John Paul ... turned previous synods into rallies for his own
policies. So this extra [sic] synod will be invited to confirm not so
much Vatican II as the pope's analysis of what the church needs
today. It is now clear what that is, and Cardinal Joseph Ratzinger,

---

[2]Whose editorial positions can be imagined if one knows that
the *Tablet* advertises Father Curran's opinion that "your publication is of great service and help to many people throughout the
world."

chief Vatican ideologue, has pronounced the key word: restoration."

"The synod could be the last opportunity for the bishops of the world to pluck up the courage to say 'enough is enough.' The restoration . . . has done whatever good it is likely to do. From now on, there is only the dismal prospect of breaking heads and careers through disciplinary measures—what the pope in Caracas called 'correcting with charity and firmness those who have erred.' No doubt the bishops will be held back by a reluctance to 'criticize the pope,' [but] treason against the papacy . . . is not a crime, it is a duty imposed on bishops and, especially, cardinals. It even has a technical name: fraternal correction; and it is the only defense against papal autocracy."

Commonweal said the same thing, as did Charles Curran in *America*, as well as *Concilium*, a group upon whose editorial board sit such figures as Schillebeeckx, Kueng, Pohier, Yves Congar, Gustavo Gutierrez, and Leonard Boff. Kueng wrote a private attack as well. In short, it was a rather old song, and wags in Rome suggested the Pope had called the Synod because he knew the Modernists would sing it; and that this would reveal even to them how exhausted their ideas were. Regardless, the only Episcopate that danced to it with any energy was Hebblethwaite's own: Cardinal Hume and the English. And, as we shall see, the Hume dance did grave damage to the Modernist cause.

Meanwhile, there were doubtless many reasons why the Pontiff felt in 1985 that he was ready to challenge the distortions of Vatican II and win the clear support of the international episcopate in doing so, against those minority episcopates that had allowed the distortions. At the same time His Holiness had, of course, read Cardinal Ratzinger's interview with Vittorio Messori, parts of which had appeared in the Italian magazine *Gesu* in the autumn of 1984. He was also aware that the interview had provoked scattered protests, and would be published in book form and in numerous languages throughout the course of 1985. Accordingly, it is not impossible John Paul had guessed that his convening of an Extraordinary Synod would have the immediate practical effect which it did in fact have; which was to make the Ratzinger interview the primary focus of intellectual debate within the Church throughout the year. Having accomplished that, there seems little doubt the Pope also succeeded in putting the Ratzinger analysis at the center of any discussion about Vatican II for at least the remainder of the century.

E.J. Dionne of *New York Times* was openly amazed by the "astonishingly clear language, unencumbered by diplomatic hedges" in Ratzinger's "remarkable indictment of what has happened to the Roman Catholic Church." Ralph McInerny called the interview "without doubt the most refreshing, sustained and sensible look at what has actually taken place in the post-conciliar Catholic Church ever to appear."

"Dr. Ratzinger is an excellent theologian," Cardinal de Lubac told *30 Giorni*, and "he is not afraid to take up in broad daylight either fundamental questions or current problems, always with calm, simplicity, a sense of measure, great respect for people and a smile." Messori himself noted in Ratzinger "the ability to listen, the readiness to let himself be interrupted by questions and the willingness to answer everything with the most extreme frankness, while allowing the tape recorder to run."

While it ran, the Cardinal told Messori that the "The Catholic who clearly and, consequently, painfully perceives the damage that has been wrought in his Church by the misinterpretations of Vatican II must find the possibility of revival in Vatican II itself. The Council is *his*, it does not belong to those who want to continue along a road whose results have been catastrophic. . . . what the Church needs in order to respond to the needs of man in every age is holiness, not management. . . . Dogmas are not walls that prevent us from seeing. On the contrary, they are windows that open upon the infinite. . . ."

Particularly striking was how His Eminence cut to the heart of the modern world's contempt for women. "Woman," he notes, "who is creative in the truest sense of the word by giving life, does not 'produce,' however, in that technical sense which is the only one that is valued by a society more masculine than ever in its cult of efficiency. She is being convinced that the aim is to 'liberate' her, 'emancipate' her, by encouraging her to masculinize herself, thus bringing her into conformity with the culture of production and subjecting her to the control of the masculine society of technicians, of salesmen, of politicians who seek profit and power, organizing everything, marketing everything, instrumentalizing everything for their own ends," and "what is the woman to do when the roles inscribed in her own biology have been denied and perhaps even ridiculed? If her wonderful capacity to give love, help, solace, warmth, solidarity, has been replaced by the economistic and trade-union mentality of the 'profession,' by this typical masculine concern? What can the woman do when all that is most particularly hers is swept away and declared irrelevant and deviant? ... It is precisely woman who most harshly suffers the consequences of the confusion, of the superficiality of the culture that is the fruit of masculine attitudes of mind, masculine ideologies, which deceive woman, uproot her in the depths of her being, while claiming that in reality they want to liberate her ... To respect biology is to respect God Himself, hence to safeguard his creatures," and so "it is no accident if the word 'Church' is of feminine gender. In her, in fact, lives the mystery of motherhood, of gratitude, of contemplation, of beauty, of values in short that appear useless in the eyes of a profane world."

And, as Cardinal Law insisted, the light must name the darkness. Thus, Cardinal Ratzinger observes of the Liberal Consensus that "Ultimately the authority on which these biblical scholars base their judgments is not the Bible itself but the *weltanschauung* they hold to be contemporary. They are therefore speaking as philosophers and sociologists, and their philosophy consists merely in a banal, uncritical assent to the convictions of the present time." Of the McBriens and the Currans: "a certain 'contestation' of some theologians is stamped by the typical mentality of the opulent bourgeoisie of the West ... it seems to them that they must choose between opposing modern society and opposing the *magisterium* ... consequently they set out on a search for theories and systems that allow compromises between Catholicism and current conceptions." But of course, as McBrien has so degradingly revealed, you cannot serve God and mammon. Instead, as Ratzinger points out, "among the most urgent tasks facing Christians is that of regaining the capacity of nonconformism, i.e. the capacity to oppose many developments of the surrounding culture."

As one might imagine, the Modernists were no longer simply displeased, they were frightened; worse, they were exposed. Accordingly, it was clear to them that Ratzinger *himself* had to be discredited, and quickly, so as to prevent his arguments if possible from being read, but at all costs from being considered: for they knew that once considered, his analysis could well lead to the restoration of Vatican II, and the end of its bureaucratic misappropriation by the spiritual heirs of Alfred Loisy and George Tyrrell.

The somewhat base lengths to which such people were willing to go received scrutiny in a 19 January 1986 *Our Sunday Visitor* article by Russell Shaw; in it Shaw disclosed the rumor suggesting close ties between Ratzinger and the Third Reich that was circulated during the Synod, despite the fact that Ratzinger was but 12 years old when World War II broke out, or, indeed, that it was the Cardinal's horror of the Nazi evil which helped convince him he had a vocation to the priesthood in the first place.

Commonweal editor Peter Steinfels was thought by some to be the source of this usually repugnant stategem, due to his insistence in the 30 November *America* that Ratzinger's views were "an intellectual scandal," whose "most revealing passage ... might be one having nothing to do with the present state of the church. It could well be the one page or two in which the Cardinal fondly recalls the church in Bavaria of his childhood," since "to anyone familiar with . . . that era—I am putting the matter delicately—the Cardinal's virtually unqualified complacency is quite remarkable."

If one might be less delicate, it is clear Steinfels sought to convince people that Ratzinger's perspectives could be ignored because at the heart of his faith was a certain complacency about exterminating Jews, which charge is especially curious coming from an editor who regularly publishes and celebrates people who are not just complacent, but positively enthusiastic about the extermination of unborn children, Jewish or not. Accordingly, there was a certain consistency in Steinfels' careful refusal actually to quote the passage that was the basis of his charge, so allow me to compensate for this omission.

"The Catholicism of my native Bavaria," His Eminence observed, "knew how to provide room for all that was human, both prayer and festivities, penance and joy. A joyful, colorful, human Christianity," especially as "I grew up in a family which really practiced its faith," that "confirmed for me that Catholicism was a citadel of truth and righteousness against the realm of atheism and deceit which nazism represented." Thus, he reminded Messori, "the poisonous seeds of nazism are not the fruit of Austrian and Southern German Catholicism but rather of the decadent cosmopolitan atmosphere of Vienna at the end of the monarchy," which is why "in the decisive elections in 1933 Hitler had no majorities on the Catholic states."

This attempt to smear Ratzinger with anti-semitism, Shaw observed in the *OSV* article, was "a small incident, but symptomatic. In recent months fantastic tales tinged with hostility and paranoia have often been told about Joseph Cardinal Ratzinger .. . he has been depicted as a reactionary, an inquisitor, and even ...

as a crypto-Nazi." People knew to whom Father Richard McBrien referred when he charged that "national episcopal conferences are under attack from far right-wing quarters." "Cardinal Ratzinger has violated notoriously the much publicized secrecy of the Vatican," as the Lutheran pastor Richard Neuhaus observed in the 14 February 1986 *National Review*. "Through lectures, articles, and interviews he has tried to communicate with critics and supporteers alike. Were the content of the communication other than it is, the style would be celebrated by those who call for an 'open Church.'"

In September the formally "pro-choice" and 1800-member National Coalition of American Nuns (NCAN) issued a press release demanding that His Eminence retract his "scandalous calumny" and "outrageous attack on the good name of non-cloistered women,"—whom Ratzinger had said were in a "grave crisis," and often unhappily distorted by a false "feminist mentality."

In May a group of French priests, with some episcopal support, issued an attack on Ratzinger called the Montpellier Appeal, which received devoted attention in the French press, but was promptly dismissed by Cardinal Lustiger as "pure absurdity that makes no sense." The English Dominican publication *New Blackfriars* (*NB*) also published a bitter jeremiad that month from hand-picked members of the newly formed "Association of British Theologians," under the direction of *NB* editor Father Fergus Kerr; its flavor can be imagined from Kerr's own quiet reflection that Ratzinger's perspectives are an "example of the long, boring tradition of hyped-up, panic-mongering hyperbole." Monsignor George Higgins, meanwhile, had difficulty deciding between directly denouncing Ratzinger and presenting as general opinion the views of priests whose apprehensions were coincidentally in accord with his own. Using the direct method, Higgins explained that Ratzinger's ideas were "dyspeptically dim," "convoluted," "extremely dispiriting," as well as "grim and doleful," whose triumph at the Synod would prove "embarrassing and slightly ominous." Taking the safer approach, Higgins adds that "I share the reaction of Fergus Kerr, O.P., editor of *New Blackfriars*," who has provided nothing less than "a fair and accurate summary of the Cardinal's overall point of view."

Meanwhile, Peter Hebblethwaite's already weak reputation as an accurate or perceptive reporter suffered perhaps fatal blows in 1985, due to his insistence, time after time, that Ratzinger's perspectives had been intellectually destroyed once and for all. In point of fact, these analyses began in late 1984, when Hebblethwaite charged in the 25 November *Reporter* that Cardinal Casaroli didn't like the document on liberation theology, and that accordingly "some sympathy is due to Ratzinger for what now looks like a misguided and utterly unsuccessful enterprise. He has had a bad two months. In September, he failed to get a condemnation of Leonard Boff, the Brazilian Franciscan . . . in any secular administration, such manifest failures would lead to resignation . . . but by now his face must be as crimson as his cardinal's robes."

On 7 December 1984 Pope John Paul II undercut Hebblethwaite's premature thesis by urging 18 visiting Bolivian bishops "to follow recent Church guidelines" because of "the dangerous uncertainty created . . . by some currents of liberation theology. In this work of clarification, you will be helped by the norms contained in the pertinent instruction of the Congregation for the Doctrine of the Faith." The Pope returned to this theme consistently during his triumphant South American tour in February 1985. On March 20, Leonard Boff's key work was formally condemned; in May Boff was silenced altogether, for nearly a year.

But Hebblethwaite was not deterred. "Curia 'defenders' undercut pope's message" ran an April headline; in June, he claimed that the fluff in *New Blackfriars* "is devastating for Ratzinger;" in August, that "when Ratzinger gets up at the synod, he will be at a distinct disadvantage." That same month he claimed that "a time bomb, carefully crafted at Regis College, Toronto, Canada, is about to go off. It is the work of Father Luis Segundo, a Uraguayan Jesuit who . . . has been called 'the Karl Rahner of liberation theology.' Segundo's book is a sustained attack on the instruction . . . by the Congregation for the Doctrine of the Faith on 'Certain Aspects of Liberation Theology.'" The time bomb turned out to be a firecracker, and a lady finger at that. And yet Hebblethwaite, apparently hoping against hope, continued to push on, claiming as late as 6 December 1985, despite abundant evidence to the contrary, that according to the mood of the

Extraordinary Synod the Cardinal's "May 1985 book the *Ratzinger Report* now appeared thoroughly eccentric."[3]

A certain insecurity about this point came to light in August, however, when the Pope all but formally endorsed Ratzinger's views as contained in the Messori interview. The Pontiff noted, as had Ratzinger himself, that "what Cardinal Ratzinger has said is his own opinion," albeit an opinion which His Holiness acknowledged is one that "corresponds to many events." John Paul further agreed with his chief Prefect that the Cardinal's views "cannot be understood [to mean] that the Council, Vatican II, was a negative influence, a negative meaning for the Church—no, to the contrary."

Headlines across the diocesan press subsequently ran: "Pope disagrees with Ratzinger on council."

Meanwhile, perhaps the most comic expression of the Modernist insecurity was the observation of Catholic Theological Association president Monica Hellwig, to the effect that though he had read and approved publication of the interview (and though numerous passages has appeared in *L'Osservatore Romano*), even Cardinal Ratzinger disagrees with Cardinal Ratzinger. "I cannot believe," she wrote in the 15 November *Commonweal*, "that some of the . . . statements in this 'report' actually came from him or represent his opinions accurately."

---

[3]To help buttress Hebblethwaite's sagging but crucial reputation, throughout 1985 a series of reviews praised his rather sad book on Pope John XXIII, though it suffered acutely from "poor scholarship" according to the American priest Father Thomas Herron, who works in Ratzinger's office, and was speaking informally when he said this. Accordingly, the ex-Jesuit's allies felt compelled to overstate their praise for the book in a manner possibly embarrassing even to Hebblethwaite himself. Father McBrien, for example, insisted not only that "the publisher has not exaggerated" in calling the book "the definite biography of Angelo Roncalli," but added that it "may be one of the most important Catholic books to appear since Vatican II," not to say "a nearly indispensible resource for anyone trying to capture the content and spirit of 20th century Catholicism." Father John Jay Hughes from Archbishop May's St. Louis *Renew* office called it "a finely drawn portrait of John's pontificate for decades to come." Xavier Rynne caught another reason for the accolades in his 24 March 1985 *New York Times* review. "What [the book] makes crystal clear," Rynne opines, "is that with the council, Pope John turned the church upside down. And that all the pope's prelates and all the pope's men cannot put its ancient intransigent imperialism together again."

Despite all the effort, however, in the end the defamatory campaign had pretty much the opposite effect of what had been intended. Throughout 1985 Ratzinger's stature continued to grow, and arguably not just despite, but also because of the contrast between his own quiet depth and dignity, not to say humor, with the not exactly admirable tactics of his enemies. The faithful, meanwhile, even began making tentative comparisons between Ratzinger and St. Athanasius, who had towered over, and conquered, another age of Arianism; and who had rescued another Council, Nicaea, from the depredations of an earlier time.

By the dawn of the Synod, the Modernist Arians of this age were desperate. Their only success had been to convince the media that Pope John Paul II intended to repudiate Vatican II, which had doubtless been arranged in order to proclaim the end of Ratzinger yet again when the Pope—yet again, this time with the Synod—announced his intention to vindicate the Council. But even this tactic would prove a failure.

Accordingly, as in the last act of a farce, Hans Kueng was trotted out onto the stage to summarize for the Higginses, the Hebblethwaites, or as one might legitimately say, for the herd; and Father Kueng's perspectives were accordingly given attention in newspapers both secular and ecclesial throughout North America and Western Europe. "For a long time, I have held myself back," his summary as published in the *Reporter* began (though less than two years had passed since Father Kueng's last long denunciation of both the reign of Wojtyla and the Papacy itself for that paper), "but it is only because I am daily made to feel how many men and women—especially fellow priests and religious—suffer under the current course that I can no longer keep silent."

"I do not wish to engage in cheap polemics against persons," but "Ratzinger is ... just like Fyodor Doestoevski's Grand Inquisitor ... his skillful argumentation lashes out on all sides, aiming at every discipline. ... Are we at the threshold of another antimodernist campaign? ... What is reflected here is the arrogance of power. From his elevated position, the ex-professor now denies the conferences of bishops all theological authority. Open-minded theologians[4] from exegetes to dogmatists and ethicists to the pastoral and liturgical theologians—are condemned by someone who is himself a former theologian and bishop." More infuriating still

---

[4]Father Kueng is himself sufficiently open-minded that in *Eternal Life?* he mused about the utility of active euthanasia.

is that "medieval usages and conceptions again recommended by Ratzinger as essentially Catholic. These include not only indulgences, Rosary, Corpus Christi processions and celibacy, but also the exaltation of Mary."

"Are these merely the private visions of an official of the Roman Curia?" he asks. "No, this book would not be worth the mention if it weren't precisely a church policy signal of the first order and if it weren't for the fact that one can also hear the master's voice in this book ... in spite of all the verbal assurances, what from the beginning have been the real intentions of this pope are becoming increasingly clear ... to be sure, Vatican II is emphatically confirmed by both John Paul II and Ratzinger. However, what they have in mind is not the progressive spirit of the council but rather the 'true council,' the one that simply stands in continuity with the past, [for] there is no more talk of a distinction between the church of Christ and the Roman Catholic church, between the substance of faith and its linguistic and historical garb, no more talk of a 'hierarchy of truths' ... For the Vatican, the coming episcopal synod in November is a suitable tactical means for a long-term strategy that aims at a comprehensive restoration."

"There can be little doubt," E. J. Dionne wrote in the *New York Times* Sunday magazine cover story about Ratzinger on the opening day of the Extraordinary Synod, that in his Doctrine Prefect "the Pope knew exactly the sort of man he was getting: brilliant, quietly thoughtful, and on a collision course with Catholic liberalism and the left." Indeed, "in choosing Cardinal Ratzinger to be the head of the Congregation for the Doctrine of the Faith, Pope John Paul made what [Joaquine Navarro Valls] the Vatican spokesman calls 'one of the most personal choices of his Pontificate.' On other important appointments, the Pope consulted widely, making bows to various constituencies; Cardinal Ratzinger ... was very much the Pope's personal preference."

"Often appearing shy in public," Dionne says, His Eminence is nonetheless "supremely self-confident ... and ready to do battle with those who disagree with the Pope." And, to be sure, "the Pope sees many of the attacks on Cardinal Ratzinger as, in fact, being aimed at himself, with the Cardinal effectively serving as a lightning rod."

"Central to Cardinal Ratzinger's disillusionment with the progressive cast of mind," the *Times* continued, "was the student revolt of the 1960's."

"For so many years," His Eminence told Dionne, "the 1968 revolution ... created ... a radical attack on human freedom and dignity, a deep threat to all that is human. At the time, I was dean of the faculty of theology at Tuebingen, and in all the university assemblies in which I participated, I could notice all kinds of terror, from subtle psycho-terror up to violence."

"This was accomplished," he continued, "in the name of freedom, with theories that were so hypocritical, if one only compared them with the praxis," and "I learned that is is impossible to discuss with terror ... as there are no premises for a discussion, and such a discussion becomes a collaboration with terror. I think that in those years, I learned where discussion must stop because it is turning into a lie, and resistance must begin in order to maintain freedom."

II. The Pontificate of John Paul II in the Year of the Synod

> *"And this is the condemnation, that light is come into the world, and men loved darkness rather than light, because their deeds were evil. For everyone that doeth evil hateth the light, neither cometh to the light, lest his deeds should be reproved."*
>
> John 3: 19-20

> *"And I say also unto thee, that thou art Peter, and upon this rock I will build my church; and the gates of hell shall not prevail against it."*
>
> Matthew 16:18

The organization of the Synod went ahead quickly. Appointed Secretary General, Czech Archbishop Jozef Tomko was put in charge of this until the death of Archbishop Ryan at the Congregation for Evangelization of Peoples, whereupon Tomko replaced Ryan and Archbishop Jan P. Schotte—said to have contributed to the composition of *Laborem exercens*—replaced Tomko. Though the Roman Pontiff is the President of the Synod, he may appoint others to act with him, and for the Extraordinary Synod did so. These were: Curial (Christian Unity) official Cardinal Johannes Willebrands, Kinshasa, Zaire Archbishop Joseph Cardinal Malula, and Philadelphia Archbishop John Cardinal Krol.

The various categories of voting participants in an Extraordinary Synod are determined by Canon Law. These 165 members included, with the Synod Secretary, 14 patriarchs, major archbishops and metropolitans outside of the Catholic Churches of the Eastern Rite; 102 presidents of national episcopal conferences, or of conferences for more than one nation (in 1985 23 of these 102 were Cardinals); the 24 members of the Roman Curia; representatives of three clerical religious Institutes, chosen by the union of Major Superiors; and 21 members chosen directly by the Roman Pontiff, of whom 2 were priests only, and ten were Cardinals. Drawn from 105 nations, and not counting the patriarchs, Curial officials and so on, 35 of the bishops were from Africa, 25 from Latin America, 19 from Western and 10 from Eastern Europe, 22 from Asia and the Middle East, 4 from Oceania, 3 from the United States, and one each from the Caribbean and Canada. Of the 165, 59 were Cardinals, five were priests, and 63 had taken part in the Second Vatican Council (as opposed to 89 of the 122 Cardinals at the Nov. 21-23 Plenary Session).

There were in addition 15 non-voting auditors chosen as observers of the Synod's plenary sessions, and participants in the linguistic smaller sessions (*Circuli Minores* as they were called) that took place the second week and were where much of the real work of the Synod was done. Notable among these auditors were Mother Teresa of Calcutta, Knights of Columbus President Virgil Dechant, and Focolare Movement Foundress Chiara Lubich. "Specially invited" but without voting rights were, among others, such eminent figures as the brilliant Catholic theologian Hans Urs von Balthasar—who in 1985 dismissed both Kueng and Leonard Boff's public positions as "no longer Christian"—Cardinals Giuseppe Siri of Genoa and Paul Zoungrana of Upper Volta, as well as Council participants and retired Cardinals Franz Koeing, Leo Suenens, Francois Marty, Bernard Alfrink (who didn't attend), and John Dearden (who did). There were also ten observer-delegates invited from Christian groups not in union with Rome, including the Coptic and Orthodox communions, Anglicans, Lutherans, Pentecostals, Baptists, and so on.

In April a series of questions were sent to the Patriarchs, Curial heads, Metropolitans, and heads of the world's episcopates, inquiring about the successes and failures of Vatican II under the various competencies: these were the questions which inspired Bishop Malone's answers as examined earlier. Brussels Archbishop Godfried Cardinal Danneels was appointed to help summarize the major points sent in from around the world in response to these questions, in preparation for the Synod. Father Walter Kasper was appointed as a special secretary to assist Cardinal Danneels in this task.

Meanwhile, after the announcement of the Synod and the enormous explosion of support he received during the February 1985 South American trip, John Paul II proceeded to confront Modernism in a more direct manner than at any time since he had become the successor to St. Peter. In March, to begin with, Franciscan friar Leonard Boff's openly Arian repudiation of Catholicism was formally condemned. The significance of this action went far beyond Boff, far beyond the fact of a specific condemnation itself, and even beyond the implicit repudiation of Brazilian Cardinals Evaristo Arns and Alosio Lorscheider, who had flown to Rome with Boff in order to help defend his theses during 1984 conversations with the Congregation for the Doctrine of the Faith. No, the real significance was that the heart of Boff's argument, apart from the dressings, was nothing less than the Liberal Consensus outlined by Thomas Sheehan in 1984.

In *Church: Charism & Power, Liberation Theology and the Institutional Church*, Boff claims his great concern for the poor, yet contradicts his claim by going on to explain that everything the Catholic poor of South America believe is to be ignored, dismissed and overcome. "The 'deposit of faith,'" which it should be noted that Father Boff considers such an undefinable concept as to merit quotation marks, is for him nothing more than "a dialectical process of history," valid only "for a determined time and determined circumstances. In another moment of the same dialectical process, the text must be able to be surpassed, to give space to the other text of today's faith." Divine Revelation, meanwhile, is merely "the 'doctrinal' understanding of revelation," and accordingly the Mass a "religious means of production and consumption" devised during "a reconciliation with the world" in a "Roman and feudal style."

As such, Boff concludes, there really has to be "a new incarnation of the ecclesiastical institutions in society," and he very clearly implies that such a new incarnation, civil as well as ecclesiastical, could be far more conveniently managed by Franciscans like himself perhaps, or Cardinal Lorscheider, or in any event the kind of people in this dialectical moment of history whom alone are qualified to say what Christianity means.

Accordingly, "The Supreme Pontiff, John Paul II, approved [the] notification and ordered [the] publication" of the Doctrine Congregation's condemnation of Boff's book. No less accordingly, when Boff himself was formally silenced the following May, *National Catholic Reporter* editor Tom Fox cried: "Let there be no mistake about it. The silencing of Father Leonard Boff was ... a serious attack ... nor can we view this as an isolated incident. It must be seen as part of a much wider and more profound development that may affect the course of church life for decades ... if Boff is attacked, we are all attacked. If Boff is silenced, we are all silenced."

In fact, the widespread corruption of the Franciscan order (OFM branch) had been festering for some time and was finally brought to a head during its June 1985 chapter meeting in Assisi. John Paul wrote something close to a tender if admonitory letter to the friars at this meeting, reminding them that "Christians expect you to love the Church as St. Francis loved it," and consequently "I exhort you therefore, to an attentive review of the theories and practices which have proved to be an impediment to the answer to such expectations ... more than ever will it be beneficial to serve the Lord in that poverty which St. Francis wished to be the particular character of this Order," which " 'highest poverty' cannot be limited to proclamations in defense of the poor, even though evangelically and socially right and proper. It receives fullness of religious significance only if it is a poverty really lived. Besides, when it is effectively put into practice, poverty requires that the fruits produced from it remain at least partially hidden, becoming in this way both humility and wisdom. It induces one to live a life more of silence than of propaganda, and avoids being boastful about oneself and self-satisfied."

The Modernist factions that have seized control of the OFM were furious; openly repudiating St. Francis and his binding Rule (which begins by insisting that all friars must distinguish themselves by "obedience and reverence to the Lord Pope Honorius, and his successors canonically elected, and to the Roman Church"), "representatives of the Order of Friars Minor rejected a Papal warning," according to the *Religious News Service* "that they ... devote more time to prayer and spiritual reflection."

"It is too late for us to turn back now!" cried the provincials, in a formal Chapter meeting response to the Holy Father. "We cannot start over again." Before that meeting came to an end, 104 of the 135 Chapter delegates had signed a letter in defense of Boff against the Pope and Catholicism; after it ended, a kind of black hysteria and even hatred began to appear in Franciscan journals. "The Holy See is not God!" former New York Holy Name province provincial Father Charles Finnegan publicly wrote, for example. In *Mustard Seed*, a Cincinnati province

newsletter "sent to every OFM friar in North America," Boff
was hailed as "one of the greatest Franciscans the Church has
ever produced," and Cardinal Ratzinger regularly denounced for
his "reactionary ecclesiology" particularly as "it seems obvious
that Ratzinger is the unofficial spokesman for the Pope."

The Pope's simple letter had provoked the as it were anti-
Francis Franciscans to expose themselves, which would make the
Pontiff's task of assisting those who sought genuine reform much
easier. Meanwhile, the Pope had done something similar with the
discalced Carmelites at the end of 1984, by recognizing the efforts
of those who wanted the constitution of St. Teresa of Avila,
against the formidable powers within the Congregation that had
sought something more "up-to-date."

In April, Cardinal Baum sent his *schema* to the NCCB and
the American universities. In May the new Cardinals were announced: O'Connor, Law, Gagnon, Hamer (following his letter to
the pro-abortion nuns), Mayer (following the indult on the Tridentine Mass), Tomko, Cardinals from Chile and Ethiopia, and
not least Cardinal Obando y Bravo of Nicaragua, that country's
first Prince of the Church.

Perhaps no less significant was the elevation to the Cardinalate of Utrecht Archbishop Adrian Simonis, leader of the
Catholic reform in Holland, on the eve of the Pontiff's historic
voyage there. The trip itself was, of course, momentous. "A Missionary Midst the Savages" is how *The Wanderer* headlined it, and
not without cause. "Demonstrators," according to the New York
papers, "smashed windows, damaged cars, and . . . threw bottles
and rocks at the Pope's enclosed car . . . 3500 demonstrators including homosexual activists and members of punk communities
clashed with police during a violent protest . . . police found two
bags of gasoline bombs . . . opponents of the Catholic Church's
ban on artificial birth control released dozens of helium filled
condoms in the air . . . made obscene gestures and shook fists . . .
another youth climbed onto a foundation and dropped his pants
. . . police fought pitched battles with hundreds of demonstrators
chanting 'Kill, kill, kill the Pope,' and posters containing death
threats have appeared in several cities . . . there was little doubt
the rioting was organized; orders were issued by loudspeakers,
and police seized a number of primitive weapons, including iron
bars and Molotov cocktails . . . several hundred Dutchmen renounced their Catholic faith in official acts in town halls
throughout the Netherlands. . . ."

"The Pope seemed weary but unruffled," the *New York Times* noted, and "essentially ignored criticism and continued to reiterate traditional Catholic teaching"—such as for example his proclamation in Amersfoort that "the Church's teaching on marital love, abortion, sexual relations before or outside marriage, or homosexual relations, remains the standard for the Church for all time. It would be easier to mouth generalities, but sometimes, in accordance to what the Gospel teaches, the Church must be loyal to high ideals, even if in doing so it opposes current attitudes."

A questioner addressed the above subjects and challenged the Prince of the Apostles, asking "whether Jesus would not be considerably gentler with these people and their problems with the Church?"

"Would it be realistic," His Holiness responded, "to imagine a Jesus who is indulgent on abortion, or sexual relations before or outside marriage or homosexual relations? Indulgence does not make people happy. The consumer society does not make people happy either."

"The early Christians who were taught by those who knew Jesus personally were certainly not permissive. And so, if the Church makes unpalatable pronouncements, it is because She is obliged to do so . . . Being a Christian has never been an easy choice and it never will be."

Many considered Holland the most striking journey of John Paul's Pontificate, comparable in its way to the trips to Poland and Nicaragua. Never before had the stark contrast between a vital and decadent Christianity, indeed between a vital Christianity and a dying West, been visually communicated so effectively.

"What seems certain," Peter Hebblethwaite wrote in the *Reporter*, "is that the psychodrama of the Dutch church, far from being a little local affair, concerns all Catholics. It involves two contrasting visions of the church . . . and of the interpretations of Vatican II."

And David Wagner in the *Washington Times*: "When Pope John Paul II ventured last week into territory known to be hostile, he did so for the same reason he has called a special Synod to consider the applications of the Second Vatican Council, and for the same reason he has taken a number of recent initiatives. He has an enterprise in hand: the real implementation of the Council as opposed to the distortions of it that have taken a deep hold."

While in Brussels, the successor to St. Peter spoke frankly to the European Economic Community (EEC). "We find ourselves confronted with the moral and spiritual decline of mankind," he told them, "particularly in your countries. It is as if human beings see life as a game, that is, whenever they are not seized by despair." This grasp of European decline is a theme to which John Paul II has frequently turned, and it arguably provides a central key to understanding the policies of his Papacy.

A striking example of this was the Pontiff's decision in June 1985 to issue not a local letter to Slavs and Eastern Orthodox bishops, but his fourth Encyclical to the entire Church, in preparation for the 1100th anniversary of the death of St. Methodius. Entitled *Slavorum Apostoli* (Apostles to the Slavs), the encyclical was almost a rhapsodic tribute to Methodius and his brother Cyril, who in the ninth century had ventured among the primitive Slavic people, converted them to Christianity, invented an alphabet for them so that they might have liturgy and Bibles, and remained constantly faithful to Rome, despite frequent betrayals and bureaucratic attempts to undermine their work. The encyclical was also portentious because St. Methodius is buried near Prague, in the Moravian town of Velehrad, where the celebration of the anniversary took place on 7 July; for "the Roman Catholic Church in Czechoslovakia is in the midst of a remarkable revival," as noted by the 5 April 1984 *New York Times*. "Repressed in the 1950's, when bishops and priests were herded into concentration camps, the Church has lately drawn young lay recruits who appear determined to guarantee its survival underground while supporting its harried above-ground priests and bishops . . . on Sundays the churches are packed and some of the faithful must even stand outside to hear Mass." Illegal publishing houses flourish, producing theological tracts, newsletters, biographies of saints and reports of government repression—which is severe: more than 500 priests have been denied licences to run parishes, and of the 13 Czech dioceses, only 3 have been filled in the past 20 years. Accordingly, underground orders and secret vows by hundreds of nuns and religious brothers are a growing phenomenon, as are ordinations by underground bishops, and a massive network of catechism classes in the home. Perhaps most intriguing of all, as the *Times* pointed out, is that not only in historically Catholic Slovakia, but also "in the Czech lands of Bohemia and Moravia, the revival is taking root in soil that has historically been known . . . for anticlericalism." "The young people love Tomasek enor-

mously," a young underground nun told the *Times*. "Before he was
not so strong, but now he has become more courageous."

There is a price for his courage, however; one was that the
government refused to allow Pope John Paul II to come to
Czechoslovakia for the St. Methodius celebrations. Hence, *Slavorum Apostoli*; followed on 7 July by the largest public Catholic
gathering in Czechoslovakia since the end of World War II. A
quarter of a million people swarmed into tiny Velehrad to honor
St. Methodius, and another 100,000 gathered in the Slovakian
town of Levoca, which—though normally a place of pilgrimage
to the shrine of the Blessed Virgin there—was on 7 July dedicated to the memory of St. Methodius. When state officials spoke
at the ceremonies, they were booed, especially when they tried to
cast Methodius into a secularly progressive role. "He is *Saint*
Methodius, he is *Saint* Methodius," the crowd continually cried: as
well as "we want the Pope," and "long live John Paul II!"
Cardinal Tomasek quietly remarked that "I am very happy about
the loyalty of the Catholics in our country to their Faith and to
the Church ... those who are true to the Church are really deeply
true."

June, meanwhile, was also the month a glum U.S. Episcopate
met in Collegeville, Fergus Kerr issued his *New Blackfriars* attack
on Ratzinger in England, and, preparing to meet those episcopal
responsibilities Peter Hebblethwaite had outlined in February,
London's Basil Cardinal Hume traveled to Bruges and gave a
speech suggesting that the doctrine of English Catholicism under
his tutelage could only mean that it was necessary to start ordain-
ing married men. The *London Tablet* published the leading headline "Ordain Married Men!"

In mid-June, John Paul projected something of a different
perspective with a trip to Venice, during which he visited St. Pius
X's hometown where according to the *New York Times* "he went
out of his way to praise not only Pius's personal virtues but also
his ideas." In September the Pontiff announced that he would
open the Vatican archives of the Saint's Pontificate to historians,
and in Rome one noticed two interesting developments: at the
Vatican bookstore the catechism of St. Pius X had been repub-
lished with a bright new cover and in prominent display; and
bishop after African bishop kept dropping by the tomb of St. Pius
X in St. Peter's, to pray there for his intercession.

The most significant event for American Catholics in June,
however—though it did not become public knowledge until the

following January—was the first formal excommunication in the United States in over a quarter of a century. Mary Ann Sorrentino, a Planned Parenthood abortion clinic profiteer, had been informed in May by her local priest that according to Canon Law, her involvement with the extermination of unborn children automatically excommunicated her. This was followed by a letter from the diocesan chancellor on 14 June formally affirming the excommunication. On at least some U.S. Prelates, the Year of the Synod was finally making its impact.

The *New York Times* was clearly upset by this development, not least because of the press conference Sorrentino held wherein she publicly asked why the same sanctions were not applied to such public figures as Senator Edward Kennedy and Governor Mario Cuomo, which, as the *Times* knew, certain bishops considered a potentially valid argument. Accordingly, the *Times* promptly called up reliable Father Richard McBrien, who insisted that: "A reasonable person would not have assumed that the Canon [in question] would apply to" Sorrentino. Later, directly attacking the authority of the bishop who'd authorized the excommunication (Providence, Rhode Island ordinary Louis Gelineau, with the subsequent confirmation of Papal Pro-Nuncio Pio Laghi), the Notre Dame theology department head told *NC News* that his position on the case "is that [Sorrentino] is not excommunicated." Canon Law Society of America executive coordinator Father James Provost made similar observations about his surprise and incomprehension; and *Reporter* editor Tom Fox lamented in his paper that "it's all so sad, so unfair, so wrong," and "will almost certainly lead to further division and suffering within the Church—despite the glee in some right-wing ranks."

In July, ecclesial matters began to heat up considerably. McBrien's heretical work got its timid slap from Archbishop Quinn, which Fox noted was "likely to frustrate the right which wanted condemnation and censure." He added that "informed sources . . . say the U.S. Bishops' doctrine committee, which probably preferred to let the whole matter go away, has now issued its criticism to appease Roman pressures, coming primarily from Cardinal Joseph Ratzinger's office. Fact: A steadily growing number of U.S. bishops are angered at the way Ratzinger is throwing around his ecclesial weight. Question: How much is too much?" Fox's question was answered the following September; Committee on Doctrine secretary Monsignor Richard Malone, who had worked in Rome, had openly expressed his admiration for Ratzinger, and was the driving force behind the even mild repudiation of the McBrien opus, was told then that his services would no longer be needed at the United States Catholic Conference when his contract expired the following summer.

Cardinal de Lubac's interview with *30 Giorni* appeared that month; on July 5, Cardinal Ratzinger went on Italian television and said the "misinterpretations" of the Second Vatican Council to which the Pope had referred in Holland included those of "some well-known theologians" who had developed "a theology that does not believe in the reality of the Resurrection . . . no longer confesses the reality of Jesus . . . no longer preaches about a God who has the ability to enter Himself into our lives." John Paul, His Eminence added, was concerned that "this type of ideological development . . . naturally has had its effect on religious life, on the formation of the seminarians, on so many other sectors of the life of the Church. One needs to clarify here," the Cardinal added dryly, "that this kind of unbelief is not the thinking of the Council."

Roger Mahoney was meanwhile appointed Archbishop of Los Angeles, which if not received with unparalleled delight in various orthodox circles, was nonetheless telling: for in February 1985 Bishop Mahoney had established rules in his Stockton, California diocese which were in effect a direct reproach to the entire post-Council U.S. Episcopate—they made clear that the responsibility for what happened in a diocese ultimately resided with the Bishop alone. "No one from outside the diocese of Stockton is to be invited into this Diocese to give teachings on the Catholic Faith," he wrote to his priests, religious and teaching personnel, "without the express approval of myself or the competent Diocesan Department. The fact that a person from outside our Diocese is well-known or popular does not substitute for the need to verify their qualifications as teachers of the Catholic Faith, nor the need to obtain express permission in each and every case."

"Special care is to be taken in designating teachers of religious education and formation of our people," he continued, and "teachers should possess a firm faith themselves." Moreover, "No parish diocesan-wide program or diocesan department is to send its personnel to a course or program of Catholic teaching unless it has been verified in advance that the course or program meets the requirements for authentic Catholic teaching." Going for the throat of the Modernists' principal organizing technique, His Excellency then added that "in a very special way, personnel are not to be sponsored to attend courses or programs outside the Diocese which deal clearly with speculative theories in theology or Scripture, which are not consistent with the teaching of the Church."

The *Reporter*, to be sure, was upset, editorializing that "Mahoney's attempt to suffocate Stockton should have no place in a Catholic community;" but others suggested the Bishop had written these rules for the sole purpose of winning the appointment to Los Angeles. Catholics would hope that isn't true, of course; but in one sense, even if it were true, it says a great deal to those U.S. bishops who might have a touch of ambition in their blood. Cardinals Law and O'Connor had clearly brought down the curtain on the era of Jadot.

In August, following the British bishops' statement almost as if it had been done on cue, *Concilium* attacked Ratzinger, a group of his former Munich priests attacked Ratzinger, and Peter Hebblethwaite predicted that Luis Segundo's attack on the historicist condemnation would mean the end of Ratzinger once and for all.

But it was also in August that Pope John Paul II spent 12 days travelling 16,000 miles visiting seven African countries, which provided a neat contrast to the Dutch visit by provoking the massive outpouring of affection that had characterized the South American tour in February. Before the literally millions of Africans who turned out to welcome him the Pontiff publicly apologized for the involvement of Christian nations in the slave trade after the Reformation; condemned the Protestant government of South Africa on the grounds that "whatever impedes human freedom or dishonors it, such as the evil of apartheid and all forms of prejudice and discrimination, is an affront to man's vocation;" beatified a Zairean martyred nun; consecrated Africa's largest Cathedral and blessed the cornerstone of its first Basilica; and became the first Pope in the history of Christendom to receive (and the first to accept) an invitation from a Moslem sovereign and religious leader, Morocco's King Hassan II, to speak in a Moslem country before an all Muslim audience.[5] "It would be a good idea for Europeans to begin learning about African culture," the Pontiff observed, not least because of African understanding that "children are God's special gift to parents, to society and to the nation. The joy that you experience in your children is like the joy Jesus felt when he called them to be near to Him." Therefore, he continued, "do not give in to the forces that weaken and destroy the unity, stability and happiness of your families. Do not follow the path of selfish materialism and consumerism which have produced so much suffering in other parts of the world," and "do not listen to ideologies which allow society or the State to take over the rights and responsibilities which belong to families . . . Your glad acceptance of your children as God's gift to you stands to your honor and glory," because "anti-life action such as contraception and abortion are wrong and unworthy of good husbands and wives."[6]

In the West, meanwhile, tension continued to rise. In September, *Commonweal* and *America* launched a plethora of anti-Synod articles from such luminaries as Gregory Baum, George Higgins, Charles Curran, Elizabeth Fiorenza, and James Malone. In October, Kueng issued his attack on Ratzinger and the Pope, and Mario Cuomo was scheduled to be the National Conference of Catholic Charities (NCCC) keynote speaker at the annual convention on justice issues. This was due, the NCCC said, to the governor's "great insight into justice issues," notwithstanding his support for the legal structure that exterminates 4000 unborn children daily of course. However, the annual convention was

---

[5]The significance of the latter action was not lost on the multinational population control apparat either. A major confrontation between pro- and anti-abortion forces had just taken place at the end of July during the U.N. Conference on Women in Nairobi, Kenya. There, as the 25 July *New York Times* reports, "Arab countries joined forces with the Vatican representative to invoke religion and cultural traditions to change paragraphs in the draft of the final conference document" and kill a pro-abortion amendment; or, as the *Times* put it, "killing a proposed amendment on the right of women to control their own lives and bodies."

[6]"In Kenya," the 11 August *Times* reported, "government officials have openly called on people . . . to use family planning," but "the attitudes of Catholics and non-Catholics alike in this country and Africa as a whole appear to be more in line with those of the Pope . . . There is also a suspicion that family planning is a Western conspiracy to inhibit the development of African countries. For that reason some Kenyans refuse to eat yellow corn donated by the United States, fearing that it will make them sterile of that it contains some contraceptives."

scheduled to be held in Pennsylvania, which is blessed with some of the best bishops in the country—Krol in Philadelphia, Bevilacqua in Pittsburgh, Timlin in Scranton, and Welsh in Allentown. They wrote a letter blasting the NCCC, rumors of a major confrontation ensued, and the Governor wisely discovered a scheduling conflict that made it impossible for him to attend after all.

The orthodox counter-attack reached something of a peak as well in October. That was the month Balthasar exposed the fraudulence of Boff and Kueng. And *The Wanderer* held a major convention in Washington, D.C., taking out a full-page advertisement in the nationally distributed daily *USA Today*. That advertisement, among other things, charged that "the powerful and magnificent teaching of the Church, reaffirmed and elaborated by Vatican II," has "too often been ignored, distorted or subverted. We have seen the Church's ... priests and religious cowering before worldly powers; Her seminaries and convents emptying; Her children in a state of religious illiteracy; Her people turning away," and accordingly encouraged Catholics to send in for and sign *The Wanderer's* Declaration Pro-Council, which by the time of the Synod some 35,000 Catholics had done.

The *Declaration* itself was a scathing indictment of the post-Council administration of the Church in the United States. Among other things it charged that "many parents who previously would make great sacrifices to see that their children received a Catholic education now no longer believe it is worthwhile to do so," and that "among the most dangerous environments for the faith of youth today is the modern Catholic college or university and the seminaries. There is scarcely a family in the United States, which, in sending its children to a Catholic college or university, has not seen a number of those offspring lose their Catholic faith." Finally, the *Declaration* charged, "those who brought us this reform lacked faith, holiness, a sense of the sacred, and, ultimately, love; some even openly hate the Church. How then could they have truly carried out the wishes of the Council? We ask the Synod to turn the Church toward authentic renewal and put an end to the destructive practices of the last 20 years.... We ask the Fathers of the Synod for nothing more than the true teaching and implementation of the promises of the Second Vatican Council."

The battle lines were just about drawn; but not quite. Among other things, there remainrd the need for a quiet and reasoned explanaton of the Council itself, of the kind that had never really been adequately provided. That is, not until 21 October, when Joseph Ratzinger rose to the occasion once again.

III. To Fr. Kueng and Friends: In Continuity with the Past

> "St. Athanasius was by instinct neither a liberal nor a conservative in theology. Indeed the terms have a singular inappropriateness as applied to a temperament like his. From first to last he cared greatly for . . . the integrity of the Catholic creed . . . devotion to the Divinity of Jesus Christ," but "the conspicuous abilities he displayed in the Nicaean debates and the character for courage and sincerity that won on all sides made the youthful cleric henceforth a marked man . . . His career almost personifies a crisis in the history of Christianity."
>
> The Catholic Encyclopedia.

> "There is no such thing as was, because the past is."
>
> William Faulkner.

Not surprisingly, Cardinal Ratzinger's *Ecclesiology of Vatican II*, was delivered to a conference on—and of—the Catholic laity. As Vatican II had particularly noted, and the Doctrine Prefect here reiterated, the Catholic Church is more than its clerics or its episcopacy, more even than the universal pastor of the Church. "All of us carry Her forward in faith," as the Cardinal put it, "just as She carries us."

But above all, he continued, "the Church is the presence of Christ . . . The Church's life springs from the fact that Christ is present in our hearts; out of this reality He forms His Church. Therefore, the first word of the Church is Christ, and not Herself; She is healthy to the extent that all Her attention is focused on Him. Vatican II placed this conception at the apex of its considerations in such a majestic way that the fundamental text on the Church begins precisely with the words: *Lumen Gentium cum sit Christus*—Christ is the Light of the world. And it is because

Christ is the Light of the world that there exists this mirror of His glory, the Church, that transmits His splendor. If one wishes to understand the reality of Vatican II, he must always start again from this beginning..."

One must also keep in mind, His Eminence proceeded, that "the Church grows from within: this is what the expression 'Body of Christ' intends to communicate to us, yet it immediately implies this other element as well: Christ has constructed a body, and I am called to enter in and become a part of it, as a humble member—otherwise it cannot be found or had—yet in a complete way, because I have become truly one of His members, one of His organs, in this world, and consequently for eternity. The liberal idea for which Jesus is seen as interesting, while the Church is viewed as an unfortunate affair, completely differs, by its very nature, from this awareness. Christ gives Himself only in His Body and never in a mere ideal. This means together with the others, with the uninterrupted communion that spans the ages which is His Body. The Church is not an idea, but a Body, and the scandal of becoming flesh over which so many of Jesus' contemporaries stumbled continues in this scandalous character of the Church. Yet here too, the phrase is valid: Happy is he who is not scandalized by Me."

"However, this community character of the Church necessarily signifies its 'we' character ... certainly no one can say 'I am the Church.' Each of us can and must say: we are the Church. And this 'we,' in its turn, is not a group which isolates itself, but rather keeps itself within the entire community of all the members of Christ, those who are living and those who have died ... in this way a group can, then, truly say: we are the Church ..."

"Finally, the idea of development, and thus the historical dynamism of the Church enters into this theme ... For Cardinal Newman, the idea of development had truly become the bridge of his conversion to Catholicism. In effect,"—and as it were against the one-time-conversion-determines-all heresy of the Evangelicals—"there is a real identity with the origin only where there is at the same time that living continuity that develops the origin and, in so doing, guards it."

Cardinal Ratzinger then addressed what would become one of the major themes in the *Final Report* of the Synod. the expression *Corpus Mysticum*, or Mystical Body, "originally applies to the Holy Eucharist ... for Paul, as well as for the Fathers of the Church." From this, "there arose an ecclesiology of *communio* as well. This ecclesiology of *communio* became the true heart of Vatican II's doctrine on the Church, the element which is new yet at the same time fully linked to the origins, and which this Council wished to present to us. . . .

\. . . the Church lives in Eucharistic community . . . The Mass is Her form . . . in every celebration of the Eucharist our Lord is erally present . . . He always gives Himself entire and undivided. For this reason the council says: 'This Church of Christ is really present in all legitimately organized local groups of the faithful, which, in so far as they are united to their pastors, are also quite appropriately called Churches in the New Testament . . . in these communities, though they may often be small and poor, or existing in the diaspora, Christ is present through whose power and influence the One, Holy, Catholic and Apostolic Church is constituted.' "

His Eminence then notes that *Lumen Gentium*, however, "does not simply say 'The Church is completely present in every community that celebrates the Eucharist,' " because "two elements are important here: the community must be 'legitimately organized' and united with the pastors, including, of course, the universal pastor.

"What does this mean? It means, in the first place: no one can make himself the Church. A group cannot simply come together, read the New Testament and say: Now we are the Church, because the Lord is found wherever two or three are gathered in His name," since "the element of 'receiving' belongs to the Church in an essential way, just as faith derives from listening and is not the product of one's own decisions or reflections. Faith, in fact, is an encounter with that which I cannot devise or produce with my own efforts, but which must be granted to me. This structure of reception, of encounter, we call *Sacrament*. And precisely for this reason, the fact that a sacrament is received and that one cannot confer it upon himself places it within the fundamental form of Sacrament. No one can baptize himself; no one can ordain himself a priest; no one can, by himself, absolve his own sins. The fact that perfect contrition by its very essense, cannot remain interior, but impels one towards the form of encounter of the Sacrament, also is a result of this structure of encounter." The one exception, of course, is the Eucharist, where "the priest, it is true, can administer the Sacred Gift to himself," but this "points back to the *mysterium tremendum* to which he finds himself exposed in the Eucharist: to act *in persona Christi* and, at the same time, to show him to be a sinful man whose whole life stems from the reception of Christ's Gift."

"The Church cannot be made, but only received, and this means received from where She already is, from where She is really present: from the sacramental community of Her Body which extends throughout history."

Consequently, "with eucharistic ecclesiology there is connected in a most intimate way the idea of episcopal collegiality, which also belongs, in the same measure, to the foundations of Vatican II's ecclesiology . . . the dispute regarding collegiality is not a dispute between the Pope and the bishops over the power each should have in the Church, even though it can very easily degenerate into such an approach . . . Neither is it properly a dispute regarding juridical forms and institutional structures. Collegiality is rather, in its essence, ordered to that service which is the true and proper service of the Church: divine service—the Mass . . ."

"The early Church had no notion of self-sufficiency as regards single communities. In fact, the presbyters who serve them are united: one with another, they form the bishop's 'council.' The communities are joined together by the presbyters, and through the bishop they are kept within the vaster unity of the whole church. . . .

" . . . this also means that the bishops, for their part, cannot act in isolation, . . . a bishop is not a bishop by himself, but only in catholic communion with those who were bishops before him, with those who are bishops with him, and with those who will be bishops after him . . . the dimension of time is included in this," because "the Church is not something that we do today, but that we receive from the history of the faithful and transmit to others in a yet unfinished form; it will only be fulfilled with the return of our Lord."

"The Council fused this idea with the other fundamental concept of episcopal ordination, with the idea of apostolic succession, in an organic synthesis . . . 'Collegiality' belongs to the essence of the episcopal ministry: it can be lived and realized only within the unified whole of those who represent, at the same time, the new People of God . . ."

"What does this involve? . . . even in the Old Testament the term 'People of God' does not simply indicate Israel in her empirical reality. At the purely empirical level no people is the 'People of God.' To make God the stamp of a lineage or to make him a sociological mark could only be—at any time—an intolerable presumption, indeed, ultimately, blasphemy. Israel is indicated with the concept of the People of God inasmuch as she is turned towards the Lord."

Meanwhile, "perhaps I may be permitted to speak in a somewhat more personal way here, since I was able, in a small way, to take part in the pre-history that led to the Council. My theology professor in the early 1940's, when the idea of the People of God had been freshly thrust into the debate, had arrived at the conclusion, on the basis of some patristic texts and other testimonies of tradition, that the 'People of God' could in fact be the basic concept of the Church much more adequately than the 'Body of Christ.' However, since he was a very meticulous man, he did not settle for such approximate certainties, but wished to see more clearly, and he resolved to assign a series of doctrinal dissertations on the question in order to conduct research at every level of tradition. It thus fell to me to treat the People of God according to Augustine, whom he especially saw as having evidenced the idea of the People of God."

"When I set to work, it quickly became clear that I would also have to include the preceding African theologians who had prepared the way for Augustine, especially Tertullian, Cyprian, Optatus of Milevis and the Donatist Ticonius. Naturally, it was also necessary to keep in view the most important theories of the East, at least figures like Origen, Athanasius and Chrysostom; and finally, it was impossible to do without a study of the biblical foundations as well."

"I came upon unexpected results: the term 'People of God' does appear frequently in the New Testament, but only in a very few places—in the last analysis, only in two—does it indicate the Church, while its normal meaning refers back to the people of Israel. Indeed, even where it might indicate the Church, the fundamental sense of "Israel" is maintained, while the context clearly implies that the Christians have become Israel. We can thus say: in the New Testament, the People of God is not a name for the Church . . . the normal name for the Church in the New Testament is the term *Ecclesia,* which in the Old Testament indicates the assembly of the people convoked by the word of God. The term *Ecclesia,* Church, is the modification and transformation of the Old Testament concept of the People of God. It is used because in it is included the fact that only the new birth in Christ causes the non-people to become a people."

"Paul then consequently summarized this necessary process of Christological transformation in the concept of the Body of Christ ..."

"What does this mean, in concrete? It means that Christians are not simply the People of God. From the empirical point of view they are a non-people, as every sociological analysis can quickly demonstrate. And God is not the property of anyone: no one can appropriate Him. The Christian non-people can be the People only through becoming part of Christ, Son of God, and Son of Abraham."

And what does it mean in terms of bishops, in particular the idea of being in union with the Bishop of Rome, and the Catholic episcopate? Is juridical union enough?

Not according to Vatican II, it would seem, if we recall that in the chapter headings of *Lumen gentium* the hierarchy, like the laity and religious, follow the chapter on the People of God, because this concept includes them all.

And "we are not the People of God," the Prefect of the Sacred Congregation for the Doctrine of the Faith concluded near the end of his address, "unless we take the body of Christ, crucified and risen, as our point of departure. We become that people only through being ordered to Him in a living way. And only in this context does the term have meaning."

By this token, the views of the Liberal Consensus may by the Body of Christ be considered parasitical or like cancer cells: for they have no Christian meaning. Common sense, of course, had already suggested as much; but it is Vatican II itself which tells Catholics that those who believe what the Consensus advocates—people like David Tracy, perhaps, or Daniel Maguire—are not the People of God, are indeed formal enemies of both the teaching of Christ and His Church. They are, in fact, enemies of the Catholic people and thus have the right to that charity Christ requires; but as St. Pius X reminds us, "the prime duty of charity does not lie in the toleraton of false ideas."

As to how much respect or obedience American Catholics owe to, say, bishops like Rembert Weakland, Cardinal Ratzinger's address to the laity on the eve of the Synod seems to provide light here as well. It is perhaps enough to consider whether Weakland's defense of men like Daniel Maguire—particularly in view of the Archbishop's overt political opposition to anti-abortionists at the NCCB meeting in November 1985—is in union with those Catholic bishops throughout the world that have preceded, are co-existent with, and will succeed Bishop Weakland; whether, in Ratzinger's words such a defense is "ordered to Christ in a living way." If a Catholic layman believes it when a press campaign tells him he has no right to make such a judgment, the solution is unfortunately simple enough; he can send his children to Weakland's schools.

Those, on the other hand, who know and accept Vatican II, know also that while they cannot form a legitimate community by themselves, and must be united with their pastors, this latter obliges them to obey only in those things which still have life because—despite the pastor's subjective impulses—they are animated by and united with the People of God: what has come before, in preparation for what will follow. In particular it means, as Thomas Aquinas and John Paul II through Cardinal Gagnon, and numerous others have made clear, that that Catholic has full rights, indeed obligations, to fight against any man, whether under episcopal or any other pretense, who poses a threat to the Faith.

But like courage, prudence too is a virtue: which is why the Gagnon, Ciappi, Oddi, Ratzinger and other episcopal interviews that went beyond platitude, have meant so much to the Catholic laity in recent years. Finally, there is again the question of Mystery, the fact that as heavy as Christ's burden may sometimes prove, it is yet lighter than any other. Vatican II provides insight here, too, as Cardinal Ratzinger points out in the concluding remarks of his address to the laity.

The Council, he noted, also gave "primary importance to a second fundamental term for the Church—together with the term 'People of God'—the Church as Sacrament. One remains faithful to the Council only when both of these central terms of its eccesiology are always read and considered together: sacrament and people of God. Here we see to what extent theCouncil still lies before us: the idea of the Church as Sacrament has so far entered into our awareness very little."

Lumen gentium, however, "ends with the chapter on the Mother of God ... in this way the point of departure for our consideratons ultimately becomes visible once again: the Church is not an apparatus; She is not simply an institution; She is not even one among many sociological entities; She is a person ... and only to the extent that faith, beyond our *doings,* molds our *being,* are we the Church, is the Church within us. Only in being Marian do we become the Church," which in the beginning "was generated when in the soul of Mary their awakened the *fiat*. This is the most profound desire of the Council—that the Church might awaken within our souls."

"Mary shows us the way."

IV. Endgame: The English Bishops and Their Friends

"Of course, defamatory campaigns always have a certain effect. What is inconceivable and wounds the Christian heart is that such things are echoed and even encouraged by some men of the Church. I don't want to dwell on this point. I only remark that this Pope—who worked hard at the council, wrote a lot and labored to make it known and to have it put into effect, both in letter and in spirit—still refers to it constantly, takes from it his reference points and follows it in exercising his ministry as bishop and successor of Peter. And to suggest anything to the contrary is, as has been only too well said, a complete imposture."

Henri Cardinal de Lubac

"At the time of the Reformation, the English had the great saint, martyr and bishop, John Fisher. Which means that the English hierarchy was much healthier in those days than these; for then there was at least one Catholic among them."

John Cardinal Wright

The preparations undertaken for the English bishops' Submission to the Secretariat of the Synod revealed as much about clerical antagonism to Vatican II in England and Wales, as did the Submission itself. There is further evidence, however. The English National Catholic Directory and the Catholic Education Council, for example, show that though the English Catholic population has increased by about 400,000 since 1965, estimated Sunday Mass attendance has decreased by 600,000 to roughly a million and a half. Baptism, meanwhile, have declined nearly fifty per cent to some 70,000 annually, as have Church marriages by the same percentage; and conversions are far less than half what they were in 1965, as are ordinations to the priesthood. And of course, always a good indication of the state of the clergy is the newspapers they allow to be published: the once great Catholic *Tablet*, as well as the *Universe* and the *Catholic Herald*, had all become raucously Modernist by 1985, which doubtless accounts for the decline in the circulation of the *Universe* from 311,512 in 1963 to 127,452 in 1984. The circulation of the other two has declined so sharply that both stopped publishing their circulation lists some time ago.

Accordingly, the last thing the English clerical bureaucracy wanted was an Extraordinary Synod, or any attempt to solicit genuine Catholic opinion about how the bishops and their priests had implemented the Council in England and Wales. The episcopacy apparently felt it important to hide these fears, however, for they announced that every Catholic in the two countries was invited to send the bishops his or her opinion on Council implementation, to help form the Episcopal Submission to the Synod. Nonetheless, this announcement was not made with a press conference and great fanfare—in fact, it was done rather quietly, and the lay response seems to indicate an understanding that the clerics did not really want their opinions, or that they would be censored if proferred. For though a dozen or so approved organizations submitted reports that the clergy had done a superb job implementing the Council in England, only six individuals—or, if you prefer, 0.0001% of the English Catholic population—took the bishops' inquiry seriously enough to answer it.

Rather than dwell on the implications of this, the Modernists chose instead to engage in open duplicity and damage control while the bishops sought to deflect attention from themselves by producing a Submission which everyone recognized as an attack on the successor to St. Peter and his colleague Joseph Ratzinger. Thus, after the survey of the six English Catholics, the *Universe* ran the headline "Vatican II Changes Welcome—Voice of the People". The *NC News* headline was "English Bishops Report Widespread Acceptance of Vatican II".

As to the Submission itself, "the first thing that strikes one about the English Bishops' [July 29] document," as the British writer Philip Trower observed, "is that it is less an attempt to answer the Holy See's questions than a theological tract in which the authors lecture the Holy See about the Church, pluralism, evangelization, and 'ministries'."[7]

---

[7]*The Wanderer*, 21 November 1985.

"There is no reflection here of the view of Cardinal Ratzinger," editorialized the 3 August *Tablet*. "On the contrary, his gloomy assessment of the state of the Church today, leading him to deplore the record of the last 20 years and to call for a 'restoration' is often explicitly opposed."

In fact, "the English and Welsh bishops differ in their assesment, point by point, from Cardinal Ratzinger," as the 20 September *Commonweal* renounced editorially. "On ecumenism, on the understanding of the church as the People of God, on collegiality and the application of the principle of subsidiarity to the church's exercise of authority, on the role of bishops both in their diocese and in episcopal conferences, on pluralism in the church and the validity of diverse theological approaches, on the need for the Holy See's support in safeguarding *both* diversity and unity in the church, on the concerted effort which must be made 'to open to the changing role of women, which has many implications for the life of the church,' on the social and political responsibilities of the church and its members—on all these points the bishops affirm the value, necessity, and essential healthiness of directions in the church's life which Cardinal Ratzinger was wont to view almost entirely in terms of excess and danger . . . the statement's high-water mark may be the remarkable respect it pays to the laity."

Accordingly, the Submission had water marks which were lower than the respect Cardinal Hume pays to the laity. One of these, as Mr. Hebblethwaite points out in the 16 August *Reporter* is that the English bishops "cleverly apply to all the bishops . . . what the council says of the bishop of Rome." They do this by asserting that *Lumen gentium* presents "the role of the Bishops as the visible foundation of the Church," when in fact it does nothing of the kind, but instead explicitly states that "the Roman Pontiff, as the successor to St. Peter, is the perpetual and visible source and foundation of unity both of the bishops and the whole company of the faithful."

To be sure, this "excellent preparatory statement" (in Msgr. Higgins' view) does mention a few difficulties—as *Commonweal* notes—"concerning liturgy, confusion of doctrine . . . decline in vocations," and "apathy toward the church." Among other things, under the curious heading "Pluralism in the Church," the English bishops also note a "lessening of reverence for the Eucharist." Nonetheless, there is no suggestion that any of this might be attributable to the maladministration of Modernist inclinations of their own rule; indeed, the impression is given that though secular society deserves some of the blame, the real source of the decline rests primarily with the Holy See.

Meanwhile, in Hebblethwaite's *Reporter* analysis we are told that the English Submission was written "to blaze a trail and put down markers," because "the Dutch are not taken seriously. The Brazilians and the U.S. bishops are too obviously involved in the various disputes about the nature of collegiality. The Italians, being closer to Rome, do not want to stick their necks out. The French could never agree among themselves. The Australians are too far away," and "the Africans are too dependent on the Congregation for the Evangelization of Peoples. But they will support what they were unable to initiate."

"Am I then suggesting collusion among various episcopal conferences?" Hebblethwaite asks. "I am. Was there a plot? There was. It cannot yet be proved, of course, but a very interesting memorandum outlining a strategy for the synod was privately sent to friends by [the Jesuit] Cardinal Carlo Maria Martini, archbishop of Milan. His ideas are reflected in the submission. It seems likely, therefore, that Benedictine Cardinal Basil Hume of Westminster will be the chief standard-bearer of the residential bishops at the synod. . . . He will go to the synod armed with his 'submission' and the favorable response it has already evoked in public opinion. . . . He's going to a synod . . . where he may well have a dream."

Hebblethwaite was wrong again. To be sure, Hume was a standard-bearer, but apart from Malone and a few others, his "dream" got virtually no support at a Synod where, like Joseph Bernardin, Carlo Martini was conspicuously absent. The interventions at the Synod made it clear this would have happened anyway, but Hume's reputation, not to say the Submission's concern that he should be allowed to run things without a "hindrance" inspired by "a lack of tolerance and a new fundamentalism", received something of a fatal blow three days after the release of that Submission.

The problem, again, was sodomy. Under Hume's leadership, Quest, the British equivalent of the homosexualist Dignity, had received open hierarchical support virtually from the time Hume became London's Archbishop in 1976.

The year Hume assumed the Archbishopric, his fellow Benedictine Bishop B.C. Butler formally addressed the 1976 Quest gathering on the theme of "Ecstatic Love." In 1977 an "open symposium" on the "homosexual catholic" was staged in Hume's own Cathedral Hall in Westminister; in 1979 a "Eucharistic service" was scheduled for the Gay Christian Movement (GCM) at Westminister's Cathedral Conference Centre, until a presumably intolerant and fundamentalist uproar caused His Eminence to cancel those plans—though not without using the faithful's money to compensate GCM for the inconvenience. Accordingly, it was not impossible the Cardinal's priests were reading Quest literature, which for example, formally asserted the goal in *Gay Catholic in Britain* that "it is entirely compatible with the Christian faith not only to love another person of the same sex but also to express that love fully in personal relations."

Thus it was not a complete surprise when London's 3 August *Daily Telegraph* revealed that Monsignor Anthony Howe, who is no less than Cardinal Hume's Chancellor of Westminster Catholic Cathedral, "was fined 30 pounds yesterday at Marlborough Street from importuning at public lavatories in Oxford Circus." Such things can happen of course; but in the case of His Eminence's top aide, "the monsignor admitted persistently importuning men for an immoral purpose," presumably for at least nineteen years, since "the court heard that he had a previous conviction in 1966 for a similar offense."

From then until the Synod, it was downhill for the Westminster Archbishop. When Jean-Luc Godard's blasphemous film *Je Vous Salue Marie*, or "Hail Mary", came to town, the English bishops did not, as in Brazil, arrange to have it banned; nor, as in New York, Paris and Boston, deplore, in John Paul II's words, "the presentation of a cinematic work that twists and falsifies the spiritual significance and historic value of the Christian Faith, and deeply wounds the religious feeling of believers and respect for the sacred, and the figure of the Virgin, Mary." Quite the opposite in fact. According to the 17 September *London Standard*, "priests and Catholics and journalists crowded into a little Soho cinema and smiled beatifically upon Godard's treatment of the Holy Family. . . . Nicolas Coote, who was representing the [Bishops'] Conference, was . . . fulsome. 'I don't find it at all offensive,' " he announced, " 'though it may be upsetting for some people's religious make-up. When I next see Cardinal Hume I shall inform him there is nothing to worry about.' "

The final public scandal came on 14 October when Victoria Gillick publicly denounced the English hierarcy for refusing to help parents protect their children from the contraceptive industry. Its "lack of leadership on Catholic principles," she charged, had "given comfort to the enemies of the family and to those who condone sexual permissiveness in society." Mrs. Gillick had been fighting to stop doctors from distributing contraceptives to girls under 16 without their parents' knowledge or consent, not least since sex with a girl that age in Britain constitutes the crime of rape.

Three days after Gillick's rebuke, the House of Lords ruled that doctors were free to give minors contraceptives if they decided it was in the child's "best interest." When the hierarchy announced it would not contest this decision, London's *Guardian* ran the headline "Catholic Hierarchy Backs Lords on Pill." Cardinal Hume disputed this, using virtually the identical argument Mario Cuomo had employed in defending abortion at Notre Dame. According to the 17 November *National Catholic Register*, His Eminence's response to the *Guardian* was that "while backing Mrs. Gillick's affirmation of moral principle as well as her concerns as a Christian parent," he was "not convinced of the wisdom of taking legal action which raised other complex issues."

Msgr. Vincent Nichols, the general secretary of the bishops' conference, added helpfully that "on the issue of parental responsibilities Catholic moral teaching holds no clear line between parental rights and the growing responsibilities of young people." According to *Catholic Herald* reporter Kasia Parham, "the way forward, say Church leaders, is through education rather than attempts to change the law."

The contrast between the English bishops' bold defiance of the Vatican and its submissive docility to the State—not for the first time in the history of an English hierarchy—ruined any hope that Hume would be afforded much respect by his brother bishops at the Extraordinary Synod. By its eve, the Cardinal understood this, and so called a press conference at his house at Westminster where—as his friend Peter Hebblethwaite headlined the 15 November *Reporter*—"England's Hume Laments Prospects for the Synod."

"Why had we been summoned?" Hebblethwaite inquired. "Largely to be warned not to expect much, indeed not to expect anything from this synod. Hume said he does not think it will be able to produce a document." Meanwhile, the extent of Hume's failure to rally serious Modernist opposition to Cardinal Ratzinger was revealed in an almost offhand lamentation he made to Hebblethwaite about a prelate far subtler than himself.

"I'm very sorry," His Eminence sighed, that "Joe Bernardin won't be at the synod this year." Consequently, the *Reporter* editorialized in that same issue that "John Paul could repair this snub" by inviting both Bernardin and Martini to remain after the universal Cardinalate's Plenary Session introduced the Synod.

But the Prince of the Apostles decided against following this advice.

In November, the flurry of discussion about the Synod continued as intensely as during the rest of the year, but among the Modernists, Hume had set the tone: aggression was replaced by damage control, insistence that the Synod couldn't really mean anything, that there was no time, it would have no impact, one mustn't have high expectations, despite the Pope's hope to destroy Vatican II he would certainly fail; and so on. The basic theme that came out of all this was that far more important than the Extraordinary Synod would be the Synod on the Laity, which had originally been scheduled for 1986, and then postponed to 1987, and where both Cardinals Bernardin and Martini would return as members of the Synod Council to influence events, and doubtless work to ensure the laity be given as much voice then as Cardinal Hume had struggled to give them in 1985.

But everybody knew, in Cardinal Krol's words, that the Extraordinary Synod would set the "agenda for the next twenty years."

There were some last minute cries, however. Viena's retired Cardinal Franz Koenig gave a book-length interview contesting Ratzinger's views, which was published in Italy to coincide with the opening of the Synod.[8] But it was so predictable (not to say dull) that even the Modernists ignored it. The Canadian Bishops' Conference issued a Submission to the Synod that was half-way between Bishop Malone's Watergate Report (as it had been nicknamed) and Cardinal Hume's bold aggression. Archbishop Lefebvre denounced the Synod on the grounds that it would "exclude all judgment or criticism of the Council." On November 6, according to the *Chicago Tribune* of the following day, "Joseph Cardinal Bernardin appealed forcefully for a continuation of reforms in Roman Catholicism. . . . The Chicago archbishop, in a bluntly

---

[8]Koenig's own role at the Council can perhaps best be discerned by noting his 1963 praise of Father Kueng's work, which Koenig called a "challenge which . . . will be received with understanding and spread far and wide."

worded address at the Catholic University of America in Washington . . . strongly expressed his support for the unfettered exchange of ideas among Catholic theologians and scholars."

The 21 November issue of *The Wanderer* had a huge front-page drawing of two Popes, St. Pius X in the background, his present successor in the foreground. The NCCB had its annual meeting in Washington, during which Montana Bishop Elden Curtiss denounced "inappropriate interference of the Pope," presumably in His Excellency's hopes to excommunicate any layman who protests the neo-Arian *Renew* program. The U.S. bishops meanwhile voted tens of millions of dollars to build themselves and the USCC a new office building; which the media immediately dubbed the "Taj Mahal." Archbishop May denied that it was a Taj Mahal, but presumably in order to help better facilitate pastorals critical of U.S. capitalism, said it "was a necessity for space reasons." The Archbishop then flew to Rome as Bishop Malone's secretary, joining nearly two hundred other bishops from around the world.

The Synod had not even begun, but its impact had already proved enormous. Never again, it seemed, would a facile invocation of Vatican II be used by a cleric to launch some new assault on the Catholic people. The assaults would still come, to be sure, but any pretence of their being connected with anything recognizably Catholic was destined to recede further and further from the public discourse. The question of collegiality had in effect been solved, as meaning what Vatican II said it meant, to wit, the obligation of bishops to make their decisions in union with the Vicar of Christ, rather than his obligation not to exercise his duties as universal pastor of the Church. Some further discussion of the role of bishops' conferences was doubtless still to be had, and there was some question how much success Bishop Malone might have in insisting they had real juridical authority, since the vast majority of bishops at the Synod would be the heads of bishops' conferences: but everybody knew Ratzinger's critique would ultimately triumph, simply because it was self-evidently true.

"It is, in fact," as E. J. Dionne wrote on the Sunday *Times* cover piece on the eve of the Synod, "one of the most remarkable aspects of the Synod that it is Cardinal Ratzinger and not the Pope himself who has been the dominant figure in the debate leading up to the gathering . . . it is not without cause that many have dubbed this meeting 'Ratzinger's Synod.' "

Thus, there was now talk of a universal catechism. And certain aspects of liberation theology were clearly in retreat, enough so that Colombia's brilliant Cardinal Lopez Trujillo could tell the 2 February 1986 *National Catholic Register* that "even for those theologians who don't accept the *magisterium*, [Ratzinger's] instruction made them more cautious. They don't say out loud some of the ideas they carelessly spoke about before. They know very well that if they want to have the people's sympathy, they won't get it in Latin America if they show a lack of obedience to the Pope. For us, Christianity without the Pope is not only a theological error, but a very serious offense to popular religiosity. Love of the Pope is very deep in the heart of our people."

Of course, rising from the rubble of Modernism would take more than a year; or an interview, however brilliant. Or a Synod, however extraordinary.

"Taking the longer view," E. J. Dionne observed in the 12 May 1985 *New York Times* Sunday magazine, "the Pope seems to believe that societies have passed through periods of decadence before, and that the Church's task is to keep alive and spread the traditional values, in preparation for a time when society will embrace them again." Amazingly, no less reluctant figures than Hebblethwaite and Arthur Jones agree. "John Paul's strength rests in the papacy itself," they wrote in a joint 24 May 1985 *Reporter* analysis, "and his own extremely forceful personality."

"What Wojtyla . . . brought to the papacy with him," they continued,[9] "was an alternative culture. And this is his theme: 'The joy of faith in a troubled world' is enough. The world doesn't need Karl Marx or Sigmund Freud. People turn to Marxism, he thinks, because they have insufficient confidence in their Catholic faith—a faith John Paul II is convinced can transform the global society if properly applied. In this tough-minded pope's view, Western culture is not much better than Marxist materialism. What Westerners regard as their 'pluralism', John Paul dismisses. Significantly, it was in materialist West Germany that the pope said the seeker after values is like a shopper in a supermarket: he doesn't know which to select. The intellectual freedom of the West is an illusion, John Paul says: faith is not."

"So through television and travel, John Paul II also sets aside the traditional church organization chart and goes over everybody's head to the people. . . . Said one Rome-based senior

---

[9]In I believe the only example of objective analysis from these gentlemen I have ever had occasion to read.

member of a religious order, 'He is a very determined man. He is like a panzer, an army tank. Nothing can stop him.' "

"To date," Jones and Hebblethwaite gloomily concluded, "nothing has."

Nothing stopped him for the rest of 1985 either, when his major purposes for announcing the Synod were accomplished. There remained, however, the formidable and fundamental task of trying to communicate to the bishops a sense of the dignity of their office, and the courage necessary to express that dignity, as *Lumen gentium* had tried before to do. To rescue them, as it were, from the indignity of Humeism.

It was this task that would engage the mind of John Paul II during the actual meetings; and which would rescue the Synod from being but an epilogue to the extraordinary events that had unfolded up to the moment it was formally convened, with a Mass at St. Peter's Basilica, on the Feast of Christ the King.

THE SYNOD

I. The Means
of Social Communication

*"The lip of truth shall be established forever; the lying tongue
is but for a moment."*

Proverbs 12:9

"If any man have ears to hear, let him hear."

Mark 7:16

*"With the exception of the 1978 conclaves that elected John Paul II
and his short-lived predecessor, John Paul I, no meeting in Rome since
Vatican II has provoked as much advance speculation as this synod,"*
Time *magazine informed its readers. And then added: "One reason is
sheer mystery; its agenda is wide open and no one knows what will happen."*

*There were a few clues to what might happen, however, as I have
sought to indicate in the course of this book. Thus, as the* National
Catholic Reporter *pointed out, "never, according to Vatican authorities,
had the Holy See's press office been besieged by journalists as it was for
this synod." Apart from 200 regulars, Pontifical Commission for Social
Communications President Archbishop John Foley revealed that there
were an additional 600 accreditations, half of them from the United
States—"and a new wave arrived for the second week of work," as the*
Register *observed. Ralph McInerny in the January 1986* Catholicism
in Crisis *added that "the press corps was said by veterans to be considerably larger than that which covered the Council."*

*And yet, one of the striking things about the Synod was how little
the media actually conveyed. Despite outnumbering the bishops by as
much as four to one, few reporters showed any grasp of the real dynamic
at the Synod; and this was particularly true of the Americans, whose tone*

of almost petulant frustration suggested that they knew something *was going on, even if they couldn't figure out what it was. Kenneth Briggs, however—whose reports in the* New York Times *had proved singularly ideological and inaccurate—nonetheless had what I believe was his only insight in a post-synodal analysis for the 24 January 1986* National Catholic Reporter.[1]

"When reporters moan and groan," he wrote, *"it is usually just like anyone else griping about the job ... but sometimes the grousing actually tells the story better than the reports that appear under their bylines. During the synod there was lots of moaning. Reporters at times wore haunted looks, stalked around restlessly and emitted mammoth sighs ... but the moans and groans testified, I think, to the fact that something much more powerful and unmanageable was going on just out of view."*

In fact, the only reason Briggs and his confreres found the real story "just out of view" is because of what Joan Lewis of the Register *called the media's "tunnel vision." Since nowadays the Western press participates in events as much as it reports them, there was much evidence at the Synod of the Vatican's—and Archbishop Foley's—post-Council sophistication for matters were arranged in such a way as to force journalists either to have to dig out what was really going on (and thus know something about Roman Catholicism), or else be content to emit sighs.*

"Some visiting reporters," as Lewis pointed out, *"looked upon the Vatican as little more than a non-profit multinational industry responsible more for the earthly than the spiritual well-being of the world's 800 million Catholics ... it was observed that many pens stop writing when terms such as ecclesiology, spirituality, transcendence, the mystery of the Church or the Mystical Body of Christ were used." Liberation theology, for example, received a little, but not very much attention during the Synod. Yet Peter Hebblethwaite ran about almost frantically insisting it was the major issue, and that the priest who briefed the English press was suppressing the fact (unlike the French and Italian briefings, he said, though he provided no quotes, and though I attended some of the Italian briefings and never heard it mentioned except for one occasion when it was noted how infrequently the subject came up). When the Synod's* Final Report *exposed the illusory nature of Hebblethwaite's perceptions, he then blamed Ratzinger for suppressing the bishops' true desires.*

Hebblethwaite was not alone with this kind of ideological posturing. Numerous reporters had their own agenda in mind, and were determined to insist it was the bishops' agenda as well, regardless of what actually took place. "Bishops' Powers Are Top Issue At Synod" Briggs's headline

---

[1]Small world. Briggs left the *Times* as religion editor in May 1985 and immediately began writing for the *Reporter*.

in the 27 November Times *read. But despite the hopes of Msgrs. Hume and Malone, that was not the top issue at all. Meanwhile, only one bishop suggested the Church ought really to wink at contraception, but the NC* News *and others gave this view much attention. Only three bishops argued in favor of ignoring Christ's dictums against divorce, but in many papers this seemed like the bishops' major concern, with the possible exception of the need to ordain women, though not one bishop brought that up. After the Pope's address to the Cardinals explaining that when the Curia speaks, it does so in his name, the* International Herald Tribune—*published in concert with the* Washington Post *and the* New York Times—*headlined the story, "Pope Says Curia Has No Authority."*

And all the while, most of the media either censored or left out the very serious and at times fascinating picture the bishops were giving of the Catholic Church, both locally and universally.

"The journalists," America *editor George Hunt remarked in his 14 December issue, "often seemed as helpless as those present at a death watch or a baby's birth, relying on hints of hope or dismay and grateful for any bulletins of progress. The difficulty stemmed from the Vatican's perennial passion for secrecy."*

In reality, for those journalists who were not (like Hunt and Hebblethwaite) mere ideological hacks, the difficulty stemmed rather more from relying on cliches about the Vatican's passion for secrecy; which thus blinded them to Archbishop Foley's nefarious trick, so to speak, of providing so much information that the poor press corps just didn't know what to make of it.

It was really quite amazing. To be sure, it was a synod of bishops this time, and not of journalists: no one said, as Council Father and Jesuit Archbishop T. D. Roberts did about Vatican II,[2] that "I know if I give my talk to the press many more of the bishops will see it and understand it than if I give it in the aula." Still, with very few exceptions (and these largely from Communist countries), the bishops provided summaries of their eight-minute interventions during the first week, which were elaborated upon immediately after each session by thorough and, in the case of the English spokesman Father Diarmuid Martin, entertaining briefings. Cardinal Danneels' report on the questionnaires, his report summarizing the interventions after the first week, the introductory reports of Krol, Garrone, and Schotte, the Pope's homilies and commentaries, the Message *and the* Final Report *of the Synodal Fathers, and much else, were published virtually immediately after their approval in the aula, or meeting hall; and not least, there were numerous press conferences, with such cen-*

---

[2]Michael Novak's, *The Open Church*, London, 1964.

tral figures as Cardinals Danneels, Krol, Willebrands, Malula, and Archbishop Schotte, as well as with some of the local bishops, such as the Americans, who held two. And though none of these interviews were quite as straightforward as Cardinal Ratzinger's, some came close; and the others revealed as much by their equivocations as had Ratzinger by his clarity.

In fact, leaving aside ideological motivations, the reason the American media failed to communicate what happened at the Synod—why, in Cardinal O'Connor's words,[3] "its representatives did an extraordinarily shabby job during the days of the Synod,"—was due at best to a kind of provincialism, and at worst to an ignorant, when not conscious, racism. The unhappy reality is that the majority of American journalists have been schooled to believe it cannot possibly matter what a Cardinal Thiandoum of Dakar or a Bishop Mkhori of Malawi has to say, else Dan Rather would certainly have told us by now. Since he has not, how could American journalists be expected to pay attention to such men, especially when their views during the Synod were presented on any given morning with those of ten or eleven other bishops from remote and strange cities from around the world? Accordingly, American Catholics were hardly told what the Synod Fathers said, much less what the Synod itself accomplished.

It was, however, there to be seen.

---

[3]*Catholic New York,* Dec. 12, 1985.

II. The First Week

1. Monday Morning, November 25:
The First General Congregation

The Pontiff's Sunday Mass opened the final week of the liturgical year before 10,000 people on November 24, and the work began the following morning. The structure of the Synod over the two weeks varied some, and will have to be explained as it evolves. Nonetheless, when the bishops gathered in the *aula*—named after Paul VI—for the plenary sessions, these assemblies were known as "general congregations." Two a day took place from Monday through Thursday, and the ninth general congregation was held Friday morning, November 29: together, they provided the Church some 150 strictly observed eight-minute interventions from Her bishops, the two summaries of Cardinal Danneels, as well as the opening addresses of Cardinals Krol and Garrone, and Archbishop Schotte. Over the weekend and through Monday December 2nd, the bishops separated into ten specific language groups, where they discussed the information of the first week among themselves, before formally presenting the conclusions of these groups in the tenth and eleventh general congregations on December 3rd.

In short, though collegiality was discussed a bit, one distinguishing element of the Bishops' 1985 Extraordinary Synod on the Second Vatican Council was how extensively it was practiced. This, one suspects, was a cause of real chagrin to the enemies of Vatican II, because it not only vindicated the Council's (and the Pope's) concern with collegiality, but also produced unnerving evidence that when collegiality is genuinely practiced by bishops among themselves—as opposed to among surrogate journalists and/or bureaucrats acting in their stead—the result is liberating and Catholic.

"A fresh experience of fraternal and collegial communion is proposed to us," Cardinal Krol observed in the Synod's opening address. "This is that communion which is lived among the faithful and among their pastors and which, sixteen years ago, on the 15th of October 1969, in the first Extraordinary Synod, one Synod Father described: 'This communion does not just entail a community or a common action, but, going into interpersonal relations, it entails a communication of goods. This is not just a communication of external goods, but the internal participation of the persons themselves, which, though largely internal and hidden, also has its external and visible aspect. And in this precise sense, the collegiality of the bishops corresponds to the communitarian nature of the Church.' That bishop was Karol Wojtyla," Krol added, "who is now here among us as Pope, and solicits this collegial collaboration."

The Philadelphia Cardinal, meanwhile, did not hesitate to indicate in this address how he thought the bishops' internal collegiality might find external and visible aspect. "Our proposals for the future will be many and varied as we listen to the discussions of the next days," he said. "I would like to propose one approach: that with courage, we implement the New Code of Canon Law," since "to use the Holy Father's words again, 'the Code is the last volume of the Council to be published and in this lies its value and force: its unity and its impact.' "[4]

Pontifical Council for Culture President Gabriel-Marie Cardinal Garrone also addressed this opening session, during which he provided his nostalgic recollections of the Council; and Archbishop Schotte gave a final review, which was in a sense a culmination of a series of press conferences he had been holding right along, reporting the progress of responses to the Synodal questionnaire sent out in April. Originally, responses were to have come back before 1 September, but by then only 18 of the 136 anticipated had arrived, due, according to Schotte, to "the desire of certain episcopal conferences to carry out a broad consultation,

---

[4]I asked Bishop Malone at the American bishops' first Synodal press conference if he thought Cardinal Krol's intervention would inspire the American episcopate to similar enthusiasm, especially over the matter off Canon 810: but the NCCB President chose to remain non-committal about that possibility.

the impossibility for certain episcopal conferences to hold a special plenary assembly during the indicated period," and "for not a few episcopal conferences, the absence of administrative structures and qualified personnel for the obtaining of good results in such a brief period of time." During the Synodal interventions, an African bishop complained that his conference had not sent in a response because it had never received one, given "the vicissitudes of the mail service" in his country. Archbishop Schotte, meanwhile, reported that by 1 October sixty-four questionnaires had been returned; by 1 November eighty-five, and by 20 November ninety-five, for a total of some 70 per cent.

The summary of these was the job of Cardinal Danneels with the help of Father Kasper and others. The First General Congregation closed Monday morning with this report, which was a most enlightening one, and on the whole startlingly frank. Under the heading "Post-Conciliar Evaluation," the bishops had expressed "disappointment," noted that "there have been problems and travails," and indeed began to make Cardinal Ratzinger sound by contrast moderate and reserved: though like him, they insisted "it would be a fundamental error of logic to affirm 'after the Council, therefore because of the Council.' "

Numerous prelates, however, indulged precisely in that gesture of logic, erroneous or not, both in private and public, not excluding Bishop Malone himself, who publicly (and erroneously) blamed *Lumen gentium* for being ambiguous over the fundamental question of collegiality. Richard Neuhaus in the February 1986 *National Review*, meanwhile, accurately reported that though \everyone wanted it understood that, if much had gone wrong after Vatican II, the Council was not the cause ... yet, delicately in public and more candidly in private, synod fathers acknowledged that Vatican II made two massive errors in judgment. The first was the vast overestimation of the solidity of Catholic teaching and practice. . . . The second error was an astonishing naivete about the nature of the modern world."

Indeed Danneels, though noting a "unanimity" about "the considerably positive fruits" of the Council, admitted that "a synthesis" of the bishops' views "is difficult because of the extreme diversity of the situations of the various Churches," though "the most convergent responses are given especially in regard to the Constitution" *Lumen gentium.* It was nonetheless a convergence hostile to the interpretations of Bishop Malone and Cardinal Hume.

Under "Negative Points" , Cardinal Danneels was forced to admit that "the responses speak with great frequency and realism here." Among other negations of the Council, the "insufficiently prepared" and "superficial" reform of the Mass was denounced, as was "a certain subjectivism" in "some priests" who "forget that the liturgy is the patrimony of the whole Church, thus neglecting certain aspects associated with adoration, worship and sacrifice." Also noted were "a crisis as regards the sacrament of reconciliation and the disappearance of many forms of public devotion."

"The emphasis on the Word of God," the bishops charged, as had Cardinal Ratzinger to the fury of Father Kueng and the Liberal Consensus, "has sometimes led to an isolation of the Bible from its vital context—Living Tradition. This has come about," they continued, in what amounted to repudiation of the majority of seminaries in North America and Europe, "because of a subjectivism that tries to take the place of ecclesial understanding and the authentic understanding of the Magisterium." The bishops then all but named the United States in charging that "in some countries there are problems with the integrity and organic structures of catechesis," and that "the gravest problem seems to be in the area of the relationships between morals and the *magisterium* of the Church. Many find it difficult to accept objective norms, and these are then passed over in silence."

Again, it is possible the bishops were collectively chiding Cardinal Ratzinger for being too gentle during his interview with Vittorio Messori; but in calling a misperception of the Council's teaching about ecclesiology "the heart of the crisis," they echoed his views, and in asserting that "there have been unilateral, superficial and ideological interpretations of *Lumen gentium*, especially regarding the concept of the 'People of God'," Their Excellencies went beyond the charges the Cardinal had made. As to *Gaudium et spes*, the bishops reasserted its essence while diplomatically distancing themselves from the strain of naivete that runs through that document. "The relationship between the Church and the world," they dryly observed, "is more difficult today than it was twenty years ago. In wealthy nations there is an increase in secularization, atheism, materialism and indifference, caused by the crisis of moral values. In developing nations there is increasing poverty and misery . . . there are new problems regarding war, peace and the sciences, such as bioethics."

After Cardinal Danneels had read his summary, the first general congregation came to an end. Whereupon he and Cardinal Krol with Father Kasper held their first conference with a bewildered press.

If Time *magazine was puzzled over what the Synod could possibly be about, the editors of the* New York Times *were somewhat more astute. Indeed, one week to the day after the Pope had announced it, the* Times *editorialized that "it cannot be coincidental that the Pope's call follows a series of chastisements of the church for what he perceives as laxity. In the first three days of his current trip to South America, for example, he has spoken repeatedly of the need for Catholics to accept church discipline."*

The interesting thing about the Times *in 1985, however, is that for the first time in years, and arguably in decades, that paper provided genuine information about the Church, instead of simply reporting how Church actions were to be interpreted by the secular and not infrequently anti-Catholic bias the* Times *represents. I have already given the example of how Kenneth Briggs attended Cardinal O'Connor's seminal 1984 press conference, but that the* Times *gave it no coverage until it made the front page three days running when Mario Cuomo criticized it five weeks later. Another example is that covering Cardinal Hamer's demand for a retraction from the nuns and priests who signed the pro-abortion ad in the* Times, *Briggs refused to print, despite an abundance of such, any statement of support for the action, though he quoted numerous opponents of it. These examples are not isolated. I have been reading the* Times *with an eye towards its coverage of Church affairs for over a decade now; and until 1985 I was never given the pleasure of learning anything about the Church beyond noting the* Times *shifting tones of prejudice and hostility.*

It is thus no exaggeration to say that I—and numerous others with whom I have spoken—were stunned by the coverage E. J. Dionne gave Catholic affairs and the Pope, and even Cardinal Ratzinger, in 1985. It can hardly be said that Dionne is biased in favor of Catholicism; but he does give a genuine picture of the struggles going on within the Church. Since this seemed to be unprecedented, and since Kenneth Briggs left the Times *in May 1985, I naturally wondered what was going on, and asked Ari Goldman, the* Times *reporter covering the Collegeville gathering in June 1985, if the* Times *had been embarrassed into finally finding a qualified reporter for its Rome beat.*

We'd had a few drinks, and Goldman said that Dionne was a fiery and eccentric fellow, as if that were an answer. Then I remembered what an old friend who had worked at the Times for years once told me; to wit, that its power elite were such essentially dull people, that they liked a few eccentrics around to make them feel the paper had a certain lively strain running through it.

It seemed as good an explanation as any, particularly when the old religion editor of the 1960's, Ed Fiske, wrote his first article about religion in years for the 17 September Times—analyzing the Synod, of all things, as if the Times brass was unsure it wished to leave such a potentially momentous event solely in the objective hands of E. J. Dionne. The theory that the Times readership—in particular other people in the media—also had to be told the ideological line on the Synod received some further substantiation when, Fiske having proved too rusty, Briggs was brought out of storage just to cover it. The latter was not rusty, having limbered up with a piece in the 22 November Reporter, wherein Briggs praised "the British analysis" as "a refreshing contrast and a hint of what might have been;" praised Archbishop Gerety's Call-to-Action Conference as nothing less than "the most extensive survey of Catholic opinion [the American bishops] had ever conducted;" and was able to describe someone openly demanding that the American bishops "secede from Rome" as "a highly respected man who attends mass regularly and perceives politics and the church with humane conservatism."

Whether Briggs return was ideologically motivated or not, the editors of the Times seemed clearly nervous about the upcoming Synod. Dionne's superb front-page story about Ratzinger for the 24 November Sunday Times magazine indicated that the ideologues on that paper had reason to be nervous; and it should be recalled that the daily paper and the Sunday magazine are completely separate operations with two different editors. Accordingly, the former's 24 November issue ran a full page of articles about the Synod employing a more standard approach. Dionne's article, on the plenary session of the Cardinalate, was the smallest of these, and at the bottom; a huge article in the middle was titled "Catholics See Synod as Key to Role of Women;" and splayed across the top was the information from the resuscitated Kenneth Briggs that "On Eve of Synod, Top U.S. Bishop Sees Possible Need for Changes." Not exactly original for the Times, suggested changes included "conditions that would warrant an end to mandatory celibacy for priests" and "a means by which Catholics who disagree with the church's ban on artificial birth control might consider the rule an 'ideal' rather than an immediate demand."

Briggs ascribed these views to Bishop Malone as well as to "*some Vatican officials,*" who "*have also appealed to that strain of tradition that regards church law as something to aspire to rather than as an enforceable policy,*" and further claimed that Malone "*also criticized Cardinal Joseph Ratzinger, the head of the Vatican Congregation for the Doctrine of the Faith, for being 'one of the obstacles' to improving what Bishop Malone described as poor relations between bishops and theologians. . . . His remarks reflect both the common loyalty among bishops to the Vatican and the considerable diversity of views among bishops who will be asked to review the effects of the Second Vatican Council. . . . Bishop Malone's comments put into sharp relief many of the issues expected to draw the attention of the 160 bishops*" at the Synod.

After Cardinal Danneels' Report was released, neither Briggs nor the Times corrected this analysis, which did not prevent Msgr. George Higgins arguing in a February 1986 column that though "*a mainline Protestant with a degree in theology, Briggs is well-informed about the Catholic Church and over the years has consistently reported on Catholic events and personalities with fairness and objectivity.*"

As the hundreds of journalists began to gather in the Sala Stampa, or Press Room, for the Danneels/Krol press conference, one noticed right away a palpable gloom among—if I might so call them—the enemies of Vatican II. Peter Hebblethwaite was surrounded by a group of earnest looking fellows, whom he lectured about the glories of Cardinal Hume and the inevitable demise of Joseph Ratzinger; but his look was not a triumphant one, perhaps not least because—unlike earlier synods—the folks gathered round him included no one of consequence. Indeed, throughout the Synod, Hebblethwaite wandered about with a kind of desperate and even tragic air, looking for all the world like faded Elvis Presley wondering why his fans had lost all their vitality.

When, after Krol, Kasper and Danneels—with Foley hovering in the background—began taking questions, the reason for the gloom became obvious. It was clear that, unlike during the Council, the journalists really had no policy beyond resurrecting tiresome and settled questions—priestesses, birth control, the acceptability of divorce—and trying somehow to arrange for a formal Synodal repudiation of Ratzinger. As Dionne had quoted Navarro in the Sunday Times piece, "the liberals will try to have Cardinal Ratzinger's book as the central document for discussion." If Navarro was right, it was an agenda based on a daunting ignorance, for it presumed that men like Basil Hume and James Malone were representative of the typical bishop around the world. Meanwhile, journalists favorable to Ratzinger—there in sufficient number to provoke complaints in Hume's Universe about their presence—also thought Ratzinger's views deserved Synodal attention.

Accordingly, question after question centered around either Ratzinger or whether the Synod meant the end of Vatican II—to the extent that at one point Cardinal Danneels rather irritably protested that "this is not a Synod around a book, it is a Synod around a Council." Cardinal Krol, meanwhile, helped the journalists demolish their straw dog by noting that "even from a juridical standpoint, there is no way that the synod can overturn the ecumenical council." But all this had been said before. Except for watching the media flip like fish on the beach trying to find the ocean, the only interesting point in the conference was Danneels' response to the question of how frequently the role of women had come up in the bishops' answers to Schotte's questionnaire.

"Many reports from the first world, the developed West," he said, had "raised this issue, but it was absent from the reports from the third world and communist nations."

Before the conference was over, everyone seemed thoroughly frustrated; and so Cardinal Danneels tried to throw the journalists a bit of an anti-Ratzinger bone. In response to whether they thought Bishop Malone's cheerful assessment of the post-Council era had been more on target than Ratzinger's, Krol answered in prelaturese: "I say both views are valid and based on their experiences and both are necessary to carry out the purpose and the goals of this council, and that it is to bring all the various concepts and ideas together. This isn't a boxing match. It's not a contest. It's an honest expression of relationships."

"Cardinals and bishops are human beings," Danneels suggested. "I think they have the right to express their emotions. And also they have a temperament. You shouldn't expect from the Synod the canonization either of Cardinal Ratzinger or of Bishop Malone. We don't make saints at the synod, and we don't make sinners. The only question that is interesting me is not what is Cardinal Ratzinger saying or what Bishop Malone is saying, it is the truth which is interesting me. Certainly you know the story about the glass of water. One man who looked at the glass said, 'it is half full,' and the other man looked and said, 'it is half empty.' What interests me is not those statements, but the statement about the exact contents of the glass. And it is that we are doing now. So Cardinal Ratzinger can say that it's half empty and Bishop Malone can say it's half full, but I would like to know how much water there is in it."

This profundity was greeted with much laughter and a smattering of applause from the gathered pressmen. But it was all they would get.

La Stampa, *which is roughly the Italian equivalent of the* Washington Post, *blazoned the headline "No Restoration!" the following day, which was representative of similar headlines in other European papers. And yet a tone of relief was missing from the accompanying articles.*

On the 25th, the New York Times *released the news that, according to a poll it took, only a quarter of Catholics "oppose" the use of artificial contraception, over half "favor" the idea of priestesses, sixty per cent "favor" the idea of married priests, and 70% "favor" permitting Catholics to divorce and remarry. These statistics were culled from but 280 people who claimed to be Catholics. I was reminded of the polls during the 1984 election campaign, which, while claiming a margin of error of between three and six points, also said, depending on the poll, that Walter Mondale would get anywhere from 30 to 51% of the vote. He got 41 per cent. Whereupon numerous papers claimed the polls had, darnit, been right again. Meanwhile, a poll of over 5000 Catholics who read* Catholic Eye *revealed overwhelming opposition to contraception, priestesses, married priests, and so on; but this one was dismissed as unscientific.*

An observation of Malcolm Muggeridge also came to mind. "Such lies believed!" he once wrote. "Never, surely, has there been credulity like it. African witch-doctors and makers of potions must look with sick envy at the impostures of our age."

2. Monday Evening, November 25: The Second Congregation

Cardinal Law was not alone in saying he considered the Synod "a most profound experience" not least because it helped put the local Church into the context of the universal Church. In particular he noted "the vitality of the young Catholic Churches in Africa and Asia."

Meanwhile the English Bishops' July 29 Submission had lectured the Pope about how "the process of the synod itself, the drawing up of the agenda and the preparatory papers, the allocation of time to the diverse elements of ceremonial celebration, set addresses, discussion in small groups and general debate all need to be arranged carefully. The process should be geared towards allowing the mind of the synod to be fully expressed and fully articulated for the benefit of the whole church." Monsignor Higgins, perhaps drawing from the general tone of the Submission, wrote in the 28 September *America* that from this passage "one can reasonably infer that the bishops of England and Wales do not expect this to happen." But they were in for a surprise.

Of course, virtually every Synod Father praised the Council, some less, some more, though there was arguably an embarrassing note in all this, especially in light of the *Final Report*'s claim that the central theme of the Synod was the "Celebration, Verification, and Promotion of the Second Vatican Council." The point was not lost on the European press, for as the sprightly if anti-Catholic Italian paper *La Repubblica* observed, "it was a bit of a strange procedure: that is, that the Synod, an inferior organism, should render a sentence about the legitimacy and validity of a superior organism; to wit, the Council."

Meanwhile, in finding their stride, the bishops addressed a variety of subjects on this first night. Their order of appearance was decided by whichever bishop first signed up; and if their interventions in the *aula* were occasionally more revealing than the written interventions supplied to the press, the briefings indicated that the latter were nonetheless revealing enough.

Of the published interventions, Peru's Archbishop of Lima Landazuri Cardinal Ricketts opened the evening with an attack on "a pessimism that gives rise to doubts and fears"—which ill-disguised shot at a certain famous brother Cardinal erased all doubt that the Fathers were free to speak their minds. The Synod was off and running.

Cardinal Sou Hwan Kim of Seoul, Korea, whose country has seen an enormous number of conversions to the Faith since the Council, accordingly cautioned against "narrow interpretations" of it, particularly since "aberrations" and "excesses" had been "minimal in the East."

Cardinal Eugenio de Arauio Sales, who would prove one of the major influences at the Synod, spoke third. Among the fifteen specially appointed Papal nominees, the Archbishop of Rio de Janeiro went quickly to the heart of what would prove the first of his many interventions, the rest written. These interventions formed the corpus of an open and dramatic debate with his Brazilian brother bishops—Boff's friend Alosio Cardinal Lorscheider of Fortalenza, also a Papal appointee, and conference president Jose Ivo Lorscheiter of Santa Maria. The confrontation had in fact begun during the Cardinalate plenary session, when

Cardinal Sales had put as it were a Ratzinger interpretation on Bishop Lorscheiter's claims that the entire Brazilian Church supports liberation theology; he did so by joining a group of Cardinals who made a point of expressing their formal thanks to the Vatican for its condemnation of historicism.

"The primacy of Peter and collegiality are fundamental in the effective proclamation of Christ to all mankind," Sales told the Synod, for only by defending "it in the person of the Pope . . . will we be true pastors of the universal Church."

"The Church is not merely a religious society," he added, echoing Ratzinger, "but also the mystery of Jesus Christ. She proclaims the Gospel but is Herself part of the Gospel proclaimed." And finally: "The foundation of ecumenism is found in the preservation of the Church's identity. Her activity in favor of man's dignity depends on that identity."

Senegal's Archbishop of Dakar Hyacinthe Cardinal Thiandoum, a veteran of Vatican II, then launched what would become one of the central themes of the Synod, as it has quietly been for this Papacy: the need for a universal catechism such as had been provided by the Council of Trent. Ukrainian Cardinal Myroslav Lubachivsky, who had granted an exclusive interview to *The Wanderer* shortly before the Synod, followed Bishops' Congregation Prefect Cardinal Bernardin Gantin, whose intervention had been of a general nature.

In *The Wanderer*, Lubachivsky had expressed contempt for Western consumerism, and noted by contrast that "the Church is flourishing in the Ukraine. The people stay Catholic," though that is illegal in the Soviet-occupied territory. "There are about ten bishops," in the Ukraine, he noted, "and between 400 and 500 priests. They can't work openly, but they are very active," and "we have many vocations," who because they "cannot study openly . . . study with older priests." He added: "We don't have the doctrinal problem—liberalism. That sickness has not spread much among us, as it has among the Latin Rite and the Protestants . . . we have the old way of catechetical teaching, and it is working well."

At the Synod, His Eminence called for a more dramatic recognition of the rights of Eastern Churches, requested the status of a patriarchy for the Ukrainian Catholic Church, and in regard to Soviet persecution of Ukrainian Catholics, appealed for the universal Church to give "proof of solidarity by stirring public opinion against this basic disregard of human rights." Another

Ukrainian bishop, Maxim Hermaniuk of Canada, proposed that the present legislative authority of the Curia be replaced by a Permanent Synod of Bishops. The idea did not catch on, but (perhaps because seen as an anti-clerical gesture) received more attention in the press than did Cardinal Lubachivsky's appeal against the Soviet persecution of his people. The latter, in fact, I saw nowhere mentioned.

Durban South African Bishop Denis Hurley spoke between the two Ukrainians, denounced injustice, inquired as to whether the principle of subsidiarity had application to the Church, and disheartened many with the facile observation that "this Synod should be more concerned with the requirements of practical evangelization rather than theology."

Polish Archbishop of Poznan Jerzy Stroba's intervention repudiated Hurley's. "The first task of the Council should be the enrichment of the faith in relation both to doctrine and to the life of Christians. This has happened for some Christians, but for others, no, because of the ever growing process of secularization. The principal reason" for this, he continued, "is to be sought in the crisis of European culture that has profoundly characterized both the diffusion and the reception of conciliar teaching. This teaching was diffused through channels of information marked, moreover, by secular thought, often leading to disinformation. For many Catholics, the consequences have been disorientation, insecurity, resignation. Some," he said, "have even become skeptical in the face of such information and await an authentic interpretation of the conciliar texts." It was a militant call that the American laity would like to have heard; but the press neglected to report it. Still, significantly, Stroba too was a Papal appointee; and the juggernaut for a universal catechism was growing. Meanwhile, His Excellency closed his intervention by insisting that "of extreme importance" is that "the concept of the 'People of God' . . . must be understood within the framework of . . . the Mystical Body of Christ."

Tamale, Ghana Archbishop Peter Poreku Dery noted that "the freedom given to us all in the Church by Vatican II has been misused by the people of some overseas countries," but felt that in Africa "the Holy See should leave enough scope and sustain the process of inculturation to allow the young Churches to grow to full maturity"—a point to which African bishops would refer, in order to protect "inculturation" from the kind of misinterpretation that has plagued such concepts as liberation theology and collegiality.

The Archbishop of San Jose in Costa Rica, Arrieta Villalobos, brought the second general congregation to a close. "The misfortunes of the Church during the last twenty years," he said, "are not due to the Council," but to those in positions of responsibility "without the Spirit of Christ and authentic love for the Church" who used the Council "as a pretext for the diffusion of their opinions" and who "erroneously interpreted conciliar teachings. It is therefore urgent that there be a profound conversion to Christ and His Church," and Her "teaching in seminaries and houses of formation," and "that there be fidelity to the letter and spirit of the Council to interpret correctly its doctrine."

Meanwhile, in an intervention that was not originally published with the rest of the Second Congregation's, but was released later in the week, Panama Archbishop Marcos McGrath foresaw some of the difficulties of "anecdotal reporting and superficiality," which would present the interventions seriously, or "gather them into a communitary vision of the universal Church." Accordingly, His Excellency suggested that the Synod's "collegial reflection, with the Pope at the head, might be considered but a beginning in the consideration of the Council; that this might produce a first general impression and directives for the continuation of this consideration in the local Churches, in communion with the Apostolic See and in contact with the Roman Departments," and not least that "further along, perhaps for the twenty-fifth anniversary of the Council's close, the Holy Father might convoke another extraordinary synodal session in order to gather together all of these efforts along conciliar lines."

"The most popular briefer by far," according to Dionne, "was the Rev. Diarmuid Martin, an Irish official of the Curia. At the least, his efforts at circumlocutions and evasions were often artful and amusing; jokes and a musical Irish brogue often filled the gap left by the paucity of genuine information." Dionne, as one can see, also has his shortcomings, since the above interventions were available to him as well, and would have provided him his genuine information had he not fallen into the media trap of rejecting them because they did not fit preconceived notions. But Dionne was right about Msgr. Martin, whose credits in addition included working for Cardinal Gagnon, and being regularly denounced as a "fascist" by an increasingly frantic Peter Hebblethwaite.

Martin's first briefing immediately followed the second general congregation. The next day, translated and reproduced in four or five different languages, the published interventions were available for the accredited members of the international media.

On the whole, they read them, scratched their heads, and wondered what was going on.

3. Tuesday Morning, November 26: The Third General Congregation

While the press gazed into the horror of its own puzzlement, the bishops were back at work. The Third General Congregation produced twenty-one published interventions. Causes for Saints Prefect Pietro Cardinal Palazzini and Non-Believers Secretariat President Paul Cardinal Poupard discussed the competencies of their Curial functions in general terms; but when I say that, or when I note that German Episcopal Conference President Joseph Cardinal Hoffner—an Opus Dei promoter—and Italian Episcopal Conference President Ugo Cardinal Poletti spoke in general terms, I do not mean to denigrate their interventions.

Indeed, a book with a more thorough investigation of all the interventions would be extremely valuable, but would probably take as many pages as I have written so far, and so I shall content myself with presenting the essence of the interventions and noting the shifting mood of the Synod as they unfold. Accordingly, when Cardinal Palazzini talks about the work of his Congregation, I sacrifice such interesting notes as that there have been 398 causes introduced to that Congregation since the close of the Council; in like manner, though the more thorough examination could explain the context of Cardinal Hoffner's observation that "the Synod of Bishops must radiate courage in a world that is tormented by fear," or Cardinal Poletti's about the urgency to clarify "the relationships of associations, movements and groups in the particular Churches with the diocesan bishop," (especially as that doubtless referred to Opus Dei), such viewpoints will here, with due respect, be "generalized."

In addition, having I hope conveyed a sense of the dynamic that was functioning in these congregations by presenting Monday night's events chronologically, I intend nonetheless to present the remainder thematically. During the Third General Congregation, for example, Philadelphia Ukrainian Bishop Stephen Sulyk "strongly emphasized the primatial authority of the Holy Father at all times and in all places," but requested that he "grant jurisdiction to all Eastern Catholic patriarchs and major archbishops over their faithful even outside their historic boundaries," and sought to have this request considered for the Eastern Catholic Code of Canon Law, presently being developed. Thematically, that is more or less outside the scope of the concerns Cardinal Ratzinger addressed in his interview with Messori; and so although Sulyk spoke first during this Congregation and the following two Synod Fathers spoke thirteenth and fifteenth respectively, their interventions will here be grouped together.

Of the two Indian bishops of the Syro-Malabar rite (that traces its ancestry to the evangelization of St. Thomas the Apostle) Archbishop Anthony Padiyara spoke before Archbishop Joseph Powathil, and though both made the same points, it was the former who was more forthright. Indian Christians observing the ancient rite, he noted, are "24 per cent of the total population of India, and it supplies 70 per cent of the missionary personnel in India . . . however, the Syro-Malabar Church is denied to exercise its fundamental right of providing pastoral care to thousands of her sons and daughters who are emigrants in the major and small cities of India. This is on account of the strict insistence of the Latin Hierarchs on the principle: one territory - one jurisdiction. This is clearly against the teaching of Vatican II regarding the Oriental Churches." And then, perhaps looking at the Prince of the Apostles (who attended all the sessions), Padiyara went on to express a kind of smoldering resentment that was not uncharacteristic of other Oriental interventions, for "though the Apostolic Visitator presented his report in 1980 to the Holy Father with appropriate suggestions, practically no effective measures have been taken so far in this regard."

Maronite Patriarch of Antioch Antoine Cardinal Khoraiche, the penultimate speaker of the morning, expressed similar alarm: "The faithful of these Churches are not second-class Christians," he charged, "nor are they shining witnesses to an outdated archeology . . . it is important to face the difficulties raised by the superimposition of jurisdictions, the diaspora of the Eastern faithful, union with their Patriarchs, etc. . . . the like of which has not been seen for thirteen centuries. . . . There exists the fear that the upcoming canonical dispositions relating to organization will neutralize the guidelines of the Council, leading to the dissolution of the Eastern faithful in the countries of emigration. The Churches of the East are in difficulty. It is necessary to save them ... by creating movements of Christian solidarity."

In an intervention that was released later in the week, Canada's Bishop of Saint-Jean-Longueuil, Bernard Hubert, proposed the idea of a formal "Message" from the Synodal Fathers, and dealt with Archbishop McGrath's idea of further episcopal meetings in the future.

Bishop Malone was the third speaker of the morning; and his intervention did receive attention in the *Final Report*, though perhaps not quite in the way he had hoped. Asserting that the Council teaching on collegiality had given "impetus" to episcopal conferences, he suggested this "should be reinforced," and urged that "advice to this effect should be given to the Holy Father by this Synod." He stated clearly that "some extension of collegiality in the direction of episcopal conferences seems warranted." And he requested that the Synod offer advice on "the limits of pluralism, the debate about episcopal conferences and their teaching authority," and ecumenism with non-Catholics.

Malone's points were answered in the final document: ecumenism was approved, pluralism condemned, and an investigation of conferences ordered—though most assumed this meant merely the formal promulgation of Cardinal Ratzinger's views sometime in the future. In the 16-page single-spaced Elaboration of his intervention Bishop Malone clearly hoped otherwise, stating that "episcopal conferences should not be thought of as just another way of achieving organization in the efforts of many individual bishops." That Elaboration was also of interest for a kind of plaintive tone in the explanation of how the condition of the Church in the United States was not the fault of its episcopacy. "Clearly the bishops were trying to keep faith with the Council," Malone wrote there more than once. "They sought to see to it that Vatican II would not be misinterpreted." He insisted that the bishops' conference was a chief means Their Excellencies came up with to achieve this desired goal; and he devoted much space to insisting that the main thing about such conferences is their contribution to the Council's call for evangelization.

There would seem to be two purposes behind this latter argument: one was that His Excellency had already backpedaled considerably by admitting in the Elaboration that the principle of collegiality could only "find *limited* expressions in bishops' conferences" (my emphasis); and the other, that by proposing another theological instead of juridical approach, he hoped still to salvage the clearly fading hope that the conferences might speak with independent episcopal authority. His Excellency's case was somewhat undermined, however, by constant references to the "ambiguities" he found in *Lumen gentium*—which few other bishops recognized.

More extreme—and thus drawing the most journalistic attention of the morning—were the interventions of Oslo, Norway Bishop John Gran and Kingston, Jamaica Archbishop Samuel Carter, representing dioceses where the Church is not exactly thriving. Reflecting Saginaw, Michigan Bishop Kenneth Untener's view, Bishop Gran decried what he perceives as "a return . . . to a new emphasis on universality which alas carries the hallmark of centralization . . . there should be fewer duties of recourse to the Holy See and a greater local say in the appointment of bishops." Carter, too, was upset about "too many decisions still made at the Roman level," and gave as examples the refusal to allow general absolution; and the agreement to allow for the Tridentine Mass. Somewhat of this calibre—though the *Final Report* betrayed some sympathy here, while wholly ignoring Gran and Carter—was Mauritius Islands Bishop Jean Margeot who waxed enthusiastic about "base communities."

Meanwhile two notable interventions came from Hanoi Archbishop Joseph-Marie Cardinal Trinh Van-Can, and the Philippines' Archbishop of Cebu Richard Cardinal Vidal. The former's dealt at length with the difficulties of liturgical and musical renewal in Vietnam, leaving one to suspect his oral additions may have been too explicit for public release.[5] Cardinal Vidal—a Papal nominee—on the other hand provided the script that would write Philippine history in less than three months.

"A faithful involvement in secular affairs with clear distinction between purely sociological and specific ecclesial dimensions will help clergy and laity in establishing balance in action. Clear

---

[5] For that matter, the reader may wish to assume that all the bishops spoke more sharply among themselves, especially in those cases where the published interventions (like Archbishop Stroba's for example) were notably pointed.

delimitation of their roles will avoid the clericalization of the Church's social action. This in turn will help the laity to become fully aware of their mission and responsibility." A neglected dimension of Corazon Aquino's amazing triumph in the Philippines, incidentally, is that she is also a firm defender of human rights for the unborn; and an opponent of the multinational population control outfits with which Mr. Marcos and his wife had been cooperating for some time.

Nonetheless, despite the historic contribution of Cardinal Vidal, the frank challenges of the Oriental Churches, the ambiguities of Bishop Malone, and the open Modernism of Msgrs. Gran and Carter, one of the more striking aspects of the Third General Congregation was the aggressive tone of the six remaining bishops who spoke that morning.

"The Council's recognition of the importance of mass media has not been followed by adequate practical results," Archbishop Foley charged. "Some Catholic publications feature dissent more than dogma, while some Church spokespersons show unnecessary secrecy, defensiveness and fear of the truth." Accordingly, "the Church should educate its members to be intelligent contributors to the media and discriminating consumers of the media," for "the message of the successor of St. Peter ... must be echoed more clearly and faithfully in the mass media."

In discussing missionary activity as defined by *Ad gentes,* Taiwan's Archbishop of Taipei Stanislaus Lokuang backed Cardinal Vidal's position, noting that the " 'mission' is not to dedicate oneself exclusively to social activities, which can also assist the work of evangelization, but it is to announce the Gospel."

French Bishop Jean Vilnet of Lille stated frankly that "the West is seeing its values crumble."

Salesian Society of St. John Bosco Major Rector Father Egidio Vigano—one of the three elected Superiors General along with Jesuit Father Peter-Hans Kolvenbach and Benedictine Father Viktor Dammertz—immediately followed Vilnet, and elaborated on his thesis. "The grave crisis which has arisen," he said, "is a phenomenon of the whole Church, as well as of civil societies, indeed of Western civilization itself."

Argentina Archbishop of Avellaneda and head of the South American bishops' conference Antonio Quarracino praised the Council, denounced the Lefebvrites as well as those who "accepted neo-Modernist positions, emptying the Church of essential values," and argued that "it is necessary to emphasize," and "to insist upon the unity and the inalienable function . . . of the *magisterium.*"

But arguably the most stirring intervention was that of Ecuador's Archbishop of Guayaquil Bernardino Echeverria Ruiz.

"A great effort," he said, "has been made to study the conciliar documents, and the fruits are apparent. Yet there is the risk that it becomes more a matter of theoretical rather than pastoral effort and that declarations take the place of actions. Indications must be given to ensure that the missionary and apostolic spirit transcend the productions of documents."

"For a new dynamism that leads the renewal to fullness, one must refer to the Mystery of the Cross," Ruiz continued. "Proposing the Cross and inscribing it in the hearts of the communities, like the first missionaries to America, will not fail to promote the most intimate and radical dimensions of the Church, and will set in motion the interior renewal of the faithful."

"The Cross," he concluded, "is also the interpretive key for the preferential option for the poor," for "the Cross liberates. If one does not look to it, with Mary, it is easy to fall into erroneous schemes of the interpretation of reality and to do work that is both socially subversive and pastorally sterile."

The bishops retired for lunch and perhaps a fine Roman siesta at about half past twelve. Father Martin arrived soon afterward in the Sala Stampa *for the briefing. By five, the bishops were back at work for the Fourth General Congregation.*

4. Tuesday Evening, November 26:
The Fourth General Congregation

Concentrating on Bishops Malone, Gran, and Hermaniuk, while ignoring everyone else, Kenneth Briggs was already reporting that "Bishops' Powers Are Top Issue At Synod," when the Synod Fathers gathered for the pivotal Fourth General Congregation. The "note of realism"—in Russell Shaw's words—that had been gathering steam during the previous Congregations, brought major conflicts of opinion into dramatic focus in the Fourth: and the major protagonists were Father Boff's two friends from Brazil; Yugoslavia's Archbishop of Zagreb Franjo Cardinal Kuharic; Conakry, Guinea Archbishop Robert Sarah;

Argentina's Archbishop of Cordoba Francisco Cardinal Primatesta; Bernard Law; and Joseph Ratzinger.

Altogether there were seventeen published speakers during the Fourth Congregation, making a published total of 38 for the entire day, which number was not equaled for the rest of the Synod. Secretariat for Non-Christians Francis Cardinal Arinze, Pontifical Biblical Commission Secretary Henri Cazelles, and Pontifical Council for the Laity President Eduardo Pironio spoke in general terms about the work of their agencies; but Cardinal Kuharic set the tone for the session with his opening intervention.

"The Council is a good tree," he said, "and bears good fruit when it is interpreted and applied in an authentic and faithful way in its integrity and with a sense of correct ecclesiology. The authentic renewal in the Church, to be promoted in line with the Council, simply requires a full adherence to the Church and to Her Magisterium, over which presides, in truth and charity, the Successor of Peter, according to Christ's mandate. . . ."

"The Council [cannot] be blamed for the errors, dissent and disturbances which occurred after the Council in some particular Churches. This tempest has other sources and causes. Some philosophies and ideologies have created the so-called 'myth of man,' as if he were a new species of superman having his own norm of good and evil, a man who must be allowed everything which pleases him," but "once the transcendence of the human person is denied and man is separated from the transcendent God, man finds himself in danger of being seduced by a civilization of death."

"Under the pressure of this mentality, some people even ask the Church to change the Creed and the Ten Commandments," but "the Church cannot change the truth revealed by God. She can only invoke the conversion of the world," and exhort it to "believe in the Gospels."

Archbishop Sarah spoke seventh, right after Cardinal Arinze, and elaborated on some of Cardinal Kuharic's, and the Synod's, themes. "The fruits of Vatican Council II are numerous," he said, in particular "the rooting of the Church in new cultures," but "the confusion of souls regarding the mystery of the Church and its hierarchical constitution, the grave difficulties brought about by divergent interpretations of the dual dimension of the Church universal and particular, the moral crisis of the world and the social disturbance born of it, and the disdain in many quarters regarding the opening of the Church to the world, suggest to us these proposals: the humble but clear reaffirmation of the evangelical mission and that of custodian of Catholic faith and morals," along with "a firm reminder as regards the teaching and certain dogmas of the Church," which seems "necessary in order that no one abuse the Love that is the real presence of God in the world."

"In truth," he continued, "our dogmas protect us from our most destructive dreams.... Dogmas have as their aim, and must have as their effect, the prevention of the transformation of the love proclaimed in the Gospel into an ideology. In this way, proclaiming what She is and Her divine mission, the Church keeps watch to ensure that the Light of Christ ... is correctly received always and everywhere."

"The most urgent need and aspiration of the Church is to have evangelical men," His Excellency added. "The supreme criterion for evaluating the youth of the Church is perfect fidelity to the whole Christ, and in this perfect fidelity, sanctity founded upon the Cross. The Church rejuvenates Herself when She succeeds in forming saints, or when She succeeds in committing Her children to the path of the supernatural."

These views were reinforced by most of the bishops who spoke between Kuharic and Sarah. Berlin's Cardinal Joachim Meisner charged that "the Church as a mystery and not an institution is yearned for by many people who feel oppressed with respect to their value in a mass society."

"The Church has been a character of a mystery and this is rooted in the mystery of the Triune God," Cardinal Simonis insisted. "Human *being*, as such, has also the character of a mystery, and it cannot be understood without its relation with the mystery of God ... the Synod has to understand these signs and to indicate ways along which our contemporaries can discover the mystery of God."

Managua Archbishop Miguel Cardinal Obando y Bravo, who is in the thick of the confrontation between the Catholic transcendent idea of man and the brute physical power of historicist ideology, was asked by the Nicaraguan hierarchy to attend the Synod in place of episcopal conference president Bishop Pablo Vega, presumably due to His Eminence's high profile in the persecution of the Church by the Sandinista junta. Dryly, he observed that "during these years an intense theological reflection concerning the identity of the priest has taken place under the weight of crises and tensions which have assailed it with a certain force." Accordingly, Obando y Bravo suggested various criteria for "the priest committed to the integral liberation of the poor and the oppressed," such as "a life of fervor, prayer and practices of piety, through ascetical witness, manifested by the practice of obedience ... with maturity in the acceptance of celibacy," and "faith in the Magisterium, whose task it is to discern the essential and permanent aspects of the priesthood."[6]

Curiously, though discussing the advance of ecumenical efforts in traditionally Coptic Ethiopia, Addis Ababa Archbishop Paulos Cardinal Tzadua, who spoke right after Obando y Bravo, gave at least a small picture of the clerical chaos to which his brother bishop alluded. "There are groups that carry out ecumenical initiatives or activities who are not under the control of the central department for ecumenism. These groups even deliberately ignore the local Church and deal directly with the other Churches and with single individuals," he charged.

"A certain coordination and order in ecumenical efforts are necessary," His Eminence added, perhaps thinking of the day when the Church in now Communist Ethiopia might be strong enough to provoke a persecution comparable or worse than the one in Nicaragua, "both for the Catholic Church and the other

---

[6]The Cardinal's contrast between the Catholic priest and Modernist clericalism was, to be sure, not only dirrected to the priests in the Sandinista junta who have abandoned their calling, but to the large number of Jesuits, Maryknollers, and priests from other religious orders who work in open opposition to the Church, and in collusion with the junta. Not least, it might well have been sending a message to Bishop Malone, whose claim in his September 16 Submission that the "NCCB and USCC have become effective instruments for collaboration among the bishops and the development of collegial relationships with episcopal conferences of other countries" is not supported by the USCC's treatment of the Nicaraguan Episcopal Conference. Chief USCC spokesman on Latin America Thomas Quigley, in fact, has provoked formal protests from the Nicaraguan hierarchy; has been quoted against it in the Sandinista press; and is on the steering committee of The Religious Task Force on El Salvador, whose July-August 1984 *Central America Report* denounced Obando y Bravo. Most recently, according to the February 1986 *Catholicism in Crisis*, Quigley joked about the junta's suppression of the Catholic paper, *Iglesia*, on the grounds that it was "not an awfully good little newspaper, it has lots of pictures of Cardinal Obando and a lot of articles about statements made by the bishops."

Along with his friend Brian Hehir, Quigley remains one of the more influential voices in the USCC.

churches. The Decree on Ecumenism likewise recommends that ecumenical initiatives be carried out under the vigilance and the direction of pastors."

Bishop Lorscheiter, on the other hand, sought a different emphasis. "Vatican Council II," he charged, "must be a light and not a limit. The principle of subsidiarity in the Church must be better studied and applied. It is necessary to study more deeply the meaning and foundation of episcopal conferences. Catholics must avoid these interpretations, published in Catholic periodicals, which might be unjust towards persons or Churches of other countries." Such as Leonardo Boff, for example?

The Bishop was backed by his cousin, Cardinal Lorscheider. "A decentralization is necessary ... the tension between the spiritual and temporal mission of the Church cannot have unilateral solutions ... the Church of the future will be the Church of the poor, not only attentive to the poor, but also identified with them ... the Church of the future must strive for justice and the integral liberation of man ... the Church of the future must recognize the dignity and the rights of women and minors...."

These were the opening salvos. The public debate with Cardinal Sales through written interventions would come later. It was Cardinal Lorscheider, however, who would get the full-page interview in *Newsweek*, which provoked one journalist at the Synod to rhetorically inquire, "why, if Lorscheider is so interested in the poor, does he always get such enthusiastic support from bastions of upper-middle class opinion like *Newsweek*?" The answer to that, I helpfully suggested, could be found in Cardinal Ratzinger's interview with Messori.

Nonetheless, the two Brazilians got some support from Malang, Indonesia Bishop Francis Hadismurta ("rather than ever stressing centralized exercise of authority, the Roman Curia should give much more encouragement [to] local Churches") and, albeit somewhat more ambiguously, from Kisangani, Zaire Auxiliary Laurent Monsengwo Pasinya. Equatorial Guinea's Archbishop of Malabo, Rafael Nze Abuy, however, gave a generalized intervention, though he did reproach "the inconsistencies which went far beyond what the Council said or sought to say, and also the unfounded resistance to the application of the Council's directives—all of this in blatant contradiction to the Magisterium of the Church."

Speaking between the two Brazilians, Raul Francisco Cardinal Primatesta also unmistakably addressed his remarks to them—and their allies—by attacking "the imprudence and the audacity with which the 'popular church' is spoken of, leaning towards Marxist positions and attacking the hierarchical structures as if they were human inventions," not to say "the theological autonomy with which many scorn the ordinary *magisterium* and the pastoral activity of the Pope. They speak of the unity of the Church, but in the abstract, and separating Her from Christ Himself, and from the center, which is the Pope."

In addition, Cardinal Primatesta insisted upon "the need to affirm the obligation of the State, as such, to recognize God and the right to promote His worship . . . where this is not the case there is a lapse into secularism that leads to practical atheism."

The main practical intervention of the evening, however, came from Cardinal Law. Speaking in Latin, the official language of the Synod—Bishop Malone had been given permission to use English—His Eminence was not, on the other hand, merely practical. "Ideas have consequences," he observed, and "today there are negative consequences flowing from a secularization of the Church's teaching and mission. We must attend to our responsibility as doctors and masters of the faith." He then revealed in what direction he felt this responsibility ought particularly to be exercised.

"Very often there is open dissent," Law noted, "even in theological faculties at Catholic universities. I understand the difficulties of linking the theologians and the *magisterium*, but the difficulty cannot justify open dissent," in particular when it becomes little more than "dissent as a theological method."[7] The Cardinal's practical Synodal suggestion was an elaboration on Cardinal Thiandoum's intervention of the night before.

"I propose," His Eminence continued, "a Commission of Cardinals to prepare a draft of a Conciliar Catechism to be promulgated by the Holy Father after consulting the bishops of the world," because "in a shrinking world—a global village—catechisms will not fill the current need for clear articulation of the Church's faith."

---

[7] I was not surprised by Law's focus on Canon 810 and, in effect, his understanding that probably the majority of (certainly the majority of Jesuit) schools in the United States that now call themselves Catholics must cease to do that if Vatican II is to have a chance here. While at Collegeville, I occasionally sported a button that read, "I love St. Athanasius," and Cardinal Law was the only prelate who made a point of verbally noting it—before remarking with sparkling eye that "I love St. Athanasius too."

This proposal would become a central focus of discussion not only amongst the Synod Fathers, but amongst the Synod journalists as well; though it was a measure of the latter's racism and/or sloth that the idea got no public attention until the American revealed it in written form. In order to know that it was in fact launched by an African, they would have had to attend the briefings.

Law was the penultimate speaker of the evening; Pironio was last. Immediately preceding Law was the intervention of the Prefect for the Congregation of the Doctrine of the Faith.

Cardinal Danneels had rightly protested that the Synod was about a Council and not about an interview; but as Richard Neuhaus observed, though Danneels "protested rightly, he protested too much." It was the interesting case of this Synod that because Joseph Ratzinger had once "learned where discussion must stop because it is turning into a lie and resistance must begin in order to maintain freedom," he paradoxically set the terms of the Synodal debates.

Morality, as Chesterton once remarked, like art, consists in drawing a line; and so, eventually, does truth. In fact, it is impossible to be a Catholic without believing that. By challenging the historicists in the document on liberation theology, and in the silencing of Boff—which announced that the seriousness of the matter had gone beyond the polite confines of academic discussion—Cardinal Ratzinger had identified, and thus set the stage for overcoming the latest infestation of Arianism in the Church; as well, it is to be hoped, in the world.

And the Synodal Fathers knew it.

"For a Catholic," Ratzinger had told Messori, "the Church is indeed composed of men who organize Her external visage. But behind this, the fundamental structures are willed by God Himself, and therefore they are inviolable. Behind the human exterior stands the mystery of a more than human reality, in which reformers, sociologists, organizers, have no authority whatsoever. If the Church, instead, is viewed as a human construction, the product of our own efforts, even the contents of faith end up assuming an arbitrary character: the faith, in fact, no longer has an authentic, guaranteed instrument through which to express itself. Thus, without a view of the mystery of the Church that is also supernatural and not only sociological, christology itself loses its reference to the divine in favor of a purely human project: the Gospel becomes the Jesus-project, the social liberation project, or other merely historical, immanent projects that can still seem religious in appearance, but which are atheistic in substance."

"The Second Vatican Council," he said at the Fourth General Congregation, "spoke of the Church in a more radical and profound way than any other Council of the past," and yet "paradoxically, it is precisely the theme of the Church that has become the most suspect in the post-conciliar period. This discrepancy between the intention and the effect of the Council necessitates an analysis."

"In the general consciousness, as well as in that of Christians, the Church appears reduced to Her institutional aspect; She encounters the same suspicions as do other international organizations. It is thus of decisive importance to learn to understand once again the Church as mystery, in Her transcendence toward Christ."

The media's comic opera continued. Kenneth Briggs needed several days, to be sure, to understand the impact of the Fourth Congregation, and the focus it gave to the rest of the proceedings. A little over a week after the fact, however, he began to catch on; and in a by-headline of the 5 December New York Times, *one reads "A Loaded Term: 'Mystery,'"—and Briggs' view that "with battle lines drawn over unresolved problems, the most loaded political term at the Synod has as anomalous"—or "abnormal" according to the* Concise Oxford Dictionary—"ring. It is the word 'mystery.'... Liberal bishops have had difficulty fighting this sentiment largely because that could be seen as an assault on mystery, which no bishop wants to oppose ... the liberals have been making their points within the semantic limits. They have spoken of the church as a 'fellowship' of 'people of God,' to underline the nonhierarchical dimensions of the church. And while affirming theological mystery, they have been more upbeat than traditionalists about the value and influence of secular culture." Briggs meanwhile forgot to mention—or did not know—that "The Mystery of the Church," is also the opening chapter of* Lumen gentium.

Dionne also took a shot at analyzing the use of language, in the 7 December Times. *"Liberals became the party of 'collegiality' " he mistakenly claimed, while accurately grasping that "like the War Powers Act in the United States Congress, 'collegiality' is invoked—politely of course—to suggest that there are limits on the powers of the man at the top ... thus conservatives rallied to another idea: they became the 'universal catechism' party." What Dionne left out is that though some invoke collegiality in the manner he describes, most bishops use it in its genuine sense, and appreciate, for example, the present Pontiff's extensive practice of it through various measures such as the Dutch Synod and the plenary sessions of the Cardinalate, and other examples that have been* noted: not to say his comprehensive use of the "ad limina" visits, through which the Pope has sought in the past seven years to confer with virtually every bishop throughout the world on a personal level. As for the false exploitation of the word "collegiality," or "People of God," or any of the other terms that came out of Vatican II, one is reminded of the racists who once invoked the expression "law and order," as a means to oppress American blacks: despite the ugly tactic. it did not make everyone who used the term a racist. Nor did it obviate the genuine need for law and order.

Accordingly, Pope John Paul II not only underscores the practice of collegiality, but its theological basis as well, for it is clearly the hinge upon which he hopes to restore a sense of episcopal dignity to timid and/or compromised bishops. "The particular churches in which and from which the one and only Church of Christ exists," he observed while visiting Loreto in Italy on 11 April 1985, "in fact find their authentic meaning and their ecclesial consistency only as expressions and realizations of the Catholic Church, the one, universal and original Church." Thus, as he told the Swiss bishops in 1984, genuine collegiality "presupposes oneness in mind about doctrine, and oneness of will about the great mission of the Church."

"There can," he elaborated in the latter address, "sometimes be a certain tension between, on the one hand, the wishes and needs of the Christians on the spot . . . and the principles and directives of the magisterium of the whole Church. The problem is similar to that of inculturation in the young churches. It is indeed true that Christians and their pastors on the spot are well placed to find the opportune way to present these principles, with convincing reasons and precise applications. But it is equally true that they are subject to pressure from their environment, and opinions and practices not deriving necessarily from the Faith, or which are not at all compatible with it."

This was a point Bishop Untener had forgotten to consider. Thus collegially assisting him in that same address to the Swiss bishops, His Holiness pointed out that "the universal Church, and notably the Bishop of Rome with the departments of the Apostolic See, provides the inestimable service—even if in more general terms and from a standpoint above particular circumstances—of tracing the sure path based on Living Tradition: takes account of the Christian mystery and Christian ethics; avoids simplifications and pitfalls: and preserves the unity of all the Churches."

Meanwhile, the journalists had contradictory interpretations even among themselves of what the Synodal terms meant. Writing for the English-language Roman Courier, for instance, the often perceptive Robert

Moynihan, who had apparently read Cardinal Ratzinger's October 21 discourse, recognized the term "communio" as one with which His Eminence was closely associated. Despite this, Peter Hebblethwaite claimed that "the synod's greatest achievement was to place koinonia *or* communio *at the heart of the Church's self-understanding"—and then made clear why he thought so, by writing in the 20 December* National Catholic Reporter *that "this was a triumph for Cardinal Basil Hume of Westminster," though "he was not crowing about it." His Eminence's uncharacteristic reticence, however, may have been because Hume knew the Synod's understanding of* communio *was not what Hebblethwaite hoped, as even the ex-Jesuit began to imply upon denouncing the Synod's "loose and imprecise language," as well as acknowledging his deep concern that "if one does not attend carefully to language, all kinds of 'ideological' elements get smuggled in, and language becomes the theatre of a veritable power struggle." Particularly guilty of this, he felt—just like Kenneth Briggs, in fact—was "Cardinal Joseph Ratzinger . . . a master of ideological language." In the end, Hebblethwaite's implications became specific when he also blasted the Synod Fathers'* Final Report *for "shrewdly" warning that "the ecclesiology for* communio *cannot be reduced to purely organizational matters or arguments about the distribution of authority in the Church." Somewhat defensively, he then added, "Who said it can?"*

5. Wednesday Morning, November 27: The Fifth General Congregation

There were eighteen published interventions in the Fifth General Congregation. If these seemed to lack the dramatic aspect of the previous evening, they nonetheless brought out some important local issues and refined certain themes that had either been earlier introduced, or had been in the background of other interventions.

The Bishop of Beira, Mozambique Jaime Pedro Gonclaves, for example, decried the war ravaging his country, and "the cruel and inhuman method of fighting this war," and spoke of his hope for "a ceasefire in order that the factions might dialogue with one another to bring peace to the people." Halifax, Canada Archbishop James Hayes urges greater efforts in ecumenical work with non-Catholics, as did Mosuma, Tanzania Bishop Anthony Mayala, who also made general observations about the benefits of

collegiality, and recommended "that greater attention be given to
the power of the liturgy in the parish community as a means of
teaching and deepening the faith of those who are already Christian."

Ivory Coast Archbishop of Abidjan Bernard Cardinal Yago
reflected some of Bishop Mayala's opinions by observing that
"tensions within dioceses between the periphery and the center,
and those between the particular Churches and the episcopal conference, are normal and signs of vitality." Sion, Switzerland
Bishop Henri Schwery asked that the Synod shed some light on
such tensions where they exist, and delineate better the specific
role of episcopal conferences.

Oruro, Bolivia Bishop Julio Terrazas Sandoval spoke in high
rhetorical flourish, albeit in only general terms, about "the solidarity of the Church with the world, the evangelical attitude of
dialogue of the Church with mankind," while including none of
the cautionary notes about the distortion of this approach that
had characterized other interventions. Questioning the value of
collegiality, His Excellency expressed his preference for
"confidence in the relative autonomy of the local Church."

The most popular intervention of this Congregation with
the press was that of Salzburg, Austria Archbishop Karl Berg,
who argued that the Church should repudiate Christ's dictum
against adultery, by readmitting Catholics to the Eucharistic
Sacrament who were conjugally involved with someone other
than their spouses. This, however, caught on only with the press.

India's Coadjutor of Calcutta Archbishop Henry D'Souza,
meanwhile, gave something of an ambiguous and arguably eva-
sive response to the forthright protests of the Syro-Malabar rite
bishops. "The problem of the three rites in India must be seen in
the perspective of" the Decree on Missionary Activity, *Ad Gentes*,
D'Souza argued, given his view that "in the mission situation,
there is no place for any one Church—Latin or Oriental—imposing its traditions and culture on the new emerging local Churches, but rather the fostering of a truly incarnate
Church emerging from the flesh and bone of the local people."
Accordingly, he concluded, "the suggestion for a study team is
welcome."

Glasgow, Scotland Archbishop Thomas Winning's intervention sounded very much like he'd been reading through Newark
Archbishop Peter Gerety's *Renew*, and decided it might prove either a compensation or diversion from some of His Scottish Ex-

cellency's more pronounced inadequacies. These latter, alas, came again to the fore after the Synod when the last junior seminary for the Catholic Church in Scotland—the 157-year-old St. Mary's College in Blairs, Aberdeen—announced that it would close in June 1986, despite the fact that it has a tradition which predates even the present site: a tradition, in fact, that goes back to the post-Reformation days, and St. Mary's founding in Morar in the West Highlands, when Catholicism was illegal and persecuted in Scotland, produced the heroic "heather priests."

About this development, Archbishop Winning expressed "great regret and sadness." He was more upbeat and confident at the Synod, however, and in spite of clerical inability to maintain seminaries that had survived overt State persecution, Winning argued that "in calling the laity to a greater awareness of our common mission to participation and co-responsibility in the life of the Church," the clergy has "the duty to equip them adequately for this role." Indeed, His Excellency feels that "what dioceses need, and what the Synod should encourage, is a programmed strategy for spiritual renewal," that would do nothing less than accomplish "a revision of diocesan and parochial structures," which he seemed to think was why "the Church in Latin America is a Church on the move."

"We too can follow," Archbishop Winning enthused.

Confronted with that sort of enthusiasm, however, the African bishops seemed slightly embarrassed by their support for genuine local community prayer groups, sometimes called base communities. Burundis Archbishop of Gitaga Joachim Ruhuna defended them anyway, but quickly added that the way to protect and ensure their effectiveness was by producing a universal catechism. Following along these lines—which Bishop Gonclaves had also touched upon—Dioulasso, Niger Bishop Anselme Sanon tried to explain to the Synod the importance Africans ascribe to the "inculturation" idea, particularly "considering the growing number of new converts and apostolic vocations within" Africa, as he not unpointedly reminded his European brethren. His clear desire to explain it carefully is doubtless because inculturation—like collegiality—has both an essential aspect, and an army of folks willing to exploit it in order to ignore Christ's demands.

The Niger Church, Bishop Sanon said, "made a fundamental option in 1977, for a Church-family, where the spirit and the ties of communion take their inspiration from the Trinitarian model and the best African traditions." Even more to the point, he added, inculturation meant that "for the first time, there has begun to resound in our languages the Word of God, of which the first translations have been made."

Elaborating on his intervention, Sanon spoke with Moynihan at the Courier the following day, and made clear "it is not the exceptions we want to inculturate, it is the central values of the African tradition . . . monogamy is more common than polygamy among my people. This is the cultural tradition we want to reinforce," though "when we instruct the young, we don't focus on individuals, we look at the group," for "the Christian doctrine of the Trinity is interpreted by Africans as a reflection of their own communities of family, tribe and church." A convert to the Faith when he was 11, His Excellency also told Moynihan that "if we measure riches according to standards of the West, then we are very poor—but it is not the quantity of wealth that gives happiness."

From across the ocean, Cap Haiten, Haiti Bishop Francois Gayot developed similar themes, asked for "a privileged place" by the Synod for the local prayer-group communities, as well as "that this mystery of communion which is the Church among men might be highlighted."

Cardinal Lustiger introduced a somewhat complicated argument that sought to tie *Gaudium et spes* and *Lumen gentium* together. "By now," he said, "it is clear to everyone that the Church does not coincide with empires. The unity that She wishes and creates is not of a political order. Today, the primacy of Peter can appear in a more evident light—a spiritual one—as a guarantee of the unity that consolidates the particular Churches, while the college of bishops structures this Catholic communion through the diversity of the various cultures." *Lumen gentium*, he added, "is emblematic of the form of unity desired by humanity: this unity belongs to the order of the person and of communion . . . the communion of the Church is the guarantee of a reunited humanity."

From a Church somewhat younger than the one in Paris, Bougainville Bishop Gregory Singkai of Papua-New Guinea and the Solomon Islands began his intervention by announcing that his conference "sends its warmest greetings to you, Holy Father." The conference's childlike enthusiasm, however, was matched by a perceptive list of recommendations, all of which seemed more concerned with problems afflicting the universal, rather than its local Church. These included "affirmation of religious instruction in government schools . . . solution to the 'confrontation' atmosphere between laity and hierarchy, better relations with the secular press and need for the Catholic press to reach more people, satellite television evangelization," and, not least, a "reintroduction of the sacred and solemnity in the Mass of Paul VI."

Among more general observations, Spain's Archbishop of Oviedo, Gabino Diaz Merchan reflected Cardinal Ratzinger's query of the previous evening, by asserting that in regard to "errors and omissions," the Church must "discern the true cause of what happened in the post-conciliar period."

Munich Archbishop Friedrich Cardinal Wetter sought to comply. "Keeping in mind the widespread religious ignorance today, we must make known the teaching of the Council and fortify religious instruction even among adults. . . . The concept 'pastoral' must not be separated from the teaching of the Church or placed in opposition to it. Following the Council, pastoral activity is based on the faith of the Church and is the application of the teaching of the Church in the concern for the salvation of men. Today's widespread image of the Church as something exterior must be contrasted by the image described by the Council—the Church as mystery: the Church as the place of the saving presence of God."

And he concluded: "Present-day difficulties in the life of the Church are not at all reason for discouragement, but are rather a challenge for a deeper faith."

Cameroon's Archbishop of Garova, Christian Wiyghan Tumi, further suggested that "we have a duty to deepen the philosophical, biblical, and theological education of seminarians. For this to be possible it is essential to have approved manuals which contain those theological principles which are permanent and irrevocable." And, as had the Council, Archbishop Tumi recommended the restoration of "the scholastic method in the study of theology and philosophy."

Finally, also addressing Archbishop Merchan's and Cardinal Ratzinger's challenge, Puerto Rico's Bishop of Ponce Juan Fremiot Torres Oliver frankly stated that though "the principal purpose of the Council was the promotion of sanctity in the Church and the salvation of all men . . . in our time, there is a grave spiritual crisis . . . the causes of which are many and complex. But among these," His Excellency noted, "we need to indicate the influence of secularism on the clergy and religious, the spread of erroneous doctrines and, above all, the abandonment on the part of many of the traditional means of sanctification. It is therefore urgent that there be a fuller application of the Council's teaching concerning the universal vocation to sanctity, that it might lead to the recovery, with new vigor, of the Christian spirit of prayer, penance, and participation in the sacraments, and of the striving for personal sanctification without which we Christians cannot be the salt of the earth and the light of the world."

Slowly, the journalists began to notice the impact of the bishops from the third world on the 1985 Extraordinary Synod—Apostles, in fact, for whose people it seemed more and more the Second Vatican Council had been intended, as the West lost its will to live.

6. Wednesday Evening, November 27: The Sixth General Congregation

It is unfortunate that some of the more interesting figures at the Synod chose not to publish their interventions: people like Cardinals Joseph Siri of Genoa, for example, or Laszlo Lekai of Esztergom in Hungary, or retired Cardinal Leo Suenens, the former Archbishop of Brussels in Belgium. And given, as Moynihan pointed out in the Courier, *that "there seems no denying the strength of the Third World group," which stood "firm behind traditional church teachings on moral issues, issues of church organization, and on the central importance of Rome and the pope to Catholicism," it would have been especially interesting to read the intervention of Guatemala Archbishop Prospero Penados del Barrio, due to the notable frankness of an open letter he sent to Ronald Reagan in 1985.*

There, he requested the U.S. President's "immediate intervention in view of the dramatic affront being committed against the Christian principles professed by the immense majority of the citizens of Guatemala."

His Excellency elaborated, telling the President that "we have given careful attention to your courageous message in the defense of the lives of millions of human beings to the World Congress on Population in Mexico City in August of 1984. At this Congress, the United States representative vigorously condemned institutions, such as the International Planned Parenthood Federation (IPPF), which use abortion as a means for family planning. The United States delegate further promised that during your administration, the government would no longer fund such agencies. When we heard this important message, we gave God thanks and hoped that the systematic invasion of all kinds of artificial methods of birth control and the indiscriminate sterilization programs, especially among our Indian population, would be halted. In Guatemala we have the most varied mosaic of ethnic, anthropological, cultural and racial groups in the entire continent, and it is, therefore, very painful for us to see ... an unforgivable act of genocide against an innocent and helpless minority."

Another "serious affront that we face today, Mr. President," Bishop Penados continued, *"is a recent agreement that has been signed by the government of Guatemala and the IPPF's affiliate ... that teaches our youth to be amoral and defies and mocks our Christian principles, the only weapons our people have left to preserve their dignity and freedom. This agreement seeks to implement a liberal, hedonistic, so-called sex education that entices the young towards promiscuity, prematurely destroying their innocence and violating the parents' right to be the prime educators of their children in matters of sex education."*

"I am certain," he added, perhaps with a touch of irony, *"that you and the American people would be shocked and scandalized to learn that such degenerate material was funded by an American foundation, the Kellogg Foundation, and is being distributed throughout Latin America by IPPF. As Christian pastors of our people, we feel that the myopic intervention of these agencies brings about a reaction of antipathy against what is perceived as a North American cultural and biological imperialism which is destroying the desire for fraternity that is the legacy of our founding fathers."*

Since so many of the Synodal Fathers who chose not to publish their interventions were said to be from countries oppressed by Communism, one wonders if Bishop Penados addressed his remarks to Bishop James Malone, whose bishops' conference has been conspicuously silent about the fashionable oppression Penados protested in his letter to Ronald Reagan. Alas, if so the story was not leaked.

The fifteen published interventions of the Sixth General Congregation, however, were of considerable interest all the same. Brisbane, Australia Archbishop Francis Rush discussed collegiality and the need for a more precise delineation of the bishops conferences' theological grounding. Greek Melkite Patriarch of Antioch Maximos V Hakim noted major contributions that Eastern Rite Catholics had made to the documents of the Council, and appealed to the Pope for direct intercession in order to ensure that the Eastern Code of Canon Law would be ready by the Jubilee of Vatican II in 1990. Cardinal Garrone gave reflections on the nature of *communion,* and noted that "since it is a question of a Living Person, the Church cannot be fragmented. Reflection and theology can distinguish this or that aspect, but not abstract it from the totality that is the source of meaning."

Bangkok Archbishop Michael Cardinal Kitbunchu asked for attention to his country's refugee problems, and discussed the difficulties of inculturation in Thailand, "due to the closed religious society and identification of Buddhism with Thai culture. Other difficulties," he added, "arise from misunderstanding of the spirit of the Council followed by abuses in practice." Tokyo, Japan Archbishop Peter Shirayanagi's intervention illustrated Cardinal Kitbunchu's point by insisting that it was the obligation of the Church to change Her values to the society around Her rather than be the leaven of renewal. In Japan, he said, it is accepted that "one should correct a mistaken marriage by beginning a new one, so it is almost impossible for a Catholic divorcee not to re-marry because most people around put so heavy pressure on him, that a Catholic would become forced to remarry according to civil law." Accordingly, he urged the Church to adopt Archbishop's Berg's solution.[8]

Meanwhile, with what looked like deliberate ambiguity, Chilaw, Sri Lanka Bishop Frank Fernando also addressed the question of Asian inculturation, by calling for "an open and positive attitude toward non-Christian religions," without defining what this meant, while at the same time arguing that "the theological foundation of this open attitude is [that] Jesus Christ, in whom all men—Christian or non-Christian—find salvation, is already operative in the hearts of all men, and also in the great religious traditions of the world," since "God's plan embraces all." Perhaps aware how painfully the imprecision of these remarks

---

[8]According to an American missionary-priest who works in Japan, and with whom I had dinner, the Japanese hierarchy has become utterly compromised, and has never, for example, aggressively denounced abortion, though Japan was the first "Western" country to legalize the practice after the War, and though there is great disquiet abbout the practice throughout the country. In consequence, this priest suggested, the Church ought to consider readopting the ancient practice of highlighting the universal nature of the Mystical Body, by a widespread establishment of hierarchies that are not native. "It would be the solution for Japan," he observed, "and I think also the United States could maybe use a few African bishops, to help bring some of its priesthood and laity back into communion with the Church."

threw Cardinal Kitbunchu's warning into relief, Bishop Fernando added that they were not intended to denigrate "the centrality of Jesus Christ, Lord of history"—and closed his written summary with the observation "that all missionary endeavor, whenever possible, has to be brought to a climax in the explicit proclamation of Jesus Christ and His Gospel."

Another strange intervention during this Congregation came from Armagh Archbishop Thomas O'Fiaich: while claiming that Council directives have in Ireland "been applied with fruitful results," he at the same time lamented that Irishmen "have not the joy and exuberance, or the enthusiasm in responses and music that one finds in the young African Churches." Without seeming to notice a possible connection between the two complaints, he added that "in addition many of our traditional popular devotions have been allowed to lapse." Falling somewhat short of Irish metaphor at its best, His Excellency concluded by expressing the hope that the Synod "will not be a policeman signing us to stop, but a helpful traffic-warden supplying the Pilgrim Church with a road-map, the documents of Vatican II"—again without noticing the contradiction contained in those two suggestions. One had the impression His Excellency may over the summer had fallen into the bad Irish habit of reading too many English newspapers.

Speaking of which, Cardinal Hume's intervention on the surface also seemed somewhat vapid, though when one considers his priests' enthusiasm for the Godard film, and other events of the summer, it was actually quite audacious. "This Synod has to show itself as having a positive vision," he boldly proclaimed, "and a message for the people of our generation." He added that "the concept of *communio* deepens our understanding of the relationship between the Supreme Pastor and each bishop, emphasizing their unity within the mystery of the Church, without compromising in any way the teaching of the First Vatican Council." But of course (to paraphrase Hume's friend) who said it did?

Jos, Nigeria Bishop Gabriel Ganaka suggested that in order to protect the priesthood from corruption, "the documents of Vatican II must be a basic textbook in all formation houses and seminaries—not just a reference book." Perhaps reading the coverage of the Synod, he also noted his hope that "because of its importance, the means of Social Communication will be a Synod theme."

Spain's Archbishop of Madrid Angel Cardinal Suquia Goicoechea rather threw down a gauntlet, charging that for the Church to "provide an example of sanctity, it is the bishops' duty to tend to their own holiness and that of their faithful," for "the Church will be incapable of realizing Her mission in the world if the faithful are not renewed—above all interiorly and spiritually." His Eminence further observed that though "the missionary consciousness of the Church has grown within the Council in some new and ancient Churches, beyond this missionary zeal has lost energy."

In addressing the matter more diplomatically, Congregations for the Evangelizations of People Prefect Jozef Cardinal Tomko at the same time clearly confronted the ambiguities, not to say open corruption, of certain Asian episcopal initiatives. After praising various post-Council missionary developments, His Eminence admitted that "however, there exist some restraining phenomena, such as the decrease in missionary vocations in the Churches having a long Christian tradition, some uncertainties concerning the motives for missionary work as it relates to the general mission of the Church and to the theology of salvation, and also concerning the relation between the Gospel proclamation and human promotion. The Council, read as an integral whole, provides the answer to these uncertainties: today, as yesterday, *lumen gentium cum sit Christus*; in Him, God and man, is found the solutions to the problems of mankind."

Consequently, Tomko continued, "it is necessary once again to propose the truth about Christ because in Him is also the truth about man. With His incarnation he is also the model and the ultimate reason for evangelization wisely inculturated—incarnated. The Church in Her mystery as the Mystical Body of Christ must bear in Her countenance and in Her mission the reflection of Christ, and of His holiness."

Venezuela's Archbishop of Caracas Jose Ali Cardinal Lebrun Moratinos spoke of the Council's particular contributions to his country, such as an increase in vocations both to the priesthood and the religious life, but added that "without a doubt the Council has not been sufficiently or adequately known." He further noted that "among the clergy and the laity there are initiatives that some view with mistrust and suspicion . . . due to the personal and arbitrary positions of some speakers and lecturers."

In consequence, "one must therefore conclude that a great effort is necessary to remove these obstacles."

In light of John Paul II's introduction of the Synod with authoritative remarks about the importance of the Curia, Education Prefect William Cardinal Baum's intervention seemed clearly to indicate the Pontiff's agreement with Cardinal Moratinos. In effect, Baum's remarks were understood to be a direct attack on both the Liberal Consensus and its chief theoretician Raymond Brown.

"There is the matter of the reception and application of the Conciliar Constitution *Dei Verbum*," as His Eminence observed. "This document appears to be poorly known and incorrectly applied."

Accordingly, "some reflections are suggested concerning the importance and the necessity of promoting the exegesis that is truly in harmony with the prescription given by the Constitution, particularly as regards the relationship between Sacred Scripture, Tradition and the ecclesial *magisterium*. It is therefore hoped that there will be a biblical renewal which emphasizes that Sacred Scripture is . . . a living Word that must be read within the Church," and "thus an exegesis that is not purely critical, but theological and ecclesial."

"This conception of exegesis," he concluded, picking up where St. Pius X left off, "shows itself to be of particular importance for theological renewal, the formation of candidates to the priesthood and the promotion of a correct ecumenism."

If Cardinal Baum's remarks were the most significant of the Sixth Congregation, however—and perhaps, given what they reveal about the mind of John Paul, of the entire Synod—the intercession of Pereira, Columbia Bishop and Latin American episcopal conference Secretary General Dario Castrillon Hoyos, was also notable in that he addressed the consequences of the postconciliar distortion of Catholicism. These included, he noted, an increasing "disdain for human life, violence, deterioration of the institution of marriage to the point of negation"—Bishop Castrillon Hoyos spoke after Archbishop Shirayanagi—"the perversion of individual, family and social morals, the decrease or the disappearance of the sense of the transcendent, refusal of ecclesiastical authority, a decrease in the practice of the sacraments, the crisis of priestly vocations, and the visible deterioration of ecclesial love."

Slowly, surely, the Synod was facing the heart of the problem. And the source of the solution. "We are not bishops for ourselves," the Columbia Apostle told his confreres, "but for the
Church."

Finally, Polish Primate and Archbishop of Warsaw Jozef
Cardinal Glemp was even more direct. "Secularization is one of
the obstacles to the Council," he charged, and "is nothing but an
accommodation to the world ... the Council's doctrine is less effi-
cacious due to a lack of courage on the part of ecclesiastics who
avoid preaching about chastity, marriage, divorce and abortion."
In addition, he added, "the conciliar concept of religious liberty
[has been] transformed into a liberty conceived in a worldly way,
often harmful to human dignity."

Nor need it be this way, His Eminence pointed out. "The
Church in Poland received the decisions of the Council with seriousness, prayer on the part of the faithful and profound study on
the part of the priests," in which the role of "the illustrious figure of the deceased Primate of Poland, who prudently guided the
conciliar reform in Poland, must be emphasized." The reference,
of course, was to Stefan Cardinal Wyszinski.

7. Thursday Morning, November 28:
The Seventh General Congregation

"For the most part," Michael Jones wrote in the February
1986 *Fidelity* of the interventions, "the proposals that were inconsistent with Catholic morals or Catholic Church polity seemed
glaringly idiosyncratic." This reality became even more apparent
in the final three congregations, though a number of bishops
from countries with small Catholic populations continued to
sound a discordant note of ambiguity from time to time.

Algeria's Coadjutor Archbishop of Algiers Henri Teissier,
for example, did make some stirring observations during the
Congregation about how dialogue with Moslems had helped
Christians refocus "our attention upon our Christian identity in
order to deepen it and savor its richness." On the other hand, his
seemingly laudable suggestion that "the Synod should invite all
the Churches to value the importance of Christian witness before
every man, regardless of his ideological or religious identity be-

cause, at its roots, the human vocation is identical," left some wondering whether he was talking about witnessing to the Kingship of Christ or to just being nice: the latter interpretation received some strength when the Archbishop insisted that "condemnation of past errors would be useless," a subject about which the tiny Church in Algeria was not previously considered expert.

Monrovia Archbishop Michael Francis, representing the inter-territorial Conference of Gambia, Liberia, and Sierra Leone (each country of which has a roughly two per cent Catholic population), said "the Conference would like to see developed the autonomy of the local Churches and expects of this Synod . . . a recognition of the autonomy of the local Churches."

New Zealand's Archbishop Thomas Cardinal Williams gave something of a contradictory intervention, by on the one hand joining Cardinal Glemp in condemning clericalism and "a clerical model of the Church," while on the other using precisely the kind of semantical distortion Modernist clerics most often invoke to defend their privileged positions. "Much remains to be done," the Cardinal opined, "in bringing about a proper balance between central authority and local autonomy." But of course, one of the first things that needs to be done is to repudiate false dichotomies that in effect reject Vatican II; for the Council did not seek a balance between Rome and the local Churches, but rather an integration, or, to be more exact, a reflection, one of the other. The *Final Report* would, in fact, reflect this unity—and repudiate the dichotomy.

The Archbishop of Dhaka in Bangladesh Michael Rozario made a general intervention about "renewal of the Christian life in Asia," and talked, as did John Paul during his February 1986 trip to India, of "the importance which Asian peoples give to spiritual values," which His Excellency called "the starting point of our dialogue." But again, a note of ambiguity was introduced when His Excellency added that "especially through our works of diakonia and the struggle for justice we are building a fruitful 'dialogue of life' with the followers of other Asian traditions."

The nature of these ambiguities, of course, was not that the bishops were saying how infrequently opportune was the possibility of fruitfully proclaiming Christ's Name to those who did not recognize His Divinity, but rather the slight hint that they were unprepared to do so even when a genuine opportunity should present itself; and their intimation that this lack of preparation was deliberate, on the grounds that fondness for Buddha was kind of like accepting the Gospel. Accordingly, the Japanese missionary's idea of establishing unindigenous episcopates[9] began to find favor among certain Catholic journalists at the Synod: if it was mentioned inside the *aula*, however, this was not publicly revealed.

The Latin Patriarch of Jerusalem Giacomo Beltritti, however, spoke after Teissier and Francis, and went beyond the vague generalities. Representing "the Episcopal Conference of the Latin Rite in Arab countries (CELRA)," which "includes thirteen Arab nations, the majority of them Muslim," he said its chief concern was "to nourish and strengthen the faith of our faithful, who are exposed for many reasons to the serious danger of losing their faith. To nourish the faith," His Beatitude pointedly added, "it is first of all necessary that it shine out in the words and life of pastors, priests and bishops. These, in turn, will try to nourish the faith of the people," by various means, including "a valid catechesis of children" as well as "a uniquely based catechism for the entire Church."

The Vicar Apostolic of Istanbul, Bishop Pierre Dubois, was not sanguine either. "The problem faced by Christians, one out of every two thousand inhabitants [in Turkey]," he said, "is that of conserving their identity." In addition to the "lack of vocations and the exodus of Christians," Bishop Dubois observed that "the number of pilgrims and tourists continues to increase, and they are obviously very welcome, but it is desired that tourists behave as Christians in Turkey, without scandalizing people with their behavior," by "showing interest only in ancient stones and the 'Club-Mediterranee'."

In the remainder of the seventeen published interventions of this Congregation, Bishop Joseph Ruzindana of Byumba, Rwanda gave a rather general talk about the importance of youth, as did Chile's Archbishop of La Serena, Bernardino Pinera Carvallo, about how "the Church must think towards the future." Benedictine Confederation Abbot Primate Father Viktor Dammertz discussed some of the problems of religious brothers, noting that their involvement "in the work of the world," and their call "to manifest the eschatological dimension of the Mystery of Christ . . . does not take place without tensions and risks." Implicitly attacking most post-Council developments in the West,

---

[9]See footnote 8.

Father Dammertz added that the chief resolution of this tension was "a solid theological and spiritual formation."

"The Brothers are more valuable to the Church for what they are than for what they do," the Benedictine continued, "and here we see the need for a permanent conversion to God. The young people at the close of the twentieth century have need of teachers of wisdom, witnesses to the absoluteness of God. And saints. This is the principal challenge to the Brothers in today's Church."

Cardinal Willebrands discussed aspects of his competence as President of the Secretariat for Christian Unity. Pontifical Commission for the Authentic Interpretation of the Code of Canon Law President Rosalio Jose Cardinal Castillo Lara picked up where Cardinal Krol had left off during the First General Congregation, and remarked that "since the Council used necessarily general formulas, there was a need to translate them into concrete norms of action. This was done by means of a long collegial effort," and accordingly "it is necessary definitively to overcome the widespread anti-juridical sentiment that has caused not a few ills for the Church," since "She cannot set laws aside," when they are "theologically founded upon Scripture and Tradition."

"Let us bring to mind the bishops' duty to safeguard the unity of the Church through requiring the observance of the laws," he concluded, "and let us promote the knowledge, love, and application of the Code."

Bishop Emilio Eid, Vice President of the Pontifical Commission for the revision of the Oriental Code of Canon Law, discussed the progress of that revision; Prefect of the Congregation for the Oriental Churches Simon Cardinal Lourdusamy also discussed his competence in general terms, while seemingly responding—however unsatisfactorily—to the charges of the Syro-Malabar Indian bishops. "In order to favor the flowering of the Oriental Churches, the Latin bishops have been exhorted, in the application of the conciliar norms, to provide—through the designation of the priests of various rites—for the care of the Oriental faithful subject to their jurisdiction," Lourdusamy said. That some Latin-rite bishops have apparently rejected this Curial directive (as they have others) seems indicated, among various instances, by the constant Ukrainian insistence on the need for authority independent of the Latin hierarchy.

Czechoslovak Patriarch Frantisek Cardinal Tomasek, meanwhile, chose understatement ("in Czechoslovakia . . . the

Church lives under particular conditions"), but in what many interpreted as a particular message for the West, he observed that "for us, it is precisely the liturgy that is the principal wellspring of religious life and pastoral activity. From this one sees the importance of an ongoing liturgical formation of both the clergy and the faithful."

In addition, he concluded, "it is necessary that everyone strive to work, pray and suffer for the sake of the Kingdom of God."

Congregation for Religious and for Secular Institutes Prefect Jerome Cardinal Hamer zeroed in, as it were, on the responsibilities of bishops vis-a-vis the professed religious in their dioceses. "In this context" he mentioned the "talks presently underway in the various dioceses in the United States between the local bishop and members of religious institutes." Whether these talks will lead bishops to exercise their episcopal authority in defense of their flock was not a subject upon which Cardinal Hamer publicly chose to venture an opinion.

Related to that development, however, Colombia's Archbishop of Bucaramanga Hector Rueda Hernandez, in observing that "Vatican Council II was eminently ecclesiological," and "the Church is a sacrament of communion," further pointed out that consequently "this ecclesia communion must exist and manifest itself in the fraternity of bishops, in the faith, in the pastoral mission and activity, and in obedience to the disciplinary norms of the Church. The Episcopal Conference of Colombia," he continued, "by the gift of God enjoys perfect unity of spirit and concord in pastoral work, always in a communion of obedience, adherence and affection with the Roman Pontiff."

Finally, the most direct synodal criticisms of the inadequacies of Vatican II were presented during this Congregation by Papal nominee and Secretary General of the International Theological Commission Monsignor Philip Delhaye.

"I wish to recall some gaps in the Council and ask that as regards these points its great work be carried forward," he wrote. "First, there was so much talk about the grandeur of man, of earthly realities, that at times the primacy of the work of Redemption, of the Cross of Christ, was forgotten. Secondly, the Council did not have occasion to propose important texts concerning the principles of Christian morals. A suitable place ought to be given to them in the synthetic exposition whose preparation has been suggested by some Fathers." Finally, Monsignor Delhaye suggested, since "Vatican II dealt very little with priests," and "there have been crises of identity, abandonment, and difficulties concerning the number of vocations, perhaps this problem should be dealt with more explicitly."

The Seventh General Congregation, however, did not end immediately after the interventions. Before retiring for lunch, the Synod Fathers decided to vote on the suggestion put forward for a Synodal Message to the Church: and it was passed almost unanimously. In consequence, the three President delegates appointed a commission of five bishops to compose the Synodal Message, who were chosen, according to *L'Osservatore Romano*, for their "geographic and linguistic variety." The five bishops were: Cardinal Lustiger (Fifth Congregation); Ukrainian Metropolitan of Philadelphia Stephen Sulyk (Third Congregation); Latin American Bishops' Conference General Secretary and Pereira, Columbia Bishop and (like Lustiger) Papal nominee Dario Castrillon Hoyos (Sixth Congregation); Archbishop of Lome, Togo Robert Casimir Dosseh-Anyron, who would not speak until the following morning in the Ninth Congregation; and the Archbishop of Karachi in Pakistan Joseph Cardinal Cordeiro, who did not published an intervention.

Until the announcement of this development, the letter from Papal Nuncio Laghi to Archbishop Hunthausen had been the topic of the day among American journalists—along with Thanksgiving. When news of the Commission was released, a palpable excitement arose briefly, as various pressmen insisted this meant the episcopal rebellion against the Papacy for which they felt all had been aching right along. More prudent voices, particularly those few who seemed to have been reading the interventions, suggested the utility of noticing the makeup of the Commission.

Eventually, this advice was followed. By Saturday, the press was angrily demanding of Cardinal Malula during a press conference why strict democratic procedures had not been established for the choosing of the Commission.

8. Thursday Evening, November 28:
The Eighth General Congregation

The fifteen published interventions of the Eighth General Congregation included some of the bluntest of the Synod. Babylonia of the Chaldeans Patriarch Paul II Cheiko spoke of the illustrious lineage of Christians who have come from the east. Jean-Marie Cisse, the Bishop of Sikasso in Mali, which has a Catholic population of less than one per cent, urged the importance of giving "more responsibility to the episcopal conferences, in order to make collegiality function." Paraguay's Bishop of San Juan Bautista de las Misiones, Carlos Milciades Villalba Aquino gave a very generalized praise of the Council's impact in his country, as did the Dominican Republic's Archbishop of Santo Domingo Nicolas de Jesus Lopez Rodriguez, though his was more detailed. Uruguay's Archbishop of Montevideo Jose Gottardi Cristelli's was more like Villalba Aquino's, however with the caveat that "it is difficult to know with precision what is the heritage of the Council and what comes from erroneous attributions." Apostolic Exarch of Sophia Metodi Dimitrow Stratiew discussed the improvement in relations between Catholics and Orthodox in Bulgaria, who even, he went so far as to suggest, "think we will realize in the future the desire of Christ: 'Father, that they may all be one.' "

The Bishop of Mohale's Hoek in the land-locked country of Lesotho—wholly surrounded by South Africa—is Sebastian Koto Khoarai. His Excellency was pleased to announce that "all liturgical books have been translated into Lesotho, and the faithful have a high level of participation, especially in the singing." He complained about the level of religious education, on the other hand, and said that, in addition to inculturation, "improved seminary training" was an urgent need. At the same time, Bishop Khoarai was able to note that "Lesotho is making its first steps of sending missionaries from among its own people to preach the Gospel beyond its own borders."

Malta Archbishop Jose Mercieca chose not to address publicly the State persecution which has been growing in recent years in his ancient Catholic country. Instead, he spoke to the concerns of the larger Church, and noted that though "it is of great help to recall the good fruits that resulted from the Council, this is not enough. It is also necessary to take into consideration the difficulties—of which some have spoken." Urgent among ways to counter these difficulties, he added, is unity among the bishops in repudiating facile suggestions that the Council must adapt itself to the passing enthusiasms of the modern world; but instead "to present to everyone the whole doctrine, without any mutilations."

There followed what everyone understood to be severe attacks against the episcopicies and bureaucratic structures of Europe and the United States.

Singapore Archbishop Yong Soot Nghean—who, as well as Singapore, was also representing the episcopal conferences of Malaysia and Brunei—was very direct. "The Second Vatican Council was meant to be a new Pentecost," he said, "to bring about the renewal of mankind in Church and society. Has this goal been achieved? Men, women, and children around the world today are hungering for a personal experience of God. The Second Vatican Council can be judged a success or a failure, as far as individuals are concerned, by the answer they give to this question: has Vatican Council II helped you to acquire, foster and increase your experience of God as a loving Father, through the merciful grace of Jesus Christ, in the fellowship of the Holy Spirit in your personal, social, and spiritual life?" That was the Archbishop's complete published intercession. One suspects it rang like a shot in the middle of the *aula*, for he made no attempt to defend or reproach Vatican II—the question of its legitimacy never seems to have crossed Archbishop Nghean's mind. Yet in questioning whether its promises had taken hold in the hearts of Christians, His Excellency was reminding his brother bishops of inquiries they would one day be obliged to answer before Christ Himself.

Chikwawa Bishop Felix Mkhori shortly afterward put Archbishop Nghean's question into context. "I speak on behalf of the Malawi Episcopal Conference," he noted, and "we are very grateful to the missionaries who preached the Gospel and implanted the Church in Malawi" However, he continued, "it seems there is a change of attitude on human development among us and some missionaries as well as some old sister Churches," since nowadays "the latter seem to overstress the material aspect at the expense of the spiritual formation and growth. We still believe that man does not live by bread alone."

The Malawi Bishops' Conference had more to say: "Human development is not limited to material considerations but rather it must be complete and integral to promote the growth of every person and the whole person. The difference of attitude is manifested, for example, when we ask for assistance to counterbalance the massive free literature against the Church. To our great surprise, we receive a negative answer, but when we propose to build a social center, we get a positive answer without delay! Mosques are coming up like mushrooms in Malawi. When we request money to build churches, seminaries, or to run programs in our Episcopal Conference, we receive regrets."

"We request therefore," His Excellency rather dryly concluded, that "the missionaries and the old sister Churches have a dialogue with us in deciding on our top priority needs."

Speaking for the Zambian Bishops' Conference, Mansa Bishop James Spaita made points similar to those of Bishop Mkhori. After praising the work of missionaries, he acknowledged however that "on the one hand, we have registered a marked drop in the number of missionaries due to the scarcity of vocations in the old sister Churches ... on the other hand, vocations are flourishing in our region both for the diocesan clergy and for the religious life."

"These changes," he continued, "have posed new challenges and problems to us and the missionaries in such a way that our harmonious cooperation is in danger." And he explained how: "Let the missionaries accept the changes in a spirit of faith and realism and resolve to cooperate. For we are all called together to build the local Church. We are called to witness and announce the Gospel in order to build the Body of Christ. This work does not overstress the material development alone but it focuses on the salvation of the total person. Missionaries should be ready to adapt themselves to the local situations and cultures and not to impose their thinking on the people."

Further insight into Bishop Spaita's concern was provided during a strange interview in the 28 February 1986 National Catholic Reporter *with Adrian Hastings, a priest who had abandoned his calling (in order to get married) after 24 years of service, 16 of those as a missionary in Africa.*

When asked, "How well do Western missionaries understand African Catholicism?" Hastings answered that "when I was there, the sort of soft theological progressivism among American, Dutch and other missionaries was becoming a problem," because they were involved "with this kind of 1960's theology which doesn't really go down at all in the typical African church context. They find it difficult to participate because of the tension produced by them saying they don't believe in angels or something. Whereas people in Africa have had a frequent experience of angels and no problem at all about believing in them." Or "missionaries say, 'there aren't any witches, there's no witchcraft' to people who are very conscious of witchcraft."

"*I don't say the answer is to say, 'there are witches,'* " *Hastings quickly assured* Reporter *readers.* "*But if you simply dismiss the thing and say, 'This is a lot of nonsense,' or 'a psychological problem,' the African can say, 'we have the Bible on our side, we have Church doctrine on our side.' The vitality and dynamism of the Church very naturally goes with what we would consider a very theologically conservative position.*"

Finally, the Eighth Congregation produced a serious reflection on the liturgy from Sacraments and Divine Worship Congregation Prefect Augustin Cardinal Mayer, as well as some alas ignored (by the media) but very astute observations on relations between the Church and the State during three separate interventions.

In noting that "the intentions of the Council will not be fully implemented if a proper sense of Mystery is not cultivated in liturgical celebration," Cardinal Mayer reminded the Synodal Fathers that "such celebration is not primarily the execution of human actions, but the celebration of the saving works of the Lord and the simultaneous actualization of our Redemption. It is this sense of participation with understanding in the Divine Mysteries which needs to be inculcated in the hearts of God's people," particularly given "that such a dimension to liturgical celebration is actively desired and sought by many of the faithful," and accordingly "should be met by the mode of celebration."

"The Paschal Mystery of Christ which embraces the realities of the Passion and Cross," he concluded, "must be celebrated in all its fullness, and the element of adoration, praise and thanksgiving should be promoted as pertaining to the primary end of liturgical action. All these matters call for careful attention in the initial and ongoing formation of clergy, with a view to providing sound catechesis for the People of God."

Meanwhile, Pontifical Commission for Justice and Peace President Roger Cardinal Etchegaray somewhat confounded *Wanderer* predictions with an engaging and thoughtful intervention; it was mostly, but not solely, about *Gaudium et spes.* "We must once again bring out not only the ethical character of every social action," he asserted, "but the religious foundation of social ethics. The rehabilitation of the social doctrine of the Church passes by way of its reinsertion in the very heart of theology."

The difficulties and rewards of the struggle for that rehabilitation were addressed by Angola's Archbishop of Huambo, Manuel Da Costa. "The last twenty years," he observed, "have without doubt been the most tormented that Angola has ever experienced, in a context of war and revolution. Initially, the war of liberation from 1961 to 1975: thousands upon thousands of the faithful, catechumens, catechists and missionaries were the innocent victims of repression. And then 11 November 1975: the proclamation of independence after a long war [of] 14 years of immolation, uncertainties and expectations. Almost immediately Marxism-Leninism took hold," and "radicalizations and extensions of the process of Marxist indoctrination." Consequently, "the Church loses her radio, her educational institutions, and so forth."

"It was in this very difficult context," Da Costa continued, "that the Church in Angola received, divulged and studied the doctrine and the spirit of the Council as a providential gift," and "its positive effects have been innumerable." Among these His Excellency noted developments more or less the opposite of the West's; that is, "a purification of the personal and community life of priests and religious," and "a Church which became more liberated with respect to the world, and at the same time more inserted in the world as a ferment of salvation."

"The doctrinal clarity of the Council," the Archbishop pointedly concluded, "warns all of our faithful against a social class concept of the Church which often seeks to impose itself." In addition, "the Church gives us the guidelines for . . . consecrated vocations, the young, families, Christians, and truly committed lay persons," all of whom "enjoy the protection of Mary, Mother of the Church, and of Angola."

Finally, El Salvadoran Archbishop of San Salvador Arturo Rivera y Damas explained the practical application of Cardinal Etchegaray's thesis. "The Episcopal Conference of El Salvador committed itself to making the conciliar documents known," he said. "This effort culminated in every diocese in the community apostolate, designed to create in every parish a community of faith, worship and fraternal love. This work was influenced in part by the phenomenon of an excessive politicization in which even some members of the clergy found themselves involved. The situation worsened with the armed conflict, which, though it had internal roots, was quickly ideologized because of external forces, becoming still more complex through internationalization. In spite of everything, the Church sought in every way to maintain Her own identity and fidelity to Her mission, favoring the poor. This earned for Her general esteem, and for this reason She is considered the most credible moral authority." After noting specific efforts to end the war, His Excellency concluded by observing that "in a particular way, we focus our attention on the call to conversion and reconciliation according to the lines traced out by the last Synod [and presented in the Apostolic Exhortation *Reconciliatio et poenitentiae*]. For this reason we expect from this Synod light and energy, so that through our work we might contribute to the Kingdom of God in our country."

9. Friday Morning, November 29: The Ninth General Congregation

While the journalists began arriving sleepy-eyed at the sala stampa *in the late morning, the bishops conducted the Ninth General Congregation: the final one during which Their Excellencies would present the eight-minute interventions. Certain elements in the media were still excited with the illusion that the collegial decision to present a Synodal Message represented episcopal antagonism to the Pope and the Faith: and Cardinal Hume's* Universe *was published that day, with the blazoned headline "No Going Back." Perhaps to assure readers what was meant by this, an article appeared on the second page of this issue, titled "Birth Control Teaching," which read: "The Church could not apportion guilt to couples who did not follow its teaching on artificial contraception, Bishop Devine of Motherwell said this week . . . 'A couple may decide to use contraception for a number of medical or social reasons. What the Church asks is, "Are they making that decision from an informed conscience or simply following the secular view which claims contraception will solve all their problems?"' . . . The bishop said the role of Catholic marriage counselling was invaluable as it helped a couple to have an informed conscience." He forgot to add that even more invaluable to that formation would be understanding how thoroughly the British hierarchies seem to have rejected Catholicism once again.*

The Extraordinary Synod, meanwhile, seemed to have that understanding well in hand. In the Ninth Congregation there were thirteen published interventions. Zimbabwe's Bishop of Gweru, Tobias Chiginya, chose prudently to speak in general terms, though the Zimbawean episcopate has been both resolute and courageous in exposing the human rights abuses of the apostate Robert Mugabe's oppressive tribal government. Less resolute and courageous about that practice has been the Cuban hierarchy, whose representative at the Synod spoke only in general terms, except to "thank the Council for not having condemned anyone." Camaguey Bishop Rodriguez Herrera said the reason he felt this gratitude had to do with nothing more than a conviction that "the serene proclamation of the Gospel and the joyous experience of faith has more power than any purely condemnatory or defensive attitude"—though some cynics wondered how the Bishop would know, since none of the above is allowed by the Castro government.

As ever, the African interventions seemed particularly moving and to the point. The Sudan's Archbishop of Khartoum Gabriel Zubier Wako wrote that "the local hierarchy in the Sudan is ten years old. They have been a difficult ten years for the local bishops, who had to rebuild a Church devastated by civil war and utterly weakened following the mass expulsion of missionaries from the country. After the first years of struggling with no older hand to guide them, the bishops drew up a National Pastoral Plan," but "at times the bishops felt they were abandoned and that often made them ask, 'Where does a Church like ours feature within the Universal Church?' "

"Vatican II very much stressed the doctrine of communion, unity and collegiality in the Church," the Archbishop continued. "The Universal Church must, therefore, see herself as a communion of all the local and particular Churches united with and under the leadership of the Bishop of Rome. This vision requires that there will be real collaboration, cooperation and mutual concern for one another among the local Churches that make up this communion." Accordingly, "the problems of growth, inculturation and self-reliance that many young local Churches face should be the concern of the universal Church—the concerns of the whole Body. The young Churches need encouragement and accompaniment in their efforts to tackle these problems."

In fact, His Excellency concluded, "if the Church has to grow organically, She should pay special attention to the local Churches that show signs of weakness," although "without conversion of heart, no change is possible in the Church."

Chad's Archbishop of N'Djamena Charles Vandame also had a *cri de coeur* against Modernism's devastation of the Western Church and its effects on the younger Churches, for despite the rapid growth of native vocations, the absence of missionary priests has left many Chad communities without the Eucharist, and allowed the growth of heresy in others. "The burst of vocations will not be able to remedy this situation," Vandame charges, and though "the permanent diaconate would permit the resolution of the first problem . . . we hesitate to proceed along this path," and "do not see clearly what the best solution would be." But the intervention was not wholly pessimistic. "The Church in Chad is the last born among the African Churches," the Archbishop noted. "She has experienced grave trials, cultural revolutions, war, famine, and thirst . . . in spite of all this, She continues to grow."

Gabon's Bishop of Franceville Felicien-Patrice Makouaka spoke of numerous benefits that have resulted in his country due to Vatican II, but added that "in spite of this, many difficulties remain: the small number of 'apostolic workers;' the absence of large seminaries and other institutes of formation; the dangerous evolution of society; the race for money, power, pleasure; spiritual insecurity; fetishism, sects, and so on; timidity on the part of the laity." Nonetheless, His Excellency noted, even with these problems, and "in spite of the recent competition of Islam, the Gabonese are very open to the Christian life."

Uganda's heroic Archbishop of Kampala Emmanuel Cardinal Nsubuga chose not to speak publicly about the murderous collapse of public order combined with brief bursts of state tyranny in his ravaged land. Indeed, his one sentence published intervention seemed clearly directed toward the few African episcopal complements of Archbishop Berg—though in speaking about "the unity and indissolubility of marriage on the natural and sacramental levels," perhaps Cardinal Nsubuga in fact had Western prelates in mind.

The Central African Republic's Archbishop of Bangui Joachim N'Dayen spoke in specific local terms about the permanent diaconate, but perhaps gazed in pointed directions when he argued that "we must avoid 'clericalizing' everything at whatever cost."

Benin's Archbishop of Cotonou Christophe Adimou devoted his published intervention to a local explanation of inculturation. "Our efforts at inculturation in Benin," he said, "proceed in two directions: catechesis and the liturgy. Regarding catechesis we have compiled the manuals in our languages. The four Gospels, the Acts of the Apostles, and several books of the Old Testament have already been translated. Regarding liturgy, nearly all our liturgical texts have been translated, both for the administration of the Sacraments, and for the Eucharistic celebration."

Not least was the intervention from Archbishop Robert Dosseh-Anyron, the African chosen by the Synod to help compose its Message.

"Togo is still experiencing the atmosphere of the Pope's recent visit," he informed his brother bishops, "a visit which gave Christians the opportunity to 'be Church with Peter,' sharing the experiences and the acquisitions of the Council. Vatican II coincided with the political birth of our nation, in which 65 percent of the population is under twenty years of age; and it coincided with the consolidation of the local hierarchy, whereby now we must be our own missionaries." Among the benefits of the Council in Togo, His Excellency among other things mentioned "an authentic ecclesial communion in which all the clergy, religious and laity, with their respective duties, learn to 'be Church,' linked in the effort towards inculturation, towards the defense of the human person—especially our young people, once tempted by the mirages of Sartre's existentialism—and towards the defense of justice and peace." In conclusion, Archbishop Dosseh-Anyron said he hoped the principal result of the Synod would "lead to our closer visible communion within the episcopal college, with the unshakeable rock that is Peter."

The head of the Curia's Sacred Apostolic Penitentiary, Cardinal Luigi Dadaglio, spoke about "the Sacrament of Penance or Confession, neglected or even disdained by many" and seemed clearly to be laying the blame for this on the priesthood. "The thought of St. Pius V remains always valid," Dadaglio concluded: "Give me good confessors and behold the reform of the entire Church."

Cardinal Oddi, the last published speaker during the interventions, discussed his general competence as head of the Congregation for the Clergy; but he also invoked St. Pius V in arguing that there should be an open indult for the celebration of the Tridentine Mass codified by the Saint in 1570.

Meanwhile, the Indian Catholics who trace their origins to the evangelization of St. Thomas celebrate two Oriental rites: in addition to the Syro-Malabar, there is also the Syro-Malankarese rite. The Metropolitan Archbishop of Trivandrum, Gregorius Thangalathil, presented an intervention on behalf of the latter, during which he too argued that the Council dictums on the Oriental Churches in India must now be applied. "The Malankara Church," he said "has benefitted much by the Vatican Council, especially in the renovation of family life. However, even twenty years after the Council, our Church does not have the possibility of having pastoral care of the faithful according to our own spiritual tradition. The clear teaching of the Council must be put into practice without any further delay. Parishes and ecclesiastical jurisdictions should be established wherever our faithful are in significant numbers."

But if, like so many of his Christian brethren in the West, Archbishop Thangalathil felt frustrated by the powerful clericalism that prevents the implementation of Vatican II, he went beyond the mere juridical aspects of the problem, and condemned clericalism's fruit, as well.

In fact, during an interview published in the 1983 *National Catholic Register* Christmas issue, His Excellency had already frankly discussed one of the matters that goes to the heart of the conflict between the Latin and Oriental Rite Churches in India.

"The oriental rites," he said then, "have a deep sense of sacred mystery. We know that the human mind is not able to fathom the mysteries of God. In the West the tendency has been to understand as much as possible. In the East, although we also try to understand the faith, we give great importance to mystery. The human mind is finite; it can never comprehend the profound wisdom of God."

"Also," he continued, "the oriental liturgy places great priority on a sense of respect. In the Latin Church now, symbols are largely eliminated. The altar is brought into the middle of the people. People stand all around. In one way, it has become so common. But once it becomes such, it's difficult to keep the interest of the people: 'Oh, we know everything. We have grasped everything.' But how little we understand. A respectful distance from the sacred mysteries will preserve the great spiritual wonder. This has helped us very much."

At the Synod, His Excellency developed these themes. "About liturgical practice after the Vatican Council," he noted, "there is, all over, a great diminution of the spirit of penance, especially bodily penance—fasting, abstinence, asceticism, etc. This is very harmful. The value of the Cross of the paschal mystery has also been lost. This is harmful and liturgy and prayer life have become insipid. The sense of mystery must be regained."

Finally, Mexico's Archbishop of Jalapa Sergio Obeso Rivera's intercession was a succinct summation of the week's events. "It would be a repetition of what has been said several times—especially concerning Latin America and Africa—to refer to the results and to the errors of post-conciliar life in Mexico. In summary, let us say that the Council continues to be a light and continues to give a valid response to the challenges of the present. The errors into which we have fallen are not due to its application, but to false interpretations, partial readings and ideological exploitation."

"We deeply rejoice in this Synod," he concluded, "because it gives us the opportunity to study the Council more deeply."

10. The Bishops' Interventions: Cardinal Danneels's Second Report

Cardinal Danneels second report, his published summary of the week's interventions, was also presented on November 29. Its tone was sharper than the first one; and indicated how much more direct the bishops' exchanges in the *aula* had been in comparison to the statements they published.

The heart of its "general summary of the interventions," for example, concluded that "the promotion of the knowledge and the application of Vatican II supposes a more profound and integral knowledge that does not separate the letter from the spirit, in the light of the integral tradition of the Church and of the signs of the times."

About "the mystery of man," the Summary pointed out that "there is an increase of secularism, which leads to immanentism," whereas "the rightful autonomy of human culture must be distinguished from an autonomist vision of man and of the world which casts aside and denies spiritual values. Many of our contemporaries, especially the young, are experiencing a spiritual crisis, particularly in the Western world . . ."

"The primary end of the Council was to make the light of Christ shine out from the Church's countenance so as to illuminate the world. This is true *aggiornamento*," in contrast to an "easy accommodation, which could lead to the secularization of the Church. . . ."

"The call of all the faithful to sanctity must be preached in a clearer and more incisive way," and "in the preaching of the Word of God, the false opposition between 'pastoral responsibility and doctrinal responsibility' must be overcome," since "in fact, the true aim of pastoral action is to actualize the truth of doctrine." Consequently the bishops stressed "distinction, not separation," because "there is a duality (not dualism) in the mission of the Church. Oppositions between natural and supernatural aspects between the spiritual mission and *diaconia* for the world, are useless and harmful."

"Liturgical renewal is not limited to ceremonies, texts, etc., but is above all interior participation in the Paschal Mystery of the Christ."

"The ecclesiology of communion was the central and fundamental idea of the conciliar documents," the Report continued, "but this reality of communion has not yet been sufficiently understood, and even less actualized," in particular with regard to "the unity of the Church," and "the faith, the sacraments, the hierarchy, with the Pope as the centre of unity," whose office is "not an obstacle but an anticipation and prophetic sign of fuller unity."

Also misunderstood in post-conciliar Catholic life is that the "pluriform aspect of the Church," wherein "the one and universal Church makes itself present in the particular Churches ... is not pluralism, which often means opposition of parts." As to episcopal conferences, "there is no doubt regarding their utility, indeed their pastoral necessity. But they are based on ecclesiastical law," whereas "collegiality is a sacramentally founded reality" that "has a meaning which is much fuller than the juridical exercise of collegiality."

In concluding its analysis of how *communio* has been undermined in both practice and comprehension, the Report summarized the bishops' observations that though ecumenical dialogue "is deeply etched in the consciousness of the Church," this is only the case when "the identity of the Church in faith and charity" is presupposed. Further, the Second Report pointed out the inadequacy in "the relationship between the magisterium of the bishops and theologians," as well as, *pace Gaudium et spes*, the "relationship between the Church and the world," since "a *theology of the Cross* is necessary" (the Report's emphasis), and "the relationship between human history and salvation history must be explained in the light of the paschal mystery. It is not a question of encouraging pessimism, but of being guided by the realism of Christian hope."

In short—recalling that well over sixty per cent of the prelates at the Synod were representing their episcopal confer-

ences—the world's Roman Catholic bishops overwhelmingly saw
the crisis of the modern world in terms virtually identical to
those outlined by Joseph Cardinal Ratzinger in his interview
with Vittorio Messori.

11. The Written Interventions

Published only after the first nine General Congregations
ended, the written interventions were distinguished primarily,
though not exclusively, for the sharp confrontations between the
Brazilians. Nonetheless, general observations about the importance of the laity and consecrated religious, as well as priests and
in particular "the formation of candidates to the priesthood"
were made by Aveiro, Portugal Bishop Manuel D'Almeida
Trindade. The Congo's Bishop of Owando Georges Singha urged
the Synod to address the questions it was in fact addressing; and
Benedictine Father Dammertz, while admitting the massive
"defections, errors, and deviations among religious," asked the
Synod not "to forget the fervour and devotion of the great majority of religious"—who, of course, are particularly heroic in this
era due to the oppression and abuse they too often suffer at the
hands of their superiors and "brethren" for holding to the Faith
and the teachings of the Council.

Apostolic Exarch for Catholics of the Armenian rite in the
United States and Canada Mikail Setian wrote that "the be-
haviour of the hierarchy, the clergy and the faithful of the Latin
rite towards their Oriental brothers—exiled and uprooted from
their homelands and established in the West—will be the tangible
proof of our catholicity, of our fraternal charity, of the genuine-
ness of our ecumenical spirit, as well as of our sincere proposal to
actualize and to live Vatican II. It is necessary that facts speak
more than sentiments."

To the dismay of the men who drew up Bishop Malone's
September 16 Submission, that last sentiment was being voiced at
the Synod in more than one context. Not least, "the twenty-year
evaluation of the Church must take into account the physical
disappearance, at least in its visible aspects, of the Church in
Cambodia. There have been no priests in Cambodia for nine
years," as Phnom-Penh's Vicar Apostolic Yves-Georges-Rene
Ramousse painfully observed. While helping to compose the

Synodal Message, Philadelphia Ukrainian Metropolitan Stephen Sulyk also made a "plea for the Church to unite in loud protest against the religious persecution against all Christians, especially Catholics in Soviet dominated countries."

One might have thought the last two interventions would cool the ardor of Father Boff's friends; but they did not. Between Bishop Lorscheiter and Cardinal Lorscheider, however, it was clear that the latter was the real theoretician; the former was, as it were, a kind of Hunthausen, full of enthusiasm, whereas the North American counterpart to his cousin was more someone like Bernardin, or Weakland.

Thus the bishop made only two written interventions, in which he asserted that the principle of subsidiarity, although it has its origin in social philosophy, can be applied to the Church." (The social principle of subsidiarity is that decisions and actions affecting the common good ought to be taken at the lowest possible level at which they can be effectively administered. In regard to the government of the Church, the argument is essentially invoked as a challenge to the Council's insistence that collegiality means a cooperative communion between the universal and local Church: it is another word for "autonomy.")

Jesuit General Peter-Hans Kolvenbach's written intervention seemed to back Lorscheiter, though following the Jesuit tendency in this century, the General's arguments were characterized by linguistic obscurity. Canada's Bishop Hubert on the other hand, was less obscure: in praising the laity, his two written interventions carefully ignored groups involved in serious attempts to implement the Council, while otherwise in awe of "certain forms of ministry exercised by the laity," which, "appear more or less to be expressions of a search for a new way of exercising the priesthood."

Bishop Lorscheiter's second written intervention gave some indication of how much more lively discussions within the *aula* must have been: for it sounded like a response to a challenge that never appeared in the published oral interventions.

"Among the positive fruits of the Second Vatican Council," he felt, "in Brazil, and in all of Latin America, there is the elaboration of a theology adapted to the specific conditions of the Church on our continent. Liberation Theology"—the Bishop's Capital Letters—"is the principal result of this effort. It represents not the product of a few isolated and more audacious theologians, but the fruit of the totality of the Latin American

Church's life. Against the false interpretations it must be clarified that Liberation Theology is not a theology of violence or one that pushes towards violence. It is not a theology that assumes or justifies Marxist ideology. Nor does it apply European political theology to Latin America. Nor does it break with Catholic theological tradition."

Who said it did? Well, Cardinal Ratzinger for one, but Bishop Lorscheiter, though claiming to speak on behalf of nothing less than "the totality of the Latin American Church's life," makes it clear he does not really care whether the above charges are true or not, given his (concluding) view that "Liberation Theology is indispensable to the Church's activity and to the social commitment of Christians, even if it carries with it risks, such as those recently indicated by the 'instruction' of the Congregation for the Doctrine of the Faith." He adds, nonetheless, that these are "risks that need to be faced seriously and responsibly."

Cardinal Lorscheider, on the other hand, sought to tie the idea of subsidiarity—without using the word, since, as Bishop Lorscheiter had neglected to notice, it was not received with much enthusiasm by the Synod—to the theological concept of *communio*, which, he insisted (and once again, who said it did?) "does not at all damage the primacy of the Roman Pontiff, but rather realizes what the ministry of the Pope is already meant to be: the service of unity."

As to who is to define that unity, "it can be said that the episcopal conferences have rendered a service to all the bishops of the world, a service that is much more complex and linked, because they have avoided isolated positions, with very broad social consequences." In addition, contrary to what *Lumen gentium* itself says, His Eminence insisted that "the Church as the people of God is the key idea of *Lumen gentium*," and "consequently, for two theological reasons, the Church must place itself in an attitude of listening to the people." His Eminence continued that "in order to listen to the people, the Church must create within herself some conditions: change of social role, attitude of listening, of humility, capacity to pick up the message of the people, to let herself be questioned by that message," and the list goes on.

One gasps at the implications of this, for throughout the century it has always been through insisting upon "listening to the voice of the people" that that voice has been most effectively silenced. Bishop Ramousse could tell us, Khmer Rouge also insisted upon that, and so one wonders: if Cardinal Lorscheider disapproves of the Khmer genocide, does he recognize as prophetic those in pre-Khmer Cambodia who denounced the imposture of listening to the people? Or does his assertion merely mean that people should listen to him?

Cardinal de Sales challenged Lorscheider at every step: both prelates delivered three written interventions, whereas except for Hubert's and Lorscheiter's two, the only other written interventions are the single ones noted.

"When a well-founded doubt exists as to whether or not some food for sale in the stores of a city has been poisoned," de Sales observed, "or constitutes some threat to public health, the police immediately prohibit its sale until its quality is tested. But in the Church there are grave errors that are sometimes taught in colleges, seminaries, etc., without the people (and the seminarians) being protected. The mass media often impose these fashionable but false ideas upon public opinion," and "there are also cases in which some pastors of the Church show themselves to be weak, or even support errors or seem to defend those who have published false doctrines."

Therefore, "it is necessary that the bishops, as teachers of the truth and of the integrity of the faith intervene with courage, even if it may cost them suffering and hate."

In addition, de Sales argued that since "not only the correct application of the Council, but also the future of the Church depends in great part on the formation given in seminaries," there must thus "be a more explicit definition of the ecclesial function of the professor, who cannot use the *cathedra* for 'his' doctrines, but in the service of the Church's faith in the name of God."

"Apostolic visitations of seminaries are urgently needed, but visitations that have practical consequences, undertaken by the competent authority."

12. The Press Conferences

On the afternoon of November 29th, after the close of the Ninth General Congregation and the release of Cardinal Danneels' Second Report, the American bishops held a press conference. Cardinals Law and Dearden were there along with Archbishop May and Bishop Malone; Cardinal Krol did not attend.

Most of the questions dealt with the media's agenda for the Synod—female ordination, married priests, divorce—and Cardinal Ratzinger's presence was still in the air, but some journalists even touched on matters germane to the Synod. In regard to the media agenda the American prelates were all quite orthodox. Malone noted that the question of female ordination had not even come up. He was somewhat ambiguous about the matter of married priests—which is, of course, not a doctrinal, but a juridical matter—but did not recommend it for the United States at the present time. And all the bishops disavowed Archbishop Berg's idea that the Church should repudiate the Sixth Commandment, with Archbishop May giving the most straightforward answer:

"It is important to realize that we believe this teaching comes from Jesus," he said. "Jesus was explicit about those who leave a partner and marry another. The Church is not free to accommodate itself by a practical approach to the modern world. . . . The Church always has been and is for many a sign of contradiction—countercultural to the age in which we live."

Meanwhile, as Ralph McInerny observed in the January 1986 Catholicism in Crisis, "Bishop Malone astonished the press by several times suggesting, albeit jokingly, that the Extraordinary Synod was a contest between himself and Cardinal Ratzinger. In considering the last twenty years," the Youngstown Ordinary observed, Ratzinger "and I are looking at the same phenomena. Where we differ is in the interpretation, or perhaps more precisely, in the tone. I take a relatively optimistic view, by which I do not wish to suggest that the Cardinal is a pessimist." There were some dutiful chuckles at this, whereupon His Excellency suggested that the real problem lay with Messori, who should have "asked [Ratzinger] to discourse on the virtue of hope and the many positive signs in the life of the Church today."

Having apparently not paid attention to the interventions, Cardinal Dearden insisted that the majority of the Synod Fathers supported Malone over Ratzinger both in regard to the Council "and how it's been implemented."

Peter Hebblethwaite suggested there had been a difference between what the heads of episcopal conferences and the fifteen Papal appointees had been saying, and seemed much distressed over the idea of an international catechism. "If an episcopal conference can't produce a national catechism, what can it produce?" he wanted to know.

But the Americans essentially ignored the question. When a similar one was posed to Archbishop Schotte after the Synod was over, he wryly noted that there could hardly be a problem, since the international catechism would be addressing doctrinal matters with which, of course, no episcopal conference would disagree.

Finally, on the matter of the authority of bishops' conferences, Bishop Malone and Cardinal Law reflected a muted example of the conflict between Cardinals Lorscheider and de Sales.

Though "the Second Vatican Council does not specifically attribute a teaching role to bishops' conferences," Bishop Malone remarked, "my own opinion is that episcopal conferences do have a teaching role, and teach with authority." He then restated his formal reasons for this opinion. Whereupon Cardinal Law remarked that "as far as the teaching authority of the conference is concerned, it is my understanding that unless it is a matter that has been given by the conferences to the Holy Father for his final decision, then what a conference has said derives its authority from the local bishops who choose to give it authority."

Over the weekend, there were other conferences, but they were striking primarily for the paucity of intelligence in the questions. During the conference held by Cardinal Malula, an ex-nun from Belgium and a woman from Fort Lauderdale helped the press compensate for this problem, by passing out obscene literature and staging a protest about the immediate need for priestesses. Later on in the week they sought unsuccessfully to stage a "mass" in St. Peter's. The media was grateful. It gave them something to write about without having to work.

On that note, David Wagner of the Washington Times and I had a rather sad conversation with Peter Hebblethwaite. We were chiding him a bit about the brilliance of Cardinal Ratzinger, when he suddenly became agitated and made a rather strange observation to both of us.

"But you're so young" he said, almost plaintively, as if the one failure he hadn't yet faced was how impressive a man of Ratzinger's depth would be to the young. My answer, if not kind, was spontaneous.

"Ah yes, Peter, and you're so old," I said. "How does it feel to have bet on the wrong horse and to see the sun setting on all you've worked for during the last twenty years?"

His answer astounded me and seriously upset the devout Wagner.

"Well, it's too late to change now, isn't it," was the gloomy, if classic reply.

And yet, it was worthy of all the other heresies Hebblethwaite had served; in fact ultimately the one toward which they all lead.

And like them, it is false.

III. The Second Week

"The lip of truth shall be established forever; the lying tongue is but for a moment."

Psalms 120:21

1. A Growing Militancy:
The Language Group Reports

"From the point of view of the press," Mike Jones remarked in the February 1986 *Fidelity*, "the proceedings went from bad to worse." The reason is that the bishops broke into ten separate language groups in order to complete the work of the Synod, without inviting any journalists to join them.

One of the groups was composed of special invitees to the Synod such as Cardinal Dearden and Father von Balthazar who did not have voting status and so did not release a report. The remaining nine groups did so on Tuesday, 3 December, in the Tenth and Eleventh General Congregations, presented by a secretary elected from within each group.

Some of these summations revealed rather little about the actual dynamics and conclusions of the group, such as Spanish Language Group B, for example, despite that it was composed of such distinguished prelates as Penados del Barrio, Quarrancino, Rivera Damas, Vigano, Obeso Rivera Torres Oliver, and Cardinal Primatesta. They reported only that "the group concentrated its work on four themes: mystery, the founts of life, the ecclesiology of communion, and the mission in the world. Each theme was developed in three complementary moments: fundamental Conciliar principles; the most worrisome aspects of the past twenty years; some working propositions for the episcopal conferences ... a dozen propositions were drawn up and offered to the Relator General as material to be used in his later summary."

The Report of Spanish Group A, on the other hand, though somewhat generalized, still became specific at points. These were of particular interest due to the makeup of this group, which, among others, included Bishops Castrillon Hoyos, Lorscheiter, McGrath and Da Costa; and Cardinals Castillo Lara, de Sales, Ricketts, Moratinos, Lorscheider, and Obando y Bravo.

Regarding post-Council problems, "we welcome the initial *relatio* of Cardinal Danneels asking that the causes be specified," and so wish "to emphasize the role of the Church as mystery; the active presence of Christ through Her that culminates in the Liturgy. From the Cross He communicates the paschal and holy life to us," and thus "only sanctity is the root and guarantee of the integral conversion of the Church, including Her structures and Her relationship with the world." In addition, apart from addressing questions of communion and evangelization, this group also stressed "the need to give human (moral) meaning to technical-scientific progress, and to proceed with the interpretation of the new signs of the the times."

Similarly different approaches affected the reports of the two English language groups. Thus though such interesting figures as Bishops Mkhori, Spaita, Malone, Winning, and Sulyk, as well as Cardinals Lubachivsky, Nsubuga, O'Fiaich, Vidal, and Williams were in English Group B, it produced only a generalized report encouraging "personal spiritual renewal, ecumenism," and the like: though it did specifically recommend that "the teaching of *Gaudium et spes* [should] emphasize the faults of secularism."

But English Group A was more specific. The confrontation—or, if you prefer, collaboration—here, included Bishops Carter, Hurley and Foley, and Cardinals Arinze, Baum, Cordeiro, Hume, Krol and Law. And it was curiously this group that acknowledged the concerns of Bishops Spaita and Mkhori, by calling upon episcopal conferences to provide "not only for economic development but also for fostering the spiritual development of peoples." In addition, while noting the importance of communio and pluriformity, the group made clear that for these to have any effect, "authentic spiritual formation is needed," and so asked that the Holy See publish "a compendium of Catholic teaching from which each country could draw its own teaching documents." Unfortunately, the Modernists were quick to seize upon the idea of a compendium as a possible means of both opposing a universal catechism, and maintaining their own control of Catholic bureaucratic structures; but, to be sure, such distortions are inevitable. Meanwhile, apart from encouraging lay participation in the Church and "a level of inculturation consistent with the teaching of Christ in the Church," the group noted tha "bishops' conferences should be recognized as a genuine but limited expression of collegiality."

"Acutely aware of the signs of the time," it concluded "the Church must proclaim, defend and promote sacredness of life, dignity of the human person, sanctity of family, justice and peace, and commit itself to service of the poor."

To some extent, the same phenomenon hit the French speaking groups. Composed of men such as Bishops Sanon, Sarah and Teissier, as well as Cardinals Thiandoum, Tomko and Trinh Van-Can, for example, French Group B did call for an international catechism, "the promotion of ecumenical dialogue with realism, in truth and mutual respect," as well as an improved "spiritual formation of priests, religious and laity"—but the remainder of the observations were of a general character. More pointed were the perspectives offerd by French Group A which included Father Kolvenbach, Bishops Hermaniuk and Dosseh-Anyron, and Cardinals Danneels, Etchegaray, Garrone, Hamer, Lustiger and Malula, as well as Monsignor Delhaye, who delivered the report.

"The Church is essentially a hierarchical communion," it affirmed. "Sacramental grace is not to be confused with organizations. The essential structures link men with Christ, the Apostles and their successors, and particularly with Peter and the Pope. Toward other religions the Church wishes to have an attitude of receptivity, recognizing some of their values. Still, she cannot fail to preach that Christ is the one Saviour." In addition, though "the preferential but not exclusive option for the poor is an evangelical requirement which asserts itself in a special way in our day, it must not, however, be polluted by political options." In affirming the value of the Council, meanwhile, the group noted that "in some regions, it is still a question of making the Council known," whereas, "in others a critical evaluation is necessary."

The remaining three language groups—Italian, German and Latin—were the most forthright. Though the Italian Study

Group included Bishop Shirayanagi and Cardinals Casaroli and Baggio, these were more than counterbalanced by Cardinals Gagnon, Gantin, Glemp, Kuharic, Oddi, and Tzadua. Together, they recommended "the necessity of promoting the knowledge of Vatican II by means of a 'Catechism of the Faith' directed toward believers; a 'Book of the Christian Faith' offered to non-believers; and a 'Book of Moral Doctrine' for everyone. Further recommendations included "a more explicit and exact knowledge of the 'collegiality of the bishops with the Pope' in the Church; of the doctrinal, sacramental and disciplinary communion of the particular Churches with the Pope and under the guidance of the Pope; of the infallibility of faith and morals promised by the Holy Spirit that is guaranteed by the Pope, as an expression of the Church even in the ordinary *magisterium* exercised by him and by the bishops in union with him . . . a positive conclusion to the Synod with precise adherence to Vatican Council II and to the *magisterium* (ordinary as well) . . . and the formulation of concrete 'propositions' concerning the religious, moral and social problems of the Church and the world to be elaborated—if, when and in the manner that the Holy Father deems opportune—in an eventual Apostolic Exhortation."

And, not least, the Italian group recommended "the precise elucidation of the bishops' responsibilities in the spiritual, doctrinal, and human formation of priests."

Bishops Berg, Gran and Cardinal Willebrands were in the German Study Group, as were Archbishop Stroba, and Cardinals Kim, Hoffner, Wetter, Meisner, Mayer, Lekai, Simonis, Tomasek, and Ratzinger.

"The Church, as the Council emphasizes," their report noted, "can be understood in Her specific form only in relation to the Mystery of Christ. From this perspective, the Council has spoken of the Church in a marvelous way," and yet "the reasons—internal and external—for the distress which often manifests itself in the Church have been examined. The group itself sought to make an examination of conscience. Has there not perhaps been too much talk of the Church and not enough of Christ? In the Church's pastoral opening to the world, has use been made of overly critical worldly categories and points of reference? In liturgical celebrations, has the value of reverence, of the sacred and of silence been sufficiently taken into account? Have the major post-conciliar pastoral instructions of the Papal *magisterium* (e.g. on catechesis, on work, on the family) been sufficiently drawn upon for the actualization of the Council?"

Perhaps having learned from Archbishop Foley's wisdom, not to say the dynamic of the Synod in contrast to the myopia of the press, "it was also emphasized that preaching, catechesis and pastoral work must stress the real problems of mankind today, and not merely the themes prevalent in the attention of the day; themes that in the last analysis fail to grasp the most profound problems of man, and especially of the young."

Finally there was the Latin Study Group, composed of Bishops Lokuang, Padiyara, and Thanagalathil (who was chosen to present their report to the Synod); and Cardinals Sabattani, Vaivods, and Palazzini.

Delicately, the Latin Group applauded *Sacrosanctum Concilium*, while noting that "the possibly too rapid rhythm with which it was carried out has produced a certain loss of the sense of the sacred, which must be restored, along with the forms of private devotion." Further, "evangelization must prepare the way for the right reception of the sacraments in order that it might be truly fruitful." In regard to such right reception, the Fathers observed that they had "particularly considered the Sacraments of the Eucharist and Penance, pointing out the need to instruct the faithful on the preparation which must necessarily precede the reception of the Sacrament of the Eucharist."

They also insisted upon the need for "the principle of subsidiarity to be suitably clarified so as to avoid incorrect interpretations which could not be reconciled with chapter III of *Lumen gentium* and the *Nota praevia.*"

"The unity of the Church is a common good to be defended and safeguarded by all the particular Churches. In the international assemblies promoted in defense of human dignity, may Christians, in every way possible, recall the right of every individual to the free profession of his own faith. In the promotion of ecumenism, which it is hoped will ever increase, let us not, however, forget the danger of indifference, which causes harm to all religions."

The last paragraph, however, was the only one of the nine reports that had the courage to assert with clarity what was not only on everyone's mind during the course of the Synod, and indeed since the elevation of Karol Wojtyla to the Papacy, but what everyone knew was going to have to be exercised frequently if

John Paul II has any genuine hope to implement the work of Vatican II.

"In promoting ecclesiastical discipline," Archbishop Thanagalathil read to the assembled Fathers, "charity cannot be weakness on the part of those who perform the service of authority. Even the threat of ecclesiastical punishment is, in the intention of the legislator, an exercise of charity towards those who are in error and the obligatory safeguarding of the flock entrusted to one's care."

The work of the Synod was not quite done. On 4 December the original Synodal Message was rejected by the Fathers. In voting *placet* or *non-placet* (pleasing or not pleasing), sentence by sentence, there was sufficient displeasure to require a redrafting of the entire message. This was done, the process was repeated, and then finally a vote on the completed document, which passed, "almost unanimously," according to Monsignor Martin. The text is not as important as the Final Report, but a couple of observations may be useful here.

Though the Fathers say "we do not fix upon the errors, confusions and defects which, because of sin and human weakness, have been the occasion of suffering in the midst of the people of God," neither are such errors wholly ignored; for the Message also note the necessity "to avoid false sociological or political interpretations of the nature of the Church," and makes clear its unity with Cardinal Ratzinger by recalling that "the first chapter of the Constitution on the Church *(Lumen gentium)* does not bear the title 'Mystery of the Church' without good reason. We are speaking here of a reality of which we must be ever more certain," for "we are aware that the Church cannot renew Herself without rooting this spiritual note of Mystery more profoundly in the hearts of Christians."

The continued calls, both during the General Congregations and in the Message, for "a deeper understanding of the true significance of Vatican II," and insistence that "it is also a question of putting them more deeply into practice," amounted to a formal repudiation of the pretense that, universally, the Council had been successfully implemented. As for the clerical campaign against the right of American Catholics to defend the faith—and when necessary to communicate with Rome—the Message sharply condemned it, as well as all vilification of the orthodox laity, since "every baptized man and woman according to his state in life and in the Church, receives the mission to proclaim the Good News of salvation in Jesus Christ. Each is therefore called to exercise his or her responsibility."

Meanwhile, on 3 December, the non-Catholic Ecumenical Observers delivered a report to the Synod, wherein they thanked the Holy Father "for the confidence you place in our churches. You have not seen us to be outsiders or rivals, and we have not felt ourselves to be so." They were also pleased that "the Synod has made it very clear that ecumenism is an essential part of the way forward, and that it does not involve a betrayal of divine truth and faith," and that "notwithstanding doctrinal differences which still exist, some questions which were once divisive have come to be seen in a different perspective, not now as church-dividing questions."

The Pope responded on 5 December with a short address during an ecumenical prayer service. "There is one center around which the human family can be united," he said. "Jesus Christ. That is the will and plan of God," and "divisions among Christians are contrary to the plan of God," although "the restoration of unity must be above all a restoration of the inner dimension of the Christian life—a wholehearted personal commitment to Jesus Christ which makes intolerable any separation among those who share that commitment. Any faltering in the movement towards unity since the impetus of the Second Vatican Council is partly due to the fact that we have not attended enough to this interior dimension."

The lay and religious auditors—Mother Teresa, Chiara Lubich, Virgil Dechant, et al—delivered two messages to the Synod: one, from the entire group, remarked upon numerous matters, not least "the universal presence of the Church, Her living within the diversity of ethnic cultures," and "Her profound unity in the same faith;" and the other, from solely the woman auditors, who discussed Synodal themes such as *communio* and "the mystery and sacrament of the Church." Among other things, they also noted that "if vocations decreased in the post-conciliar years, we see that young people are again entering religious life, in increasing numbers in some continents, but slowly in others as well."

On the evening of 4 December Cardinal Danneels introduced the first draft of the *Final Report*. As with the Synodal Message, the Fathers went over it sentence by sentence, *placet* by *non placet*, until it too received a "near unanimous" vote of support, on Saturday morning, 7 December. That evening, the Fathers watched a film on the work of Mother Teresa in Calcutta.

When the matter of the would-be priestesses began to peter out, the media could have relayed the story of the language group reports: but they did not, presumably for the same reasons they chose not to report the Synod at all. Apparently confident that no one would read—or report—the source of his assertions, Hebblethwaite announced in the Re-porter that "only the Western English-language groups refused to support the pessimistic line of the prefect of the Congregation for the Doctrine of the Faith, Cardinal Joseph Ratzinger, that seemed to dominate the language-group reports."

"The Westerners," he pretended, "boldly and publicly raised their issues, collegiality and a role for episcopal conferences. But in the language groups, as distinct from the general openness on the synod floor a week earlier, the odds were stacked against the progressives." All this was pure fantasy, of course, though perhaps I should say desperate fantasy; for just as "progressives" are shocked to discover that it is precisely young Catholics who are often most appreciative of Joseph Ratzinger, so I think they were wholly unprepared to discover which views the bishops of the world really consider eccentric—and contemptible. Thus men like Peter Hebblethwaite had to come up with some—or rather any—explanation to account for what happened at the Synod: to account for why every prediction they made from the moment of the Synod was announced had been proven not just wrong, but ridiculous. Remember the alarmed American bishop who pompously announced that the "fundamental issue" of collegiality "will revolve around the question of who gets to write the documents that will come out of the two-week session"? Or the English Submission insinuation that John Paul would prevent the bishops from saying what they really thought? But the bishops were free, and they did produce the documents, all of which were thorough repudiations of virtually everything men like Hebblethwaite, Higgins, McBrien, Curran, Hume, Weakland—alas, the list in this tedious era is a long one—stand for. That is what the Hebblethwaites get paid for.

John Paul II had produced the ecclesiastical equivalent of Muhammed Ali's Rope-a-Dope: the Modernists had flayed and flayed, only to collapse from their own efforts—or rather to be defeated by the very rules they had insisted upon. So an explanation had to be invented, new tactics were required.

Indeed, it is no small indication of what the Synod accomplished just to read the lengths to which such men are driven. "Liberation theology," Hebblethwaite charged, *"was viciously condemned in a Spanish-language group that contained ... Lorscheider and ... Lorscheiter,"* who *"had no voice."*

The explanations did not begin until after the Synod, however. Up to the release of the Final Report, *the media continued to believe that, whatever this incomprehensible interlude was about, the bishops would eventually get around to reproaching Ratzinger formally. Even Hebblethwaite was claiming as late as 6 December that the bishops had in effect already done so; in the 12 December* America, *editor George Hunt announced that "If the Cardinal had hoped to steal a march on the Synod, then his was a tactical error. Instead of stealing a march, he was, more accurately, trampled to death."*

Well, not exactly. Meanwhile, Kenneth Briggs announced in the 5 December New York Times *that "a major clash has broken out among Roman Catholic bishops at the extraordinary Synod here over the form and substance of the assembly's final documents." This major clash was according to Briggs between those bishops who wanted Danneels' third Report—*The Final Report—*released as the formal and public observations of the Synodal Fathers to the Roman Pontiff; and those who didn't want it publicized. But where Briggs led, others followed. It was, of course, taken for granted that the Prince of the Apostles was implacably opposed to the publication of such a document, given—in the media's view—that it would almost assuredly call for Ratzinger's resignation. There was even talk of a vote on the question, until His Holiness announced that he would, obviously, release the third* Report, *as had been done with the other two.*

Then everybody was in for a surprise.

2. The Final Report

If the Synodal Fathers felt compelled in their *Final Report* on Vatican II occasionally to exaggerate by, for example, asserting that "the large majority of the faithful received the Second Vatican Council with zeal," they were quick to add qualifying realities such as that "in truth, there certainly have also been shadows in the post-conciliar period." The first shadow mentioned, one to which the Fathers continually refer, was a clear repudiation and indeed a reproach against the dishonest clerical Submissions from the English and the U.S. Episcopates.

"In a particular way," the Fathers begin the fifth paragraph, after the pleasant introductions, "the question must be posed as to why, in the so-called 'First World', following a doctrine of the Church which has been so extensively and profoundly explained, quite often a certain estrangement is manifested towards the Church."

This book, to be sure, has been an attempt to answer that question. The Synodal Fathers, however, needed no helping hand. "In the wealthy nations," they point out, "we see the constant growth of an ideology characterized by pride in technological advances and a certain immanentism that leads to the idolatry of material goods (so-called 'consumerism')," which manifests nothing less than "the work of the 'prince of this world' and of the 'mystery of iniquity.' "

In consequence, the bishops frequently drove home that the essence of *Gaudium et spes* was not its passing tone of naive optimism, in particular because since the Council, "there has also been a lack of the discernment of spirits, with the failure to distinguish correctly between a legitimate openness of the Council to the world and the acceptance of the secularized world's mentality and order of values." The importance of that Pastoral Constitution rather lies in its condemnation of "an immobile closing in upon itself of the community of the faithful. Affirmed instead is a missionary openness for the integral salvation of the world." What this meant in practical terms had perhaps been best explained during the crucial Fourth General Congregation by Cardinal Primatesta when he noted "the need to affirm the obligation of the state, as such, to recognize God and the right to promote His worship," since "where this is not the case there is a lapse into secularism that leads people to practical atheism."

"The separation of the Gospel and culture was defined by Paul VI as the drama of our age," is how the Synod Fathers put it—"as it was for other ages. It is therefore necessary to make every effort towards a generous evangelization of culture, more precisely of cultures. They must regenerated with the good news," and "the Church must prophetically denounce every form of poverty and oppression, and everywhere defend and promote the fundamental and inalienable rights of the human person. This is *above all* [my emphasis] the case where it is a question of defending human life from the time of its very beginning, of protecting it from aggressors in every circumstance and of effectively promoting it in every respect," with the understanding that "besides material poverty there is the lack of liberty and of spiritual goods, which in some way may be considered forms of poverty, and is particularly grave when religious liberty is suppressed by force."

This refocusing of *Gaudium et spes* continued given, as the Fathers dryly put it, that "the signs of the times do not exactly coincide, in some points, with those of the time of the Council. From among these special attention must be paid to the phenomenon of secularism . . . the secularism that consists of an autonomist vision of man and the world, one which leaves aside the dimension of mystery, indeed neglects and denies it. This immanentism is a reduction of the integral vision of man, a reduction which leads not to his true liberation but to a new idolatry, to the slavery of ideologies, to life in reductive and often oppressive structures of this world."

"Among the internal causes, [in the Church]" the *Report* continued, "there must be noted a partial and selective reading of the Council, as well as a superficial interpretation of its doctrine . . . on the one hand, there have been disappointments because we have been too hesitant in the application of the true doctrine of the Council. On the other hand, because of a partial reading of the Council, a unilateral presentation of the Church as a purely institutional structure devoid of Her Mystery has been made," but "the ecclesiology of communion cannot be reduced to purely organizational questions or to problems which simply relate to powers."

"When we Christians speak of the Cross," the Fathers accordingly point out, "we do not deserve to be labelled pessimists, but we rather base ourselves upon the realism of Christian hope. From this paschal perspective, which affirms the unity of the cross and resurrection, the true and false meaning of so-called 'aggiornamento' is discovered. An easy accommodation that could lead to the secularization of the Church is to be excluded," and thus "it is necessary to distinguish pluriformity from pure pluralism. When pluriformity is true richness and carries with it fullness, this is true catholicity. The pluralism of fundamentally opposed positions instead leads to dissolution, destruction, and loss of identity."

With that in mind, certain Asian bishops were reminded that "dialogue must not be opposed to mission," since "all Christians have received from Christ the mission to make all people disciples of Christ . . . it is thus necessary to put aside the false and useless oppositions between, for example, the Church's spiritual mission and 'diaconia' for the world."

Consequently, "it is not licit to separate the pastoral character from the doctrinal vigor of the documents. In the same way, it is not legitimate to separate the spirit and the letter of the Council. Moreover, the Council must be understood in continuity with the great tradition of the Church," for "the Church is one and the same throughout all the Councils," and so "the false opposition between doctrinal and pastoral responsibilities must be avoided and overcome. In fact, the true intent of pastoral work consists in actualizing and making concrete the truth of salvation, which is in itself valid for all times. As true pastors, the bishops must point out the right way to the flock, strengthen the faith of the flock, and keep dangers away from it," while remembering that "ecclesial communion with Peter and his successors is not an obstacle but the anticipation and prophetic sign of a fuller unity," and that "in the whole theological question regarding the relationship between primacy and the college of bishops, a distinction cannot be made between the Roman Pontiff and the bishops considered collectively, but between the Roman Pontiff alone and the Roman Pontiff together with the bishops,"—as *Lumen gentium's Nota praevia* had already made clear.

There is much more in the *Final Report*, which the reader may find in the Appendix, and which is admirable also for its economy of expression, while still addressing the major and even (when serious) minor concerns of the world's bishops. It notes, for example, that "the more ancient Churches can learn much from the new Churches, from their dynamism, from their life and testimony even unto their shedding of blood for the Faith," and the anomaly that, unlike the consumerist nations, "where the Church is oppressed by totalitarian ideologies or where the Church raises Her voice against social injustices, She seems to be accepted in a more positive way. Yet it cannot be denied," the bishops added in a perception even Peter Hebblethwaite admitted was directed against certain aspects of liberation theology, "that even in such places not all the faithful fully and totally identify with the Church and Her primary mission."

Two final and related points: In condemning an obsession with Church structures that in effect ignores both Christ and the world that needs Him, the Synodal Fathers reminded their brother bishops that "the message of the Church, as described in the Second Vatican Council, is Trinitarian and Christocentric." Consequently they noted and indeed closed their *Final Report* with a call for a deeper grasp and elucidation of "the theology of the cross," which is not separate from the resurrection—just as the resurrection is not separate from the theology of the cross.

Thus "in our day above all," they charge, "when so many people feel an interior void and spiritual crisis, the Church must preserve and energetically promote the sense of penance, prayer, adoration, sacrifice, self-giving, charity and justice," for which "popular devotion, rightly understood and practiced, is very useful in nourishing the holiness of the people. It therefore merits greater attention on the part of the pastors."

Some thought this a quiet appeal—among other things—to the universal pastor of the Church for the restoration of the prayer to St. Michael at the end of the Mass. Others remarked that should the Vicar of Christ make that collegial gesture, it would doubtless aid what the Fathers understood must prove a major confrontation, if the laity in the West are ever truly to be allowed popular devotion, a devout Mass, the overcoming of their spiritual crisis by nourishing holiness—in short, if they are ever to be allowed the fruits and reality of Vatican II.

Archbishop Thanagalathil's Latin Study Group had reminded the Church—and His Holiness—that ecclesiastical discipline is an act of charity, both for the aggressor, and for the faithful who suffer at the aggressor's hands. Because of their power with the media and in the bureaucracy, Modernists are able to portray Vatican attempts to check predatory attacks on Catholics as if the Vatican action were the tyranny: men like Thomas Sheehan and Richard McBrien are forever decrying the cruel regime of Pope St. Pius X. But if Popes are on occasion intimidated by such power, it should be remembered that Christ never was; in the Gospels, His mercy to the sinner is often rivalled by His asperity against the oppressor.

It is thus of some consequence, as Peter Hebblethwaite kindly points out, that "the final report contains no echo of Archbishop Godfried Danneels' splendid remark the opening day of the synod," that "the remedies to post-conciliar difficulties cannot be reduced to disciplinary or administrative measures. Post-conciliar weaknesses cannot be put right by pre-conciliar methods.

"If words mean anything," Hebblethwaite wrote in 20 December *National Catholic Reporter*, "that reference was to the Franciscan Father Leonardo Boff case. That may explain its absence from the final text."

Yes, and it might also explain the Synod's open call for a confrontation with the Liberal Consensus, and the Modernists take-over of so many Western seminaries.

"The Dogmatic Constitution *Dei Verbum,*" the Fathers state, "has been too neglected . . . in particular the exegesis of the original meaning of Sacred Scripture, most highly recommended by the Council, cannot be separated from the living tradition of the Church. . . . It is necessary already in seminaries and religious houses to give a formation that educates the candidates not only intellectually, but also spiritually; they must be seriously introduced to a daily spiritual life (prayer, meditation, the reading of the Bible, the sacraments of Penance and the Eucharist)."

"Therefore," the Synod adds, "a new effort in evangelization and in integral and systematic catechesis is required," and "the formation of candidates to the priesthood must be looked after in a particular way. In it, the philosophical formation and the manner of teaching theology proposed by the Decree *Opatatium totius* n. 16 merit attention."

Notably, the opening line of n. 16 in the Decree on the Training of Priests insists that "Theological subjects should be taught in the light of faith, under the guidance of the magisterium of the Church," and "in such a way that students will draw pure Catholic teaching from divine revelation, will enter deeply into its meaning, make it the nourishment of their spiritual life, and learn to proclaim, explain, and defend it in their priestly ministry."

When he announced the Extraordinary Synod on 25 January, Pope John Paul II said that its purposes would primarily be "to exchange and examine experiences and information about the application of the Council at the level of the universal Church and the particular Churches; to promote the further study and the constant incorporation of Vatican II into the life of the Church, in the light of new exigencies as well," and, not least, "to revive in some way the extraordinary atmosphere of ecclesial communion, which characterized the Ecumenical Council, in the mutual sharing of sufferings and joys, struggles, and hopes, which are typical of the Body of Christ in the various parts of the world."

"The Synod has accomplished the purposes for which it was convoked," His Holiness announced at its formal closing during a Mass at St. Peter's Basilica on 8 December.

On 7 December, after the approval of the *Final Report*, the Pontiff spoke for the first time in an official manner during a General Congregation. There, he expressed "my real gratitude to all of you who have taken part in this assembly of the . . . Extraordinary Synod of Bishops: to you Cardinals, Archbishops, Bishops and Priests who, according to the current norms of the Church, have taken part in the Synod as Members. You have brought the Synod to conclusion with fraternal cooperation, open and free communication, intimate communion."

"I greet also the male and female religious, the laymen and laywomen who are present, since through them all the levels and living forces of the Church have been present here in this Hall." He also expressed gratitude to the non-Catholics who took part.

"The interventions made in the Hall and in the small discussion groups," he continued, "were deserving of appreciation," in particular since "liberty was in no way an obstacle to the substantial unity," through which "you manifested collegial spirit in an excellent way. Therefore with joy and with sincere gratitude I accept from your hands the *Message* and the *Final Report* which demonstrate this sense of communion: with my consent these documents will be made public. May the Lord see to it that they bear abundant fruit. . . ."

"As regards the valuable suggestions which have come to light during this Synod I wish to underline some: the desire expressed to prepare a compendium or catechism of all Catholic doctrine, to serve as a point of reference for catechisms or compendia . . . in all the particular Churches [which] desire responds to a real need both of the universal Church and of the particular Churches; the deepening of the study of the nature of the Episcopal Conferences," and "the publication of the Code of Canon Law for the Oriental Churches, according to the tradition and norms of Vatican II. . . ."

"As you know, this Synod was preceded by the General Assembly of the College of Cardinals. It dealt with an aspect of great importance in the life of the Church, that is, the restructuring of the Roman Curia . . . on this subject the Presidents of the Episcopal Conferences were also consulted. Since the Roman Curia is an organic instrument of the Roman Pontiff in the exercise of his pastoral ministry for the good and the service of the

Catholic Church, it seemed particularly opportune to seek to know fully the needs and the requirements of the Church in their regions."

"It is now your task to ensure that the great force and the awareness of the importance of the Council penetrate deeply into the universal Church, into your particular Churches and into the various communities. . . . It is the duty of the Bishops, as pastors of souls, together with their priests, to instruct their people concerning the things which the Synod has considered good, and to exhort them to draw with renewed fervor from the treasures of the Council the inspiration to live a Christian life in a manner which is ever closer to the principles of the faith."

"Tomorrow, 8th December, Solemnity of the Immaculate Conception of the Blessed Virgin, Mary, is the twentieth anniversary of the conclusion of the Council. I invite you to concelebrate with me in St. Peter's Basilica in the Vatican; at Vespers we show our veneration for the Virgin Mother of God, Mother of the Church and Queen of the Apostles, in the Basilica of Santa Maria Maggiore. I have said Mary, Mother of the Church: to her, who is particularly present in the Mystery of Christ, we wish to commend this epoch in the life and the mission of the Church."

After Cardinal Krol gave a concluding address, the assembly rose, and closed the Sixteenth and final Congregation by praying the Angelus, and singing the Magnificat of the Blessed Virgin Mary. "My soul doth magnify the Lord . . . for He that is mighty has done great things, and Holy is His Name. And His mercy is on them that fear Him, from generation to generation. . . ."

IV. Aftermath

> *"Every human work is imperfect. The Synod has reached a good point. But I would have liked greater clearness and decision on some points."*
>
> Alosio Cardinal Lorscheider

> *"It was a stupendous Synod. The union, the brotherhood among the Synod Fathers, the strong union with the Pope and among ourselves. It was truly an extraordinary Synod in every sense."*
>
> Miguel Cardinal Obando y Bravo

    Kenneth Briggs headlined his 7 December New York Times *piece, "U.S. Bishop Calls Synod a Success, Saying it Backs More Autonomy." Since the Synod said first the opposite, however, Briggs toned it down the next day to "Compromise Report Issued by Bishops, Welcomed by Pope." On the op-ed page was a piece entitled "Good News for Catholics" by Andrew Greeley associate William McCready; in effect, McCready suggested the Synod had somehow endorsed Greeley's view of an "American" approach to Vatican II, defined as loyalty to the Church accompanied by disagreement with all Her tenets—or at least those which priests (and their friends) are expected to oppose if they wish to be published on the op-ed page of the* New York Times.

    Father Richard McBrien, despite having written and spoken extensively on the Synod throughout 1985, chose to produce but one column on the subject after it ended. Titled "What the Synod Really Said," McBrien informed diocesan newspaper readers across the country that its major thrust was a neat balance which "contradicts the brooding fears of the left and the bellicose expectations of the right." In other words, Modernists were wrong to fear the Synod, Catholics were foolish to have been hopeful about it. Monsignor Higgins titled his analysis "Synod Not Question Of Winners and Losers." Michael Novak, however, now struggling to shed his "progressive" past, blew the cover on the Briggs/Higgins thesis, and the many who imitated it. "The strongest ally of the 'progressives'," he noted in the January 1986 Catholicism in Crisis (CinC), *"is the media; when progressives claim a tie, you can be sure they lost."*

In Europe, though they often sought to maintain a mythical view of the Council, the newspapers chose not to protect their readers from what really happened at the Synod. *"Ratzinger Has Won!"* La Repubblica proclaimed. *"The Church Will Have Only One Catechism!"*

"So it is over," the article read, *"this extraordinary Synod called to celebrate the twentieth anniversary of Vatican II. There was heard, naturally, a general chorus of praise for the Council. Everybody wants to put it into practice and to gather its fruits. Nobody wants to turn it around. The bishops will leave Rome, they say, happy. Happy also is Cardinal Ratzinger since, with the proposal for a universal catechism accepted by the Pope, he may perhaps have fewer worries about safeguarding the area of faith and morals. And in reality this is the most solid result of the Synod."*

And on the same page: *"Requiem for the People of God: The Synod Restores the Separation Between the Sacred and the Human Put Aside by the Council."*

"In vain did the Brazilian Cardinal Alosio Lorscheider remind [the bishops] that the Church as the People of God is the key idea of Lumen gentium ... *the Synod has listened to the complaint of Ratzinger ... [Yves] Congar was invited by the Pope to the Synod. But the old Dominican theologian lies paralyzed on his bed in Paris. He has not come to Rome. In this way perhaps he has been spared the grief of seeing the shipwreck, in a Synod, of the concept so dear to him."*

Meanwhile, numerous papers expressed their surprise that a group of prelates composed primarily of bishops' conference heads did not demand an expansion of their roles. *"An extraordinary synod?"* wrote Le Monde *in the most comprehensive analysis. "Well, at least a paradox. Calling together the 102 presidents of the episcopal conferences of the whole world, it has planned to limit their role so that they will not have the temptation to exalt themselves into national churches ... [the conferences] might express the viewpoint of a group of bishops in a region, a country, a continent, but the episcopal collegiality as understood by the Council is of an absolutely different nature: on the pattern of the college of the Apostles, gathered around Christ, collegiality unites each bishop in his diocese in a universal solidarity around the first among them who is in Rome, that is, the Pope."*

"In other words," Le Monde *continued, "the Church is not a representative democracy, where one observes the bishops of a particular country delegate their power to some elected representatives who are enabled to speak in their name. The president of the French bishops' conference is*

not the 'head' of the Church of France ... the authority of the episcopal conferences, in each country, in every continent where they are found, will be weakened."

At the American bishops second Synodal press conference, before the formal approval but after the essential thrust of the Final Report was known to Bishop James Malone, His Excellency sought to put on as brave a face as possible. "It seems clear," he said then, "that the Synod concurs on the importance of episcopal conferences in the future of the Church ... on the theoretical and theological levels many important questions about episcopal conferences have come to the fore since Vatican II. It appears to me from this Synod that there is universal agreement that these are indeed important questions which must continued to be studied. I am more than content with this outcome."

"Malone, of course was right," observed Michael Jones in the February 1986 Fidelity. "The synod did think that episcopal conferences raised important questions in the life of the post-conciliar Church; however, the synod clearly did not endorse the position that Malone took a week earlier at his first press conference ... one of the ironies of the Malone intervention was the high place he gave to consensus building. This declaration was followed by his inability to create anything approaching a consensus on an issue that would have seemed to have been popular across the board. It shouldn't take a super salesman to sell the idea of more power to the episcopal conferences to the assembled heads of those conferences; however, Malone couldn't do it. Cardinal Ratzinger, on the other hand, seems to have done the opposite without even trying."

Indeed, though "most English-speaking bishops—from South Africa and Australia to Britain and the United States—wished to claim more autonomy for the national conferences of bishops," as Novak wrote in the 31 January National Review, "third world bishops were not swayed." The reason they were not, he suggests, is because Latin and African bishops "desperately desire to speak with the authority of the Pope and as an International Church, rather than in their own weak voices. For them, the papacy is a liberating authority. The English-speaking bishops were quietly but steadily rebuffed."

In the 14 February National Review, the Lutheran Richard John Neuhaus dug even deeper. "In terms of numbers, growth and spiritual vitality, the Roman Catholic Church is predominantly a Church of the Third World," he pointed out, and so "bishops from the poor countries minced no words in indicating that they held the churches in the industrialized societies responsible for most of the 'deficiencies and difficulties' afflicting contemporary Catholicism. Whether the point under discussion was the 'decadence' of feminism, or the exportation of oppressive ideologies, or *the desire to increase the power of national episcopal conferences, the bishops from Africa and elsewhere wanted it understood that the British/European /America agenda was not theirs."* As one African bishop put it, according to Neuhaus, *"you Americans have thc money, you have the United Nations, you have the power to blow up the world. Now you want the power to blow up the Church."*

Doubtless the Africans had also noticed the U.S. bishops' penchant, as Michael Jones put it, to *"consider themselves courageous when issuing documents that are binding on no one, and show themselves spineless"* where they could bring the Gospel to bear—as shown, for example, by their fear of *"implementing the mandate given to them by the new code of Canon Law on Catholic education."*

"The swing vote on the catechism came from the African bishops" as well, according to the 10 December Boston Globe; although *"the catechism idea proved so popular that many liberals decided to get on board,"* according to Dionne. Nonetheless Canadian Bishops Conference Vice President Archbishop James Hayes (the third bishop at the Synod to challenge Christ's teaching on adultery, incidentally, though he did not do so in the aula) admitted, as he put it, that *"there certainly is a divergence of views between those bishops who have called for such a catechism and others who insist on the rights of the local Church with the local bishop as head."*

Peter Hebblethwaite did not like the African bishops for this, since he remembered Cardinal Ratzinger's visit to France in January 1983 where His Eminence attacked the French catechism—and in one sense got the whole restoration rolling. *"Heart-rending stories are told of bishops in small countries with few theological resources who pleaded for such a catechism,"* he scorned in the 20 December Reporter. *"But everyone knew Ratzinger had been at odds with the French and Italian bishops concerning catechisms. He now had what he needed to impose his will."* Some remembered Ratzinger's conflict with American catechisms as well; though another Hebblethwaite oversight was his suggestion that the catechism idea had come from Cardinal Law, when in fact it first came from Cardinal Thiandoum.

But just as the Modernists were making the somewhat desperate argument that the chief thing about the Extraordinary Synod was how unimportant it was in comparison to the forthcoming 1987 Synod on the Laity, so were they maintaining that the thing to remember about the catechism was, in Dionne's words, *"that such a document would take a long time to write and would keep Cardinal Ratzinger's office busy."* Bishop Malone, for example, told John Thavis of the NC News that *"when I came to the Synod, I was not prepared to vote for that proposal, but I*

was persuaded to vote for it." According to Neuhaus, on the other hand,
" 'Don't worry about that,' Bishop Malone told a 38-year-old reporter.
'You won't live long enough to see it completed.' " During the Synod, I also
overheard Father Vincent Giese of Our Sunday Visitor *expressing his*
fear over this question to Monsignor Higgins.

"There's a lot of money in catechisms," Giese said.

"There won't be one in my time," Higgins chuckled complacently.

"Think of all the money American catechists would lose," Giese re-
sponded, apparently too upset to have heard the distinguished Monsignor.

But five days after the Synod had ended, just prior to his
mandatory retirement (he is 75), Cardinal Oddi announced "when
I arrived here as Prefect of the Congregation for the Clergy, I already had some experience of the serious problems which the approval of catechisms was giving us: some of them did not present
certain truths, others were not sufficiently clearly expressed. I
said to myself, we need a basic catechism," whereupon, with the
approval of the Pope, his Congregation began to compose one.

"It is divided into two parts," he told *La Repubblica*, "one
dealing with doctrine, the other with morals, just as the Synod requested. The doctrinal part is already finished. The second part is
just about ready ... there are 160 points that develop the doctrinal
part and 60 points in the moral part. There will be about 70 pages
... in everything that we mention we scrupulously make reference to Vatican II, wherever the Council spoke of these things,"
though "we must remember that Vatican II was a pastoral Council, not doctrinal. In our text, therefore, there are references to
everything that concerns doctrine and morals: Old and New Tes-
taments, the Council of Trent, Vatican I, and, in particular, the
Second Vatican Council. And of course, the documents of the
Popes, from Pius XI to John Paul II."

The National Catholic Reporter *was horrified. The editors dug*
up what they called "religious education authority Thomas Groome," who
"told NCR Dec. 17 that such a catechism would be impossible to write
and a disservice to the church. Groome, associate professor of theology
and religious education at [the Jesuits'] Boston College and author of
Christian Religious Education, *said the idea of a universal catechism*
'violates all the insights we've learned in psychology, anthropology (and
other disciplines) over the last 100 years,' " as well as being, in his view,

"totally contrary to church doctrine over the last 20 years ... Oddi's decision not to reveal the existence of the catechism draft during the extraordinary synod shows the lack of real integrity that undergirded the suggestion ... it was a political ploy to advance a conservative cause."

Monsignor Higgins said much the same in his syndicated column. "I would guess," he wrote, "that those who spoke at the synod in favor of a universal catechism were surprised, perhaps even offended, by Cardinal Oddi's unilateral decision to bypass the various episcopal conferences. In fact, I suspect if the cardinal had shown his hand during the synod, he would have been called to account by at least some of the bishops, including some who favor a universal catechism."

All this merely revealed, however, that neither the *Reporter* nor Higgins had done their homework. Giancarlo Zizoni—a kind of Italian version of Hebblethwaite—had been warning all year that His Eminence had a catechism ready, and Oddi himself observed that with the Extraordinary Synod, "I said to myself, this is the time to launch the idea. I first proposed it to the Italian language group and it was unanimously approved ... then I consulted the other language groups, and saw that they were not opposed," so "I announced that we have a basic catechism almost ready. A few days later we heard the reports of the other language groups ... and now here we are with our catechism almost ready ... it has been a task which lasted five years, and it seems to me, with good results. Now we are putting it in the hands of the Holy Father."

John Paul II, doubtless, will still proceed with Cardinal Law's idea of a Commission of Cardinals working at the universal catechism in consultation with episcopal conferences: but if certain elements within those groups struggle principally to ensure that it does not come out until such time as Monsignor Higgins and Bishop Malone are no longer with us, one can suppose the Pontiff may remind them there is a catechism already at hand. One can further suppose that Cardinal Oddi's efforts may help bring clarity wherever the collegial effort is tempted to be vague, particularly in light of the Pope's remarks to a general audience on 9 January 1985 that "in the face of resistance that he meets, one who is dedicated to catechesis could be tempted to retreat, not to expound the Christian message in all its truth and all its demands on life, and to limit himself to some more admissible points. But it is then that he must remember that he has been charged with a teaching that surpasses him: he must strive to propose it as he has received it: and he must above all be aware that in his work of catechesis he has at his disposal a Divine Power that enables him to transmit the Faith; and that in the heart of his listeners the Holy Spirit makes the word penetrate to the extent that it is faithful to the truth that it has to express." Not least, of course, when the catechism is released, it will have the authority of the Papacy and the universal episcopate behind it. Father Giese is no doubt right that the professional catechists are liable to lose some money at that point.

Meanwhile, in the United States, the press, and others, had still not caught on. In December, Newsweek *reported "The continuing Revolution: Two decades after Vatican II, the world's Roman Catholic bishops gathered in a special synod to reaffirm their break with centuries-old tradition."*

That same month Archbishop Weakland gave a discourse on the economic pastoral before Novak's American Enterprise Institute, charging that whereas "Cardinal Ratzinger, Prefect of the Congregation for the Doctrine of the Faith of the Roman Curia, has called . . . for a new kind of withdrawal from the world, a new *fuga mundi* . . . the bishops gathered at Vatican Council II had grappled with that question and come out with a different solution in their document, *A Pastoral Constitution on the Church in the Modern World.* In paragraphs 40-45 in that document a more nuanced vision of the way in which the earthly city and the heavenly city compenetrate each other is given. There it is stated that the church, acting through her individual members and her whole community, believes she can contribute greatly toward making our world and our history more human."

Doubtless hampered by the fact that none exists, His Excellency failed to give an example of where Cardinal Ratzinger opposed this view. Neither did he quote from the cited passages in *Gaudium et spes,* though the reader could do worse than to look them up and consider how faithfully Rembert Weakland has responded to what they say; such as for example the demand that "all pastors of souls be mindful to build up, by their daily behavior and concern, an image of the Church capable of impressing

men with the power and the truth of the Christian message."
Nonetheless, apparently having yet to absorb the results of the
Synod, Weakland further told the Institute of his anticipation
that the economy pastoral might "bring us as a church closer to
the people of the Third World:" with equal insight he hinted, according to the *NC News*, that "the U.S. bishop's pastoral on the
economy could effect a papal encyclical on social justice in 1991
. . . to mark the centenary of Pope Leo XIII's *Rerum Novarum*."

*In the Brooklyn diocese—to give an example of a local re-
sponse—reaction to the Synod, though confusing, was also at least temporarily edifying. In January, the diocesan* Tablet *published some very
uncharacteristic opinions by for example editorially endorsing a universal
catechism, admitting that since "Ratzinger's claim that some had over-
stepped the bounds of the Council was heard . . . Catholics are more likely
to make certain that what they now advance as sound theology is firmly
rooted in documentation from the Council," and even by arguing the need
to "grasp anew the Church as a mystery, a community and a hierarchical
structure," leading to "a renewed commitment to the Catholic Church
rooted in a renewed understanding of Vatican II's Constitution on the
Church and Constitution on the Church in the Modern World. The synod's
call for such renewal was on target."*

More characteristic was the 31 January Tablet Forum *choice of
Kenneth Briggs, the Jesuit Father George Hunt of* America *and Peter
Steinfels of* Commonweal *to explain the Synod. That Forum, despite its
absence of serious catholic opinion, was strikingly revealing all the same.*

*"Steinfels said that his reaction ranged from apprehension before
going to the Synod, to wonderment during the proceeding and finally uncertainty when it was all over," according to* Tablet *editor Ed Wilkinson.
Forum chair and* Tablet *columnist Monsignor Howard Basler added
that "Peter Steinfels said directly that the results and impact of the synod
are uncertain."*

*"Father Hunt," Wilkinson added, "felt that the Synod 'ended on an
upbeat level,' but Briggs claimed that it 'ended on a very somber note.' The*
Times *correspondent said that 'I did not experience nor did I sense that
there was great joy or a sense of elation over what had happened,'" indicating that Mr. Briggs' contacts are somewhat different than my own. "I
would like to report," he continued, "that the Synod was a show of unbe-
lievable, perhaps unsurpassing, unity, and a great step forward, and that
all of what Vatican II did has been reaffirmed as the final word, but
that's not the way it struck me."*

Hunt, according to Basler, also "said that the second draft of the document was so far out of line from the testimony it was to summarize, because it was written before the synod began." Basler himself argued that "the English reports contrasted with the other four language groups, especially those of the Latin and German discussions." These sentiments indicated that neither Hunt nor Basler had paid any attention what the bishops actually said, but chose instead to rely on as it were the quasi-official Modernist line being developed by Peter Hebblethwaite. Further evidence of this could be seen in Hunt's enthusiasm for the clerics on the Laity's Synod's preparation committee—Martini, Hume, Bernardin, Lorscheider, and Etchegray compose a third of it—whom he said "are some of the most progressive and respected bishops in the world." In fact, Basler seemed not even to have read the Final Report, *since he wrote "it is unfair that the synod didn't attribute some of the post-conciliar confusion to the tactics of obstructionists"—when, as we have seen, such attributions existed in abundance.*

Stranger still, however, was Bishop Malone's remark on a 20 January Catholic Television Network of America (CTNA) program, which indicated he had never read the Council's Constitution on the Liturgy, *Sacrosanctum Concilium.* Appearing nationwide with two women advocating female ordination, His Excellency inaccurately claimed that "Vatican II clearly established the vernacular as the language in which the Mass is to be celebrated," when it in fact did just the opposite. The error vindicated, however, the point His Excellency had made upon releasing the September 16 Submission four months earlier, that "fewer people have studied the Council's doctrine than speak of it, and fewer have made it fully their own than have studied it."

Back in Rome, the Pope's sermon at Santa Maria in Maggiore on the Feast of the Immaculate Conception revealed that His Holiness had been listening carefully to the analyses of his brother bishops during the course of the Synod. He accordingly urged a return "to the unity of ecclesial communion those who have strayed from it or broken it through rebellion, disobedience, and sin." And since some would refuse this appeal, the Pontiff further appealed to God to "defend your children in the struggle against the power of darkness and against the insidious power of error and falsehood." In addition, he announced plans to visit the tombs of St. Francis de Sales, St. Margaret Mary Alacoque (to whom our Lord revealed the devotion to His Sacred Heart) and the Cure of Ars, St. John Vianney, in the coming year.

On 12 December Cardinal Ratzinger held a press conference announcing that "on the occasion of the twentieth anniversary of Vatican II, the Congregation [for the Doctrine of the Faith] thought that it could make a useful contribution to this significant celebration by collecting in one volume all the texts that it has published over the last twenty years," which, he added, "are not merely the documents of a determined historical moment," for "they root themselves in Tradition and have their permanent function in the constant work of evangelization." Accordingly, some noted, they could prove helpful in the composition of a universal catechism. The Doctrine Prefect himself, however, pointed out that "bishops would be able to find in them, often as an echo of their own concerns and views, assistance in their ministry of teaching for the benefit of the faithful entrusted to their pastoral care." Theologians, on the other hand, would find "an invitation to develop their research or to verify their hypotheses in the light of the teaching of the *magisterium*, for the greatest good of the whole People of God."

Meanwhile, by January, not a few Modernists were beginning to understand something awful had happened. Hebblethwaite, though engaged in damage control, had realized it as soon as the Final Report *was published, as demonstrated, after months of optimism, by the 13 December* Reporter *headline, "Tension, uncertainty mark synod end." Surprisingly, given its tradition of anti-Catholic bigotry (according to the Catholic League for Religious and Civil Rights), some of the most perceptive coverage of the Synod came from the* Boston Globe. *To be sure, the* Globe *sent its version of Kenneth Briggs in the person of Xavier Rynne, but, like Dionne at the* Times, *the* Globe's *James Franklin was more interested in reporting what happened, to the extent he could grasp it. Thus by 5 December, Franklin was already letting his readers know that "Cardinal Ratzinger, the Vatican's guardian of doctrine since 1982, has emerged as the single most influential voice in the current synod of bishops . . . if he has not literally authored a script for bishops taking part in the synod, which ends Sunday, Cardinal Ratzinger has said first what many bishops later voiced in the synod in complaints about decadence in Catholic life since the council and in questions about the role of modern church agencies such as bishops conferences." At the Synod's end, Franklin reported that "Pope John Paul II yesterday concluded an extraordinary synod of bishops in which he successfully demonstrated the unity of the Catholic Church in the face of strong regional problems, and strengthened his hand in leading the church toward the end of the century."*

By 24 January, Rosemary Ruether was fulminating in the Reporter *that "the basic question that needs to be asked about the* [Final Report] *is: Who thought these things needed to be said? Most of the truths of the Vatican council, which it claims to verify, did not need to be verified for most of us who, in fact, have interiorized and have been promoting them with somewhat more authenticity than many of the writers of the document. The Roman Curia," the pro-abortion Ruether added, "is primarily amiss in this interiorization and promotion of the teachings of the Second Vatican Council." Thomas Sheehan enthusiast Tim Unsworth was equally penetrating: "That meeting was really about power," he wrote, "and there wasn't much time to get into anything else."*

In Commonweal's *31 January "Theology After the Synod" series, Maryknoll School of Theology teacher Father Robert Imbelli humbly suggested that a better way to understand Vatican II might include "drawing upon the thought of Friedrich von Huegel"—who, though a layman, was the close collaborator and in effect padrone of Modernists George Tyrrell and Alfred Loisy. "Might I hazard the belief," Imbelli added, "that a contemporary depiction of Christ is portrayed with Buddha on one side and Mohammed on the other? Despite this broadening of the horizon, the conversation on the mount of transfiguration will remain as in Luke's account: 'the exodus which Jesus would accomplish in Jerusalem.' " In the same issue, the pro-abortion Elizabeth Fiorenza denounced what she considered to be the Synod's "patriarchal sexism."*

The editors of diocesan newspapers across the country voted the Synod the top story of the year in an *NC News* poll. On 31 January, the Vatican announced there had been—despite continued decline in the West—a 7 per cent increase in ordinations to the priesthood in 1984 over the previous year. A group of South American bishops—Cardinal Law was also invited—met in Lima, Peru to discuss a more Catholic framework for the just expression of "liberation theology." Cardinal Obando y Bravo suggested the term "theology of reconciliation."

In February, due to the (for once) unified intervention of the Brazilian hierarchy, the Godard film *Je Vous Salue Marie* was formally banned in Brazil. The U.S. National Conference of Diocesan Directors of Religious Education—whose president, Newark's Monsignor Thomas Ivory, had in his own diocese promoted *Christ Among Us* but banned the use of orthodox catechisms such as those published by the Daughters of St. Paul—called for "international consultation" on the preparation of the universal catechism. Also that month, as revealed in the 7 March *Reporter*, editor Tom Fox joined numerous other editors as well as a number of bishops for a meeting in Tampa, Florida, ostensibly "to open more channels of communication between the U.S. bishops and Catholic press editors."

Surprisingly, Fox divulged what looked like the real purpose of the Catholic Press Association-sponsored gathering, upon reporting that "judging from comments made during last week's meeting, the U.S. bishops are increasingly disturbed about the distorted picture of U.S. Catholicism painted in *The Wanderer*—and airmailed weekly to all the Vatican congregations." The *Reporter* editor duly proceeded to denounce "Wanderer supporters" for possessing "judgmental, legalistic, anger-based attitudes [that] are closing them off from the rest of the church." Proof of *Wanderer* isolation from what the *Reporter* considers "the rest of the church" could presumably be discerned from the CPA's decision not to invite the editor of the nation's oldest Catholic weekly to the Tampa *con-spiratio*.

In March, the decisions of the Synodal Fathers began to take form—as did the opposition. The second pro-abortion ad appeared in the *Times* on the 2nd. Bishop Malone promptly announced that in regard to "whether a Catholic can legitimately dissent from the Church's teaching on abortion, the response can be stated simply. In view of the consistency and the universality of this Catholic teaching, there is no such thing as legitimate dissent by a Catholic from the proposition that to seek or perform a direct abortion is, objectively considered, a grave moral evil . . . there is no room for dissent by a Catholic from the Church's moral teaching that direct abortion is always gravely wrong in itself."

The general secretariat of the Synod of Bishops met to discuss implementation of the recommendations in the *Final Report*. Pope John Paul appointed six Cardinals to a commission whose purpose would be the restructuring of the Roman Curia: among them, Nigeria's Cardinal Francis Arinze, Cardinal Castillo Lara, and Edouard Gagnon. The Vatican announced it would henceforth release its budget figures.

In mid-March, after a year of *ad limina* visits with nearly the entire 358-man Brazilian episcopate, the Pontiff held a meeting with 21 senior bishops, including Lorscheider and Sales.

According to Porto Alegre Bishop Alfredo Cardinal Scherer, the meeting reduced inter-episcopal tensions, though it revealed "that the problem is not between Ratzinger and them, but between the bishops themselves." It was this, he added, that prevented the bishops from addressing the heresies of Leonardo Boff, which is why "it was left up to Rome to do it." Accordingly, at Easter, the Vatican lifted the formal silence imposed on Boff a month earlier than expected. Cardinal Lorscheider announced that Boff must "now change his ecclesiastical theses and emphasize that the Church is a hierarchical community in which Jesus established who should orientate and guide in His Name."

Just after Easter, Cardinal Ratzinger's elaboration of his 1984 condemnation of historicism was released. "The new document was composed after a long process of gathering information," the 23 March 1986 *National Catholic Register* reported. "All the world's episcopal conferences were polled for their views about liberation theology," and "the document was composed entirely by Cardinal Ratzinger and his staff." His Eminence signed it "with the approval of the Pope," according to the 16 March *New York Times.*

The *Instruction on Christian Freedom and Liberation* was no less forceful than its predecessor, condemning both exploitation of the poor by the privileged and by "new forms of servitude ... inspired by concepts which ignored the transcendental vocation of the human person and attributed to man a purely earthly destiny." In addition, though only reflecting Church tradition, the Instruction noted that "in the extreme cases where there is recourse to armed struggle, which the church's *magisterium* admits as a last resort to put an end to an obvious and prolonged tyranny which is gravely damaging the fundamental rights of individuals and the common good ... the concrete application of these means cannot be contemplated until there has been a very rigorous analysis of the situation."

This passage seemed particularly applicable to the intensifying abortion battle in the United States, given the Instruction's further observation that "in loving the poor, the Church also witnesses to man's dignity. She clearly affirms that man is worth more for what he is than for what he has. She bears witness to the fact that this dignity cannot be destroyed, whatever the situation of poverty, scorn, rejection or powerlessness to which a human being has been reduced. She shows Her solidarity with those who do not count in a society by which they are rejected spiritually and sometimes even physically. She is particularly drawn with maternal affection toward those children who, through human wickedness, will never be brought forth from the womb to the light of day, as also for the elderly, alone and abandoned."

Meanwhile, as George Weigel observed in the 23 March *Register*, "three months after an Extraordinary Synod of bishops met in Rome to celebrate the 20th anniversary of Vatican II's formal closing, we might well say, 'the synod is over; the synod has just begun.'" The Modernists had finally converged about an interpretation, as indicated by Weigel's coverage of a 17 March seminar at the Woodrow Wilson International Center for Scholars in Washington D.C. Among others, the seminar featured Xavier Rynne (Father Francis Murphy),[10] who maintained that "the synod was a reprise of the conciliar battle between progressives' and conservatives,' with Cardinal Ratzinger taking the Prince of Darkness' role," wherein "the synod was a triumph for the 'progressive/conciliar' forces over the 'conservative/rollback' men of the Roman Curia."

That the Modernists knew better, and had to compensate, came to light in a February 1986 *St. Anthony Messenger* report that "more than 15 New Testament scholars have launched a potentially controversial project to develop a consensus on the words Jesus probably said or did not say and those attributed to him. The consensus will be sought by voting—proverb by parable by pronouncement story—on the likeliest authentic sayings. After six years, members of the 'Jesus seminar' hope to have considered 500 sayings attributed to Jesus in biblical and non-biblical sources. Both the active and corresonding participants (which include many of the leading researchers in mainstream biblical studies) contend they are guided by the weight of biblical critical scholarship, plus their own insights in determining what words were actually spoken by Jesus and what words have been put on his lips by gospel writers or Church tradition."

"Dr. Robert Funk, former director of Scholars Press and a prominent New Testament scholar," the article continues, "organized academicians to 'report their work to a broader public.... They have hesitated to broadcast the asssured results of historical-critical scholarship out of fear of public controversy

---

[10]Rynne had written a book on the Synod expounding his thesis; as has Peter Hebblethwaite. Msgr. Higgins has written the introduction to the Rynne book.

and political reprisal.' . . . Eventually the group hopes to publish a Bible with Jesus' sayings printed in colors symbolizing the degree of acceptance by the scholars. Red means 'authentic'; pink 'may be authentic'; gray, 'probably not'; black, 'no.' At the initial balloting, the beatitudes 'Blessed are the peacemakers . . . ' and 'Blessed are the meek . . . ' were blackballed. The first voting session was held last October. The next one will convene March 6-9 at the University of Redlands in California."

The desperation of such measures reveals how effectively the Synod (and its preparations) had been. "Pope John Paul II had never intervened" as Hebblethwaite noted in the 13 December 1985 *Reporter*, "and never lost control. . . . Louvain Professor Jan Grootaers described the pope's implementation of Vatican II in this way: In Poland, Karol Wojtyla had to apply the council step by step among a people who had not been prepared for it. Now, the pope is extending the same principle to the whole church, for it is true that there is now another generation that needs to be reintroduced to the council."

"All along," E. J. Dionne wrote in the 9 December *Times*, "the pope said he was seeking a celebration of Vatican II, not partisan wrangling. A sharply divided meeting could only weaken John Paul's position; a happy end suggested a search for a kind of synthesis that the pope himself has been seeking, and left him without a major bloc of challengers." And indeed, as Ralph McInerny pointed out in January 1986 *Catholicism in Crisis*, "one can follow through from the summary of the pre-synodal statements, to the individual statements and then the reports of the [language groups] to the Final Report and the Message a movement from almost provincial concerns to the perspectives of the universal Church."

"Above all," Dionne concluded, "and in contrast with many of the partisans, John Paul tends to take a mystical view of Vatican II and the church. This often leads him in directions that seem to be—and often are—conservative. But his papacy is, more than anything, an attempt to assert the primacy of the spiritual over the material in an increasingly secular world. If there is any message that permeates the synod's statement, it is this one."

Accordingly, with the support of the Synodal Fathers, the Pope was ready to challenge the enemies of that message as Charles Curran and the Modernist Establishment in the United States were about to discover.

PREPARATIONS
FOR THE THIRD MILLENIUM

I. The End of an Historical Era

"The harvest is past, the summer is ended, and we are not saved."

Jeremiah 8.20

"What is most frightening about the phenomenon of religious modernism is the way in which its largely negative energies are being harnessed for what is perhaps the last, most openly nihilistic phase of modern culture."

James Hitchcock

According to the 18 March 1985 *Newsweek*, the standard categories of the eight-billion-dollar-a-year U.S. pornography industry "include films and magazines devoted to: group sex, oral sex, anal sex, gay and lesbian sex, sex with pregnant women, sex with crippled women, bestiality, child porn, and sadomasochism. S & M in turn has its own peculiar racial subcategories including black women bound and struggling against their tormentors; Asian women bound and hung from various objects, and white men bound and masked.... And spread across all these categories," according to UCLA psychology professor Neil Malamuth, is "the eroticization of violence. We found that a substantial percentage of the population is more aroused by themes that involve domination and conquest," than by "equally explicit but nonviolent material." This may explain why, along with child porn, sadomasochistic pornography is the fastest growing part of the industry, netting some two billion American dollars annually at last count. "The violence," *Newsweek* reveals, "takes many forms: rape, beatings, whippings, dismemberment and, as can best be determined, simulated murder. In the highly specialized subgenre of

Nazi porn, sexual torture and rape are presented with the Holocaust as background."

"Once the transcendence of the human person is denied," Cardinal Kuharic told the Synod, "and man is separated from the transcendent God, man finds himself in danger of being seduced by a civilization of death." The strange and indeed mystical terror about sex is that if it does not worship life, it will invariably worship death. Men and women have throughout history struggled with that reality, but when society as a whole loses a transcendent sense of sexuality, a proper sense of awe about what is responsible for being in the first place, then its days are numbered. "Dogma sounds so narrow," as Sobran observes, "and pluralism so broad. But the Age of Dogma gave us art in which man still appears sublimely great, a little lower than the angels, while the Age of Pluralism offers an image of man that keeps getting smaller and more degraded."

"In the American context," he adds, in the 18 January 1986 *Catholic Eye*, "opposing contraception is seen as a strictly Catholic thing to do, and even as a diehard position within Catholicism, rather than the stance of historic Christianity. . . . But in fact the vast majority of Christendom still stands where it always did: against artificial prevention of human life. And not only Christendom. Orthodox Judaism rejects contraception. So does Islam. An Indian friend tells me that Moslems and Hindus alike in his country regard contraception as a monstrosity from the West: they don't see it as 'progressive,' despite the missionary efforts of their liberal Western preceptors. They deeply resent it. The obstacle to worldwide population control is not native ignorance but native reverence for life." In March, according to the NC News, "Zambian bishops have asked the U.S. government to stop its plan to introduce sex education in schools." In Kenya, "the school children here had been warned by their parents: if a strange car pulls into your schoolyard, it is the 'family-planning people.' The children would later say that their parents had warned that these family-planning people would give away milk laced with birth-control drugs, that they would administer injections that would make the children sterile." Perhaps the parents had been reading the increasingly public support for coercion in the "family-planning" literature.

"The key fact of our time," according to Ben Wattenberg, "is that the important, modern, free, powerful nations of the world are not having 2.1 children per woman [which is the number necessary for a population to reproduce itself]. Not even close. In the U.S. the rate is 1.8 child per woman. In England it's 1.8; in France 1.9; in Japan, 1.7; in Italy, 1.6; in West Germany 1.4. This is the first time in history that a collection of nations—without the stress of war, famine, or disease—have opted not to reproduce themselves.

"It has been said that the Church was defeated," Pope John Paul II told the VI Symposium of the Council of European Episcopal Conferences on 11 October 1985, "because it did not succeed in bringing about the acceptance of its moral norm [in regard to abortion]. But I think that in this very sad and regressive phenomenon it was man, it was woman, who was really defeated. Doctors are defeated, who have renounced the noblest oath and claim of medicine, that of defending and saving human life. The 'secularized' State has truly been defeated, renouncing the protection of the fundamental and sacrosanct right to life in order to become the instrument of a supposed collective interest, and sometimes showing itself to be incapable of safeguarding the observance of its own permissive laws. Europe will have to meditate on this defeat."

Indeed, in the 21st century, that meditation may have to take place while the European serves mint tea to his Moslem conqueror. "The demographic fall in the birth rate and increasing age of the population can no longer be ignored or held to be a solution to the problem of unemployment," the Pontiff continued. "If the current demographic trend continues, the European population, which in 1960 constituted 25 per cent of the world population, would by the middle of the next century drop to a level of 5 per cent. These are figures that have led some European leaders to speak of the 'demographic suicide' of Europe. If this regression constitutes a source of concern, for us it is even more so, because, observed in depth, it appears to be the grave symptom of a loss of the will to live and of prospects for the future, and even more, of a profound spiritual alienation."

Another historical age is coming to an end. Like a plague of locusts, historicism swept through the rich glory of Christian Europe, and left it barren, empty, without art, without culture, worshiping a technology that will not save it. Modernism joined the Death Ride and drove Christendom from the West. But through the seed of Vatican II the Faith settled on other shores, took root, grew and began to flower twice as fast as it had withered in its former home.

II. The Devil in Miss Jones (and in her Troops)

> *"Historicism, by relativizing fundamental values, leads to an unfounded primacy of freedom over truth, practice over theory, becoming over being. It results in ideological and moral relativism."*
>
> Pope John Paul II

> *"They manipulate the fundamental truths of our faith, taking upon themselves the right to reinterpret and even to rewrite the word of God, in order to make it fit their own ideology and use it for their own ends."*
>
> The Nicaraguan Bishops Conference

"Among the many things Cardinal Ratzinger has told me," Vittorio Messori remarked about the famous interview, "there is one area which, while it is not absolutely central, has evidently attracted the attention of very many commentators ... many articles (and their corresponding titles) were devoted not so much to the strictly theological, exegetical and ecclesiological statements of the Prefect of the Congregation for the Faith as to remarks made—a few paragraphs, totaling perhaps ten pages—concerning that reality to which Christian tradition applies the terms devil, demon and Satan."

"Does this show a liking for the picturesque," Messori inquires "a curiosity about something which many people regard as a vestigial piece of folklore, as something which is at all events unacceptable to a mature faith? Or is there perhaps something deeper behind it; uneasiness beneath a veneer of laughter? Is this urbane lightheartedness or is it an exorcism in the cloak of irony?" Whatever, Messori adds, "it is a fact that no other topic unleashes such a storm of indignation among the mass-media of secularized society as that of the devil."

"The evil which exists in the world," Pope Paul VI observed on 15 November 1972, "is the result and effect of an attack upon us and our society by a dark hostile agent, the devil. Evil is not only a privation but a living, spiritual, corrupt and corrupting being. A terrible reality, mysterious and frightening ... he is the sophistical perverter of man's equipoise, the malicious seducer who knows how to penetrate us, through the senses, the imagination, desire, utopian logic or disordered social contacts, in order to spread error." The Pontiff consequently called for a "return to a study of Catholic teaching on the devil and the influence he is able to wield."

The reaction to this proposal, as Messori suggests, was not one of unalloyed enthusiasm. In fact, he notes, it was rather "one of uproar and protest: and strangely enough it came from precisely those newspapers and commentators which should have been unconcerned about the renewed emphasis on an aspect of a faith which they claimed to reject totally. From their point of view, irony would have been understandable; why the anger?"

Why, indeed? A similar anger is expressed by such as Father Matthew Fox—and others who believe "there's a lot of wisdom in witchcraft"—when Catholics go so far as to suggest an enthusiasm for Satanism in Wicca. It is but innocent paganism they say, when the Wicca priestess chants that "in the center of the earth fire and earth combine to make molten lava and fire ... feel that healing, transforming fire in the center of the earth ... bring that energy up, through your roots into your body ... the energy can handle whatever comes to you, all you need to do is call it up."

But that of course may be politics. Where it seemed unlikely a few years back that any priest would in the name of the Church be urging Catholics to absorb the wisdom of witchcraft, so might it seem strategically unwise at the moment to encourage open adoration of the angel Christ called the Enemy.

Even so, open flirtation with this possibility has already been seen. Rosemary Ruether, for example (who we may recall gave the keynote address at the Women's Spirituality Conference covered here earlier, which concluded with the Wiccan worship ceremony), wrote recently in the Gregory Baum-edited journal *Journeys* that, "having dwelt in the households of the suppressed faiths for a time, I felt I was on more sympathetic terms with the

Ba'al worshipers. I knew that Ba'al was a real god, the revelation of the mystery of life, the expression of the depths of Being which has broken through into the lives of people and gave them a key to the mystery of death and rebirth. . . . As for the defects of Ba'al, were they more spectacular than the defects of the biblical God or Messiah, or perhaps less so?"

Given this query—and Miss Ruether's dedicated promotion of the idea that abortion, sodomy, and various other enthusiasms of the Consumerist ethic should be endorsed by Catholicism—it is not insignificant that the Jesuits' foremost publication in the United States allowed her to rally the troops by presenting the Modernist strategy in the post-Synodal era, in an article considerably "lengthier than those in *America* generally are." Those were the words of Father George Hunt in his 1 March 1986 editorial praise of Miss Ruether's "lucid, cogent presentation of a point of view that is widely shared."

Although "we see alarming evidence of retrenchment by a Vatican leadership," Ruether wrote, "we also see renewed a right-wing Catholicism organized internationally . . . and nationally by groups like Catholics United for the Faith (CUF)," and "although historical-critical thinking and social justice issues generally are on the hit list of these groups, the chief victims are those concerned with sexual rights, namely reproductive rights . . . gay rights and optional celibacy."

Miss Ruether is unhappy with this development due to her sense that "Catholicism has a unique opportunity to bring a universal ethic to the conflicting values that divide the capitalist, socialist and third world countries. It is not insignificant," she notes, "that the Pope is probably the only global leader in the world today who could get an enthusiastic reception in all three regions. If this world religious leader could speak credibly, out of a deep conviction of the best in both civil libertarian and socialist values, and the need to unite the two in a comprehensive vision of a free and just society, he would provide an invaluable witness to a world bereft of credible moral and political leadership. But it is not at all clear that Catholicism will be able to rise to this occasion," especially since "it seems that the hierarchy, particularly in the Vatican, is far from understanding dissent and freedom of conscience, as not only a private, but also a public right. This has become most evident in the recent American dispute over the public right of dissent and open discussion on the question of abortion."

"Many Catholics in recent years," she continues, "have found the resistance of the hierarchy to these challenges so discouraging, their own position in the church so untenable and the expectations of change from the top so unlikely that they ask, 'Why bother with the church at all?' Is not the effort to work within it simply helping to perpetuate a bad system? Why not get out of it and work for change in secular society? Such questions can not be taken lightly," she adds, but "although I am not totally against forming new churches what is clear to me is that forming new churches never did much to reform the church that one left. It is precisely reforming this particular historical institution that concerns me," for though "it is assumed that if only we, the critical ones, disaffiliate with the Catholic Church, it will dry up and disappear, on the contrary, the history of Western Christianity since the Reformation shows that Roman Catholicism goes along the same as ever when dissatisfied people leave it, happily relieved of their critical presence."

And so, "why even bother to try to reform it, if we are already doing 'our thing?' It is at this point that Catholic liberal-leftists need to gain greater respect and understanding of the function of historical institutions. Because we have been so deprived of meaningful political participation in our church leadership, we easily become naive anarchists. We forget that no matter how great our living-room liturgy may be, it is going to last only a few years. The parish will go on and will continue to be the main vehicle for gathering and socializing Catholics[1] throughout the world and down through the generations. Unless we manage to insert what we are doing in more autonomous settings back into these main institutional vehicles of ministry and community, breathing new life and activity into them through sharing the fruits of our work, it will have no lasting historical impact ... so it seems to me extremely important that critical and justice-minded minorities stay in the church and use whatever parts of it they can get their hands on to respond appropriately to these critical challenges...."

"Moreover, these critical minorities will have far more impact, both on the church and on the world, if they continue to find ways to work through this church than they could possibly have if they separated from it. One might only think of how few liberation theologians there are in Latin America and yet what

---

[1]As, incidentally, Archbishop Peter Gerety understood when he devised the parish program 'Renew'.

an enormous impact they have already had, precisely because what they do is broadcast through this global network call the Roman Catholic Church. This is like the difference between shouting with the unaided human voice and speaking through a global system of telecommunications. We need to figure out how to use institutional networks creatively, rather than to feel powerless before them."

"We can do this," Ruether concludes, "by creating new vehicles of ministry, community and communication, and then 'attaching' them to the edges of the existing historical church so they become new vehicles within and for the whole Catholic community. American Catholicism has been particularly adept at doing this ... one has only to think of ... the Catholic colleges ... and the independent Catholic press—all vehicles of the struggle. More recently, there have been the network of peace and justice centers, the networks of Catholic women, both religious and lay, such as the National Association of Religious Women and Chicago Catholic Women, and Catholic advocacy groups of various kinds, such as Dignity, Catholics for a Free Choice and the Association for the Rights of Catholics in the Church, not to mention the Chicago Call to Action."

"I believe a failing these parallel groups have is a tendency to get too separated from the ordinary vehicles of Catholic life, particularly the parish. Whenever possible, one should use these ordinary structures for such activities (although, if this is blocked, one should not hesitate to meet in other structures while still calling oneself Catholic). If one organizes a liberation or feminist theology lecture series, one should try to hold it in a Catholic college or parish. If you are producing a new newspaper, you should try to distribute it in parishes. If you have a study group that is open to new members, you should advertise it in the parish bulletin. In this way new initiatives interpenetrate and renew ordinary Catholic life and, in turn, critical minorities are kept in touch with ordinary Catholic life ... the ability of its critical minorities to find creative ways to use the church, and to express their vision through it, will make the difference."

III. The Gathering Storm

The fundamentally reactionary ideology—since its only goal any longer is to react of such as Miss Ruether and the Modernists, has not eluded the successor to St. Peter. "The cultural systems, institutions and ideologies which have characterized the Europe of this century, and originated naive utopias," he told the European bishops' conferences on 11 October, "have gone into crisis under the blows of [their] instrumental rationality and of the empire of science and technology. The university—that glorious European institution to which the Church gave birth—shows itself incapable of elaborating an acceptable cultural project. This indicates that in modern society culture has failed in its very function as guide. Today, people live and struggle above all for power and material well-being, not for ideals."

The result, His Holiness added, is that Western man "who would like to be so adult, mature and free is also a man who flees from freedom in order to settle down into conformism, a man who suffers from loneliness, is plagued by various disturbances of the soul, seeks to get rid of death and experiences a frightening loss of hope."

It would appear that Catholic life in the United States in the post-Synodal era is about to undergo a transformation. Some have felt that, confronted as he is with the vast suffering and heroic witness of Catholics in such places as China, Eastern Europe, the Middle East, South America, and Africa, Pope John Paul II has felt a measure of contempt for the superficiality of Catholic life in the West since the Council; and, particularly because the momentary financial wealth of West Germany and the United States help to fund essential human services to the thriving but poor sister Churches in the third world, cynics have suggested the Pontiff has preferred to let the Western Church stew in its own juice for awhile, rather than provoke the economic assault the Modernists will invariably launch when their hegemony in the West is directly attacked.

And, not least, there has been the fear of *de jure* schism, as opposed to the de facto one even Paul VI recognized, according to Cardinal Gagnon. For though the Catholic Church has ever been resolute about upholding the truths bequeathed to Her by Christ, She has never been content to hold them smugly in a vacuum, and thus—though eminently fallible in this prudential judgment—She has always been hesitant to provoke a confrontation if it seemed that more souls might be saved in the long run by avoiding one. Speaking of his youthful friendship with Karol Wojtyla, Rett Ludwikowski noted in the February 1986 *Catholicism in Crisis* that "as a teenager I often asked questions to provoke him. He always tried to find some point which harmonized our positions rather than disagreeing with me. From this common ground he used to steer the discussion in such a way that you unconsciously agreed with his arguments. Suddenly you would find yourself much closer to his starting point than to your own, and, most amazing, you never had the impression that you had lost the argument. He made it in such a kind-hearted way, that no one could have a shade of doubt that his 'victory' gave him any personal satisfaction. Of course I was not much of a partner for him, but in those discussions he always seemed to treat me very seriously, without the visible condescension so typical of great men."

There has always been a tension within the Church between this gentle approach, and Cardinal Ratzinger's understanding that if "discussion becomes a collaboration with terror" then "discussion must stop because it is turning into a lie, and resistance must begin in order to maintain freedom."

To be sure, the Pontiff's intention to continue discussion even (nay, particularly) with lost sheep and terrorists is unlikely to end, but it is likely to take a different form in the closing years of Christianity's second millenium. In the early years of his Papacy he has used common ground to steer a discussion with the world back to a renewed understanding about basic Christian truths. Given the decayed condition of the Church in America, people sometimes forget what an enormous accomplishment this has been, or indeed, that Americans represent only seven per cent of the world's Catholics—a figure that declines each day. Accordingly, if it seems to some that the Pope has moved slowly, he has nonetheless moved effectively. The universal catechism will soon arrive, Hans Kueng has become a joke, nary a word has been heard from the former media star Raymond Hunthausen since November 1983. More importantly, with the Synod, the Prince of the Apostles has successfully isolated the Modernist bishops and their timid episcopal supporters, so that John Paul is now free to take necessary measures with little fear that there will be a schism, or in any event one that will last beyond the generation of those few unlikely bishops still inclined to go that route. Even Rosemary Ruether understands that.

The problem, of course, is that she and her confreres understand it all to well; yet despite all the talk of Papal contempt for American decadence, it seems the Pontiff has heard the cry in the letters American Catholics have sent him by the hundreds of thousands; and has grasped, in E. J. Dionne's words, that "traditional Catholics no doubt have a legitimate complaint when they contend that, outside the Vatican, their views on sexuality do not get much of a hearing." For the Pope has gone about as far as he can in triumphantly removing the bushel that in 1978 seemed to be covering the Light of Christ's truth. "If ambiguity is the mark of the demonic," Cardinal Ratzinger told Messori, "the essence of the Christian's struggle against the devil lies in living day by day in the light of faith's clarity." Thus, if those Catholics faithful to Vatican II—priests, lay, and religious—are to be spared further formal oppression by a clericalism whose chief aspect is this deliberate and demonic mark, then juridical moves will be necessary.

It would appear the Modernists have grasped the nature of the gathering storm: and intend either to win or to lose. That they also understand the intrinsic importance of the massacre of abortion to their cause is clear from the public positions that

Charles Curran insists must be considered arguably
Catholic—because those positions, for all the inevitable talk of
nuance, in fact represent the warp and woof of the Abortion
Culture. Accordingly, after a six-year dialogue with the Sacred
Congregation for the Doctrine of the Faith, Cardinal Ratzinger,
with the approval of John Paul II, wrote to Curran on 17
September 1985 asking him "to reconsider and retract those positions which violate the conditions necessary for a professor to be
called a Catholic theologian. It must be recognized that the authorities of the Church cannot allow the present situation to continue in which the inherent contradiction is prolonged that one
who is to teach in the name of the Church in fact denies Her
teaching." His Eminence concluded "In your letter you indicated
that you had not taken the positions you have without 'a great
deal of prayer, study, consultation and discernment.' This fact in-
spires us to hope that by further application of these means, you
will come to that due adherence to the Church's doctrine which
should characterize all the faithful."

When I spoke with Bishop Howze in June 1985 I did not
know the Vatican was investigating Father Curran, nor did I
know, when I wrote the previous commentary about the priest in
this book, of the 17 September letter, or that said investigation
was near its completion. It was not until Curran held a press conference on 11 March 1986 revealing these developments that they
came to my attention. At that time, announcing that he would
not retract his positions, Father Curran also repeated what they
were.

"On the question of contraception and sterilization," he
said, "I have maintained that these actions are not intrinsically
evil." On abortion, he denied Catholic teaching that human life is
sacred and inviolable from the moment of conception. On the
matter of euthanasia, he was ambiguous. "Masturbatory acts," he
maintained, "are ordinarily not very important or significant and
usually do not involve grave matter." On fornication, with exceptions, "I justify premarital sexuality on the basis of the theology
of compromise." Though Father Curran "does not accept or condone homosexual acts without personal commitment," he believes
there are some circumstances when sodomy "can in a certain
sense be objectively morally acceptable." And as to Christ's dictums against divorce and adultery, Curran thinks they should be
repudiated, and "that the Catholic Church should change its

teaching on indissolubility and allow divorce in certain circumstances."

These positions, he argued at that press conference, "are neither radical nor rebellious, but are in the mainstream of contemporary Roman Catholic theology." Knowing these positions to be but axioms to the Liberal Consensus, and apparently fully understanding the implications of the Curran case to its own power, the Modernist establishment rushed to his defense.

"Thank you, Father Curran" was the formal 21 March editorial in the *National Catholic Reporter*. Curran's Rochester, New York ordinary Matthew Clark promptly published a statement in his 13 March diocesan *Courier-Journal* calling Curran "a man deeply committed to the spiritual life," and adding that "as a theologian, Father Curran enjoys considerable respect, not only in our diocese, but across the country, He is unfailingly thorough and respectful in his exposition of the teaching of the Church. Indeed, I have heard it said that few theologians have a better grasp of or express more clearly the fullness of the Catholic moral tradition. In instances when Father Curran offers theological views which *appear* to be [my emphasis] at a variance with the *current* official statements of the Church [again], he always does so in a responsible manner"—such as presumably the strike he helped organize at Catholic U. in 1967. Bishop Clark added: "He is respectful of authority in the Church, treating and referring to persons in authority in a most Christian manner."

"It is, I believe, commonly accepted in" what the prelate called "the Roman Catholic theological community that Father Curran is a moral theologian of notable competence whose work locates him very much at the center of that community and not at all on the fringe. I believe that perception is true."

Bishop Clark's use of "appear" and "current" and "Roman Catholic theological community" are crucial to the debate here. All the Pope is saying at this point is that Curran may no longer consider himself a Roman Catholic theologian. The Modernists, on the other hand, are insisting on nothing less than that the Church must formally acknowledge the basic moral tenets of both Modernism and the Abortion Culture to be within the purview of the Faith itself—of Roman Catholic theology. They have, of course, tacitly and in practice been insisting upon this right along, but Ratzinger's intervention has brought the moment to its crisis: what the Modernists now demand is not unlike what

Thomas Sheehan called for in June of 1984—the formal end of Catholicism.

"The Curran case is a genuine scandal, an action so dismaying that it requires something beyond outrage," editorialized the 28 March 1986 *Commonweal*: it feeds "conservatives who would conduct a purge of theologians on the scale of the Modernist crisis—and who denounce the bishops for not leading the way. . . . If an outstanding Catholic and one of the nation's most respected moral theologians cannot be designated 'Catholic,' the fact will only devalue the designation. . . . Curran's positions are well within the mainstream, indeed often stand as moderating alternatives to much more radical positions."

Monsignor George Higgins and Catholic Theological Society of America (CTSA) President-elect Monica Hellwig signed a Catholic University alumni letter "affirming publicly" their conviction that Curran is "a man of deep faith and powerful witness." The Monsignor, in fact, so thoroughly understood the urgency of the matter that he, Bernard Haering, and CUA's School of Religious Studies Dean William Cenkner joined Curran for a trip to Rome and a meeting with Ratzinger urging His Eminence to back down. Since the Cardinal seemed reluctant to do this, Curran offered what at the March 11 press conference he called his compromise—which would entail a complete retreat on the part of the Supreme Pontiff, in exchange for Curran not changing anything at all. "My compromise," he said, "was my willingness not to teach sexual ethics here at Catholic University in the future. I noted that I had not taught the course in sexual ethics in the last 15 years and had no intention of teaching the course in the future." He also graciously "expressed my willingness to have the congregation issue a document pointing out what they judge to be the errors and ambiguities in my theological teaching"—which was in any case accomplished that day since Curran released Ratzinger's 17 September letter—"while still recognizing that I am a Catholic theologian in good standing." Curran added: "Unfortunately . . . Rome was unwilling to accept this compromise."

"Cardinal Bernardin" on the other hand, according to the *NC News*, "who is chairman of Catholic University's board of trustees, said he supported the compromise and that the Vatican should be open to reconsidering it." *America* magazine, fresh off Ruether's contribution, thought this an excellent perspective, and editorialized that "at the very least, the compromise endorsed by Cardinal Bernardin should be accepted by the Vatican."

The *Brooklyn Tablet*, doubtless representing the approach of dozens if not hundreds of diocesan papers across the country forgot its January editorial arguing that because of Cardinal Ratzinger "Catholics are more likely to make certain that what they now advance as sound theology is firmly rooted in documentation from the Council." Regressing to its pre-Synodal opposition to the Council, the *Tablet* editorialized instead that "U.S. theologians' defense of Father Charles Curran has been on target and persuasive. . . . At no time has [Curran] been contentious, nor disloyal. The support of church authorities, including his own bishop, attests to that. At no time has he dissented from matters of faith or doctrine." This, of course, can only be considered the case if you take the somewhat oxymoronic position that what the ecumenical Councils—not to say Christ Himself—infallibly teach, cannot be considered a matter of faith or doctrine. But of course, the *Tablet*, like the rest of Curran's supporters, is only talking about the Catholic Church in the way that Ruether talks about it. Accordingly, *Tablet* editors "continue to support the compromise offered by Father Curran and supported by Cardinal Joseph Bernardin, Bishop Matthew Clark of Rochester and a growing number of responsible theologians."

Shortly after Easter, Catholic University's School of Religion faculty by a surprisingly slim 15-member majority vote (support for Curran in 1967 recall, had been unanimous) endorsed a statement asserting that "if Father Curran's status as a Catholic theologian were denied, it would be a setback for Catholic education in this country," and formally requested the entire faculty Senate to join in urging the Vatican to reach a compromise. The psychology department also issued a statement saying that depriving Curran of the right to represent his views as if they were Catholic would mean that "the standing of Catholic University in the academic community will be severely damaged." Somewhat dubiously, Marjorie Hyer in the *Washington Post* reported on 5 April that "more than 600 Roman Catholic theologians around the country have signed a statement of support for [Curran]." On 25 March Curran held a press conference with Notre Dame's pro-abortion Elizabeth Fiorenza during which, according to the *NC News*, the priest "said Catholic theology faculties around the country will be urged to make the week of April 21 a time for special seminars and public discussions on issues of academic

freedom and responsible dissent from church teaching authority."
As for those tempted to dissent from the dissent, Thomas
Sheehan has shown us the ferocity of intolerance with which the
Liberal Consensus responds to such people; in case anyone had
forgotten, Arthur Jones was careful to refresh memories in the 4
April *Reporter*, by quoting an anonymous priest who threatened
that soon, "people will begin looking to see who among the
prominent did not come to Curran's defense."

To Catholics, depriving Curran of the right to claim that
Christ and His Church do sometimes positively favor adultery,
fornication, sodomy, contraception and so on, hardly seemed like
a major development: indeed, the frustrating thing about it was
that it took so long. The bishops should have done it in 1967, and,
if they feared the media more than they loved their flocks or
their God, then the Vatican should have intervened and resolved
the matter in two or three years at most. Things are not that easy
of course. There are other places in the world, it is not all that
sure the Vatican even knew about the Curran case in 1970, there
were many Currans those days, and, not least, these were the
catatonic final years in the reign of Paul VI.

The Modernists, however, understood the profound implications of the move against Curran, or, more to the point, the profound threat this move was both to their own reputations and
their continuing ability potentially to control Catholic money
and institutions in order to advance the Modernist cause.
Accordingly, some of their more prominent figures decided to
take the crucial step of publicly challenging John Paul II either
in effect to endorse Modernism, or else to take on its entire powerful and entrenched establishment throughout the United States.
It is likely this decision was influenced by the significant miscal-
culation that due to fear of widespread resignation and protest,
the Vatican had been soft with the nuns who signed the pro-abortion ad in the *Times*. There was, doubtless, a certain degree of
chivalry or chauvinism (depending on how you look at these
things) in the painstaking manner by which Cardinal Hamer
sought to extricate these women from their folly: but it should be
recalled that of the nineteen out of twenty-four cases that had
been reputedly resolved by early April, all of them had met the
specific terms established by Hamer when he first called for re-
cantation in December 1984. Not only is it possible that John
Paul—chauvinistically or chivalrously—considers Charles Curran

a freer agent than the foolish nuns, there remains the critical difference that, unlike them, Curran is not going to retract.[2]

Nonetheless, the Modernists sought to frighten John Paul away by making it clear that if the Roman Pontiff did not capitulate, then he had better be prepared for massive confrontation. Thus, one of the first public defenses of Curran came in a statement from nine past presidents of the CTSA and the College Theology Society, among them the Jesuits Walter Burghardt (editor, *Theological Studies*) and Richard McCormick, Bernard Cooke from the Jesuits' Holy Cross, and, as ever, David Tracy, Gerard Sloyan and Richard McBrien. The challenge they issued was a formidable one; indeed, however different his motivations, it is arguable St. Pius X could have said it no better.

"Of Father Curran's views on the various issues mentioned in [Ratzinger's] letter are so incompatible with Catholic teaching that he must be declared no longer a Catholic theologian," they wrote, "justice and fairness would dictate that other Catholic theologians who hold similar views should be treated in exactly the same fashion. Indeed, the credibility of any action on the part of the congregation would be seriously undermined by a failure to identify and act upon other such cases."

In a letter McCormick wrote to Catholic University chancellor and Washington D.C. ordinary James Hickey, the Jesuit elaborated on the Modernists strategy of seeking to intimidate the Vicar of Christ: speaking of the West, McCormick told the Archbishop that "if Cardinal Ratzinger's letter were to be applied to theologians throughout the world, it is clear that the vast majority would not qualify as Catholic theologians." However, in a 5 April *America* piece, McCormick presented the other side of the coin, demanding complete Papal and indeed Catholic submission to the basic philosophical precepts, such as they are, of the heresy called Modernism.

"Scandal, it must be remembered," the Jesuit wrote, "is not surprise or shock at the discovery of a skeleton in someone's closet. It has a technical theological sense, and the Congregation is using it in that sense. It refers to an action or omission that provides another or others with the occasion of sin. We must ask, therefore, what sin is occasioned [by Curran's perspectives]. The first possible answer," McCormick goes on, "is that it occasions or facilitates those actions condemned by official teaching but ap-

---

[2]Three of the nineteen later denied that they had met these conditions.

proved by the dissenter. But that begs the whole question," since "it assumes that the actions condemned by official teaching are, indeed, morally wrong."

In his not terribly subtle construction, McCormick also—one could say inevitably—drew on the work of Karl Rahner, who in 1980 had asked "what are contemporary moral theologians to make of Roman declarations on sexual morality that they regard as too unnuanced? Are they to remain silent, or is it their task to dissent, to give a more nuanced interpretation?" Having developed—allow us to recall—the idea of the "second magisterium" of theologians, Father Rahner felt the second course was much to be preferred. What McCormick neglected to note about the master, however—though one suspects he had not forgotten it—came to light in the 30 March 1986 *Our Sunday Visitor*, when the Catholic theologian Germain Grisez drew attention to Rahner's contention "that by not acting against theological dissent, the Vatican was tacitly accepting it." One finds in that observation perhaps as good an explanation as any for the massive apostasy in the United States and Europe since Vatican II.

Nonetheless, not all Modernists were sanguine; for there is every indication that John Paul II and his friend Joseph Ratzinger—not to say the world's bishops—fully understand the nature and implications of the challenge; and indeed had every intention of meeting it even before it was formally proferred. Father Burghardt seemed to understand the possibilities when he complained that "this could be the beginning of a process where ultimately only those who conform to the congregation's understanding of Catholicism will be allowed to teach theology in Catholic institutions." That is, of course, the way the Modernists will try to explain it when it happens, while, *contra* Vatican II, depreciating the "congregation" on the grounds that John Paul II, or Cardinal Ratzinger in his name, has no right to speak definitively in the name of the Church.

Cardinal Ratzinger has put it more cogently. Clearly endorsing Cardinal Baum's *schema* for Catholic universities that would enforce Canon 810, the Doctrine Prefect deliberately (and as it were by introduction) tied that matter to the Curran case in his 17 September letter. Noting there that "artificial contraception and direct sterilization are forbidden as intrinsically wrong," that "every true Catholic must hold that abortion and euthanasia are unspeakable crimes," and so on, His Eminence also pointed out that "the apostolic constitution *Sapientia Christiana* makes specific application of these principles to the particular requirements of theological instruction and says that Catholic theologians, hence those teaching in theological faculties, do not teach on their own authority, but by mission they have received from the Church. In order to guarantee this teaching, the Church claims the freedom to maintain Her own academic institutions in which Her doctrine is reflected upon, taught and interpreted in complete fidelity. The freedom of the Church to teach Her doctrine is in full accord with the student's right to know what the teaching is and have it properly explained to them. This freedom of the Church likewise implies the right to choose for her theological faculties those and only those professors who, in complete intellectual honesty and integrity, recognize themselves to be capable of meeting these requirements."

As we saw from his observations to the European bishops at the beginning of this chapter, it is unlikely that the successor to St. Peter would find the standard secularist arguments against Ratzinger's thesis very convincing. Nonetheless the CTSA signers charged that relieving Curran of the formal right to represent his views as legitimately Catholic "raises serious questions about the academic integrity of Catholic institutions of higher learning," because "for many years enemies of the Catholic Church in the United States have argued that Catholic colleges and universities are not independent academic institutions, but are nothing more than educational arms of the official church. If Father Curran were removed from his position as a professor of theology at The Catholic University of America, it would be far more difficult to rebut this charge and particularly as it might apply to that national institution."

Pope John Paul II seems fully aware of that fact, and does not seem to mind. Accordingly, the deeper implications of the Curran case were reflected on the front—page article Kenneth Briggs wrote for the 4 April 1985 *National Catholic Reporter* on "the recent response by presidents of U.S. Catholic colleges to the Vatican's latest proposed guidelines [Cardinal Baum's April 1985 *Schema*] for higher education . . ." That Response (as we shall call it), Briggs says, "assails any attempt on the part of the Vatican to give bishops more control over Catholic educational institutions," and anticipates the issues that emerged "in the ultimatum served on Father Charles Curran to retract certain of his teachings on sexual morality or be stripped of his right to be a Catholic theologian." David Johnston, in fact, an associate director of the Association of Catholic Colleges and Universities, which is according to the American response, told the 28 March *New York Times* of his fear that, should Baum's *schema* be implemented, "a professor at Georgetown or Notre Dame could run into exactly the same problem that Charlie Curran has."

"Others have also worried," the *Times* added, "that the church has attempted to control differing views too rigidly. An advertisement in the 2 March issue of *The New York Times*, for instance, condemned the church 'reprisals' against academics and activists who took positions contrary to the Vatican's. The 1000 Catholics who signed the advertisement said such incidents were having a 'chilling effect' on academic freedom in Catholic colleges. That prospect worries educators in those universities who complain that adoption of the new document could further antagonize Catholics already concerned about academic freedom." The *Times* neglected to mention that the "position contrary to the Vatican's" was support for exterminating unborn children: or that the "1000 Catholics" included abortion clinic operators, excommunicate doctors who were directly involved in the extermination, heads of explicitly pro-abortion outfits, and so on.[3]

The Response, meanwhile, clearly reflected rising panic in the Modernist camp. Speaking of the *schema*, it charged that "what is proposed here is contrary to the American values of both academic freedom and due process, both of which are written into most university statutes and protected by civil and constitutional law" and accordingly, "there is no way within the statutes of our universities that teachers or administrators who lack something as vague as 'doctrinal integrity . . .' could be dismissed." As to Vatican II and Canon Law, both, according to the response, must be subject to the opinions of the boards of trustees. Besides, "the university is the home of the theologian, not the bishop, and the bishop must respect that fact"—whether the university is organizing experiments on exterminated and unborn children or not. As to the Pope, the academicians "would find it more advantageous to the work of the church in American higher education if this kind of juridical document were not issued at all." The question, of course, is whether theirs is really the work of the Church.

---

[3]Even this rather blood-spattered crew, it might be remarked, took some fourteen months to assemble.

No, that is not even the question anymore. "With respect to the Church itself," James Hitchcock observed in the December 1985 *Catholicism in Crisis*, "there is no doubt a kind of nihilism at work—the modernist Catholic soul will not rest until it has finally destroyed every last vestige of doctrinal certitude, moral authority, and disciplinary order. The modern Catholic's very motivation for remaining in the Church is negative." Or as Christendom College's academic dean Robert Rice (a supporter of the *schema*) told the *Times*, "they don't want to be bound by Catholic doctrine but they still want to call themselves Catholic schools." Rosemary Ruether has told us why.

The Pope, for reasons even as simple as those mentioned by the cynics earlier in this chapter, may eventually decide to drop his challenge, and continue to allow Catholicism in the United States to drift into oblivion. Make no mistake that if he does not abandon the Church in this country, the battle will be fierce. Rather obviously fearing for his own position, as well as dutifully echoing the Modernist position, Father McBrien nonetheless in one of his columns provides a picture of what is likely to happen. If it is true, he writes, that Curran's views "are incompatible with the canonical mandate to teach Catholic theology, then let the Vatican really clean house. Presidents, rectors, deans, and department heads in Catholic Universities, colleges, and seminaries know that they would stand to lose many, if not most, of their moral theologians and many other faculty members besides."

"Able theologians may abandon Catholic institutions altogether in order to avoid embarrassing confrontation with Church authority," wrote Bishop Clark, which fear also appeared in the Response. The latter went further, of course, also expressing the fear that if Vatican II is implemented then "the favorable decisions regarding public aid to Catholic colleges or universities" would be reversed. Most of these universities would first make *de jure* their *de facto* repudiation of Catholicism, and that, indeed, is doubtless the point of this dispute: when it is over, the some 220 colleges and universities that now call themselves Catholic, will no longer have that privilege. Some of them will restore their Catholic witness, and those that have it now, though poor, will doubtless flower just as the parochial school system did in the 19th century when Catholics were poorer, but had more faith. Experiments on murdered children, however, will no longer be conducted in the name of Catholicism with the feigned endorsement of Christ and His Church.

The battle, meanwhile, should begin soon. On 10 March Cardinal Ratzinger asked Father Curran for his final answer. Archbishop Hickey announced on 11 March that the matter was in its "conclusive phase." Bishop James Malone, in a statement one hopes was inspired by the courage he witnessed among his brother bishops at the Synod, noted on 14 March that Curran's "positions have been evaluated in depth by the Congregation for the Doctrine of the Faith. The central issue identified in this process concerns the fact that someone who does not accept the teaching of the Church's *magisterium* on crucial points cannot reasonably expect to occupy a position which requires that he teach what the Church teaches. It is clearly the right and duty of the Holy See to safeguard the authenticity of Catholic teaching throughout the world."

One suspects the media will be inclined to hide the fact, but the Vatican action against Curran has received widespread support, including from, among others, even Catholic University's student newspaper and *Our Sunday Visitor*, whose editorial was entitled "Restoring Sanity." In fact, even the *New York Times* felt compelled to acknowledge that "to those who oppose premarital sex, birth control and divorce, the church can hardly be faulted for holding to views it has maintained for centuries."

And so, in April 1986, this brief history of the post-Council era comes to an end. The Catholic Church teaches that, in regard to time—as opposed to eternity—Church history itself will only end with the return of Christ, the hour of which, He said, we cannot know. The responsibilities of a Christian, however, are at base no different whether Christ returns tomorrow evening or in ten thousand years; and it is doubtless a function of *hubris* to believe that return is imminent simply because the corpulent West no longer honors Christ's somewhat leaner, though more luxuriant, vision.

Because of the political instability that characterizes African and South American governments, it seems difficult today to imagine those continents being the harbingers of the twenty-first century's cultural and spiritual vision; doubtless forgotten Roman emperors felt that way about the insignificant Christians of their era. While Africans abandon animism for the potentially creative tension between Islam and Christianity, however, it is less difficult to imagine a Western social breakdown that will make the southern hemisphere appear to be a paragon of civil organization by comparison. The tragedy of man, as a reading of the Old Testament indicates, is that upon establishing cultural strength through the pursuit of truth, he then abandons that pursuit in the smug conviction that such strength must be his natural condition.

Depriving anti-Catholic universities of the right to pretend they are Catholic will of course only begin to solve the problem of neo-Arianism; perhaps better to say, this would be but an essential component of the battle for Vatican II. Ultimately, if the universal pastor of the Church is going to show American Catholics the kind of solicitude he has shown the African Church, then—as in Africa—he will also have to relieve some bishops of their sees. Peter Hebblethwaite told the 4 December 1985 *Washington Times* that five bishops have been deposed in Africa; and though we may not be as deserving as that, the effect of deposing one or two might do more to help the U.S. episcopate than all the Pontiff's superb efforts to show what it means to be a man. Love is the best approach to holiness, but if that fails, fear has often been known to save a man's soul.

Meanwhile, American Catholics faithful to Vatican II, to the Church, to what Cardinal Ratzinger calls "the sacramental community of Her Body that extends throughout history," will not soon be relieved from the spiritual diaspora of their country, nor of the Modernist clerical takeover of their Church. As they grow more militant—heretics were dragged from the altars in the Middle Ages—doubtless the Pope will help them more, as he sees their willingness to back him, and the Church. More importantly, of course, it is in their very suffering, as they struggle to remain faithful and practice mercy, whether within their families or jobs, fighting abortion or helping the poor, in whatever quiet or dramatic ways, that they most intimately serve truth; for it is then when their lives most closely reflect the human experience of Christ. And indeed as Christ's words and life made clear, never is this more true than when Christians are persecuted for their fidelity, especially when the persecution comes from a decadent clergy that hates them because it sees in them a charity the priests no longer have the courage to embrace. "In these communities," as *Lumen Gentium* teaches, "though they may often be small and poor, or existing in the diaspora, Christ is present through whose power and influence the One, Holy, Catholic and Apostolic Church is constituted."

Indeed, to the extent American Catholics "maintain their ties with the universal Church," according to Joseph Sobran, "they will be aware of themselves as the true heart of Christianity." Consequently, as the exhausted condition of both historicism's socialist and liberal idolatries becomes more and more apparent, such Catholics will also prove the seed through which North America maintains its only serious contact with the next historical era.

Appendix:
The Final Report of the 1985 Extraordinary Synod

"THE CHURCH, IN THE WORD OF GOD, CELE-
BRATES THE MYSTERIES OF CHRIST FOR THE
SALVATION OF THE WORLD"

I. Central Theme of this Synod: Celebration, Verification, Promotion of Vatican II

1. Spiritual experience of this Synod
    At the conclusion of this second Extraordinary Synod we must first of all give great thanks to the benevolence of God, who deigned to lead the Sovereign Pontiff to convoke this Synod. We are also grateful to the Holy Father John Paul II, who called us to this twentieth anniversary celebration of the conclusion of the Second Vatican Council. The Synod has been for us an occasion which has allowed us once again to experience communion in the one Spirit, in the one faith and hope, and in the one Catholic Church, as well as in the unanimous will to translate the Council into the practice and life of the Church. We likewise have participated in one another's joys and hopes, as well as in the sufferings and anguish too often undergone by the Church throughout the world.

2. Attainment of the Synod's aim
    The end for which this Synod was convoked was the celebration, verification and promotion of Vatican Council II. With grateful hearts, we feel that we have truly obtained this fruit, with God's assistance. Unanimously WE HAVE CELEBRATED the Second Vatican Council as a grace of God and a gift of the Holy Spirit, from which have come forth many spiritual fruits for the universal Church and the particular Churches, as well as for the men of our time. Unanimously and joyfully we also VERIFY that the Council is a legitimate and valid expression and interpretation of the deposit of faith as it is found in Sacred Scripture and in the living tradition of the Church. Therefore we are determined to progress further along the path indicated to us by the Council. There has been full consensus among us regarding the need to further promote the knowledge and application of the Council, both in its letter and in its spirit. In this way new progress will be achieved in the reception of the Council, that is, in its spiritual interiorization and practical application.

3. Lights and shadows in the reception of the Council
    The large majority of the faithful received the Second Vatican Council with zeal; a few, here and there, showed resistance to it. There is no doubt, therefore, that the Council was embraced with heartfelt adherence, because the Holy Spirit was prompting his Church to do so.

Moreover, even outside the Catholic Church many people payed careful attention to the Second Vatican Council.

Nonetheless, although great fruits have been obtained from the council, we have at the same time recognized, with great sincerity, deficiencies and difficulties in the acceptance of the Council. In truth, there certainly have also been shadows in the post-council period; in part due to an incomplete understanding and application of the Council, in part to other causes. However, in no way can it be affirmed that everything which took place after the Council was caused by the Council.

In a particular way, the question must be posed as to why, in the so-called "First World", following a doctrine of the Church which has been so extensively and profoundly explained, quite often a certain estrangement is manifested towards the Church, even though in this area of the world the fruits of the Council abound. Instead, where the Church is oppressed by totalitarian ideologies or where the Church raises her voice against social injustices, she seems to be accepted in a more positive way. Yet it cannot be denied that even in such places not all the faithful fully and totally identify with the Church and her primary mission.

4. External and internal causes of the difficulties

In many areas of the world the Church lacks the material means and the personnel for carrying out her mission. To this must be added the fact that not infrequently the Church is forcibly impeded from exercising her mission. In the wealthy nations we see the constant growth of an ideology characterized by pride in technical advances and a certain immanentism that leads to the idolatry of material goods (so-called "consumerism"). From this can follow a certain blindness to spiritual realities and values. In addition, we cannot deny the existence in society of forces capable of great influence which act with a certain hostile spirit towards the Church. All of these things manifest the work of the "prince of this world" and of the "mystery of iniquity" even in our day.

Among the internal causes, there must be noted a partial and selective reading of the Council, as well as a superficial interpretation of its doctrine in one sense or another. On the one hand, there have been disappointments because we have been too hesitant in the application of the true doctrine of the Council. On the other hand, because of a partial reading of the Council, a unilateral presentation of the Church as a purely institutional structure devoid of her Mystery has been made. We are probably not immune from all responsibility for the fact that especially the young critically consider the Church a pure institution. Have we not perhaps favored this opinion in them by speaking too much of the renewal of the Church's external structures and too little of God and of Christ? From time to time there has also been a lack of the discernment of spirits, with the failure to correctly distinguish between a legitimate openness of the Council to the world and the acceptance of a secularized world's mentality and order of values.

5. A deeper reception of the Council

These and other deficiencies show the need for a deeper reception of the Council. And this requires four successive phases: a deeper and more extensive knowledge of the Council, its interior assimilation, its loving reaffirmation and its implementation. Only interior assimilation and practical implementation can make the conciliar documents alive and life-giving.

The theological interpretation of the conciliar doctrine must show attention to all the documents, in themselves and in their close inter-relationship, in such a way that the integral meaning of the Council's affirmations—often very complex—might be understood and expressed. Special attention must be paid to the four major Constitutions of the Council, which contain the interpretative key for the other Decrees and Declarations. It is not licit to separate the pastoral character from the doctrinal vigor of the documents. In the same way, it is not legitimate to separate the spirit and the letter of the Council. Moreover, the Council must be understood in continuity with the great tradition of the Church, and at the same time we must receive light from the Council's own doctrine for today's Church and the men of our time. The Church is one and the same throughout all the councils.

6. Suggestions

It is suggested that a pastoral program be implemented in the particular Churches for the years to come, having as its objectives a new, more extensive and deeper knowledge and reception of the Council. This can be attained above all through a new diffusion of the documents themselves, through the publication of studies that explain the documents and bring them closer to the understanding of the faithful. The conciliar doctrine must be proposed in a suitable and continued way by means of conferences and courses in the permanent formation of priests and seminarians, in the formation of men and women religious, and also in the catechesis of adults. Diocesan Synods and other ecclesial conferences can be very useful for the application of the Council. The opportune use of the means of social communication (mass media) is recommended. For a correct understanding and implementation of the Council's doctrine, great help will be had from the reading and the practical implementation of what is found in the various Apostolic Exhortations, which are, as it were, the fruit of the Ordinary Synods held in the beginning of 1969.

II. Particular Themes of the Synod

A. The Mystery of the Church

1. Secularism and Signs of Return to the Sacred

The brief twenty-year period that separates us from the conclusion of the Council has brought with it accelerated changes in history. In this sense, the signs of our times do not exactly coincide, in some points, with those of the time of the Council. From among these, special attention must be paid to the phenomenon of secularism. Without any doubt the Council has affirmed the legitimate autonomy of temporal realities (cf. *GS* 36 and elsewhere). In this sense, a correctly understood secularization must be admitted. But we are speaking of something totally different from the secularism that consists of an autonomist vision of man and the world, one which leaves aside the dimension of mystery, indeed neglects and denies it. This immanentism is a reduction of the integral vision of man, a reduction which leads not to his true liberation but to a new idolatry, to the slavery of ideologies, to life in reductive and often oppressive structures of this world.

Despite secularism, signs of a return to the sacred also exist. Today, in fact, there are signs of a new hunger and thirst for the transcendent and divine. In order to favor this return to the sacred and to overcome secularism we must open the way to the dimension of the "divine" or of mystery and offer the preambles of faith to mankind today. Because, as the Council affirms, man is a question to himself and only God can give him the full and ultimate answer (cf. GS 21). Does not the spread of sects perhaps lead us to ask whether we have sometimes failed to sufficiently manifest the sense of the sacred?

2. The Mystery of God through Jesus in the Holy Spirit

The primary mission of the Church, under the impulse of the Holy Spirit, is to preach and to witness to the good and joyful news of the election, the mercy and charity of God which manifest themselves in salvation history, which through Jesus Christ reach their culmination in the fullness of time, and which communicate and offer salvation to man by virtue of the Holy Spirit. Christ is the light of humanity! The Church, proclaiming the Gospel, must see to it that this light clearly shines out from her countenance (cf. LG). The Church makes herself more credible if she speaks less of herself and ever more preaches Christ Crucified (cf. 1 Cor 2:2) and witnesses with her own life. In this way the Church is sacrament, that is, sign and instrument of communion with God and also of communion and reconciliation of men with one another. The message of the Church, as described in the Second Vatican Council, is trinitarian and christocentric.

Because Jesus Christ is the Son of God and the new Adam, he at once manifests the mystery of God and the mystery of man and his exalted vocation (cf. GS 22). The Son of God became man in order to make men children of God. Through this familiarity with God, man is raised to a most high dignity. Therefore, when the Church preaches Christ she announces salvation to mankind.

3. The Mystery of the Church

The whole importance of the Church derives from her connection with Christ. The Council has described the Church in diverse ways: as the people of God, the body of Christ, the bride of Christ, the temple of the Holy Spirit, the family of God. These descriptions of the Church complete one another and must be understood in the light of the Mystery of Christ or of the Church in Christ. We cannot replace a false unilateral vision of the Church as purely hierarchical with a new sociological conception which is also unilateral. Jesus Christ is ever present in his Church and lives in her as risen. From the Church's connection with Christ we clearly understand the eschatological character of the Church herself (cf. LG 7). In this way the pilgrim Church on earth is the messianic people (cf. LG 9) that already anticipates in itself its future reality as a new creation. Yet she remains a holy Church that has sinners in her midst, that must ever be purified, and that moves, amidst the persecutions of this world and the consolations of God, towards the future kingdom (cf. LG 8). In this sense there are always present within the Church the mystery of the Cross and the mystery of the resurrection.

4. The universal vocation to holiness

Because the Church in Christ is mystery, she must be considered a sign and instrument of holiness. For this reason the Council proclaimed the vocation of all the faithful to holiness (cf. *LG* 5). The call to holiness is an invitation to an intimate conversion of heart and to participate in the life of God, One and Triune, and this signifies and surpasses the realization of man's every desire. In our day above all, when so many people feel an interior void and spiritual crisis, the Church must preserve and energetically promote the sense of penance, prayer, adoration, sacrifice, self-giving, charity and justice.

Men and women saints have always been founts and origins of renewal in the most difficult circumstances throughout the Church's history. Today we have tremendous need of saints, for whom we must assiduously implore God. The Institutes of consecrated life through the profession of the evangelical counsels must be conscious of their special mission in today's Church, and we must encourage them in that mission. The apostolic movements and the new movements of spirituality are the bearers of great hope, if they properly remain in ecclesial communion. All the laity must perform their role in the Church in their daily occupations such as the family, the workplace, secular activities and leisure time so as to permeate and transform the world with the light and life of Christ. Popular devotion, rightly understood and practiced, is very useful in nourishing the holiness of the people. It therefore merits greater attention on the part of pastors.

The Blessed Virgin Mary, who is our mother in the order of grace (cf. *LG* 61), is an example for all Christians of holiness and of total response to God's call (*LG* chapt. 8).

5. Suggestions

Today it is extremely necessary that the Pastors of the Church excel in the witness of holiness. It is necessary already in seminaries and religious houses to give a formation that educates the candidates not only intellectually but also spiritually; they must be seriously introduced to a daily spiritual life (prayer, meditation, the reading of the Bible, the sacraments of Penance and the Eucharist). According to what is expressed by the Decree "Presbyterorum Ordinis", they should be prepared for the priestly ministry in such a way that they find nourishment for their spiritual life in pastoral activity itself (cf. *PO* 16). Thus, in the exercise of the ministry they will also be capable of offering the faithful the correct counsel for their spiritual lives. The true renewal of the Institutes of consecrated life must be favoured in every way. But the spirituality of the laity, founded on baptism, must also be promoted. In the first place, it is necessary to promote conjugal spirituality, which is based on the sacrament of marriage and is of great importance for the transmission of the faith to future generations.

B. Sources of the life for the Church
a) The Word of God
1. Scripture, tradition, magisterium

Hearing the word of God with reverence, the Church has the mission of proclaiming it with faith (cf. *DV* 1). Consequently, the preaching of the Gospel is among the principal duties of the Church, and especially of the bishops, and today it takes on the greatest importance (cf. *LG* 25). In this context is seen the importance of the Dogmatic Constitution "Dei Verbum", which has been too neglected, but which Paul VI nonetheless reproposed in a more profound and timely way in the Apostolic Exhortation "Evangelii Nuntiandi".

For this Constitution, too, it is necessary to avoid a partial reading. In particular, the exegesis of the original meaning of Sacred Scripture, most highly recommended by the Council, (cf. *DV* 12) cannot be separated from the living tradition of the Church (cf. *DV* 10).

The false opposition between doctrinal and pastoral responsibilities must be avoided and overcome. In fact, the true intent of pastoral work consists in actualizing and making concrete the truth of salvation, which is in itself valid for all times. As true pastors, the bishops must point out the right way to the flock, strengthen the faith of the flock, keep dangers away from it.

2. Evangelization

The mystery of divine life that the Church brings to all peoples to participate in must be proclaimed. The Church is missionary by her very nature (cf. *AG* 2). Thus the bishops are not only teachers of the faithful but heralds of the faith which leads new disciples to Christ (cf. *LG* 25). Evangelization is the first duty not only of the bishops but also of priests and deacons, indeed, of all Christians. Everywhere on earth today the transmission to the young of the faith and the moral values deriving from the Gospel is in danger. Often, knowledge of the faith and the acceptance of the moral order are reduced to the minimum. Therefore, a new effort in evangelization and in integral and systematic catechesis is required.

Evangelization does not regard only the missions in the common sense of the word, that is, "ad gentes". The evangelization of non-believers in fact presupposes the self-evangelization of the baptized and also, in a certain sense, of deacons, priests and bishops. Evangelization takes place through witnesses. The witness gives his testimony not only with words, but also with his life. We must not forget that in Greek the word for testimony is "martyrium". In this respect, the more ancient Churches can learn much from the new Churches, from their dynamism, from their life and testimony even unto the shedding of their blood for the faith.

3. The relationship between the magisterium of the Bishops and theologians

Theology, according to the well-known description of St. Anselm, is "faith seeking understanding". Since all Christians must account for the hope that is in them (cf. 1 Pt 3:15), theology is specifically necessary to the life of the Church today. With joy we recognize what has been done by theologians to elaborate the documents of Vatican Council II and to help towards their faithful interpretation and fruitful application in the post-conciliar period. But on the other hand, we regret that the theological discussions of our day have sometimes occasioned confusion among the faithful. Thus, communication and a reciprocal dialogue between the bishops and theologians are necessary for the building up of the faith and its deeper comprehension.

4. Suggestions

Very many have expressed the desire that a catechism or compendium of all Catholic doctrine regarding both faith and morals be

composed, that it might be, as it were, a point of reference for the catechisms or compendiums that are prepared in the various regions. The
presentation of doctrine must be biblical and liturgical. It must be sound
doctrine suited to the present life of Christians. The formation of candidates to the priesthood must be looked after in a particular way. In it,
the philosophical formation and the manner of teaching theology proposed by the Decree "Optatam Totius" n.16 merit attention. It is recommended that the manuals, besides offering an exposition of sound theology in a scientific and pedagogical manner, be permeated by a true sense
of the Church.

b. The sacred liturgy
1. Internal renewal of the liturgy
The liturgical renewal is the most visible fruit of the whole conciliar effort. Even if there have been some difficulties, it has generally
been received joyfully and fruitfully by the faithful. The liturgical renewal cannot be limited to ceremonies, rites, texts, etc. The active participation so happily increased after the Council does not consist only in
external activity, but above all in interior and spiritual participation, in
living and fruitful participation in the paschal mystery of Jesus Christ
(cf.SC 11). It is evident that the liturgy must favour the sense of the sacred and make it shine forth. It must be permeated by the spirit of reverence, adoration and glory of God.

2. Suggestions
The Bishops should not merely correct abuses but should also
clearly explain to everyone the theological foundation of the sacramental discipline and of the liturgy.

Catecheses must once again become paths leading into liturgical life
(mystagogical catecheses), as was the case in the Church's beginnings.

Future priests should learn liturgical life in a practical way and
know liturgical theology as well.

C. The Church as communion

1. The meaning of communion
The ecclesiology of communion is the central and fundamental idea
of the Council's documents. Koinonia/communion, founded on the Sacred Scripture, have been held in great honor in the early Church and in
the Oriental Churches to this day. Thus, much was done by the Second
Vatican Council so that the Church as communion might be more
clearly understood and concretely incorporated into life. What does the
complex word "communion" mean? Fundamentally it is a matter of
communion with God through Jesus Christ, in the Holy Spirit. This
communion is had in the Word of God and in the sacraments. Baptism is
the door and the foundation of communion in the Church. The Eucharist is the source and the culmination of the whole Christian life (cf.
LG 11). The communion of the eucharistic Body of Christ signifies and
produces, that is, builds up, the intimate communion of all the faithful in
the Body of Christ which is the Church (1 Cor. 10:16).

For this reason, the ecclesiology of communion cannot be reduced
to purely organizational questions or to problems which simply relate to
powers. Still, the ecclesiology of communion is also the foundation for

order in the Church, and especially for a correct relationship between unity and pluriformity in the Church.

2. Unity and pluriformity in the Church

Just as we believe in one God alone and one mediator, Jesus Christ, in one Spirit, so we have but one baptism and one Eucharist with which the unity and the uniqueness of the Church are signified and built up. This is of great importance especially today, because the Church, inasmuch as she is one and unique, is as a sacrament a sign and instrument of unity and of reconciliation, of peace among men, nations, classes and peoples. In the unity of the faith and the sacraments and in the hierarchical unity, especially with the centre of unity given to us by Christ in the service of Peter, the Church is that messianic people of which the Constitution "Lumen Gentium" speaks (n. 9). In this way, ecclesial communion with Peter and his successors is not an obstacle but the anticipation and prophetic sign of a fuller unity. On the other hand, the one and unique spirit works with many and varied spiritual gifts and charisms (1 Cor. 12:4ff), the one Eucharist is celebrated in various places. For this reason, the unique and universal Church is truly present in all the particular Churches (CD 11), and these are formed in the image of the universal Church in such a way that the one and unique Catholic Church exists in and through the particular Churches (LG 23). Here we have the true theological principal of variety and pluriformity in unity, but it is necessary to distinguish pluriformity from pure pluralism. When pluriformity is true richness and carries with it fullness, this is true catholicity. The pluralism of fundamentally opposed positions instead leads to dissolution, destruction and the loss of identity.

3. The Oriental Churches

In terms of this aspect of communion, the Catholic Church today holds in great esteem the institutions, liturgical rites, ecclesiastical traditions and discipline of Christian life of the Oriental Churches, because they are resplendent in their venerable antiquity and because in them is present the tradition of the Apostles through the Fathers (OE 1). In them, dating back to ancient times, the patriarchal institution is in effect, an institution which was recognized by the first ecumenical councils (OE 7). It should also be added that the Oriental Churches have given testimony with the death and the blood of their martyrs for Christ and his Church.

4. Collegiality

The ecclesiology of communion provides the sacramental foundation of collegiality. Therefore the theology of collegiality is much more extensive than its mere juridical aspect. The collegial spirit is broader than effective collegiality understood in an exclusively juridical way. The collegial spirit is the soul of the collaboration between the bishops on the regional, national and international levels. Collegial action in the strict sense implies the activity of the whole college, together with its head, over the entire Church. Its maximum expression is found in an ecumenical council. In the whole theological question regarding the relationship between primacy and the college of bishops a distinction cannot be made between the Roman Pontiff and the bishops considered collectively, but between the Roman Pontiff alone and the Roman Pontiff together with the bishops (LG expl. note 3), because the college exists with its "head" and never without him, the subject of supreme and full power in the whole Church (*LG* 22).

From this first collegiality understood in the strict sense one must distinguish the diverse partial realizations, which are authentically sign and instrument of the collegial spirit: the Synod of Bishops, the Episcopal Conferences, the Roman Curia, the "ad limina" visits etc. All of these actualizations cannot be directly deduced from the theological principle of collegiality; but they are regulated by ecclesial law. Nonetheless, all of these other forms, like the pastoral journeys of the Supreme Pontiff, are a service of great importance for the whole college of bishops together with the Pope, and also for the individual bishops whom the Holy Spirit has made guardians in the Church of God (Acts 20:28).

5. The episcopal conferences

The collegial spirit has a concrete application in the episcopal conferences (*LG* 23). No one can doubt their pastoral utility, indeed their necessity in the present situation. In the episcopal conferences the bishops of a nation or a territory jointly exercise their pastoral service (*CD* 38; CIC can. 447).

In their manner of proceeding, episcopal conferences must keep in mind the good of the Church, that is, the service of unity and the inalienable responsibility of each bishop in relation to the universal Church and the particular Church.

6. Participation and co-responsibility in the Church

Because the Church is communion, there must be participation and co-responsibility at all of her levels. This general principle must be understood in diverse ways in diverse areas.

Between a bishop and his presbyterate there exists a relationship founded on the sacrament of Orders. Thus priests in a certain way make the bishop present in the individual local assemblies of the faithful, and assume and exercise in part in their daily work his tasks and his solicitude (*LG* 28). Consequently, friendly relations and full trust must exist between bishops and their priests.

Bishops feel themselves linked in gratitude to their priests, who in the post-conciliar period have played a great part in implementing the Council (*OT* 1) and they wish to be close with all their strength to their priests and to give them help and support in their often difficult work, especially in parishes.

Finally, the spirit of collaboration with deacons and between the bishop and the religious who are active in his particular Church must be favoured. In addition, from Vatican II has positively come a new style of collaboration between the laity and clerics. The spirit of willingness with which many lay persons put themselves at the service of the Church is to be numbered among the best fruits of the Council. In this is experienced the fact that we are all the Church.

In recent years there has often been discussion regarding the vocation and the mission of women. May the Church do its utmost so that they might be able to express, in the service of the Church, their own gifts, and to play a greater part in the various fields of the Church's apostolate (cf. *AA* 9). May pastors gratefully accept and promote the collaboration of women in ecclesial activity. The Council calls the young the hope of the Church (*GE* 2). This extraordinary Synod addressed young people with special love and great confidence and expects great things from their generous dedication. It exhorts them that they might embrace and dynamically continue the heritage of the Council, assuming their role in the mission of the Church. Because the Church is communion, the new "basic communities", if they truly live in unity with the Church, are a true expression of communion and a means for the construction of a more profound communion. They are thus cause for great hope for the life of the Church (*EN* 58).

7. Ecumenical Communion
Basing itself on the ecclesiology of communion, the Catholic Church at the time of the Second Vatican Council fully assumed her ecumenical responsibility. After these twenty years we can affirm that ecumenism has inscribed itself deeply and indelibly in the consciousness of the Church. We bishops ardently desire that the incomplete communion already existing with the non-Catholic Churches and communities might, with the grace of God, come to the point of full communion.

Ecumenical dialogue must be carried out in diverse ways at the diverse levels of the Church, whether by the universal Church, the particular Churches or concrete local organizations. The dialogue must be spiritual and theological. The ecumenical movement is particularly favoured by mutual prayer. Dialogue is authentic and fruitful if it presents the truth with love and fidelity towards the Church. In this way ecumenical dialogue causes the Church to be seen more clearly as a sacrament of unity. The communion between Catholics and other Christians, although incomplete, summons everyone to collaborate in the numerous fields and thus makes possible a certain common witness to the salvific love of God for the world, so in need of salvation.

8. Suggestions
a) Because the new Code of Canon Law, happily promulgated, is of great help to the Latin Church in the application of the Council, the desire is expressed that the Oriental codification be completed as quickly as possible.

b) Since the episcopal conferences are so useful, indeed necessary, in the present-day pastoral work of the Church, it is hoped that the study of their theological "status", and above all the problem of their doctrinal authority might be made explicit in a deeper and more extensive way, keeping in mind what is written in the Conciliar Decree "Christus Dominus" n. 38 and in the Code of Canon Law can. 447 and 753.

c) It is recommended that a study be made to examine whether the principle of subsidiarity in use in human society can be applied to the Church, and to what degree and in what sense such an application can and should be made (cf. Pius XII, *AAS* 38, 1946, p. 144).

D. The mission of the Church in the world

1. Importance of the Constitution "Gaudium et Spes"
The Church as communion is a sacrament for the salvation of the world. Therefore the authorities in the Church have been placed there by Christ for the salvation of the world. In this context we affirm the great importance and timeliness of the Pastoral Constitution "Gaudium et Spes". At the same time, however, we perceive that the signs of our time are in part different from the time of the Council, with greater